AF516146

Changing Village India

Changing Village India

Edited by

Brij Raj Chauhan
A. Satyanarayana

RAWAT PUBLICATIONS
Jaipur • New Delhi • Bangalore • Hyderabad • Guwahati

ISBN 978-81-316-0531-8

© Contributors, 2012

No part of this book may be reproduced or transmitted in any form or by any means, electronic or mechanical, including photocopying, recording or by any information storage and retrieval system, without permission in writing from the publishers and the editors.

Published by
Prem Rawat for **Rawat Publications**
Satyam Apts, Sector 3, Jawahar Nagar, Jaipur 302 004 (India)
Phone: 0141 265 1748/7006 Fax: 0141 265 1748
E-mail: info@rawatbooks.com
Website: www.rawatbooks.com

New Delhi Office
4858/24, Ansari Road, Daryaganj, New Delhi 110 002
Phone: 011 2326 3290

Also at *Bangalore*, *Hyderabad* and *Guwahati*

Typeset by Rawat Computers, Jaipur
Printed at Chaman Enterprises, New Delhi

Contents

Foreword

Professor Brij Raj Chauhan served for three years at the G.B. Pant Social Science Institute, Allahabad to complete a very important work on village studies, which culminated in a seminar on "Intensive Village Studies" bringing scholars working in the field. The seminar became important as the veteran scholar presented an 80-year perspective on village studies. The papers presented in this volume are a compendium of re-study/study of villages covering the role of developmental administration, political events, constitutional amendments, empowerment of marginalised groups, and the socio-psychological probing of villages.

Village studies are important as they have the inherent capacity to bring out the pluriverse in our societies as against the universal principles that have come to dominate the social sciences, especially where *rural* is concerned. Seemingly monolithic institutions such as the caste panchayats have varied formations, as discovered by Chauhan in his work on "Chokhla". Such institutions have disparate interface with formal institutions and the marginalised sections of the society.

It is my contention that the village studies, rather than drawing commonalities with one another and coming to a theory of their work, may celebrate the pluriverse in the society and make local and other institutions respond to the pluriverse.

I am sure that the readers of this volume will enjoy the painstaking work.

Pradeep Bhargava
Director
G.B. Pant Social Science Institute, Allahabad

Acknowledgements

In editing this volume we have acquired numerous debts, both intellectual and personal. This volume is an outcome of the National Seminar on "Intensive Village Studies" held on February 29th and March 1st 2008 at Gobind Ballabh Pant Social Science Institute, Allahabad, where Brij Raj Chauhan served on an ICSSR fellowship for two years along with Ramashray Roy and J.P. Singh. This volume is a companion to *Rural Life: Grass Roots Perspectives* (2009) by Brij Raj Chauhan. The authors express a deep sense of gratitude to the Institute and its faculty which provided intellectual climate during the seminar that enlarged our visions and sharpened our skills and presentations. The support of the library was helpful in several ways in extending help in search of relevant documents. Rama Charan Tripathi, Director of the Institute, had shown keen interest in the fellowship-related project on intensive studies in villages. At the concluding stage of the fellowship, Pradeep Bhargava joined the Institute as Director who mooted the idea of a special seminar on the theme. He also showed enthusiasm for this volume and extended his willingness to contribute time to write the foreword to this volume. We express our thanks to the faculty, directors, and the library staff of GBPSSI for this. A working group comprising Rana P.B. Singh and the authors was formed in which Rana played a significant role for which we extend our thanks to him. The ICSSR extended financial help to organise the seminar and the *EPW* helped in advertising about the seminar within a short notice. We extend our thanks to both.

Special thanks to Rajen Gobind Harshe, the Vice Chancellor of the University who presided over the seminar and also encouraged at each and every movement to finalise the volume. We would also like to thank Yogesh Atal, D. Sundaram, Debal, Shankar, Abha, Rana and Dreze for their comments and suggestions on different occasions. The editorial staff at Rawat Publications also deserve our thanks for their professional support and seeing this volume in print. We also would like to thank S.K. Sharma and Ms Pant, faculty members in the English Department, who were kind enough to edit the earlier drafts of the papers. Many of the suggestions have found their way into the text and have added value. Thanks are due to the writers whose works find a mention in the text. However, the responsibility for the presentation of this material lies with the author and not with the editors or the Institute. We also extend our thanks to the invisible voices of the villagers who gave much of their time in sharing their life experiences with the paper writers and enhancing the value of their contributions.

Finally, a word of thanks to the co-workers of the guest house of the Institute whose efficiency and courtesies have now become a talking point among those who have attended the deliberations in the Institute over the years.

List of Contributors

Brij Raj Chauhan, Former Head, Department of Sociology, Meerut University, Meerut.

Ramashray Roy, Honorary Fellow, Centre for the Study of Developing Studies, New Delhi.

Yogesh Atal, a distinguished social-scientist who worked for many years as UNESCO's Regional Advisor for Social and Human Sciences in Asia, and retired as its Principal Director.

Giri Raj Gupta, Professor Emeritus of Sociology, Western Illinois University, Macomb, Illinois, USA.

Susan S. Wadley, Ford Maxwell Professor of South Asian Studies, Maxwell School of Syracuse University, Syracuse, USA.

Ravi S. Singh, Associate Professor, Department of Geography, Faculty of Science, Banaras Hindu University, Varanasi.

Kavita Jaijan, Research Scholar, Department of Geography, Faculty of Science, Banaras Hindu University, Varanasi, UP.

R. Gopinath, Research Scholar, Department of Economics, Bharathidasan University, Tiruchirappalli (Tamil Nadu).

Pankaj Gupta, Senior Research Officer, Institute of Integrated Himalayan Studies (UGC Centre of Excellence), Himachal University, Shimla.

P. Mishra, Professor, Department of Sociology, Rani Durgavati Vishwavidhyalaya, Jabalpur.

R. Shankar, Professor and Head, Department of Sociology, Bharathidasan University, Tiruchirappalli (Tamil Nadu).

Jagdish Kumar Pundir, Professor and Head, Sociology, Social Work and Mass Communication, Chaudhary Charan Singh University, Meerut.

Arun Chauhan, District Coordinator, Total Sanitation Campaign, District Water and Sanitation Committee, Zila Parishad, Udaipur.

Shashi Bhushan Singh, Assistant Professor of Sociology, Sri Venkateswara College, University of Delhi, Delhi.

Atanu Sengupta, Associate Professor of Economics, University of Burdwan, Burdwan, West Bengal.

Md. Salauddin Khan, Reader in Economics, Dr B.N. Dutta Smriti Mahavidyalaya, Hatgobindapur, Burdwan (West Bengal).

A. Nageswara Rao, Assistant Professor, Centre for the Study of Social Exclusion and Inclusive Policy, Maulana Azad National Urdu University, Hyderabad.

M. Gurusamy, Research Officer, Department of Political Science and Development Administration, Gandhigram Rural University, Gandhigram (Tamil Nadu).

Prachi Ghildiyal-Dwivedi, Assistant Professor, Department of Curriculum Development, Evaluation and Vocational Education, North East Regional Institute of Education, Shillong.

R.C. Tripathi, Former Head, Department of Psychology, University of Allahabad, Allahabad.

Sanjay, Associate Professor, Director/President, Sri Mangal Group of Institutions, Kanpur.

A. Satyanarayana, Professor and Head, Department of Sociology, University of Allahabad, Allahabad.

Sunil Kumar Verma, Assistant Professor, Department of Psychology Studies, Sikkim University, Gangtok, Sikkim.

D. Punetha, Professor, Department of Psychology, University of Allahabad, Allahabad.

Atul Singh, Reader, Department of Psychology, Allahabad Degree College, Allahabad.

Abha Chauhan, Head, Department of Sociology, University of Jammu, Jammu.

Shahul Hameed Hasbullah, Senior Lecturer, University of Peradeniya, Sri Lanka.

K. Sekhar, Faculty Head, SHANU Division, Rajiv Gandhi National Institute of Youth Development, Sriperumbudur (Tamil Nadu).

V. Sreemannarayana Murthy, Assistant Professor of Sociology, Centre for SAARC Studies, Andhra University, Visakhapatnam.

T.R. Singh, Former Reader, Department of Sociology, B.M.S. College, Roorkee.

Rabin Deka, Associate Professor and Head, Department of Sociology, Tezpur University, Tezpur (Assam).

Pragyan, Guest Faculty in Social Engineering Course, Department of Sociology, University of Lucknow, Lucknow.

D.R. Sahu, Professor of Sociology, Ravenshaw University, Cuttack.

Introduction

Brij Raj Chauhan, a pioneer of village studies in India, discussed the outline of this volume with his student, the second author of this volume, during his stay at Allahabad, Bhopal and Udaipur. An effort is made here to put his ideas together while treating social interactions as laboratory of experimentation to sharpen sociological imagination. Brij Raj Chauhan had insisted on the tradition of fieldwork and motivated his students over six decades (1949–2009) from the days of his undergraduate teaching at Udaipur, P.G., M.Phil and research at Meerut and even after his superannuation till his last breath. In this way he derived meaning of life. He further insisted on the significance of treating society as a laboratory for sociological comprehension of events in their natural settings when they occur and imparted scientific temper in the derivations of sociological imagination among his students. He questioned the validity of the concept of little community of Redfield (1953) in his thesis work on Ranawaton-ki-Sadri village in Chittorgarh district of Rajasthan which later was published as *A Rajasthan Village* (1966/ 1999). His sociological imagination is further manifested in his works on *Towns in Tribal Setting* (1970), *Scheduled Castes and Education* (1975), *Bharat Mein Gramin Samaj* (1988), *India: A Socio-Economic Profile* (1989), *Rural-Urban Interactions* (1990), *Samaj Vigyan ke Preraka Srot* (1994), *Four Decades of Rural Development in Etawah* (1998), and *Eastern Anthropologist: Special Number on Village Studies* (2005). He visited almost all the villages that made sociological history and contributed to the growth of sociology in India during the 1950s and 1970s. These villages became shrines to him. Even through revisiting these villages he repeatedly used to send reminders to the profession both in seminars and personal interactions that village studies need to be renewed to understand changes and continuities through restudying the earlier studied villages.

Brij Raj Chauhan submitted a project proposal to the Indian Council of Social Science Research (ICSSR) as a manifestation of such reminders at the age of 79 years and expressed the need to restudy the villages. ICSSR though acknowledged his contributions to the village studies in India and also the relevance of restudying these villages, but asked to modify the proposal to review the literature on village studies in Uttar Pradesh over the last 80 years by taking into account his age and deteriorating health. The Gobind Ballabh Pant Social Science Institute (GBPSSI), Allahabad became a centre for his rejuvenated social interactions in an institutional framework with academia in and around the institution in sharpening his sociological imagination. He interacted with the senior fellows like Ramashray Roy and J.P. Singh, the faculty members such as Badri Narain, Bhaskar Majumdar, S.K. Pant, K.N. Bhatt, Kripa Shankar, Jean Dreze, Kalpagam, Sunit Singh, A.R. Mishra, G.C. Rath, R.M. Tripathi, Ram Charan Tripathi and Pradeep Bhargava, and the visitors during seminars.

While reviewing the village studies in Uttar Pradesh over the last 80 years, Chauhan's inner urge to relate the review with the tradition of fieldwork motivated him to organise a workshop in the last week of October 2007 to discuss the feasibility of organising a seminar on intensive village studies. Some of the participants in the workshop besides Chauhan and myself were Tulja Ram Singh, Jean Dreze, P.B. Singh Rana, Pradeep Bhargava, Pankaj and Rajesh Mishra. In the deliberations not only some significant contributions of scholars on village studies during the 1950s and 1970s were discussed but its later decline and the current need to carry out such studies in the contemporary period with diachronic perspective were also emphasised. Finally, the deliberations culminated in taking decision to organise a seminar on February 29 and March 1, 2008 in GBPSSI to bring out some studies that were carried on villages after 1970s. March 1 coincided with the 82nd birthday of the first author of the volume. Deliberations in the workshop and the papers selected for inclusion in this volume are dealt with briefly here.

Deliberations in the Workshop

Village as an idea, an organising principle and the basis of life remains powerful in the popular conception and in the works of many academicians. Intensive village studies were carried from 1950s when the twin disciplines of Sociology and Anthropology were gaining roots in the Indian academia. This line of research also helped Indian scholars to come closer with expatriate researchers working in India. These studies stressed on participant observation and intensive microcosmic studies in the ethnographic tradition. Of course, they were supplemented with secondary data and historical evidence and insights (Atal, 2003; Beteille, 1975; Breman, 1997; Chauhan, 1974). These studies made endeavours to provide field view of the village in contrast to the "book view and upper caste view" (Srinivas, 1976) and have been extensively used as teaching material in university curricula as well as training kits for the development workers. Social sciences, thus, began contributing to a better understanding of the Indian society. In many ways these studies exploded several myths about village India as being static, self-sufficient, homogeneous and little republic (Metcalfe, 1830, quoted by Srinivas, 1955). They even challenged the Marxist interpretation of Asiatic Mode of Production (Avineri, 1969), which depicted village as static and governed by the communalistic nature of life and a hydraulic system of wet rice production. Such prevailing conceptions about the romanticised traditional village life were questioned by Popkin (1979); the conception of the village as a little republic has been extensively challenged (Dewey, 1972; Dumont, 1966) and village self-sufficiency is also questioned (Srinivas, 1955; 1960, Majumdar, 1955; Dube, 1955 and Marriott, 1955). Studies like those of Andre Beteille (1965) brought events happening in the village as related to the political and social movements at the state level. Srinivas (1955) and Marriott (1955) attempted serious work in studying the village life and exploring its links with the regional and the national or classical levels. Thus, the village studies focused either on the internal organisation of the village as a combination of groups and institutions or as units interacting with similar units and towns again through constituent elements in terms of cooperation, competition and conflicts (Chauhan, 2009). In the words of Mines (2010), "Villages as social entities are always going to be the outcome of multi-local processes and networks along meaningful social relations and identities. These processes need to be understood historically with their differential consequences on diverse sections of society".

In these studies, while some scholars were interested in documenting and understanding the structure of village India before the waves of development and modernisation transformed it (Atal, 2003; Beteille, 1975; Breman, 1997; Chauhan, 1974), others were interested in documenting the process of change, particularly of directed culture change; still some others were engaged in carrying out specific project-related studies such as evaluation or impact of innovations (Dube, 1958). The economists mostly used the survey method and focused on documenting the processes of social and economic changes in micro-settings, usually covering more than one village. Thus, it is felt that the real strength in the subject be assessed both for their internal refinement and redefining the interrelationship of sociology with economics, with historical approach, and with geographical mapping of rural settlements. Recently, the rise of development studies, and to an extent management studies, has opened a new dimension for rural research through selective case studies and their interrelations with the wider world. In order to comprehend the interconnectedness of the village with the state, the wider aspects of society in economic and historical terms are also being examined in a systematic manner.

In the words of Atal (2005), "In more recent years, attention has shifted to communication links, flows of information, voting behaviour, health practices and family, and economic transactions in the village communities. Thus much more differentiated pattern of village studies in India have emerged. The interest in social research in India is increasingly getting oriented towards the urban studies with a neglect of village studies. Such shift is appreciated but the neglect of village studies cannot be commended. Most of the data generated regarding village is discrete, descriptive and discipline-specific and little has been done to consolidate and codify it with raising and debating methodological questions along with the formulation of conceptual frameworks". Thus, in the workshop deliberations, it is realised that village is going to remain a key fact and the need to rejuvenate village studies was felt.

In the same way a need to reinvigorate village studies was also noted by many scholars earlier to these deliberations (Atal, 2005; Madan, 2005; Marriott, 2005; Shah, 2005; Wadley, 2005). The village has been cast aside perhaps more due to changing academic fashion. Two-thirds of India's population still reside in the villages and contribute to the production of primary goods for industry and cereals for consumption. The villagers have their own political, social and cultural worlds and to be seen as "an area for forces operating at regional, national and international levels" (Chauhan, 2003). Certain political changes like those of the introduction of adult franchise at the national level, and agrarian reforms like abolition of zamindari, consolidation of landholdings, and land ceiling, changes in cropping pattern and sources of irrigation, increasing intensity of indebtedness, changes in technology, Information and Communication Technology (ICT), and other forces have greatly influenced village life. Effect of such changes on the structure needs systematic in-depth comparative historical studies. Community development and its latter versions indicate state initiated development programmes and later the civil society initiated development activities have again raised questions as to how far the progress reports of macro-data are indicative of the realities on the ground. Only intensive enquiries could provide answers to such questions. There is a need for careful investigation of the outcome of the recent amendments to the Constitution related to empowerment and changes in the normative pattern of interaction between SCs and non-SCs and also women and men. There is also a need to study as to how these constitutional provisions have affected the nature of leadership, pattern of group dynamics, and factionalism in the village social structure in relation to villages and hamlets within a statutory village panchayat, block, district, state and national level group dynamics. Besides these changes, the village is also experiencing the emergence of new occupations, proliferation of middle men (Shah, 2005); Dalit awakening and civil society initiated development programmes (Madan, 2005); technological changes (Marriott, 2005); meanings associated with the interactions (Mines and Yazgi, 2010); and social and cultural processes emanating from outside the village and their differential consequences on various social units (Atal 2005; Chauhan, 2009). Systematic and in-depth studies are needed for a better understanding of group dynamics at the village level as also of the effect of rural-urban interactions. The spread of ICT, policies of liberalisation, privatisation and globalisation have their own impact on rural life as it increases the intensity of 'moral density' between rural and urban dwellers. Finally, in the workshop, it was decided to hold a seminar on intensive village studies focusing not only on the literature review of village studies but also inviting scholars carrying their studies on the tradition of fieldwork to contribute papers. Based on that the present volume is being brought out as a tribute to our friend, philosopher and guide—Professor Brij Raj Chauhan.

The Seminar Proceedings and the Volume

A seminar on intensive village studies was held on 29 February–1 March 2008 at GBPSSI, Allahabad that was attended by more than 50 scholars from different parts of the country and also from neighbouring Sri Lanka. Of the total papers presented in the seminar, 26 were selected for inclusion in this volume. The volume is divided into five sections. The first section deals with perspectives on village studies, followed by the restudy of villages and development administration in the second section. The third section is concerned with changing political scenario in Indian villages, while the fourth section looks into the socio-psychological probing of villages, and the last section focuses on war and war-like situations and social movements.

Of the six chapters comprising the first section three deal mainly with the review of literature on village studies. Brij Raj Chauhan reviewed village studies for 80 years and generated not only 10 prepositions that need empirical testing but also stressed the need for extension of intensive village studies to sister disciplines. Ramashray Roy emphasised on the limitations of village studies in the colonial period and early independent years through his phenomenal perspectives. He further emphasised the need to carry out village studies in the contemporary period also. Ravi S. Singh and Kavita Jaijan reviewed articles published in *Economic and Political Weekly* from 1995 to 2007 to find out the themes and regions that are neglected in the village studies. Yogesh Atal identified different forces operating in the villages and asserted the need to comprehend the effect of such forces on the social structure of villages. In the same tone, Susan S. Wadley reasserted not only the need for the restudy of those villages that were studied during the 1950s and 1960s but also to promote interactions with sister disciplines besides rejuvenating interactions with foreign scholars. Giri Raj Gupta tried to compare the village communities of India with USA.

The second section has again six chapters. While three are village restudies from different parts of India, the remaining three are related with developmental administration of state policies at grass roots level. The restudy of a Tamil Nadu village from 1979–80 to 2004–05 by R. Gopinath highlights the transformation of irrigation in a dry village dependent on tanks and wells and exemplified with case studies the coping mechanisms of marginal and medium size land owners to such transformation in irrigation. The implication of this study on the future of agriculture and the livelihood of such communities need to be assessed. On the other hand, the restudy of a village Shakori in 2007 in Himachal Pradesh taking the data collected by the Director General in 1961 as a benchmark by Pankaj Gupta reveals the declining significance of indigenous knowledge related to medicinal plants, bio and crop diversities, resettlement traumas of development of dam and cement factories and collective actions of Mahila Mandal of the Village Panchayat. The third restudy of a village in eastern Uttar Pradesh by P. Mishra brings out the differential patterns of social mobility among the middle and upper ranking castes as a consequence of remittances by emigrants from the metropolitan centres in India and abroad to their kin in the village.

Regarding developmental administration of governmental programmes, R. Shankar made an effort to see the role of primordial identities and cooperatives in development and their relations with bureaucrats, political leaders and beneficiaries at the grass roots level in his comparative study of Uttar Pradesh and Tamil Nadu villages. Social networks involved in borrowing loans from formal lending agencies like banks and the difficulties and costs the beneficiaries incur in the process was attempted by Jagdish Kumar Pundir. Finally, Arun Chauhan systematically analysed and evaluated the role of officials, NGOs and coordination between stakeholders and problems faced in different settlements in panchayat both in planning and execution of sanitation facilities.

The third section comprising four chapters is concerned with the bearings of political changes taking place in the statutory village panchayat and outside the village on dispute resolutions, interaction with other institutions, empowerment of poor, patterns of interaction emerging between the SCs and non-SCs after the 73rd constitutional amendment besides the effect of collaboration between modern and traditional institutions on village development. Interplay between traditional social and modern legal orders and their relevance in ongoing social and political life in four statutory village panchayats in Rajasthan from 1960s to 2000 are assessed by Shashi Bhushan Singh to understand the emergence of parallel institutions and their role in power sharing and channelisation of social conflicts in villages. The study of Shyampur panchayat in Bengal from 1978–2008 by Atanu Sengupta and Md. Salauddin Khan reveal that the empowerment of poor peasants and landless labourers is a distant dream as the decision-making bodies are dominated by middle peasants even in the regime of Left Front. The implications of 73rd constitutional amendment on the rural power structure and the constraints emerging in the functioning of four panchayats from three regions of Andhra Pradesh are analysed by A. Nageswara Rao and found emergence of four different trends in the normative interactions between SCs and general castes; women and men in the process of transfer of power to the cumulatively deprived sections of society. He also analysed the frequently observed derogative behavioural patterns towards SCs by non-SCs. M. Gurusamy studied two villages of Tamil Nadu and found that both traditional and modern institutions are functioning in collaboration with each other and promoted village development in collaboration with other modern institutions.

The section on socio-psychological probings into village life has also four chapters. The first chapter by Prachi Ghildiyal-Dwivedi and

R.C. Tripathi examines the impact of educational development at the macro level on levels of happiness and hopes and aspirations of villagers belonging to upper, backward and scheduled caste groups. The less educated are more happier than those who are relatively more educated and prosperous and are living in 'Fool's Paradise' because they evaluate their bad living conditions inaccurately as good or tolerable.

Sanjay and A. Satyanarayana, in a comparative study of suicide victim households and indebted normal cultivator households in Sangrur district of Punjab, reveal that indebtedness may be a necessary condition but other social and psychological factors seems to be the sufficient condition to explain suicides among cultivators. Similarly, the study of families in Reotipur village by Sunil Kumar Verma and A. Satyanarayana reveals that as a consequence of differences in priorities or values between generations tensions and stresses emerge. On the basis of differences in coping mechanisms to such tensions and stresses, the patterns of intergenerational relations also differ from integration, ambivalence and conflicts. Relationship between self-images of women as members and non-members of Self Help Groups (SHGs) is focused in the next paper written by D. Punetha and others. The study reveals that women members of SHGs have acquired better linguistic skills and are more self-assertive than the non-members of SHGs.

In the last section on war and collective actions, which contains six chapters, Abha Chauhan analysed the narratives of day-to-day experiences of women affected by wars (in 1947, 1971 and 1999) and war-like situations living in villages near the international border in Jammu and Kashmir and their coping mechanisms to such crises in terms of taking care of their children and neighbours. Shahul Hameed Hasbullah analysed the transformation of initial harmonic relations among Tamils and Muslims living in the undeveloped area of Sri Lanka and Singhalese becoming majority, break up of civil war, the ceasefire and tsunami, and resumption of state actions and finally coping of the villagers to such situations. The author however has some confidence in traditional institutions through which reconciliation may still work. Classification of scheduled castes into separate enclosures with each group entitled to a fixed percentage of quotas within the broad category and their consequences on the Dalit movement and Dalit consciousness with special reference to Mala and Madiga in Andhra Pradesh was dealt by K. Sekhar and V. Sreemannarayana Murthy. The hanging of the 1857 'insurgency' or 'revolt' activists by British rulers, the consequences of untimely death and localised efforts to keep the spirits calm through the Hindu and Muslim classical traditions, and the Arya Samaj and the Sanatan Dharma sects were discussed by T.R. Singh. Rabin Deka analysed the role of 'Raij Mel' or the people's assembly (traditional socio-political institution) in the mobilisation of peasants of Phulaguri in the Nagaon district of Assam in 1861 against the British policies related to the enhancement of land revenue, banning the cultivation and sale of poppy (opium) on private account. The dynamics of intra- and inter-caste social capital and its relation in continuum with collective action, development in terms of both functional and dysfunctional externalities and social conflicts in two villages of Uttar Pradesh was addressed by Pragyan and D.R. Sahu.

References

Avineri, S. (ed.) 1969, *Karl Marx on Colonialism and Modernization*, New York: Double Day.

Beteille, A. 1965, *Caste, Class and Power: Changing Patterns of Stratification in a Tanjore Village*, Berkeley: University of California Press.

Breman, J., P. Kloos and A. Saith (eds.), 1997, *The Village in Asia Revisited*, New Delhi: Oxford University Press.

Chauhan, B.R. 1996 [1999], *A Rajasthan Village*, Udaipur: A.C. Brothers.

——. 1970, *Towns in Tribal Setting*, Delhi: National Publishing House.

——. 1974, A Trend Report, in ICSSR (ed.) *A Survey of Research in Sociology and Social Anthropology*, Vol. I, Bombay: Popular Prakashan.

——. 1988, *Bharat Mein Gramin Samaj*, Etawah, Udaipur: A.C. Brothers.

——. 1990, *Rural-Urban Articulations*, Etawah: A.C. Brothers.

——. 1998, *Four Decades of Rural Development in Etawah*, New Delhi: ICSSR.

——. (ed.) 2005, "Rural Profiles Scenario 2005", *Eastern Anthropologist*, Vol. 58, Nos. 3–4, July–December.

Dube, S.C. 1955, *Indian Village*, London: Routledge and Kegan Paul.

——. 1958, 1967, *India's Changing Villages*, Bombay: Allied Publishers Ltd. (Ist Indian Edition).

Madan, V. (ed.) 2002, *The Village in India*, New Delhi: Oxford University Press.

Majumdar, D.N. (ed.) 1955, *Rural Profiles*, Vols. I and II, Lucknow: Ethnographic and Folk Culture Society.

Marriott, McKim. 1955, "Little Communities in an Indigenous Civilization", in McKim Marriott (ed.), *Village India*, Chicago: Chicago University Press.

——. (ed.) 1955, *Village India*, Chicago: Chicago University Press.

——. 2005, "Guest Editor Poser on Intensive Studies in Village: In Retrospect and Prospect", by B.R. Chauhan (ed.), *Rural Profiles Scenario 2005, The Eastern Anthropologist*, Vol. 58, Nos. 3–4, July–December, pp. 300–01.

Mayer, A.C. 1960, *Caste and Kinship in Central India*, London: Routledge and Kegan Paul.

Mines, D. and Yazgi, N. 2010, *Village Matters: Relocating Villages in the Contemporary Anthropology of India*, New Delhi: Oxford University Press.

Shah, A.M. 2005, "Intensive Studies in Villages: In Retrospect and Prospect", *The Eastern Anthropologist*, 58 (3–4): 295–99.

Srinivas, M.N. 1952, *Religion and Society Among the Coorgs of South India*, Bombay: Asia Publishing House.

——. (ed.), 1955, *India's Villages*, Bombay: Asia Publishing House.

——. 1955a. "The Social Structure of a Mysore Village", in M.N. Srinivas (ed.), *India's Villages*, Bombay: Asia Publishing House, pp. 21–35.

——. 1960 [1955], "The Social Structure of a Mysore Village", in M.N. Srinivas (ed.), *India's Villages*, 2nd revised edition, Bombay: Asia Publishing House, pp. 21–36.

——. 1987, "The Indian Village: Myth and Reality", in M.N. Srinivas (ed.), *The Dominant Caste and Other Essays*, New Delhi: Oxford University Press, pp. 20–59.

Part I

Perspectives on Village Studies

1

Eighty Years of Intensive Field Studies in Uttar Pradesh

Strong Beginnings, Indifferent Present and Promising Future

Brij Raj Chauhan

A Drawing Master Sahab teaching us in Class V, stood near the blackboard with a piece of chalk, drew a scene through some strokes, looked at them; then walked two metres away to look at the way details were related to each other; again back to the board, two or three strokes readjusted, and then again two metres … and then after four to five sets of corrections … moved four metres back to satisfy himself of the balance of the drawing as a composed work. The continuous interchange of the points of observations, re-examining the combination, and introducing or inserting corrections in the course of making a composition, have a lesson for all efforts; artistic, scientific, humanitarian or any combination of them.

In the present context, the position of the blackboard indicates the micro-dimension, the stance at two metres the meso-dimension and that at four metres the macro-dimension. These dimensions, according to space and time, vary from context to context. The position of the village is at micro level, its position among similar units covering a group of related villages, say a group of hundred villages or so is the meso zone, and probably a state or the nation constitute the macro one.

Micro studies, involving direct observation by the scholars concerned, have been carried out over nearly eight decades in the state of Uttar Pradesh. These studies cover districts such as Mirzapur, Jaunpur, Varanasi, Basti, Lucknow, Raibareli, Etawah, Mainpuri, Aligarh, Moradabad, Bijnor, Bulandshahr, Meerut, Muzaffarnagar and Saharanpur. A few villages such as Senapur (Jaunpur), Rankhandi and Jhabiran (Saharanpur), Karimpur (Mainpuri) and Palanpur (Moradabad) have been repeatedly studied by a number of scholars. Thus, they have been instrumental in making available material for more than five PhD dissertations each for different universities in the US and India, besides dozens of research articles. These studies brought Indian scholarship into direct contact with the situation on the field and abstracted significant points to interact with the international deliberations. These enabled the participants in several experiences to become respectable partners at equal levels, for at least a quarter of a century. Such a source of strength, it appears, is drying up a bit, and it is time that its strength and further possibilities be assessed, and the smell of the field reincorporated in ongoing research. After eighty years it is now time to stand apart and have a look at the mosaic that these micro studies present before us. It is also to visualise the contribution of studies to abstraction and conceptualisation; and whether certain general propositions can be drawn from there. Ten propositions may be abstracted from these studies.

The Set of Ten Propositions

Proposition I: Villages have a history of formation, control over resources and obligations for maintaining law and order

Villages were formed through the settlement of vacant land or conquests or grants from the state for services rendered in either the secular or the sacred realm. The foundation of the village is known to the people, there is a founding deity of the village as well, and an awareness of historical connections merging into mythological links. All these connections are spread over a period of time, ranging over seven to eight centuries to recent formations.

The initial formation of the village thus gets linked to a few leading families that, over a period of time; get distributed over neighbouring villages, in which some awareness of common origin continues to be shared in a meso region. At the level of conceptual analysis these lead to the formation of 'a village and its region' (Mayer, 1960).

Proposition II: Agriculture has been the main occupation of the villages with landowning groups cultivating the land themselves (as in western UP) or getting it cultivated through peasants and workers under different arrangements (as in middle and eastern UP)

Supplemental needs for cultivation are met through the services of the artisan groups distributed among a few caste groups; and domestic needs through the services rendered by similar, other specialised groups. The pattern of the interrelations linking the patrons and clients into the *jajmani* pattern lasted almost till the first half of the 20th century when the market forces began to make their presence felt. The pattern, in a rather loose form, continues its significance particularly in the ritual sphere, and a few scholars seem to suggest that patron-client relations have entered the political sphere as well!

Proposition III: Formations of villages follow two processes – the centrifugal and centripetal

When a founding family grows and diversifies, and spreads to new areas, new settlements are formed. Natural calamities and human interactions play a part in such a diversification. For example, a flourishing village (Jasohan in Etawah district), with seven hundred weavers producing cloth for the market, was located on the banks of Yamuna in the fourth quarter of the 19th century. The construction of railways ten kms away replaced the river as a means of communication and transport. Canal irrigation from the river reduced its navigability and, at least once, flooding in the rainy season proved destructive. Centrifugal forces began operating as weavers lost their jobs because commercial manufacturing in textile started taking place. A large number of boatmen became unemployed; and leading peasant families began moving nearer to their fields. As a fallout, the boatmen and weavers took to agriculture in different resettled villages and the leading families set up their new establishments nearer their fields. This gave rise to ten villages. These settlements, identifiable in a centrifugal manner, again had to be furnished with the paraphernalia of the required artisans and the service groups, ushering in the centripetal forces again into operation. In the process a number of small hamlets grew up and, over a period of time, these too developed a sort of reorganisation sometimes bordering on their own autonomy.

The developmental schemes of the state, which tend to provide schools in every hamlet, besides a few other institutional facilities like the construction of roads and other special programmes, tend to appear to provide an increasing scale of identity to these hamlets, moving at least half way to formation of a village community. On their part, the residents of these hamlets strengthen their feelings through the adoption of rituals specific to their hamlets.

Proposition IV: The social composition of a village consists of a number of castes put together in a defined locality surrounded by fields

Landowning groups usually come from the higher castes and working peasants and some artisan castes from the middle group, with a few agriculture workers and service groups coming last, corresponding to their caste positions arranged hierarchically, presenting the villagers a vertical unity of different castes. Thus, each caste has a network of its own relations at a horizontal level in the meso region of the villages. The fact of being together in the village is shared, as also the memory of events like a grand marriage or a ritual or a secular event, which becomes a reference point for locating milestones in the collective life and calendar of the village. Certain annual festivals enable common participation and the sharing of thoughts and feelings.

Proposition V: Village life, in the traditional setting, had its interconnections with other villages in the neighbourhood

Villages in the state are normally exogamous in character which means that the girls of the village are married outside the village, preferably to the spouses in the western and northern directions; and likewise the boys of the village get their wives preferably from the eastern and southern sides, thereby bringing in a total replacement of the women folk of the village. A few exceptions are reported in the case of the Muslim population where marital ties among the close kin are permitted. In general, a village gets linked to a hundred other villages with two effects, one being the widening of the kinship ties and the second providing an occasion to the villagers to exhibit their unity at the wedding functions. When an event like this takes place in the village in any caste, a son-in-law of any family is treated as a son-in-law of the whole village in terms of deferential respect and regard. As the Ganga and Yamuna form the lifelines of the state, certain common rituals associated with sacred bathing assume the form of a *mela* at pilgrim centres, with groups of villagers enriching their spiritual benefits, getting exposure to the temporarily set up urbanised centres at the river banks, and enjoying the holiday mood along with many participants from other villages. At times these occasions also provide an opportunity to look for spouses.

The implications of the propositions, for re-examining the received academic and administrative wisdom from 19th century scholars which partly continued till the middle of the 20th century also adopted in the Gandhian formulations that the village was once a self-sufficient unit, are by now clear, even in the traditional organisation of the social life for the purposes of establishing marriage relations with a hundred other villages. In the other traditional sphere of ritual life, pilgrim centres and connections of local festivals and deities with the regional and national ones had been an integral part of rural life. Thus, the traditional structure of social organisation was inclusive of extra-village ties. Therefore, any idea of self-sufficiency needs a revision.

Proposition VI: Significant events in the political life have an impact on rural life over a period of time

Over a historical period, collections of land revenue and maintenance of law and order have remained the primary concerns of a state. From one-sixth to one-half of the produce could be taken over by the state directly or through the intermediaries. During Alauddin Khilji's (1296–1316) rule, a sort of compulsory levy of food grains to sustain military and urban centres has been recorded (Thapar, 1975, 2006). For later periods, grants by the rulers as rewards for military or spiritual services have been known. In the Mughal period, especially, transfer of land control had been frequently adhered to (Habib, 1963). The successor British government devised its own pattern of revenue collection, conforming to *zamindari* rights in one case and *ryotwari* in the other. Beyond these arrangements, certain significant military operations ensured with consequences on multiple aspects of life. Selectively reference could be made to two such events; first, the 1857 struggle and its being crushed by the colonial power, and second, the struggle for Indian independence.

The events of 1857 had two impacts: (1) With some castes and lineages fighting against the British and the others siding with them. The rulers on their part rewarded their supporters through land grants and punished the fighters for their role by depriving them of their land resources. In case of Uttar Pradesh, there is a strong feeling that the differential economic development of the western part to the neglect of the eastern part is one of the implications of state action (Singh, 1997). On the other hand, within the western part of the state, the memory of opponents and supporters of different castes and lineages persists and gets linked to their differential participation in the peasant movements of the late 20th and 21st century (Satyanarayana, 2006). Gandhi's influence on rural organisations during the freedom struggle was felt in a peculiar manner, almost unanticipated. Certain caste groups responded earlier, but the stress on *khadi* had an effect of strengthening the weaver groups economically and politically. In Uttar Pradesh, the weavers came from among the Muslims who had begun to call themselves Ansari and got aligned to the Deoband School and the Indian National Congress.

After independence, the introduction of the adult franchise, abolition of the *zamindari,* adoption of ceilings on the landholdings, schemes of community development and later the devolution of powers to Panchayati Raj institutions (PRIs) have been significant events. The responses of the villagers to these initiatives have been recorded by sociologists and social anthropologists, besides scholars from sister disciplines. The enquiries reveal that, in the first phase of the introduction of these measures, the traditional power holders substantially managed to hold on to power positions and control the benefits, and only marginal gains flowed to the others formally put on the equal status (Singh, 1978; Dube, 1958; Imtiaz, 1976; Singh, 1985; Jetley, 1977) These studies related to events happening in the first quarter of independent India and their contributions have to be read with caution as they are related to the things that happened at the time of writing.

At the state level, power was initially held by a single party where the struggle for power was also limited within it. Internal groups began to be related to caste formations, leading individuals splitting the party into various groups, and the emergence of coalition politics in which sub-regional caste formations became significant actors (Brass, 1983, 1985). In the first phase, there was a specialisation of voting patterns leading to differential allocation of power within the party for the state assembly and the national parliament. But later the differences began to get reflected at the centre too. The organisation of the state and new combinations among political parties began to work themselves out. Towards the end of last quarter of the 20th century, the mobilisation of lower caste groups became a factor to be reckoned with. Scholars from the London School of Economics paid special attention to the process. Failures in the first phase now gave rise to the success in the second and still raise a question on the manner in which the new combinations get worked out in gaining power. The mobilisation of the peasants and the lower groups has its connections with rural life. Co-operative societies for brick making and dairying have been successful on the economic front with the consequence of their becoming para-political forces. The spread of education in high school and intermediate colleges is largely in the private sector managements in which new rural leadership has a stake and is becoming the spring-board for political mobilisation. State policies, in providing housing, water supply and the electricity to the rural areas, have a consequence reaching not merely the central villages but also its satellite units called *Majara* and *Purva* in different parts. Sociological interest lies in the extent to which units of planning the village or hamlet would count significantly and a substantial number of hamlets gets characterised by the larger presence of hitherto deprived sections. New priorities get worked out in these state policies. On their own part, after getting a school and allied facilities, the hamlets also try to develop their ritual identity disconnecting them from the main village and asserting their own autonomy as shown in recent studies in Jaunpur district.

The implications of this proposition for sociological understanding of the rural life are found in Bailey's (1957, 1963) assertion that in Orissa the economic forces cut across the village, and political processes pass over the village tangentially. This has to be placed in a proper time and space perspective, with the struggle for power being considered the master key for all the state directed efforts reaching the rural areas, and specially the hitherto deprived sections, by the beginning of the 21st century in Uttar Pradesh.

The legislative measures of prescribing consolidation of land holdings had their implication for the state and have had positive consequences at the rural level. Economists and administrators in the first half of the 20th century had detailed accounts of how the rights of ownership were being affected for every plot at different places (Mukerjee, 1925). The consolidation of landholdings for the owner at one place was effected, though not easily, but had significant effects on farming practices. Farmers, initially in western UP, and then in eastern, could afford to have tube wells where electricity was available or diesel operated pumping sets otherwise, to ensure regularity in the irrigational practices. This led to the adoption of commercial farming, increased use of improved seeds and fertilisers and additional scope for women's contribution to productive activities among such castes that did not consider women participation in the agricultural process as a taboo. A series of improvement followed, including the purchase of tractors both for their own use and renting them out with tractor trolleys, which worked as means of transport both for conveying produce to sugarcane factories or the market, as well as providing a facility for visits by members of family to neighbouring areas on ritual occasions (Chauhan, 1990). Consolidation of the landholdings was updated in about twenty years making the necessary adjustments and can be considered as a success story of state efforts.

In the area of peasant mobilisation a new agenda has appeared with regard to demand for regular supply of electricity (Satyanarayana, 2010), ensuring the release of fertilisers on time and reassessing the cost of production in relation to the price fixed by the state. The spread of urban and industrial areas and acquisition of land for that purpose have added to the agenda of the peasant struggle for getting justifiable remuneration or dispensing with the process itself.

The second aspect of the interest of the state has been maintenance of law and order in the rural areas for which, in the Middle Ages, institutions like *zamindari* and, later in the British period, *taluqdari* were created. They dealt with the problems of law and order and imparted local justice in both formal and informal ways. During the discussion on Zamindari Abolition Bill in the state legislature and preparation of the *ZAC Report*, Begum Aijaz Rasool in her separate note pointed out the implications of abolition of *zamindari* on the maintenance of law and order at the local level. Of course the police always existed from the British time but within the village the new *pancha* could hardly fill in the vacuum. Gradual depletion of resources of formal controllers added to the problem. Introduction of the competitive politics in the villages have intensified the power struggle and in the election to the panchayats, pressures to withdraw subsequent styles of adopting successful candidates by political parties, and the undeveloped political culture in which the electoral verdict is accepted by all concerned for a specified period, create conditions of continuous conflict that are at times tried to be solved through mechanisms of no confidence and realignment of forces or even by resorting to physical action. While such events have got ample coverage in the press, concentrated attention in sociological enquires has only begun to take shape.

Proposition VII: Developmental activities in the village have several starting points ranging from the self-initiative of the people, positive examples and economic support of kinsmen, the state and the market forces

State initiatives came through community projects in the early 1950s. In Mirzapur district factions within the village provided difficulties for undertaking development tasks. A similar situation in Mysore was examined by Beals (1955) who thought that in some villages though conflicts were present, but development had also occurred. S.C. Dube's full-length work, *India's Changing Villages* (1958), took note of a Rajput village and a Tyagi village in Saharanpur district. The dominant thought in social science, based upon the Theory of Culture Lag (Ogburn, 1932; Parsons, 1965), considered that changes in the technology come faster than the changes in values of the people. In villages people acted according to their values and habits. Thus Dube thought that the values of the people have to be respected and changes introduced within their parameters of thinking. The pilot project in Etawah, through the efforts of Albert Mayer, an engineer from the US, planned to widen the village streets and pave them. The villagers refused to accept the plan of work, saying that a more pressing problem, in the wake of some foot disease among animals was their immediate concern. Mayor (1958) changed his plans, went in for inoculation of the animals, and the cure once affected, had his bona fides accepted in the village. This led to the concept of judging the 'felt needs' of the people before introducing the plans of development.

State plans had to be educative in nature and the manner in which the message from the state reached the people became a matter of concern for social scientists. Writing of slogans on the wall had little meaning for the illiterates. The style of language used in the communication in standard Hindi was different from the dialect used by the people (Gumperz, 1957). The key functionary of the village at the village level was called the Village Level Worker (VLW), who was perhaps the weakest link in the chain, and his diary over the week was maintained by S.C. Dube (1958), which indicated the nature of pressures that different officers and public men exercised over him. The initial success of the Etawah project was charismatic. Within two decades, the scheme got routinised. In the third phase a little bit of indifference crept up in official dealings (Chauhan and Singh, 1999); and the latest position was that the Village Level Worker himself graduated to the new level of the Village Level Officer (VLO). Interesting case-studies of the Etawah project reveal the setting up of the peanut chilling factory and its giving up; an instruments repair unit having a similar fate, its machinery left free for all to be taken away. Well-intentioned moves like setting up a *Charmakar Kendra* in the village with a large Chamar population backfired. Chamar was translated as *Charmakar* whereas a substantial majority among them happened to be agricultural workers who had undertaken some sort of agricultural work. They were also affected by the movement of sanskritisation. The *Charmakar Kendra* happened to be located in a locality which had no meaning for those people as the actual workers lived in another locality. Hence, there was a need for a deeper understanding of the nature of the social units before planning for schemes based on formal nomenclatures. The Etawah project had positive aspects as well in the introduction of the high yielding varieties of wheat, potato and peas. Besides encouraging the operation of the tubewells, D.P. Singh as Project Officer set personal examples and was instrumental in encouraging local leaders to come together to set up two agricultural colleges in the district with the consequence that an agricultural graduate could be found in most of the large villages of the district.

Villagers had the capacity to understand new processes, benefited from them and later, the Agricultural University at Pant Nagar, through its experiments on the new seeds, became a place to be looked upon for more ideas. At the social level, a somewhat well-to-do section described as *khate-pite log* began to emerge, causing concern to social scientists committed to the ideology of equality, leading to a lot of discussion whether the green revolution had sown the seeds of the red revolution.

State efforts in the development of individual areas, beginning with the idea of the community development projects, developed a special branch of study in extension education. The overall result was diversification in the efforts of development, with the agricultural component becoming more and more professional. Michel Mahar, an American social scientist initially connected with the Cornell project in Deoband *tehsil* of Saharanpur, after his revisit three decades later, was asked a question by this writer, 'How do you look at the community development now?' He answered, 'Development: Yes ... Community: No ... !'. Among the studies of development, mention may be made of Surendra Jetley's (1977) work on the comparison of developed and underdeveloped villages through statistical techniques and Durganand Sinha's (1968) efforts through developed psychological techniques on people's perceptions in developed and underdeveloped villages in Allahabad district. A few geographers also attempted similar questions in Allahabad which suggested that the response of the social scientists had begun to be widespread and gained its due place in the syllabi in Indian universities. Dube's book (1958) was easily available as the first instance of a full work on Applied Sociology or the Sociology of Planning.

Beyond the state initiatives there have been a number of efforts initiated by the people themselves, like making a tubewell in an area of

Etawah prior to the introduction of the pilot project (Chauhan and Singh, 1999); purchase of tractors by a few families in the Meerut region, some even travelling to Andhra Pradesh to purchase a second hand variety of it (Satyanarayana, 1985). As development proceeded further, the representatives of manufacturers began sending their sales representatives to villages with depots on their own even at tehsil levels in Meerut region. Arrangements for different machinery for tube wells and pumping sets were made, with the rise of networks between peasant and marketing agencies (Satyanarayana, 2010). Of further significance is the rise of the cash crops which have a long history since the irrigation system was established in western UP in the second half of the 19th century, and even earlier in some parts. Improvements in the quality and amount of wheat production and extension of sugarcane cultivation have a long history of more than 150 years by now in western UP (District Gazetteers: Saharanpur, Muzaffarnagar and Meerut).

Improvements in the variety of sugarcane have come through special efforts on the part of the mill owners as they directly benefit from it, and some varieties of cane from Coimbatore have been introduced. Towards the second half of the 20th century, supply from the sugarcane factories began to be worked out through some sort of cane growers' union, with the factory allocating the quotas of the date and supply of the cane to the factory gates and the cane society taking care of the distribution of slips to farmers. Special tarred roads were also constructed, primarily to facilitate the transport of cane from the villages to the factory, with minor help from the state. On their own part, the cane growers of the Rankhandi decided to impose a cut on returns to provide a corpus fund for setting up an intermediate college in the village. They further added a brick-making co-operative unit to have the building ready for the purpose. On the railway line between Ghaziabad and Saharanpur practically every station has a sugar factory and an intermediate college. The factories cannot consume all the raw materials, hence preparation of *kandsari,* sugar and *gur* are so common that on a road journey in the winter night, one can keep smelling odours produced during the entire journey.

The rural-urban context has two dimensions. Urban areas provide avenues for further occupation, higher education, specialised medical facilities and supplies of oil and gas. Graduate students from the rural areas studying in colleges and universities in urban centres serve as links.. Aspects of rural-urban connections have been studied in detail for UNESCO project by Brij Raj Chauhan (1990). The towns themselves show migration from rural areas as the houses are built in the urban areas for migrants, some of whom bring with them the milk cows. The patterns of interrelations among women and families in a locality in Meerut have received pointed attention in the work of Sylvia Vatuk (1972). Worth noting here is a comment by a Jat villager working in an office in Meerut, 'If agriculture prospers, towns also prosper. In a good season we arrange marriages and make a lot of purchases in town. The *mandis* of the town receive grain and *gur* to sell and make profits from them helping the towns to grow further!' But to cap it all he said, 'The towns grow on the strength of the villages.' The villages themselves have begun to receive some branches of banks in leading villages. Whereas the youngsters prefer an account in town where they can use their savings and time with greater liberty; some who have made good and moved to town keep on visiting the village periodically improving the general knowledge of the people. They also think of building a respectable house in the village, which if built in the city would hardly receive public notice whereas the one in the village would be demonstrative of their new prestige. The village extension of municipal limits in the surrounding rural areas has had its own consequences. With decent compensation received by the people, one section purchased land and built house on them, another used that money for purchasing land in more distant villages, increasing their agricultural prosperity, and a third section became operators of minor transport or set up cold storage plants. Some of the youth could not adjust to the new situations, began to while away their time in their neighbouring town restaurants, and became a social problem that called for separate attention.

Proposition VIII: Education and health in the early phases of development presented alternative channels of indigenous and modern varieties that ultimately resulted in the widespread acceptance of the latter with the supplemental role assigned to the former

During the last quarter of the 19th century and the first half of the 20th century, Dayanand's influence in the spread of Vedic education particularly attracted the rural areas of western UP. Anglo-Vedic schools and colleges were set up and parallel developments in the rise of the *Sanatan Dharma* schools and colleges also ensued. Likewise, among the Muslims, the Deoband School emphasised the classical and Aligarh Muslim University the changing aspect of education to suit the needs of the modern era. At the behavioural level, in the rural areas, the Jats in particular began observing family rituals of *havan* popularised by Dayanand and found it helpful to keep ritual restrictions on direct participation in manual agricultural work at a distance. The Brahmins and the Rajputs particularly of western region too followed with no taboo on self-cultivation of land. Among a few lower groups, local priests emerged, dispensing with the centrality of the Brahmin, particularly in the Agra region. Increasing contacts between urban and rural areas had their own effect in creating a progressive section among various castes. Our enquiries in the city of Agra revealed that the parents of the girls from amongst the Bhangi and Chamar families did not want them to be married to spouses in the rural areas and the explanation offered was that in the rural setting the women would be obliged to follow the traditionally degrading work and observe the related behaviour therewith. A Jat student pursuing sociology courses in Meerut University questioned the very rationale of *sanskritisation* which defined the Brahmin at the apex of society with his standards of behaviour serving as role model for the rest of the society: 'In what way are the Brahmins superior? We have land, developed tools of agriculture; even in reciting *shlokas* during the *havan*, we are not inferior as compared to semi-literate Brahmins; and we have the numbers and public influence!'. In another Jat village a grandfather was teaching the five-year-old youngster, '*bhojan ka mantra*' and was proud of the success of the child in being able to recite it. These are illustrations of supplemental education to that which is imparted in the schools. The state maintained schools had two types of teachers, (a) permanent, and (b) temporary ones, hired under the *Shikshak Mitra Scheme*. A field visit in 2006 was addressed to the relative performances of the two sets of teachers. The work of temporary teachers was assessed as being of good quality, and they were found to be hard working and enthusiastic. Regarding the permanent teachers, with nobody to question them; their performance was summed up in one sentence, 'They behave like sons-in-law of the village.' A few English teaching schools, nick named English medium schools, have also sprung up through the private efforts of some teachers. They are beginning to receive clientele from the leading families of the villagers in the neighbouring town. High schools with greater stress on English teaching have sprung up and important neighbouring villages send their children there in specially hired auto vehicles. The dependence of the town schools on a regular supply of students from the rural areas is indicated by the reply of one of the students from village Jhunjhini in Meerut district, 'If our village and the other neighbouring village

(Nagla) do not send the students, the school would collapse.' Yet another school developed in the town and the principal and his staff was seen visiting another village canvassing for greater enrolments on the plea that the school had managed to send a batch for high school examinations that year. The leading intelligent villager remarked, 'If your results are good, you will get more students', suggesting thereby that the guardians had a stake in the delivery of quality performance in the emerging sectors, a definite change in the felt expectations of the people.

Social scientists have paid interest to the quality of the schools in the private and the public sector, the distance that the students have to travel and the relation among teachers and students. For village Palanpur in Moradabad district, Jean Drèze (2007) recognised the existence of a school with its furniture taken away and wondered whether the school could be considered as functioning. The presence of the school teachers has had both positive and negative consequences with teachers paying their normal share of attention to both the school and the agricultural operations. In addition to the personal attention being given to the students, some sort of relation among them, reminiscent of the *jajmani* pattern, is also visible. In case of teachers coming from the neighbouring villages, the teacher's presence at fixed hours, sometimes being adjusted to travel time, remains formal in nature and limited in influence. For pursuing education beyond the high school and availing of the facility at the district headquarters, the villagers are obliged to make arrangements for the residence of students in town. Where two or three children are involved, they even think of hiring a room with a lady member out to take care of the boarding and ultimately even setting up an additional household in the town. In the eastern part of UP, with over three lakh candidates appearing in the civil service competitions of the state, some repeating performance at Indian Civil Service examination at the national level as well as other, the stage is well set for a mass migration of rural youth to the university centres and arrangements for private residence and distinctive coaching centres. The process itself is tortuous and statistically over 90 per cent would never be able to get through it, creating youth problems that need a separate policy formation. Meanwhile, the questions of accommodation, coaching, and occasionally going on side-by-side, postgraduate education, create their own set of problems. Besides causing strain on their inter-generational resources and relations among the youth and their parents, the spread of intermediate and degree colleges in the rural areas has raised the problem of the quality of management, with increasing personal interventions. Yet, to a question as to the increasing number of first divisioners, our respondents merely laughed, saying, 'Oh! That can be easily managed.' At the village level, some success is visible, with students doing jobs in urban centres, maintaining rural-urban connections, and thereby serving as agents of urbanisation at the initial stage and also helping others. At least in the first generation, some investment occurred at the agricultural front and the spread of knowledge and a decent house (from the rural standards) was built there, enhancing the status of the family. The same quality of rural house would hardly attract notice, if built in the urban area.

These developments get associated with the new middle class in the village in terms of inter-family relations. The success of one leads to the rise of a feeling of relative deprivation among others, the intensity of which increases among close siblings in the wake of the rather well-known sibling rivalry, setting up a fresh agenda for social science enquiries.

In the health sector, in the early phases of the 20th century, a local physician almost amounting to a '*jhola*-type doctor' served the multifarious needs of the local people on the spot earning a reputation of his own from the neighbouring villages as well. Preliminary training in Ayurvedic medicines, with occasional use of tablets and injections from other fields, met the immediate needs of the local people. Over the next half of the new century, the other alternative of Allopathic medicine has begun making in-roads in the village. During the freedom struggle, the social workers were supposed to carry a medicine kit with them including Homeopathic medicines. In social science research, Charlotte Wiser made elaborate notes on simpler medicines and medical care, and set up an additional tent for rendering medical aid to the people of Karimpur in Mainpuri district (1963) in the second quarter of the 20th century. This move made the couple acceptable in the village and established a long-lasting relationship between the social scientists and the villagers. A few other scholars adopted the same technique of supplying some medicines on the spot. Increasing use of the Allopathic system, with continued acceptance of grandmother's recipes and alternative systems of medicines continue to be a feature of rural life, as either simultaneously or sequentially, a balance is struck by the villagers in dealing with medical problems. On the part of the state, Allopathic, Ayurvedic and Yunani centres are being selectively opened to cover a group of villages; the number of health centres with facilities for child birth is on the increase, even though the role of traditional *dais* continues. *Aanganwadi Kendras* are set up for supplementing child nourishment with differential success that catches the attention of social scientists. There are a few villages from where young doctors in different streams of treatment have come up, becoming available for advice during the visit. During serious ailments, there is a tendency to catch the sympathy of the wider social structure trying to share the intensity of the situation.

Experiments of education and medicine in rural areas become an exercise of selection among alternatives, opening new dimensions of rural-urban relationships and determining the strength and weakness of the social groups that get concerned or remain indifferent. Even the limited success in education has the consequence of the rise of a limited middle class and intensification of kinship rivalries, all attracting the notice of the villagers and the social scientists alike. One sees a sort of dialectics between the traditional and the new values, which will be dealt with in the next proposition.

Proposition IX: Educational developments have a close connection with the received wisdom of the classics, the folklore, and practical advice subsumed in couplets and idioms in the shaping of the value patterns, with ample field of interaction and decision making in the rural settings and providing norms for appropriate actions

In the context of UP, the land of Yamuna and Ganga, the gradual advancement of the Aryans and their mixing with the others, apart from producing the 'Hindustani' elements or configurations, created classic literature in the form of the Vedas, particularly the last three and subsequent commentaries (Thapar, 2006). Contributions in Sanskrit are remembered by people on ritual occasions even today. Even though Valmiki composed the *Ramayana* in and around Chitrakut, the popular version in Avadhi by Tulsi Das (1574) became the most widely read and sung form of the classic story. A copy of the text (in middle size print which has been published from Gorakhpur in 25.75 lakh copies from 1948–2006) is usually found in all Rajput and Brahmin families and its norms of behaviour cited frequently. The text and the stories were effectively used during the freedom struggle against the British. During the *Eka* movement among the peasants Baba Raghav Das Jassal (1980) used the idiom of Ramayana to great effect. The national Hindi poet from Jhansi, Maithilisharan Gupta, brought out *Saket* in standard Hindi version in a poetic form, recalling the imprisonment of Sita in Sri Lanka and symbolically extending it to the British empire he put it like this,

'*Bharat Lakshmi padi abhi bhi rakshason ke bandhan mein*' (Bharat Laksmi, or mother India, is still languishing in chains of the demons). It was his publication, *Bharat Bharati*, that became popular in most of the literate houses in an effort to revive the self-confidence of the nation and resurrect it to the extent that the publication was banned from circulation by the state. Gandhiji's constructive programmes and values percolated through his autobiography, as did the literary skills of Premchand (1988, 2005) through stories and novels, and the poetic contributions of Sohanlal Dwivedi. The rise of Hindi prose and its refinements through magazines like '*Hans*' and daily newspapers like '*Aaj*' and '*Pratap*' are relevant beyond the material published to the rise of feelings of nationalism. Historical novel *Ajat Shatru* of Prasad makes Sanskrit references important, with the marching song in highly sanskritised Hindi having a great sound effect:

हिमाद्रतुंश्रृंग से प्रबुद्ध शुद्ध भारती
स्वयं प्रभा समुज्वला स्वतंत्रता पुकारती

From the peaks of the great snow-clad Himalayas, the enlightened and pure spirit of Bharat (India) self radiant and spreading brightness all around equally, the embodiment of freedom itself beckons thee [the youth] and tells them to march on, march on.

Apart from the meaning of the words, the sounds of R, S, P and T have the onomotopoeia effect, i.e., the sound conveys the sense of the drum beat and movement of the feet. In Kamayani and Nirala'a literary genius brought further glory to the great Himalayas, drawing attention to nature and the ground level realities. Among other historical events, the story of Rani Jhansi got wide attention in Subhadra Kumari Chauhan's popular script:

चमक उठी सत्तावन में वो तलवार पुरानी थी
बुंदेलें हरबोलो के मुँह हमने सुनी कहानी थी

Chamak uthi san Sattavan men, who talwar purani thi,
Bundele Harbole ke muh, hamne suni kahani thi

In the year 1857, the old sword began to shine brightly! From the mouths of the Bundela fighters/singers, we had heard this story.

What is important for the present level of analysis is that there was a great deal of interaction between the popular singers and the literary figures as is apparent from the second line.

बुंदेलें हरबोलों के मुँह हमने सुनी कहानी थी
खुब लड़ी मर्दानी वह तो झांसी वाली रानी थी

We had heard the Bundela soldiers/singers telling the story ... she had waged the war in a manly fashion, had fought hard, she was the Rani of Jhansi.

The phrase *'Bundele Har Bole'* needs an explanation. Pooling together information from three different sources, it may be said that the Bundela represent a fighting group that supported the Maratha rulers. The Rani of Jhansi had an exquisite temple of Lord Shiva in the fort, and a military action started after paying obeisance to the Lord. The Lord is frequently mentioned in the battle cry of *'Har Har Mahadeva'*. The group of Bundela soldiers uttered the words in full throated style before launching the march. Thus, they are referred to as *Bundele Har Bole*. They also sing songs in praise of their sovereign in popular language, and the song of *Jhansi ki Rani* became a part of their heroic deeds. In effect they have added to their public performance, other historical ballad like the *Alha Udal*, based on the resistance to Prithvi Raj Chauhan of Delhi by the regional chiefs of Bundelkhand area. Sometimes they compose *improptu* devotional songs that are woven into performances. An upgraded version of the story or the song on *Jhansi ki Rani*, recomposed by Subhadra Kumari Chauhan, through the use of standardised Hindi, was spread wide beyond the point of regional origin, and incorporated into the treasury of inspiring songs that spurred the people to action at the national level during the freedom struggle. It even inspired Subhash Chandra Bose to form the Lakshmibai regiment in the *Azad Hind Fauj* during the armed struggle against British rule in 1942. Indicating the secular dimension of the upward flow of an idea or a story in what Marriott had termed as 'universalisation' in the ritual context (1955).

At the popular level, the story of the *Ramayana*, through *Ramcharitmanas*, its various editions, abstracts and short stories, reached the illiterate people through the organisation of *Ramlila* every year at the end of the rainy season culminating in *Vijaya Dashami* and wrapped up with *Bharat Milap*. Mass participation in the events, coupled with organisational skills providing First Street and public level performance by locals in towns small or large, attract a lot of villagers, sharing an advantage both secular and sacred, bringing cheers and affirming certain elements of faith centring around victory of virtue over evil. As places associated with the story lie in the central part of UP like Ayodhya, Prayag and Chitrakut, with Tulsi Das' *Ramayana* composed in Ayodhya (1574) and authenticated in Varanasi, along with their periodic enactments every year, the epic has special appeal in continuing to provide the normative standards of behaviour and actions in UP and neighbouring Bihar, the home land of Janak and Sita.

The *Mahabharata* as an epic has its centre of action in Mathura and Gokul, associated with Krishna and the *Yaduvanshi* lineages with their centre of power in Hastinapur and Indraprastha. Kurukshetra, the scene of war, lies across the Yamuna. These places associated with the epic story provide a nearness to the people. The sages who occupied the chair of Vyas composed the epic. Its popular version has not come, except in translated prose, but the epic later got popularised in a TV serial. Several places connected with Pandava's *vanavas* (forced confinement to forests) are mentioned with their final victory and ultimate retirement to Himalayas recorded in the *Mahabharata Kathas* that are specially enacted by certain families celebrating significant events in life. These are staged in rural areas and have effective messages for people and also serve as a source of recreation. With the struggle amongst the brothers being the central theme, people fear similar scenes could be enacted in every family. During a fieldwork observation, when two brothers entered a detailed discussion on distribution of property, with tempers raised occasionally, the investigator posed a question, ' What is all this happening?' and the elder brother answered with some guilt and a bit of relieving tone, 'Nothing ... we were just having a Mahabharata here'. This much is on the flip side. However, on the positive side, the composition of the *Gita* remains an eternal contribution to the value system of the people, especially during the rituals following death.

The story of *Mahabharata* is carried forward by the first generation of sociologists in India. G.S. Ghurye told us during a meeting in his chamber that the Indian society was intrinsically linked to *Mahabharata* and students of Indian society would not be able to do justice to their enquiries if they ignore the prime source, the *Mahabharata*. A keen student of kinship organisation in India, Irawati Karve, used the epic to great effect and an American anthropologist remarked about her, 'She reads the *Mahabharata* more regularly than the *American Anthropologist*.' She took the genealogies of the Kaurava and Pandava dynasties as the starting point for her principal sociological work *Kinship Organization in India* (1953) and developed the ideas in the work *Hindu Society: An Interpretation* (1961).Carrying the story forward till the end of the Hastinapur dynasty a few generations after the battle of *Mahabharata,* Karve used her literary skills to perfection in describing how an era had ended with the writing of '*Yugant*' (1974) which earned her top literary rewards. A majority of readers now raise the point, 'We are aware of her literary contributions, how come you sociologists also take her name!'.

Popular literature appealing to historical figures and their consequences on the spread of different lineages in several parts of UP, along with some historical references has come to be known. Towards the beginning of 2nd millennium of the Christian era, a number of raids from outside occurred, with some of the raiders entering the complex Hindu social organisation and incorporated as Rajputs, some of the existing Rajput clans spread from central India and Rajasthan toward the UP, Bihar and the hilly regions (Thapar, 2006), it being generally believed that the purest form of Rajput exists in Rajasthan and their further diffusions adds some local strings affecting their original purity. The name of Prithviraj Chauhan, and the spread of his kinsmen, after his defeat, in various nearby parts of UP leading to a number of lineages, has been commented upon. The court poet Chandbardai had his composition *Prithvi Raj Rasau,* which became more popular in Rajasthan. Two lines from his work, describing the distance of the victim for the blinded prince in captivity, have remained popular all over. On the resistance side, Alha and Udal brothers in Bundelkhand region are frequently mentioned in the poetic composition *Alha Udal,* which is widely sung in a ballet by a few specialists during the rainy season in large parts of Uttar Pradesh. The poetic rendering in public places is more prominent in the Bundelkhand region where a group of regional specialists called the *Har Bole* enact a few acts of bravery, making challenging statements in exciting tones, bringing the audience to great enjoyment and even sometimes to action. A frequent refrain is '*Hiyan ki baten hiyana rahi gain, ab age ke suno hawal*', which means, 'Let this part of the episode be left here now and come to the next one.' The folk singers combine devotional songs with the performance or recite them separately too. Certain common stories at regional levels are a part of folklore independently, describing the unhelpful role of a husband and helpful role of his younger brother; the story of *Sakat* and *Makar Sankranti,* how devoted worship by a woman brought her results and its imitating action by a jealous woman produced contrary results. The *Katha* of *Satynarayan* is enacted after a small worship on any occasion of thanks-giving in rural areas. A *katha* can be organised through a local *Pundit;* a series of four stories impresses upon the audience the value of being truthful to the deity or, in consequence, suffer the loss through violation, with the possibility of regaining the loss through the efforts of worship by a junior member of the family. The story is popular well beyond UP and its enactment in any home is associated with the rituals connected with the first arrival of a bride in a home in Andhra Pradesh as well.

In describing the ritual life of people at the village level, scholars like Marriott (1955), Srinivas (1952) and Bhatt (2005) have traced the links of the local practices with something written in classics, thereby providing them a fresh legitimacy as well as justifying a regional variation. At times events get described in materialistic terms and with elaborate linguistic analysis of songs and stories connected with certain events. In a broad sense, one gets reminded of Wordsworth's sentence, 'We murder to dissect'. In actual research process, some of the rituals are best studied through silent observation trying to fathom the feelings of the people by looking into the mind through their faces. The case in point is of the *Magh Mela* in Prayag on selective days, as also the procession of *Gangajal* carriers during the month of *Shravan* by the *Kawadias* who follow their own norms of behaviour. During the *Magh Mela* days of special bathing, people of all generations and castes from villages walk the last 10 km on foot with great feeling, zeal and devotion towards the *Sangam*. They return with glowing faces, take a dip there along with a bottle of sacred water, as if their longings of the year have been spiritually taken care of by the Almighty, and with satisfaction and blessings on the face, return not as briskly as they had come, but really satisfied with their spiritual encounter as it were, and adding a bit of fun and pleasure on their return journey. The combination of the spiritual and material in the struggle for reaching the place, gaining supreme benefit, returning with some sort of holidaying, is an aspect of life which is described in the preparatory phase *'mela hai'*, and all the members of the family have to take due care of this. Such an understanding of life needs no questionnaires, no sampling, no interviews, just silent observation on the part of the investigator to let things happen on their own and arrive at conclusions in one's own mind. Beyond the observation of material and external aspects of life, one has to reach the meaning of actions of the actors. This is best described in Sanskritic pursuits as a search of the essential elements somewhat symbolically as *Lakshnik;* since a lot of discussion gets concentrated on the material composition and arrangements, but their symbolic meanings get less attention from the wider social structure trying to share the intensity of the situation.

In the era of publishing literature and prose novels, stories on rural life have made their appearance. Premchand's *Panch Parameshwar* (1988, 2005) sets a norm for panchayats, Suradas in the novel *Rangbhoomi* sets a model for resistance (Chauhan, 2000) besides others, seeming to invite practitioners of literary skills to cover rural areas. The movement for *Anchalik Sahitya* or regional literature has produced insightful works like *Raag-Darbari* by Shrilal Shukla (1983, 1999), *Aadha Gaon* by Rahi Masum Raza (1966, 2006) and in the neighbouring state of Bihar *Maila Anchal* by Phanishwar Nath Renu (1984, 2005). To a social scientist, the literature is insightful, but a depiction of the real state of affairs and the authenticity of the events is under a question mark. A historian of English literature said, 'Sincerity we may expect from an artist but not the truth'; Rahi Masum Raza's work *Aadha Gaon* carries a warning on the flap that it is composed of '*aadha such and aadha jhoot*' that is, 'half truth and half falsehood'. However, his another work *Neem ka Ped* appears very relevant to Sociology of Conflict within families in the rural situation, with the tree in the courtyard is treated as a witness symbolically, describing intense conflict among two kinsmen, their mobilisation of human resources, teasing the opponent of one of the relatives, etc.

Proposition X: A group of scholars drawn from the rural background, with exposure to university education, has emerged providing fresh perspectives on rural studies, which usher in new methodological and theoretical issues

The first generation of scholars of rural studies in India and their immediate students had come from urban India, and were brought up in the metropolitan centres. They took time in getting used to the rural setting, spending a good part of their time in establishing a rapport with the villagers and developing the required skills in studying a society other than the one they were used to living in. On most of the occasions their contacts with the village got confined to the time they spent in fieldwork. They maintained elaborate field notes and even when they continued to write on the same village, they relied mostly on their field notes for the data gathered intensively for two years. Further developments in the field and happenings over the next two or three decades were not available to them. The galaxy of scholars consisted of G.S. Ghurye, who for a change also looked into secondary data of *A Century and a Quarter*. Scholars like Srinivas (1952), Karve (1963), Majumdar (1955, 1958) and Dube (1955, 1958) began as externals to the village and the first three seldom revisited the areas once the studies were over. We come across a slightly different situation when persons born and brought up in the villages maintained connections with their own villages throughout their studies in urban areas. Some of them, having been trained under the first generation, began writing about their own villages and included the personal experiences of more than a generation in addition. Thus, Rudra Dutt Singh (1956) not merely studied his own village of Senapur in Jaunpur district, but invited a host of other scholars from the USA and Lucknow University to visit that village and write learned articles on the basis of fieldwork there. Singh could trace the movements of families over generations and point out that the departure from the village of a member of the family for education or an occupation did not result in the breach of relations with the parental family immediately and reciprocal relations were maintained for a generation or two. The mutuality of obligations continued from both the sides as villages too began to receive doses of urbanisation through these contacts. Roy (1987) found it expedient to write a term paper on the political situation over a generation for a term paper in Berkeley. Gupta (1974) chose his wife's village for intensive studies and was otherwise also a frequent visitor. Gould (1988) developed a similar association with the village he called 'Sherupur' after his son's name. Chauhan's accounts as a regular visitor to his parental village, which spread over summer vacations for 16 years, are recorded in a companion volume. Singh (1978) has included his parental village, Chanukhera in Basti district among the six villages he studied for his PhD dissertation, and in our conversations and seminars frequently used the advantages of new information gathered during his several visits to the village and the visits of the villagers and the relatives to his own residence in Jawaharlal Nehru University, attending to their comforts and meeting such emergent needs as had to be taken care of in the national capital. The new generation of scholars from villages in Uttar Pradesh now finds itself pursuing courses in sociology in universities of the state.

A few methodological questions arise here: Can the student maintain impersonal relations and attitude while writing about his own village? The danger is always there. There are two difficulties involved in the process. First, the student might suffer from the complex of familiarity breeding contempt in the sense that everyday happenings may be considered too trivial to deserve research effort for an urban centre of learning. Secondly, he might consider it an easy thing to write about his village, if need so arise, even without sustained inquiries. These problems are remediable to some extent. For training in fieldwork tradition, it is recommended that the student be exposed to at least two different situations, preferably in two states. Secondly, he has to become a regular reader of field accounts published already from different areas. Training in theory and methods is assumed to be a part of the process of learning other skills in any discipline. Once that aspect is taken care of, studies in one's own village enable a student to handle data covering three generations in his village. A depth in perspective marks the questions that arise over these years, and a continuous interaction with the field structurally built into the process has the potential for raising new questions with greater facility. Methodologically, this rich resource needs greater exploration, and the richness of the data and their availability can be used for sharpening the intellectual pursuits. The undertaking of such studies at an advanced age of the scholar has begun and received attention of senior scholars, who have communicated their inclinations in that regard to the present writer in 2008. Singh mentions his interest in writing a monograph on Chanukhera, and S.S. Sharma has produced preliminary notes on Garhi Chaukhandi in the NOIDA area. J.K Pundir has begun noting the present position of different institutions of his village Karondi in Uttarakhand. H.P. Joshi has started working on his paper on village Marevada in Bhilwara district of Rajasthan tracing the successful attempts of the migrants from the village in social matters and their contributions to village development, almost in the fashion of non-resident Indians helping a few developmental activities in India, and extension of wider links of the villagers through their caste organisations. Parvez Abbasi has communicated his understanding of the series of panchayat elections held in village Chandanpur in Maharaj Ganj district of UP to this writer. A few students of M.Phil from Lucknow University have chosen different aspects of social life in village Palanpur which has been periodically studied by Jean Dreze and associates in Moradabad district. Interest in periodical studies undertaken by other writers and teams of research workers is already in fashion.

Methodological Issues

As sociological enquiries moved from the study of isolated tribes to that of the mainland rural settings they had to confront a large and varied volume of existing information for which they were suddenly not ready enough. Even though Evans Pritchard had combined historical material with field studies of Nuer (1951a) of Sudan, and argued for a slant in favour of an anthropologist also being a novelist (1951b) the remark has been noted but seldom practised in India. The institution of caste over the ages has been studied by G.S. Ghurye (1957) and the classics form the base of his writings as also of K.M. Kapadia and Irawati Karve (1963). This trend was called 'Indological' (Das, 2003) in approach. Lack of familiarity with the original language in which classics were composed was a factor in ignoring the rich source on the one hand and on the other hand they were treated as norms for action rather than accounts of actual behaviour of the people in day-to-day life. The growth of serious field studies led M.N. Srinivas (1955) to assert the 'field view' as against the 'book view', even as the very concept of sanskritisation (1955, 1956) involved the interaction between classical norms and actual behaviour of people in the rural area, and extended the study of dominant lineages in Africa to cover ground realities of the Indian situation through the study of caste (1959). The two concepts formed the key around which academic efforts got centred, with serious debates ensuing in seminars and conferences well over a quarter of a century. The point of view being advanced here is using the terms from biology: fieldwork was the dominant trait and references to classics presented a recessive strain, not quite absent. History and Mythology continued to provide insights; but with the insistence of historians to rely on recorded history and a bit of pre-history, the influence had a limited time zone for consideration. Resort to the classics in translated forms became additional sources of reaching a distant past. The classical writings in the form of a series of stories encompassing all the nine *ragas* for description were considered authentic by people themselves as their *itihas.* The discussion is kept alive at the international level. The significant sociological reference is that Srinivas (1952) in the closing chapters of religious society among *Coorgs of South India* refers to the nature of this *itihas* probingly, besides including the *Kaveri* myth in the appendix.

The Chicago anthropologists paid special attention to the existence of the little communities, namely the villages, in the context of an indigenous civilisation, which means not merely the old tradition but the written one as well. Special studies of Marriott (1955) in the village he called Kishangarhi in western UP in Aligarh district and subsequent chain of discussions generated have been referred to earlier from the methodological point of view. Using Nadel's phrase the classical tradition is 'sufficiently relevant' for encompassing the complexity of rural life.

Written history, which earlier used to be centred on invasions, establishment of empires, their disintegration and their reorganisation, has left important sources of information on the formation of villages and caste in different regions as well as patterns of agrarian relations. In these writings sociologists do not enter into discussion of the historical sources, but feel content in using the works of a few established historians, as sources or treatment of factors that are of interest to them, though some historians and sociologists have commonly approached these questions in almost interdisciplinary character. Accounts of administrators particularly during the British period are studied with an open mind for familiarising the social trends. On their authenticity and relevance for current use, discussion on peasant movements relies on officially recorded information (Dhanagare, 1983) supplemented by the participants' own versions (Oommen, 1972). A student of village affairs today is confronted by massive census information and occasional state sponsored services and reports. While the former are used for defining the broad parameters of social life, only one serious work by a sociologist, on linking social trends with demographic ones, has come to light in Kingsley Davis' work on *Population of India and Pakistan* published in 1951. The effort needs to be rejuvenated for the country and states: A series of publication on *Castes and Tribes of India* remain a reference point for some knowledge about them at the time of publication in pre-independent India. More serious studies with greater authenticity appeared later as isolated works of social scientists, both Indian and foreign.

The freedom struggle in India was *total* in the sense of mobilisation of social and academic resources. As mentioned earlier; from the methodological point of view references to classics, popular literature and a near renaissance in literary styles and composition brought new interaction at a time when sociological pursuits were only beginning to take shape. Economic enquiries in the rural areas concentrated on rural indebtedness, fractions of inherited property, the role of the moneylenders and the land revenue structure (Jathar and Beri, 1946, 1948; Ganguli, 1977). Through such economical and political bases sociological pursuits had also begun which later acquired a more specialised character. In some of the enquiries the conditions of origin persisted, and in others got diversified into specialties. In dealing with these questions for rural areas in independent India, sociological literature concerning land reforms and developmental activities on the part of the state, as well as self-initiative and market forces has grown.

A question often raised by participants in the seminar room is, 'After the presentation what?'. They are also concerned with the implications of the presentation for a development and change studies, a question persistently raised by Yogesh Atal in several seminars: 'What have substantive in-depth studies told us in accumulated form, and

'How many such studies would be needed?' To the first question, if the current presentation is an answer, then it is necessary that the strength of the intensive studies be reaffirmed through special inclusion by the university teaching departments. Next, the users of research have to be oriented to these facilities. Whereas Social Anthropology and Sociology provided the first groundings in the methods and techniques, these need to be continuously reflected in the wake of interest in rural studies among different disciplines producing 'sufficiently relevant' material, depending upon the capacity and the inclinations concerned, combining a variable mix through the extension of the method to other disciplines, as a part of their enquiries would have to be gone through, and call for greater promise. To the last question, How many intensive studies of the villagers ..., ideally the answer would be two villages in each development block and in two blocks of each district to begin with. Frequent interaction among producers and users of research and exercises periodically would be the next step in understanding rural India.

When M.N. Srinivas (1952), Irawati Karve (1953), D.N. Majumdar (1955) and Andre Beteille (1965) had started reporting the results of their intensive field studies in rural areas in the 1950s, they had to make special efforts in establishing rapport with the local people as they were scholars coming from an urban background and dealing with rural life mostly in different cultural or sub-cultural zones of India. Objectivity was thus built into the research design to the extent that the diversity of India, the scholar's readings and training and references to gazetteers and administrative reports, the census material and other accounts permitted. Karve's work (1953) introduced the scholar's own perception of the region to which she belonged and its relevant social trends, enriching the study of objective external social facts. Majumdar's (1955, 1958) multiple studies, combining summer vacations and shorter annual camps along with the students, provided a time depth and variety of even cultural experiences. The later growth of the disciplines in UP began to be marked by Indian scholars born in villages, and entering the universities thereby getting exposed to two cultural streams. Some of them began to use their intimate personal knowledge of rural life combining it with theoretical and methodological orientations of universities and urban living, in a period when struggle for national freedom was on, and a few policy changes affecting *zamindari* abolition, ceiling on land holdings and their consolidation, besides emerging political dimensions through parties, and through literary and popular writings, were the order of the day. Yogendra Singh (1978) from Chanukhera, himself a part of the legal process affecting a family even during his studies in the intermediate class, later developed strong liking for Parsonian classification and theories, and contributed articles to works edited by A.R. Desai and K. Ishwaran (1970). Chauhan used a part of his summer vacation participation in the life of village in Etawah district for over 20 years to develop a pinpointed attention to differences in social patterns in families and caste rankings in *A Rajasthan Village*, and later used the home material with facility to contribute portions to the study of the Etawah project (1999) and the present work. Similar exercise in a comparative study of Uttar Pradesh and Andhra Pradesh villages has been attempted by A. Satyanarayana (1985) who has now extended his interest to peasant studies, and, as the Convener of the Research Committee on Peasant Movements of Indian Sociological Society, and has begun co-coordinating widespread emerging studies in different parts of the country. S.S. Sharma (1988) concentrated attention on the political process in his own village and compared the findings in the neighbouring district with an insight extended to a series of panchayat elections held in 1988. Prakash (2005), besides his own village, extended the inquiries to three other villagers in Meerut region to cover the interest of the scheduled castes in the panchayats even before the introduction of the 73rd amendment to the Constitution. J.K. Pundir (2005) has used his skills enforcing seven steps required to be gone through by a scheduled caste recipient of a bank loan from the beginning to repayment, and the complexity of involvement of actors, and in the proceeding for the current seminar (1976), has contributed a piece on his own village. Female education in differential repetition in three caste-dominated villages in Meerut region has received notice in the work of M.S. Prakash (2005). Naresh Singh (2006) has studied a village covered by Cornell University and included his own and neighbouring villages with the latest interest leading him to the problems and prospects of micro-financing and management studies. Methodologically, the efforts for that objectivity and study of the external based on their own training and exposure to diversity of researches as reported and studied, try to put them in to mainstream, but by combining the long-term experiences of living in the area and participating in the dialect and the idiom of the people have provided a depth through some local history and their own varying capacities for the input that Evans-Pritchard (1951a) had attempted in his famous remark.

On the praxis side, three sets of stakeholders are involved. First, the senior faculty of departments of universities who have to participate in the field operations, like senior surgeons with junior doctors (staff) and trainees (research scholars) closely watching and acting as assistants, a point brought to our attention in conversations with A.K. Saran in the 1970s while on a visit to Meerut. A culture of mutual deliberations before and after each operation has to be generated. The universities may develop certificate and diploma courses for two purposes along two lines: (1) defining parameters of research in terms of time and space, making full use of existing multidisciplinary resources at the meso and macros levels, and (2) concentrating on field studies of a minimum of 30 night halts in a village, that could be spread over 45 to 60 days in case of Sociology and Social Anthropology; and half of that duration for sister disciplines that can be made an additional or minor course. At the university level, one course in M.A. may be offered from related optional subject. In case of M. Phil too this may be encouraged as a minor course from a field of related topic for students as per requirement. Department of Economics at Lucknow University, M. Phil programmes at Meerut and Department of Psychology in Allahabad University having a micro space for sociology, are pointers in this direction. Some of the classical studies in Uttar Pradesh have gone out of print. Their reprints have to be thought over in a programmed way. The exercise needs to be extended to a few journals and important articles selected for publication. It may be considered how, at proper levels, even translations can be introduced as 'term' papers. The second set of actors comprises students whose preparatory readings may include at least two quality field studies in book length treatment, and half a dozen research articles/reviews/field notes. Term papers by students would form a part of performances. The third set of actors in consumers of research: the state at various levels, the private industries, Institutes of Management, short report series of project reports prepared by international agencies and the media which may centre on village-based intensive studies as a whole, or encouraged to include references in boxed items. Frequent interaction among the stakeholders in the form of workshops, joint programmes and seminars will add variety to the efforts, perception of their relevance, and generation of skilled human resources to reach common goals in a cumulative way.

The concentration of scholars on specific problems has a different focus from those of the villagers studied, for whom all intellectual enquiries come under one basket. For academicians, the division of labour does not coincide with the multifarious aspects of life acting together in the rural settings, thereby posing fresh questions for producing a combination with an explanatory power for the understanding of rural life. The current presentation argues that such multifarious activities can be addressed through event-based specific case studies; and that such case studies acquire their strength when combined with the sufficiently relevant attributes classified through a combination of insights and parameters, offered through related subjects and their techniques. A number of combinations would get worked through, some imaginative effort calling for continuous academic experiments in varied situations, continuous path-breaking efforts in the spirit of the Sanskrit dictum 'Chairaiveti .... Chairaiveti' (keep on marching ahead for ever and ever), as we keep on attending to the specifics, taking a few steps, brushing up a few strokes and then again standing at a meso level having a look at the composition created in the manner of a drawing master referred to in the beginning.

References

Bailey, F.G. 1957, *Caste and the Economic Frontier: A Village in Highland Orissa*, Manchester: Manchester University Press.

——. 1963, *Politics and Social Change of Orissa in 1959*, Berkeley: University of California Press.

Beteille, A. 1965, *Caste, Class and Power*, Berkeley: University of California Press.

Bhatt, G.S. 2005, "Use of Ethnography: Trends and Issues", *The Eastern Anthropologist*, Vol. 58, No. 3–4, pp. 403–18.

Beals, A. 1955, "Interplay among Factors of Change in a Mysore Village", in M. Marriott (ed.), *Village India*, Chicago: Chicago University Press.

Brass, P.R. 1983, *Caste, Faction and Party in Indian Politics*, Vol. I, Delhi: Chanakya Publications.

——. 1985, *Caste, Faction and Party in Indian Politics*, Vol. II, Delhi: Chanakya Publications.

Chauhan, A. 2000, *Surdas and the Blind: A Comparative Discourse in the Writings of Prem Chand and Ernesto Sabato of Argentina, Dream and Vision in the Novels of Ernesto Sabato and Other Essays*, Udaipur: A.C. Brothers.

Chauhan, B.R. 1966, 1999, *A Rajasthan Village*, Udaipur: A.C. Brothers.

——. 1970, *Towns in Tribal Setting*, Delhi: National Publishing House.

——. 1974, "Rural Studies: A Trend Report", in ICSSR, *A Survey of Research in Sociology and Social Anthropology*, Vol. I, Bombay: Popular Prakashan.

——. 1988, *Bharat Mein Gramin Samaj*, Etawah, Udaipur: A.C. Brothers.

——. 1990, *Rural Urban Articulations*, Etawah: A.C. Brothers.

——. 1998, *Four Decades of Rural Development in Etawah*, New Delhi: ICSSR, mss.

——. (ed.) 2005, "Rural Profiles Scenario 2005", *The Eastern Anthropologist*, Vol. 58, No. 3–4, July–December.

Das, V. 2003, *The Oxford India Companion to Sociology and Anthropology*, New Delhi: Oxford University Press.

Davis, K. 1951, *The Population of India and Pakistan*, Princeton: Princeton University Press.

Dhanagare, D.N. 1983, *Peasant Movements in India, 1920–1950*, Delhi: Oxford University Press.

Dreze, J. 1998, "Economic Development in Palanpur", in J. Breman (ed.), *The Village in Asia Revisited*, Delhi: Oxford University Press.

——. 2007, "Palanpur 1957–93 Occupational Change, Land Ownership and Social Inequality", in J. Breman et al. (eds.), *Village in Asia Revisited*, Delhi: Oxford University Press.

Dube, S.C. 1955, *Indian Village*, London: Routledge and Kegan Paul.

——. 1958, 1967, *India's Changing Villages*, Bombay: Allied Publishers Ltd. (First Indian Edition).

Evans-Pritchard, E.E. 1951(a), *Kinship and Marriage among the Neur*, Oxford: Clarendon Press.

——. 1951(b), *Social Anthropology*, London: Cohen and West.

Ghurye, G.S. 1943, *The Aborigines So-called and Their Future*, Pune: Gokhale Institute of Politics and Economics.

——. 1957, *Caste and Race in India*, Bombay: Popular Book Depot.

——. 1969, *Caste and Race in India*, 5th edition, Bombay: Popular Prakashan.

Gould, H.A. 1988, *Caste Adaptations in Modernising Indian Society*, Delhi: Chanakya Publications.

Gumperz, J.G. 1957, "Language Problems in Rural Development of Northern India", *The Journal of Asian Studies*, Vol. XVI, No. 2, February, pp. 251–59.

Gupta, G.R. 1974, *Marriage, Religion and Society*, Delhi: Vikas Publishing House.

Habib, I. 1963, 1999, *The Agrarian System of Mughal India 1556–1707* (second revised edition), New Delhi: Oxford University Press.

Imtiaz, A. 1976, "Caste and Kinship in a Muslim Village of Eastern Uttar Pradesh", in Imtiaz Ahmad (ed.), *Family, Kinship and Marriage among Muslims in India*, Delhi: Manohar.

Ishwaran, K. 1966, *Tradition and Economy in Village India*, London: Routledge and Kegan Paul.

Jetley, S. 1977, *Modernizing Indian Peasants*, New Delhi: Asian Educational Service.

Karve, I. 1963, *Kinship Organisation in India*, 3rd edition, Bombay: Asia Publishing House.

——. 1968, *Hindu Society, an Interpretation*, Poona: Deshmukh Prakashan.

——. 1974, *Yuganta: The End of an Epoch*, Poona: Sangam.

Majumdar, D.N. 1937, 1950, *A Tribe in Transition: A Study in Cultural Pattern*, Lucknow: Universal Publication.

——. (ed.) 1955, *Rural Profiles*, Vol. I and II, Lucknow: Ethnographic and Folk Culture Society.

——. 1958, *Caste and Communication in an Indian Village*, Bombay: Asia Publishing House.

Marriott, M. 1955, "Little Communities in an Indigenous Civilization", in McKim Marriott (ed.), *Village India*, Chicago: Chicago University Press.

——. (ed.) 1955, *Village India*, Chicago: Chicago University Press.

——. 1990, *India through Hindu Categories*, New Delhi: Sage Publications.

——. 2005, "Guest Editor Poser on Intensive Studies in Village: In Retrospect and Prospect pp. 300–01", in B.R. Chauhan (ed.), "Rural Profiles Scenario 2005", *The Eastern Anthropologist*, Vol. 58, No. 3–4, July–December.

Mayer, A.C. 1970, *Caste and Kinship in Central India*, Berkeley: University of California Press.

Mayor, A. 1958, *Pilot Project India: The Study of Rural Development at Etawah, Uttar Pradesh*, Berkeley: University of California Press.

Mukerjee, R.K., 1925, *Borderlands of Economics*, London: Allen and Unwin.

Ogburn, W.F. 1922, *Social Change with Respect to Culture and Original Nature*, New York: B.W. Huebsch.

——. 1932, *Social Change*: New York: Viking Press.

Oommen, T.K., 1972, *Charisma, Stability and Change*, New Delhi: Thomson Press.

Parsons, T. 1955, 2003, *Family, Socialisation and Interactive Process*, London: Routledge and Kegan Paul Ltd.

Prakash, M.S. 2005, Impact of Education and Household Technology on Rural Women, Unpublished PhD Dissertation, Meerut University, Meerut.

Premchand, M. 1988, 2005, *Pratinidhi Kahaniya: Representative Stories of Prem Chand*, selected and edited by Bhishma Sahani, New Delhi: Rajkamal Prakashan Ltd.

Pundir, J.K. 1976, 2008, Commercial Banking and the Peasants and the Workers in a Village in Western Uttar Pradesh, paper presented at XIII All India Sociological Conference Held at Punjab University, Chandigarh.

——. 2005, Banking for the Scheduled Castes in Rural Areas. INCOMPLETE

Raghuvanshi, M.S. 1980, "Education and Modernity among the Rural Youth", *Indian Journal of Social Research*, Vol. XXI, No. 1, pp. 8–18 and Vol. XXIV, No. 3, pp. 276–89.

Raza, R.M. 1966, 2006, *Aadha Gaon*, 7th print, New Delhi: Rajkamal Paperbacks.

Roy, R. 1987, *Perspectives on Indian Politics*, Delhi: Discovery Publishing House.

Satyanarayana, A. 1985, *Technology, Work and Social Relations in Agriculture*, Meerut: Sociology Workers' Sangam.

——. 2006, Differential Participation of Kisans in the BKU Movement of Western Uttar Pradesh, paper presented in the RC-17: Social Movements of 32nd All India Sociological Conference Held at Chennai: Department of Sociology, University of Madras.

Sharma, S.S. 1988, *Factions in Northern Rural India*, New Delhi: Shree Publishing House.

Shukla, S. 1983, 1999, *Raag-Darbari*, 8th reprint, New Delhi: Rajkamal Prakashan Ltd.

Singh, N. 2006, Discussion Paper: From Cycle to Boeing: Memories of a Sociologist from Ranakhandi (Khalapur) Village and its Linkages with US Universities, Gurgoan: ICFAI Business School, mss.

Singh, R.D. 1956, "The Unity of an Indian Village", *The Journal of Asian Studies*, Vol. XVI, No.1, pp. 10–19.

Singh, R.L. 1971, *India: A Regional Geography*, Varanasi: National Geographical Association of India, Silver Jubilee Publication.

——. 1971, 1997, *India: A Regional Geography*, New Delhi: UBS.

Singh, R.S. 1985, *Rural Elite Entrepreneurship and Social Change*, Jaipur: Rawat Publications.

Singh, Y. 1978, "The Changing Power Structure of Village Community: A Case Study of Six Villages in Eastern UP", in A.R. Desai (ed.), *Rural Sociology in India*, Bombay: Popular Prakashan.

Sinha, D.N. 1968, *Indian Villages in Transition*, New Delhi: Associated Publishing House.

Srinivas, M.N. 1952, *Religion and Society among the Coorgs of South India*, Oxford: Oxford University Press.

——. 1956, "Sanskritisation and Westernisation", *Far Eastern Quarterly*, Vol. 14, pp. 481–96.

——. 1955, *India's Villages*, Calcutta: West Bengal Government Press.

——. 1959, "The Dominant Caste in Rampura", *The American Anthropologist*, Vol. 61, pp. 1–16.

Thapar, R. 1975, 2006, *Bharat Ka Itihas*, 21st reprint, New Delhi: Rajkamal Prakashan.

Vatuk, S. 1972, *Kinship and Urbanization*, London: University of California Press.

Wiser, W.H. 1958, *The Hindu Jajmani System*, Lucknow: Lucknow Publishing House.

Wiser, W.H. and C.V. Wiser, 1963, *Behind the Mud Walls*, Berkeley: University of California Press.

2

An Appraisal of Village Studies

Ramashray Roy

Can a student of Political Science say anything that is sophisticated and meaningful about village studies which belong to disciplines quite dissimilar to his own? It can very well be suggested that politics is also a defining characteristic of village life. But, Beteille (1965) has argued that politics at the level of the village is informal and requires entirely a different method than what is prevalent in the discipline of Political Science. What Beteille is, in effect, disputing is the common sharing of what we know as the scientific method. Denying this commonality underlining different perspectives on politics, Beteille (1965) goes further and asserts, "… it may be questioned whether the word 'politics' means the same thing at the level of the village and of the state. And if politics at the village level is quite different from that at the state level, does a political scientist have to contribute anything to the appraisal of village studies, a major enterprise in both Anthropology and Sociology in India?

Leaving this question for discussion later, it can also be said that a political scientist restricts himself to the reconstruction of political aspects of collective life and relations, and that also a very shadowy one. Focusing on the way the political things work, he leaves alone, or touches only tangentially, on the factors and forces operating at the village level. It is the interaction among these forces that defines the essential features of the community of the people inhabiting the lowest level of the territorially organised socio-cultural, economic and political entity. It is at this level that fundamental existential factors and forces interact to create necessary conditions for politics to make its appearance. The concatenation of all these factors and forces operating in hundreds of villages in India leads to a very large extent, the tone and texture to political life and relations at higher levels.

Thus, village studies concern themselves with the real world of people who are busily engaged in sorting out the problems of the mere act of living. The unvarying reign of everydayness that firmly grips the existence of the people living in villages, symbolizes a reality that constitutes the subject matter of village studies. These studies aim at uncovering the face of this reality. By doing so, they ascertain and elucidate the forces that secure life in the village against the anarchic forces of change as well as propel the village community to tread the unmeasured and unshared path of change. Of course, the factors that shake the village community off its moorings are not the same as those that ensure its stability.

However, communities change and the thought – ways and work-ways too change. As such, village studies carried out by anthropologists and sociologists have necessarily to take into account forces making both for stability and change. The political scientist also concerns himself with such forces but at levels that are largely immune to the unvarying tenor of everydayness. He deals, as already hinted, with factors and forces in their abstraction, representing the shadow of the real world. In contrast, village studies depict the life of the village people at the grassroots, the people who confront the thunder and dreams of the rainbow on a daily basis. The political scientist, on the other hand, commits himself to the unrewarding exercise of chasing the tails of events and asking them to reveal their meaning to construct a likely tale of political life and relations at levels above the village. Or else, he depicts reality in the hues of prejudice; as such, he tends to distort reality as well as to prevent meaningful action.

Circumscribed by the limitations that a political scientist suffers from, he looks beyond his own bailiwick to other sister disciplines, particularly Anthropology and Sociology, as they reconstruct the character of village life and relations, with the hope that their insights, experience and observations would feed some substance into his shadowy world. This hope impels him to set on a journey to discover and, if possible, profit from the world, which village studies seek to map and measure. The expectation of reaping a good reward propels the political scientist on this expedition, to be sure; however, as the journey gets longer, the terrain gets extremely varied and arid and the expectation of a good reward slowly eviscerates and erodes. This brings to mind William Wordsworth's famous poem "Yardley Visited". Why does the expedition turn not so well rewarding? This is a question that confronts not only the political scientist but also anthropologists and sociologists and a rare student of Philosophy like the Late Professor Daya Krishna. To answer this question, one needs to take into account several factors that have a very important bearing on village study. The first factor concerns the subtle transformation reflected in the unconscious slide from "my village" to "the village". This slide is a prominent feature of village studies. There are more than five hundred thousand villages in India but they are not alike. Numerous differences related to several important characteristics of the village community and interaction patterns within them operate. It is not at all possible to study life and relations, in every village in India. The village in India, it is suggested, epitomizes the essence of Indian civilisation as it is considered a repository of traditional mores and folkways. It is in this sense that we can appreciate Mahatma Gandhi (1936) when he observes, "India is to be found not in its few cities but in its 700,000 villages and if the village perishes, India would perish too. It will no more be India. Her own mission in the world would get lost". However, B.R. Ambedkar designated villages as the den of exploitation and oppression whereas Jawaharlal Nehru described them as sites of backwardness (Bhalla and Bumke, 1992).

Even during the lifetime of Mahatma Gandhi, the village, as the repository of traditional mores and folkways, had begun its inexorable journey towards a goal which made it turn away from the mission that Mahatma Gandhi spoke of by becoming something else than traditional. In its currently lived social reality, the village provides an arena where experiments in social creation are made and unmade and made again. It has become a framework for economic planning and social development and other related efforts at modernising the traditional ways of life. It has decidedly taken several steps to embrace modernisation as an institutional concomitant of technologically induced economic growth. As a consequence, the village is caught between two entirely different stones of the grinding wheel, i.e., tradition and modernity. It is the confluence of tradition and modernity that has rendered Indian society more complex, more varied, and more difficult to conceptualise. As a result of this, Indian villages manifest extreme variation in their structure, institutional arrangement, and interaction patterns both within and in their relationship with the larger social, economic and political environment in which each of them is embedded.

Despite variations in villages, the village has come to occupy a strategic position in the consciousness of both scholars and politicians. It was not only under Mahatma Gandhi's influence that the village came to be viewed as the pivot on which the regeneration of India as a distinct civilisational entity could be firmly pegged. When economic growth- driven modernisation came to occupy a central place in planned development, village studies came to be promoted. The objective was to know the social, economic and political situation at the grassroots level for better planning and plan execution. If the British rulers were interested in acquainting themselves with an alien civilisation with a view to strengthening their rule, the Indian rulers were prompted to promote village studies with a view to translating into reality, their vision of what Indian society should be. The British rulers were interested in exploiting resources, collecting taxes, and making necessary changes in the village as an administrative unit. The indigenous rulers, on the other hand, aimed at radical refashioning of life and relations in the village. Both these concerns boosted village studies and treated the village as central to Indian civilisation. As Madan (2002) notes, the village increasingly came to be identified as the '... microcosm of Indian society and civilization' and the distance from being a microcosm to a nodal entity was not very far.

It is this transformation that provides the stimulus as well as the theme of large number of writings about Indian villages. The fact is ignored that the village as the model surrogate for Indian civilisation does not exist. What we can at best say is that the village is just one instance, among numerous others, of Indian civilisation; it does not completely represent it. Like the sparks of a bolt of fire, villages do reflect some of its attributes. However, they do differ from each other in certain vital respects. Notwithstanding this, every village studied by anthropologists and sociologists, turns out to be the exact replica of India. As Niranjana (1991) puts it, "... the village assumed the status of a metaphor, standing for India as a whole'. This metaphor became instrumental in constituting an individualistic fallacy. It signifies an act of drawing the picture of the whole from a part of it. As Dumont (1971) puts it, "It is once again the old fallacy of producing the whole from the (constitutive) elements".

The second factor concerns the very image of the village community that anthropological study has built up since the introduction of anthropological studies in India. It should be emphasised here that, "... Indian Anthropology of contemporary period by and large leaned heavily towards the west" (Danda, 1995). The very condition of the birth of Anthropology in India and the socio-economic and political changes overtaking India since then signify that the sociological and anthropological constructions of village communities would necessarily undergo important changes involving both theoretical approaches and conceptual apparatus brought to bear upon village studies. Add to it the two other factors of great import that have made for differentiation and diversity in cognitive construction of village community. Under the impact of positivism, what assumed a central importance, epistemologically and ontologically, is what Eric Voegelin (Cooper, 1999) calls "phenomenalism".

Phenomenalism signifies that "reality is what appears, but what does not appear is not real; on the other hand, what does appear does not appear to everybody and, if it does so appear, nevertheless does not necessarily appear in the same way" (Cooper, 1999). As a result, the textual approach to reality in the village came to be jettisoned because it did not confront reality as it appeared. This led to a shift in focus. This shift was defined by a movement away from the textual approach toward fieldwork, a movement characterised by Srinivas as a shift from the book view to the field view (1996). This shift signified the irreparable breakdown of a common language for apprehending and expressing the characteristic features of the village community. Once the shared universe of discourse dissolved, differences in attitudes, sentiments, and experiences became impenetrable barriers to understanding, an understanding that yielded a shareable commonality. As a result, 'the massed choirs of chanting creed communities' supplanted the universal language of discourse. Theories proliferated, approaches multiplied and concepts became numerous.

The second factor concerns the dual identity of Anthropology as a field of study. As early as 1910, Haddon (1910) had pointed out that we must at least implicitly recognise the existence of two separate identities of anthropology: one, as a body of knowledge and, the other, as an academic discipline. The village is not only the object for anthropological studies. It is also the instrument that can be profitably used for consolidating the field of anthropological knowledge. Village studies have thus a two-fold utility. On the one hand, they provide the dominant framework that is available for sociological and anthropological researches and, on the other; they provide specific information for identifying specific characterisation of Indian society as a whole. The dual identity of the village denotes (a) that is, as an empirical social reality to be apprehended on its own term or (b) as a creation of sociological/anthropological imagination through the projection of a theoretical perspective on to the reality of the village community as an important aspect of the extant anthropological studies. As such, this involves the presence of a thing, on the one hand, and the cognitive apprehension of the thing present, on the other. This dual characteristic of village study has made for confusion insofar as the character of the village community remains tinged with indeterminacy and eludes clear understanding.

All these factors have combined to create a situation in which the status of the village as a reality that is empirically given appears to be uncertain. Note, for example, that the image of the village community has undergone several transmutations since they first made their appearance. We can identify three different phases in this transmutation. The first phase, beginning with British administrators, presented a stereotypical picture of the Indian village. It depicted the villages as "little republics," self-sufficient and self-contained. Conceptualising the village in terms of the little republic leads to the treatment of rural society as an integral organic whole. And, as an integral whole, the village community is nothing less than a republic with certain specific features. These features are, as Redfield (1967) identifies, (a) distinctiveness (b) small size, (c) homogeneity, and (d) self-sufficiency. The mythic view of the village continued to hold a firm grip on the students of village society for almost half a century. However, as empirical studies of village communities offered evidences to the contrary, questions about the validity of the village in terms of the little republic began to be raised. These questions pertain to (a) the attribution of the village as a modal entity representing the Indian civilisation as a whole; (b) the village as a self-sufficient and self-contained community; and (c) the village as an empirically given entity embracing a distinctive social reality. With respect to the question of the village as a modal entity, the observations arrived through empirical research, forcefully brought out the insubstantiality of such a claim. That is why, Marriott (1955) questioned whether understanding one village can contribute to the understanding of the larger pan-Indian culture and society in which the village is embedded.

Obviously, the answer to this question was in the negative inasmuch as Redfield's work saw a significant relationship between tradition and modernity. This revealed a reality which he conceptualised as a "folk-urban continuum.' Majumdar (1958) underlined the fact that the village social structure needs to be seen as integrated at different levels of the total social system of the country in order to be fully understood. Contesting the thesis of village self-sufficiency, Srinivas refers to the contradiction between the fact of subsuming the village in the wider polity and the notion of the economic self-sufficiency. Explaining why the impression of village self-sufficiency took such a deep root, Srinivas observes: "In an economy, which is, non-monetized or minimally monetized, where poor communications confine the flow of goods and services to a limited area, the wants are few and are such that can be satisfied locally. The appearance of self-sufficiency was enhanced by caste-wise division of society".

If the village is neither the modal entity of Indian civilisation nor does it contain a self-sufficient community of people, what exactly is its status? This question has certainly evoked responses. However, they fail to provide a firm basis for generalisation about the status of the village. The village is obviously a part of the larger society but does it mean that it cannot claim any self-identity? In the event that the answer to this question happens to underline the fact that, despite being a part of a larger society, the village does retain a distinctive identity, then other questions need to be satisfactorily answered. Two questions among the other assume significance in this respect. One, what kind of community of people does the village constitute and, two, does the village, as a part of a larger society, only react and respond to the impulses and stimuli corning from its external environment or does it retain some degree of autonomy in internal affairs?

What kind of answers do we get from village studies? Numerous studies give unambiguous evidence to the fact that the village community does not conform to the picture that the concept of the little republic conveys. The village community manifests inequalities in the distribution of material possession, political power, and social prestige. Knowing, as we do, it is the distribution of such societal resources as wealth, power and prestige which animates human motivation and behaviour today. The pattern of the distribution of these resources underpins social life and relations these days. We also know that it is the pattern of distribution of these resources that happens to be the focal point of political activities. These activities revolve around the question of the fairness and justness of the prevalent distribution pattern. And politics has deeply influenced community relations in the Indian village. It is in this context that the question arises whether the Indian village deviates sharply from both the idealistic connotations of the traditional *varnashrama dharma* characterisation of the Hindu society and its practical ramifications. These studies are quite unequivocal about the inapplicability to Hindu social order of the idea of its being the replica of *yajna* (sacrifice) signifying cooperation, interdependence and harmony. Whether the social order conforming to Commaraswamy's vision of *yajna* was ever an empirically determinable order or not is debatable (1975). In contemporary India, the *varnashrama dharma* ideal of society remains, as numerous village studies note, simply an ideal without any possibility of its being realised (Krishna, 1992).

However, the pale reflection of the characterisation of this idea can be observed in the growingly dissipating *jajmani* system and the eroding economic dependence of the deprived and dispossessed sections in the village population on wealthier sections. It is clear from numerous anthropological accounts that inter-dependence or rather the dependence of the weaker sections of the village society on the stronger ones has given way to cleavage and conflicts. With this, solidarity as one of the defining attributes of the village community has been laid to not undeserving rest. As a consequence, different easily noticeable constitutive elements of the village community come to be identified as very useful in village studies. Although village studies provide detailed descriptions of everyday life in the village, the tendency to focus on caste has been most prominent as well as quite extensive.

This has lent an element of lopsidedness to village studies. Beteille (1969), for example, points to the shadow of caste that has hung over most of the village studies. Inden (1990) also takes note of how the interest in caste has created an impression of the village being just an economic arena and a living space. Dumont and Pocock go still further and argue that caste is the defining aspect of village life. For them, the village is nothing more than a social space; caste is what makes it a social reality. Even Srinivas (1959) talks in terms of the dominant caste as being the principal defining category for understanding life and relations in the Indian village. The magic of caste has spread its wing far and wide; it seems that most anthropologists agree that without a clear understanding of the role of caste, whether in its undifferentiated form or as a dominant caste or as a cluster of sub-castes, social reality as it obtains in Indian villages will ever elude apprehension.

Caste is no doubt a sociological reality in India and its centrality in ritual and religious matters often spills over in other areas of life. However, it must be emphasised that caste does not always happen to be the mainstay of relations in the village community. For one thing, caste does not always prove to be a cohesive category insofar as a particular caste group, even when it happens to be a dominant caste, becomes highly differentiated. Also, intra-caste interactions often turn out to be fractious and contentious. For another, the power and influence of one caste, even if it is dominant, stop stet at the border of the village. Also, the internal affairs of another caste, which, in many cases, has its own caste-based institution, often affect rather deeply life and relations in a village. It should also be added here that it is the conjunction of caste and economic power that accounts for the power and influence of a particular caste in many of the Indian villages. And it is here in the conjunction of caste and economic power, that ritual-based superiority loses its significance.

It is against this background that the characterisation by Dumont and Pocock (1957) of the village as a physical entity that provides only a space for a caste relation appears so jejune. This is so for several reasons. First, while Dumont condemns the act of generalising about the whole from only a part of it, he himself speaks of the caste as the only explanatory category in the village on the basis of observations relating to only a few villages. Second, they contend that caste constitutes the only reality in the village. As Dumont and Pocock (1957) observe, "Village solidarity is nothing other than the solidarity of the local section of the dominant caste, and the members of the other castes are loyal not to the village as such but to the dominant caste which wields political and economic power".

Dumont and Pocock do not only commit what we have earlier called "individualistic fallacy"; they also create a mythological *faux pas* by arguing that social reality in the village is merely the product of sociological fact. Asking the question whether the village indeed is a social fact, which it has for so long been assumed to be, Dumont and Pocock (1957) argue, "A field worker takes a village as a convenient centre for his investigation and all too easily comes to confer upon that village a kind of sociological reality which it does not possess".

For Dumont and Pocock (1957), only caste has social reality. The village is only the dwelling place of diverse and unequal castes. They confuse between the thing and its representation treating the latter as the only means through which the identity of the village can be established and confirmed. The fact is ignored that in a situation where reality is two steps removed from the observer, its representation can take numerous forms. Each of these forms claims truth value for itself. The fact is also lost sight of that the use of the scientific method for apprehending reality yields only a partial, not in any sense a total, picture; as such all such accounts are only partial and tentative. It is hoped that numerous representations of the village society will ultimately yield total knowledge. However, this hope is such that it cannot be realised. And, the variety of perspectives derived from the act of representation would, it is hoped, yield enough material to generate unified knowledge by collecting the requisite social, economic, political and religious information about Indian society.

This expectation is, however, frustrated not only because perspectival differences yield information that is incompatible and incapable of being fused into a unified, homogenous picture of Indian society, in general and Indian villages, in particular. This is so for the reason that the reconstruction of the village community proceeds by imposing upon it a sociological reality, a reality that is the product of the observer's creative imagination. This reality is grounded in a perspective that presupposes a standpoint which, looking at the village from outside, objectifies a given reality. Once the village community is treated as having an objective status, the factors and forces that animate it are lost sight of. More importantly, when inequality and dominance are considered to be the only worthwhile attributes of the village community for anthropological/sociological reconstruction, the totality of the village community is sacrificed at the altar of such phenomena such as division and dominance. The fact is ignored that, despite division and domination, collective village purposes retain their primacy. It inspires, when required, cooperative efforts by the entire village community. Moreover, as Srinivas (1959) observes, it is true that the dominant caste was real. Its leaders had the maximum stake in the local community and they took a leading role in its activities. However, the dependent castes also had a loyalty to the village and were considered by the villagers themselves to have membership in it. Inclusion and exclusion operated (and continue to operate) at all levels of a caste society, and the exclusion of Harijans from certain important activities, areas, and facilities cannot therefore be interpreted as an evidence of their not being a part of the village community.

Even if a village happens to be merely a link in the great chain of being, i.e., Indian society, it retains its distinctiveness and autonomy of operation as a distinct village community. It is true that its earlier political isolation has been brought to an end, perhaps forever. It now constitutes a prominent player in the great game of politics. As such, it has been exposed, to a very large extent, to forces that emanate from its external environment and impinge on it in several ways but not quite comprehensively and in every respect. However, Beteille (1965) would like us to believe that the political connection of the village with the outside world of influences shapes all the aspects of the village community. As he says, studies analysing political conflicts at the village level in term of cleavages within its structure "tend to view the village as an autonomous unit and to divert attention from broader political forces which operate from outside. Any study of political processes within the village will be incomplete unless it shows how such processes are articulated with the regional political system." It must be pointed out here that not all political conflicts in the village are emanations of what he calls "broader political forces," quite a number of such conflicts have their origin in village specific issues. It is entirely another matter that when some of these issues divide the village in certain well-defined antagonistic groups, these groups may seek support and gain strength from broader political forces (Beteille, 2002).

We must recognise the fact that politics in a village community may be informal but it does not have different objectives from those that we associate with the regional or national political system. After all, as Harold Lasswell defines it, politics is concerned with who gets what, when and how and, as a process; politics is involved with the distribution of wealth, power and prestige. And as Roy (1987) as shown, factional conflicts in the village are concerned with such a process. It is in this sense that we can talk of the village community retaining its distinct identity as a community and being animated largely by forces integral to the village per se. This is despite the fact that the village forms only a tiny part of the greater Indian community.

This fact gets pushed in the limbo of consciousness when sociological and anthropological studies shift their focus from the relationship among different social groupings within the village to the status of the village vis-à-vis the phenomenon of planned development. It is recognised that the village, as a relatively closed system, is gradually opening up under the press of development that was launched after India gained independence. However, the coming of independence robbed the Indian village of its existential autonomy reducing it to the status of a mere site for receiving certain stimuli from its external environment, reacting, responding to these stimuli and changing in accordance with the spirit of these stimuli. Most studies that treat the village as a site seem to have unthinkingly accepted the goals and objectives of economic growth-led development as not only desirable but also necessary. They deem it essential that villages in India must change in directions desired by the rulers at the national level.

Dube (1958), for example, saw development, particularly the Community Development Programme (CDP), as a pioneering venture, emphasised that efforts had to be mounted to keep up the momentum and argued that it was in the interest of the rural population to accept changes signified by the CDP. The recognition that the village must change, shifted the role of the catalyst of change from the village to the state, from the local people who knew the reality prevailing in the village to the politico-administrative functionaries who saw this reality through the wrong end of the bureaucratic telescope. By the same token, the village community was reduced to the status of the Pavlovian dog that must make appropriate responses depending on the kind of signals it receives. This has meant a heavy loss of the collective sense of responsibility along with its corollary of the intensification of conflict for acquiring divisible benefits. In effect, then, the rural sector has remained largely outside ... the discourse and debates on economic reforms ... the rural population is somehow meant to adapt, to sort itself out, to carry on, or just take away.

What is distinctive about these studies is that while they are focused on the village, it is not the village community that they explore. They examine what happens in the village when it is made to respond to certain stimuli coming from its external environment. As Chauhan (1974) noted, ... Examination of the concept (rural studies) has made the critics feel that something other than the village is in operation in society and that those processes are more relevant than the fact of the community ... whether the village itself is a problem of study or is merely a context within which (social) processes are studied, the need for taking the village as a base for studying the links and processes is recognised by those who acknowledge that tradition.

What should also be added here is that most of such studies catch the village on one point of time in the long journey of state-sponsored economic growth/development and treat their observation at that point in time as true for all times. The freezing of eternity into a moment is a distinctive mark of village studies taking the notion of the village vis-à-vis development as their theme. This is much more pronounced in those studies, which concern themselves with villages caught in the unsettling process of change induced by state-sponsored development. Take, for example, the observation, "No doubt, a village was constantly adjusting to its changing socio-cultural and political environment, yet customs and traditions underlying its social structure gave it stability and a sense of history (Singh, 2002). What is bothersome in this observation is that customs and traditions are treated as if they are immune to change. As such, no matter how deeply is the impact of change felt by the village community, disturbances caused by the process of change would, it is believed, be moderated, even neutralised, by the benign influence by its customs and tradition. In short, it is suggested that the village can never be fully modernised since customs and traditions are quite secure from the corrosive influence of change (Singh, 2002). Two things more need to be noted in this connection. First, customs and traditions may persist; however, the animating experience that lends them significance, meaning, and relevance may erode and leave behind only the form, the outer shell. It is the animating experience that nurtures the cocoon of the primordial experience. Second, subsequently even the outer shell may undergo revisions, depletions and finally may die out. Village studies do not reflect any awareness of these two significant factors.

These studies are quite clear about what it is that becomes instrumental in bringing about significant changes in the village community in terms of caste relations, distribution of power, thought-ways and work-ways. It is also recognised that at the root of these changes lies the phenomenon of economic growth and the press of modernisation. It is true that the benefits of economic growth have not been equitably and fairly distributed. However, the process of economic growth coupled with modernisation has wrought certain far going changes in the rural society. These changes are noticeable in the relationship between the privileged castes and deprived castes, in the distribution of power since the basis of power has shifted from ascriptive to achievement criteria, and in the other aspects of the village life. However, studies focusing on these changes do not go beyond mere recording of the dimension and the direction of these changes. These do not explain why the people living in villages that remained unchanged for so long have embraced these changes.

Obviously, Indian villages have now undergone numerous changes both in their internal relations and their interaction with the external world. As is clearly indicated by newspaper reports and serious academic studies, most villages in India are credited with urban life styles, so much so that a considerable number of village people are reported to be suffering from hypertension. However, is it enough to say that village life and relations are changing because of the changing patterns of economic production and distribution and by the growing impact of modernisation? There are evident structural changes, changes in the patterns of institutions and their operation and also in inter-personal and inter group relations. These changes can be easily perceived. However, one finds in village studies only a discursive account; no explanation accounting for these changes is offered. After all, institutions and relations change not because they have the in-built capacity of auto-direction; they change because man changes, his thought-ways and work-ways change. But, as Martin Buber underlines, Anthropology has no idea of who man is. Lacking this idea, anthropological studies focusing on change cannot become anything but discursive.

It is not that attempts at explaining change are lacking. However, failing to develop the idea of who man is and under what circumstance man's attitude and behaviour change, such explanations suffer from two very grievous shortcomings. On the one hand, these explanations are couched in jejune generalisations and, on the other hand, they are framed in descriptive categories. To take just a few examples, Srinivas' concepts of sanskritisation and Westernisation, Marriott's concepts of universalisation and parochialisation, Linton's 'core' and 'fluid zones' of cultural forms; all these are generalities that fail to account for the factors that give these descriptive categories their *raison d'etre* and make for change in their fortunes. The concept of sanskritisation is a reflection of Robert Merton's, theory of reference group. However, it lacks the rigour and substantiality that we find in the reference group theory. And, if we take note of the other concept, that of Westernisation, two things have to be explained. One, why the people located at lower rungs of the caste hierarchy began to emulate the behaviour pattern of those located at higher rungs and, two, what caused the change over from one reference group to another as indicated by sanskritisation and Westernisation. They are, however, never offered.

To take another aspect of the problem, it is true that both caste behaviour and caste relations have undergone several significant changes. It is also true that all those caste groups which remained, for long, under the thumb of the privileged, usually upper castes, have acquired some degree of independence. Thus there is in evidence a shift from what Robert A. Dahl calls "cumulative inequality" to "dispersal of inequality". One can, however, ask whether this is solely due to the introduction of democratic elections or something else too is involved? Similarly, Mencher talks of the strengthening of caste solidarity, not only within the village but also beyond it in many instances, even while caste rigidities are collapsing. But we do not have any explanation as to why this is happening and under what circumstances it is likely to happen. The feeling grows very strong that all such studies have left something hanging in the air and the poor reader must grope for satisfactory answers.

To sum up, then, on the whole, village studies do not reflect a very salubrious condition. They seem to suffer from several shortcomings as detailed above. The term "village" in this context seems to be nothing more than an inflatable balloon in which a sociologist or an anthropologist can blow such air as he wishes to and claim that a balloon is fully blown. The colonial research about Indian villages stopped, as Cohn shows, at the boundaries of villages instead of penetrating into the domains of everyday life. Later on, the village was subsumed in inter-caste relations and still later, it lost its soul by mortgaging its body to forces beyond its boundaries.

References

Beteille, A. 1965, *Caste, Class and Power: Changing Patterns of Stratification in a Tanjore Village*, Bombay: Oxford University Press.

—. 1969, *Caste Old and New: Essays in Social Structure and Social Stratification*, Bombay: Asia Publishing House.

—. 2002, "The Distribution of Power", in Vandana Madan (ed.), *The Village in India*, New Delhi: Oxford University Press.

Bhalla, A. and Bumke, P. (eds.) 1992, *Images of Rural India in the Twentieth Century*, New Delhi: Sterling Publishers.

Bremen, J. 1997, *The Village in Asia Revisited*, Delhi: Oxford University Press.

Chauhan, B.R. 1974, "Rural Studies: A Trend Report", in ICSSR, *Survey of Research in Sociology and Social Anthropology*, Bombay: Popular Prakashan.

Coomaraswamy, A.K. 1975, *Hinduism and Buddhism*, Delhi: Munshiram Manoharlal Publishers Ltd.

Cooper, B. 1999, *Eric Voegelin and the Foundations of Modern Political Science*, Columbia: University of Missouri.

Danda, A.K. 1995, *Foundations of Anthropology in India*, New Delhi: Inter-India Publications.

Dube, S.C. 1958, *India's Changing Villages: Human Factors in Community Development*, London: Routledge & Kegan Paul.

Dumont, L. and Pocock, D.F. 1957, "Village Studies", *Contributions to Indian Sociology*, 1.

Dumont, L. 1966, "The 'Village Community' from Munro to Maine", *Contributions to Indian Society*, 9, reprinted in Vandana Madan (ed.), *The Village in India*, New Delhi: Oxford University Press.

—. 1971, "On Putative Hierarchies and Some Allergies to it", *Contributions to Indian Sociology*, 14, p. 5.

Geertz, C. 1972, "Village", in *International Encyclopedia of Social Sciences*, London: Macmillan and Free Press.

Haddon, A.C. 1910, *History of Anthropology*, London: Walts & Co.

Harijan, April 4, 1936.

Harijan, August 29, 1936.

Inden, R.B. 1990, *Imagining India*, Oxford: Basil Blackwell.

Karve, I. 1956, *Caste in Modern Times, Report of the Seminar on Casteism*, Bombay: Indian Conference of Social Work.

Krishna, D. 1992, "The Varnashrama Syndrome of Indian Sociology", *Contributions to Indian Sociology* (n.s.), 26, 2, pp. 281–98.

Madan, V. (ed.) 2002, *The Village in India*, New Delhi: Oxford University Press.

Majumdar, D.N. 1958, *Caste and Communication in an Indian Village*, London: Asia Publications.

Marx, K. 1963, "The British Rule in India", in S. Avineri (ed.), *Karl Marx on Colonialism and Modernisation*, New York: Doubleday.

Niranjana, S. 1991, "Conceptualizing the Indian Village: An Overview of the Village Studies Tradition", *Indian Journal of Social Science*, 4, 3.

Petropoulos, W. and Weiss, Gilbert (eds.) 2003, *The Collected Works of Eric Voegelin Vol. 32: The Theory of Governance and Other Miscellaneous Papers, 1921–1938*, Columbia: University of Missouri Press.

Redfield, R. 1967, *The Little Community*, Chicago: Chicago University Press.

Roy, R. 1987, "Cooperation Conflict and in a North Bihar Village", in *Perspectives on Indian Politics*, Delhi: Discovery Publishing House.

——. 1993, *Captive Vision: Ideas as Weapon*, Delhi: Ajanta Publications.

Shah, A.M. and Desai, I.P. 1988, *Division and Hierarchy*, Delhi: Hindustan Publications.

Singh, Y. 2002, "Chanukhera: Cultural Change in Eastern Uttar Pradesh", in Vandana Madan (ed.), *The Village in India*, New Delhi: Oxford University Press.

Srinivas, M.N. and Panini, M.N. 1971, "Development of Sociology and Social Anthropology in India", *Sociological Bulletin*, 22, 2, pp. 179–215.

Srinivas, M.N. 1959, "The Dominant Caste in Rampura", *The American Anthropologist*, 61, pp. 1–16.

——. 1996, *Village, Caste, Gender and Method: Essays in Indian Anthropology*, Bombay: Oxford University Press.

——. 2002, "The Indian Village: Myth and Reality", in Vandana Madan (ed.), *The Village in India*, New Delhi: Oxford University Press.

3

Rethinking Villages

An Interdisciplinary Discourse on Development, Modernity and Change

Yogesh Atal

The seminar on village studies is a reassurance that the village is not yet forgotten, and that there is a genuine concern for village India. The trickle down theory that failed in the realm of economic development is still being pursued in the field of social development. Hope is expressed that the information revolution and the overall urban ethos will speedily pervade all over India. In that enthusiasm, however, rural India has suffered grave neglect.

This explanation has a parallel. When the first World Summit on Social Development was organised by the United Nations in Copenhagen in 1995, as a culminating event on the review of five decades of development under the UN auspices, it was acknowledged that despite the years of development, following either the capitalist, or the socialist, or the mixed model there were deficits in the area of social development. The message was clear that the gains in economic development were not enough to wipe out poverty, unemployment and tendencies toward social disintegration and disruption related to social development in both developed and the underdeveloped countries. There was not a single country in the comity of nations that did not have these problems. Needless to say that their profiling differed from country to country and that no single recipe could be found to be universally applicable. The summit highlighted the view that while countries share common problems, there are no common solutions for them. These will have to be found by each country in its own cultural and social context. And, it was this acknowledgement that led the summit to officially recognise the role of the non-economic social sciences. The summit also endorsed the view that economic development must subserve the cause of social development, which is the ultimate goal of all developmental efforts.

"Uncommon solutions to common social problems" turned out to be a key phrase at the summit. If the deficit on the social front is to be made up, we must know the populations that are affected the most, i.e., the poor, the unemployed, and the socially marginalised. In other words, the women, the minorities, the ethnic communities, the refugees and the street children. Naturally, our attention will have to turn to the illiterates and the semi-literates, to those living in remote rural and tribal areas, who had remained unreachable. In a way, social development is all about reaching the unreachable or the unreached; or helping those who had been denied access to the benefits of development.

Where do we find the marginalised? Most certainly, the marginalised are found in rural areas. Of course, they are also the inhabitants of the slums in urban conglomerates. This must have been the concern of our political leaders and planners that prompted them to devise strategies for community development in the early years of our independence. Not only did the India of the 1940s live in villages, even today the majority of Indians live in them. Gandhi's clarion call to go back to the villages seems still valid. Attributing defeats of the ruling parties in states such as Karnataka and Andhra Pradesh which had spearheaded IT revolution and ushered in the cyber era to the neglect of the village populace serves as a timely reminder. Let us not forget the villages.

In the 1950s, with the launching of the Community Development Programme (CDP) there was a sudden spurt of interest in the villages. Amongst the social scientists, economists have a long history of working on the rural sector. But theirs were the studies based largely on official data and focussing more on agriculture than on rural life. People used to remark in a lighter vein that the agricultural economists can reel out economic data relative to agriculture but are unable to distinguish between the plants of wheat and barley – implying thereby that they were armchair analysts without having the feel of the field. But because of their contribution to agricultural economics of India, they were the first to be roped into the programme of community development.

The training for the CDP workers at the grassroots, however, required much more than mere economic facts. The knowledge of village social structure and culture was regarded as essential and for this trainers from other social science disciplines were hired. It is at this stage that the absence of fieldwork-based studies of rural India was keenly felt. It may be recalled that when colonialism spread, the colonialists felt the need to train their administrators in the culture of the colonies. That gave rise to the discipline of Anthropology and encouraged scholars to write ethnographic accounts of various tribal societies. It was a similar need that encouraged village studies in India in the 1950s. Of course, there existed studies of tribal groups that were mostly done by foreigners. There were also some works on villages such as those of Henri Maine, Charles Metcalfe, Baden Powell, Darling and Ibbetson. But these studies painted Indian villages as "little republics", more or less static, and practitioners of some sort of primitive communism. The description of social structure in them represented what Srinivas called the "book view" and the "upper-caste view". The village was seen as a homogeneous community with little or no connections with the outside world. The economists did not bother about the changes brought about in inter-caste relations as a consequence of economic activity. The village was portrayed idyllically as a place of happy innocence or rusticity.

Sociologists and anthropologists entered almost simultaneously the rural terrain – the anthropologists moved in from the study of the tribals and the sociologists drifted in from Indological studies and the studies of urban phenomena. The village became the meeting ground for them. To this list may be added the field-work-survey-oriented economists. The period from the 1950s through the 1970s saw a spate of village studies done by scholars drawn from different social science disciplines and focusing on various aspects of village life, and on the dynamics of change initiated by the planned programmes of development.

These studies challenged the prevailing stereotype of the Indian village. Although populated by largely illiterate peasants and landless labourers and relatively cut-off by communication from other habitats in the region and beyond, the studies indicated that the village is both a unity and an interlinked entity through its various extensions in the religious, social and political spheres (Srinivas, 1955; Majumdar, 1958). The "little traditions" of the villages could not be seen in isolation, and without regard for the "great traditions" of India's indigenous civilisation (Marriott, 1955). Using the field material from a village near Aligarh, pseudonymed *Kishangarhi*, McKim Marriott, for example, outlined the processes of universalisation and parochialisation to explain the dynamic relationship between the great traditions and the little traditions. In the sphere of castes, the studies suggested that in terms of inter-caste relations, the village represented a vertical unity but in the area of intra-caste interactions (Srinivas, 1955), caste represented a horizontal unity extending to several villages of a cultural region (Chauhan, 1966; Pradhan, 1966). The village was described as a vertical unity of castes, and the caste was seen as a horizontal unity extending to several contiguous villages. In Northern India, such extensions were demonstrated by drawing the "range of marital ties", and by the concept of "*Seem Seeem Na Bhaichara*". The peripatetic salesmen, the mendicants and the sadhus served as couriers of the outside elements into the fabric of village society and culture. The election process of free democratic India has created additional bridges to erase its image as an isolate. The political process has empowered the villager in certain ways. Literacy deficiency notwithstanding, the villagers have engineered a revolution via the ballot.

Writing in 1955, Srinivas said the following about India's villages: "The villager's social field is thus much wider than his village. Kin, economic, religious and other social ties enlarge the field to include a circle of neighbouring villages. But ever since the beginning of the British rule, political and economic decisions taken in London and Manchester have affected the Indian peasant in his remotest villages. And in Independent India, not a day passes without some fresh evidence of government's solicitude for the rural folk. The social anthropologist who studies a single village should not only bear in mind its ties with other villages, but also that political and economic forces set in motion in large society affect it fundamentally."

The villages studies carried out and published in the 1950s and 1960s have been extensively used as teaching material in university curricula and as training kit for the development workers. Social sciences thus contributed to a better understanding of the village society in India. In many ways, these studies exploded several myths about village India. The motivations to carry out village studies were different. Apart from academic factors influencing the shift of priorities, there were practical considerations. Some scholars were interested in documenting the "present" of the village India before the waves of development and modernisation transformed it. Others were interested in documenting the process of change, particularly of directed culture change; and still others were engaged to carry out specific project related studies such as evaluation or impact of innovations.

But somehow the interest in villages got lost in the mid-1970s, when scholars shifted to other areas such as studies of movements, including *Kisan Andolans*, or of processes of urbanisation and globalisation. It appeared that the area of village studies was saturated, as that of tribal studies, and that other priority concerns began to attract the researchers.

In the last forty years a good deal has changed in our villages and the tribal areas. Literacy has spread, so has urbanisation, along with the reach of the mass media. There is better connectivity in terms of kilometres of rail and road, and even the postal and telecommunication facilities have become better. There is also evidence of migration of people from the rural areas to the urban areas. The spread of urbanisation has taken within its fold many villages through the processes of *suburbation* and *conurbation*. And, the implementation of Panchayati Raj and the provision for the participation of women in the local self-governing bodies has certainly affected the nature of leadership, pattern of group dynamics and factionalism in the village social structures.

The slow appearing but definitely dramatic changes in rural India have made the village studies of the 1960s and 1970s somewhat outdated in the same fashion as the old ethnographies of our tribal groups. Reading Majumdar's work on the HO or Dube's on the Kamar, or Haimendorf's on the Chenchus has a different meaning today than forty years ago. Verrier Elwin's Gonds do not tally with today's Judeo Singh. Shibu Suren or Babu Lal Marandi of Jharkhand, or N.S. Sangma of the Northeast can claim a tribal status genealogically, but their portrayals will not correspond to their ancestors reported in the ethnographies of their communities published in the 19th century and the early 20th century. Those studies provide a good and dependable benchmark to contrast with the situation of today but they cannot be taken as "representative" of the studied group of our times.

The same is true of village studies. Already some scholars are planning to restudy Shamirpet village which got reported in S.C. Dube's famous book published in 1955 under the caption *Indian Village*. The impact of the cyber city of Hyderabad in the last ten years must have radically transformed this village to defy any match with what Dube had described. The same must be the fate of Marriott's Kishangarhi, Oscar Lewis' Ranikhera, Srinivas' Rampura, Majumdar's Mohana, and several other notable villages studied in the past.

Raising methodological issues regarding the representativeness of a single village study, Brij Raj Chauhan had invented a mythic village called Hindpur based on the 1951 Census data. This typical village, if it existed anywhere, was "18 miles from the rail, 6 miles from the *pucca* road, 4 miles from *kachcha* road and 33 miles from the city, with 269 males and 260 females it is inhabited by 529 persons". In 1951, the rural population constituted 82.7 per cent of the total population. The literacy rate for the country as a whole was a low 18.33 per cent.

Although I had no time to review the 2001 data relative to the few indicators that I have mentioned above, no one will question the assumption that in the last five decades considerable progress has been made. 1991 figures tell us that the rural population ratio has declined to 74.3 per cent, and literacy rates have soared up to 52.21 per cent in 1991 and to 65.4 per cent in 2001. The same must be true of the data relative to roads and railroad. I can safely assume that in today's *village* India there is a high literacy rate compared to the 1950s, most of the villages are better connected through roads with improved transportation, radio and television have also reached several villages, and several villages have been electrified. Living on the outskirts of the National Capital Region of Delhi, I know that my house is built on a land that must have been tilled for ages and that is gone. The entire area's green fields are replaced by high rise buildings; occasional visitation by field rats in those quarters is one sign of the area's prehistory. The erstwhile farmers have become rich through the sale of their landed property, and have shifted to new occupations. Even the material culture of their houses has radically changed with electricity, new electric and electronic gadgets, motorbikes, and a ubiquitous cell phone. The massive transformation of this class of farmers and landless labourers who present a new intermediate category between the village and the town offers a good example of the redefinition of the village.

In the 1950s, the classification of India into urban, rural and tribal made good sense because it represented a sort of continuum. Although some of us were unhappy even then with such a simplistic separation, none offered any other classificatory device. I had recently been to Nagaland. Visiting Dimapur and Kohima one does smell a different flavour, but one cannot club these urban centres with the remotely located tribal villages. Our tribal areas have both rural and urban settlements. The high incidence of literacy in some of the tribal groups makes different kinds of demands on the wider society. No longer does the old colonial attitude of patronage towards the tribal's seem valid. Nor are the tribals an exclusive domain for anthropological studies of the colonial mould. There are now studies by scholars from various social science disciplines, and by the tribals themselves, who have impeccable social science credentials. There is certainly a need for preparing good ethnographies of contemporary tribal societies, using modern social science techniques and an interdisciplinary approach. The old ethnographies are dated and need to be replaced. This is necessary if the prevalent stereotypes about the tribal groups generated by old ethnographies are to be challenged.

There is a need to draw an elaborate but doable tentative list for work in the rural and tribal areas. The tasks of urgent concern are:

1. Review and systematisation of our understanding about village India. There are a large number of village monographs, including those prepared by the Office of the Registrar-General of India during the 1961 Census. No effort has been made to cull out the similarities and differences that exist and to develop a social science profile of the Indian village.
2. Initiating a programme of re-studies of the villages and the tribal groups that have been studied and reported earlier. These villages need to be revisited to document the changes that have been experienced by them at the micro level.
3. Identify the gaps that exist in our knowledge – in terms of areas or regions not covered earlier, or the topics/themes not yet investigated.
4. Developing a specific programme of urgent action to research those communities that are being/or are likely to be engulfed by the processes of urbanisation.
5. Initiating studies of those new communities that are coming up.
6. An important area of research is the changing relationship between the rural and the urban. Of particular interest would be the changing economic ties, reach of the urban ethos in the village, and the impact of migration not on the point of destination but on the point of origin.

References

Chauhan, B.R. 1966, 1999, *A Rajasthan Village*, Udaipur: A.C. Brothers.

Dube, S.C. 1951, *The Kamar*, Lucknow: Universal Publishers.

——. 1955, *Indian Village*, London: Routledge and Kegan Paul.

Elwin, V. 1939, *The Baiga*, London: John Murray.

Furer-Haimendorf, C. von, 1943, *The Chenchu*, London: Macmillan and Co.

Lewis, O. 1958, *Village Life in Northern India*, Urbana: University of Illinois Press.

Marriott, M. (ed.) 1955, *Village India*, Chicago: Chicago University Press.

Majumdar, D.N. 1958, *Caste and Communication in an Indian Village*, Bombay: Asia Publishing House.

Pradhan, M.C. 1966, *The Political System of Jals of Northern India*, London: Oxford University Press.

Srinivas, M.N. 1955, *India's Villages*, Calcutta: West Bengal Government Press.

4

Village Studies

Some Observations on Fifty Years of Research

Giri Raj Gupta

It was 1955 when a student from a town with population 22,600, formerly the seat of a princely state, in Southeastern Rajasthan went to Udaipur, Rajasthan, over 400 km away, to study Art as an undergraduate (to complete B.A.) with a mission to become a freelance artist. Rajasthan has more than 22 dialects. He was new to *Mewari* as he came from a *Haruati*-speaking area. However, he did not speak *Haruati* fluently either. He chose Sociology, one of the three subjects, a student had to take at the undergraduate level. Very soon he was fascinated by the teachings of some of his professors; one of them was Professor Brij Raj Chauhan who taught Sociology, not only in the classroom but wherever he was with his students. He was sort of a Gandhian who wore *khadi* and practiced most of the principles that Mahatma Gandhi espoused. Wherever he was, he was surrounded by students, whether it was a street corner, a cafe, a cricket field, or someone's home. He also commanded profound respect. He treated and respected students as if they were part of a team. Often he knew a student and his life story better than the student knew himself. He quietly assessed each student's potential and subtly cultivated his strengths so that he could effectively pursue his life goals. Encouraging a student to be a student of a certain professor at a different university in the country was not commonly heard of in those days, but he advised his students to do so. Genuinely, he lived Sociology. I became part of this fortunate process.

During 1950s, several pioneering village studies were published. Among them were S.C. Dube's (1955) *Indian Village*, McKim Marriott's (1955) *Village India*, and Oscar Lewis's (1955) *Village Life in Northern*

India. The difference between earlier studies and these new studies was that the latter were empirical; they were grounded in theory and offered new concepts for rural studies. These village studies were conducted by scholars who were skillfully trained to comprehend the ethos of the rural life. Professor Chauhan often brought up examples from these studies in his lectures as well as from his own fieldwork. He made special efforts to invite scholars who were involved in village studies. Udaipur has had a name and attraction where most foreign scholars come and often visit the Department of Sociology and talk about their research. My fascination with rural communities tremendously increased when in 1956, I lived for ten weeks in a village in Kota district, Rajasthan under the auspices of the Ministry of Community Development, Government of India. I attended panchayat meetings, fairs and festivities, weddings as well as funerals, and watched and participated in common encounters in the village and the area. That firmed up my notion of embarking on my sociological journey.

I began taking notes, not in public but whenever I found free time for myself alone. Talking with all kinds of people, irrespective of age, gender, caste or creed, was my motto. There was always an inherent intent to understand behaviour, ritual, custom or worldview. Stopping at a small shop of a barber, tailor, grocer, cloth merchant or betel vender or even a leather worker was fun, insightful and informative. There was no hurry. However, sometimes, people felt that I was a little too curious. But everyone respected me and answered questions because they did not see any harm in divulging information they thought was probably common knowledge, and also because I was a college student and accustomed to friable. The ritual practices, traditions, beliefs and superstitions, ideas about sacred and profane, though I was brought up with many of those, now raised questions in my mind. In a way, I started feeling that Durkheim, and his compatriots, such as Raymond Firth, Malinowski, and Radcliffe-Brown in the guidance of Professor Chauhan, were directing me to observe social phenomena totally differently. I had questions such as, "Why do womenfolk go outside the village to worship a pile of rubbish, as a part of a series of wedding rites?". Or, why does the bridegroom have to mount a horse and act as a valorous warrior during his first visit to bride's home? Beyond being inquisitive, the attempt was to explain "meaning" behind the practices and how they sustained and changed the structure of social relationships within the village and beyond. In early 1959, this resulted in my Master's Thesis, "Rituals in a Rajasthan Village." Professor S.C. Dube, who was one of the external examiners of the thesis, conveyed to Professor Chauhan that this work can be extended to a Ph.D. dissertation. In fact, the credit goes to Professor Chauhan and his uncanny ability, perseverance, scholarship and guidance. Often, intellectual interest in students turns to be ephemeral, and for professors who are dedicated to teach it is very frustrating. For dedicated professors, it is like turning a small piece of gravel into a diamond by polishing it as perfectly as possible. Unfortunately, in case of students, the piece of rock also has human element and personal vicissitudes. I recall that several of my classmates had the potential but did not have the forbearance of going through the arduous task of achieving academic excellence.

As a follow up, I pursued the same topic for my Ph.D programme but limited it to the study of marriage. That opened up opportunities to look beyond the village, kinship networks and linkages beyond the village and region. In a sense the village in India is not an isolated entity, an organism in itself. Professor Chauhan's field of study, a village in southern Rajasthan in the early 1960s, gave me another insight. During a field trip we found that people from at least 20 surrounding villages attended the feast on the death of a Jat chieftain. There are controversies associated with maintaining the so-called identity of a village community and its contact with the outside world. After more than forty years of irregular but frequent contact with the village I have been associated with, I have noticed that greater contact with the outside world has steadily changed the quality of life materially as well as culturally. Marriage linkages beyond the village and region have given people more political influence, education, and resources to do business with. Now there are paved roads, TV sets, cell phones, electricity, water pumps in the homes and fields, a few tractors and other harvesting machines, better housing and a good number of college-going youths. There is an effort to find well-educated mates for the children that were commonly discouraged before. There is more greenery around in the community than I had ever seen before. The worldview has changed dramatically as some people watch national and international news and programmes, while some of the womenfolk watch soap operas. Probably, TV programmes and cell/mobile phones have opened the village to the whole world. Professor Chauhan's teaching does not end here.

In 1969, I was offered a faculty position to teach Sociology at Western Illinois University in the USA. This gave me opportunities to meet Professor Milton Singer, McKim Marriott and Bernard S. Cohen at the University of Chicago. Professor Singer, who was the doyen of the studies of culture, offered me an invaluable advice. He asked me to study some small communities in the USA and compare them with Indian village life. He said, "You have this advantage." A community of up to 2500 population in a farm setting is officially known as "rural" in the USA, representing about 2.5 per cent of over 300 million people in 2007. About 20 per cent jobs are associated with the farming industry. Over the years the farm size has been growing, ownership of small farms is declining partly due to mechanisation and the economics of farming (a 100 acre farm is considered small). States like Illinois and Iowa can feed and Wisconsin can provide all the dairy products for the whole country. Innovation and agricultural research guides the farmer who is better educated and significantly prosperous compared to anywhere in the world.

During 1972–1980, with the assistance of five graduate students, I attempted to study the themes of rural life in the US, the mid part of the country known as 'Midwest,' about 400 km from the metropolitan city of Chicago. American Sociology has a long history and probably as much sociological research is applied to simple local problems as to international issues in diverse fields, such as, what kind of environment increases productivity in an assembly line or prediction about 'who is going to be the next President? It took high ethical standards, rigour and refining of methodological tools and brilliant minds to accomplish the respect it deserved.

The American rural population lives a simpler life compared to elsewhere in the US, of course not with the same amenities as urbanites do, such as popular museums, parks, medical facilities, shopping centres, theatres or universities. But they have comfortable housing, running water and electricity, paved roads, schools, cable TV, telephones, computers, regular newspaper delivery and church services. The infrastructure transformation has rapidly changed the small community life in the last century. Currently, household size is large 4.1 persons to 2.7 in the rest of the nation. Contrary to what some believe, individual freedom is encouraged in life choices. Seventy per cent people in rural areas help their immediate relatives in need materially and psychologically. Although mate selection is theoretically open, over 75 per cent tend to marry in their own class, and 61 per cent find their mates within 30 km from their home. The rural population is relatively more religious, not necessarily tradition bound. There are almost no restrictions on food. Interpersonal relations are fairly secular, the practice of untouchability does not exist, class-based hierarchy is present but is not very conspicuous. Max Weber's indices of income, prestige and power determine class. Gender-based boundaries are limited at home as well as at places of work. Those who work in the farms rarely make a major move and some take jobs around the area during off-season. The new generations of farmers are educated with high skills in their trade. Over 90 per cent of the rural communities are well connected by transportation systems of rail, water and road. There are more cars and trucks in the families than people. There are political lobbies to seek support for farm subsidies (government subsidies to farmers to produce less to stabilise prices) but no farm movements. Due to increasing oil prices, farmers now are cashing on by diverting corn, soybeans and other farm products to produce ethanol to replace petroleum as energy source.

This brief and very cursory comment highlights the rural scene in the two largest democracies of the world. I should conclude that there is no doubt that we need to understand the rural communities in India better to embark on any planned or incidental change for better life. Educating the rural masses can be a formidable task but what they can learn and accomplish if they know what is in their interest can be equally amazing. Planned change agents have to look at what infrastructure can support, sort out secular areas of change first to initiate small scale efforts. For example, the dairy industry in the USA is run by farmer-owned cooperatives that supply processed butter, cheese and milk to the whole country and beyond.

India is a great country with a remarkable history and immeasurable potential in which social scientists can play a vital role. Science research needs to be accountable to those for whom it is intended!

References

Dube, S.C. 1955, *Indian Village*, London: Routledge and Kegan Paul.

Marriott, McKim (ed.) 1955, *Village India*, Chicago: Chicago University Press.

Lewis, O. 1958, *Village Life in Northern India*, Urbana: University of Illinois Press.

5

Intensive Village Studies in India

Susan S. Wadley

Intensive studies in and of villages in India have strong traditions. Serious work in the direction during the third quarter of the century put Indian scholarship at international standards, providing opportunities for interactions at equal levels. That appears to be a strong base for the growth of Sociology and Anthropology in India. Such a tradition of the villages appears to be on a decline. It is felt that the springs of the real strength in the subject should be reassessed both for their internal refinement and redefining the interrelationship of approach to other forms of enquiry. Ramkrishna Mukherjee had regretted that economists and sociologists had not been able to interact with each other and the great promise in that direction had been passed over. Bardhan tried to establish a link between Economics and Anthropology in the first serious attempt in the Bangalore seminar. Among the other subjects, interaction between field studies and the historical approach was attempted by B.S. Cohen. Besides these, scholars in other disciplines have perceived their enquiries in isolated manner; R. L. Singh's initiative brought geographers to map out rural settlements with good effect. Attention has also gone to the manner in which men of letters have portrayed rural life, which is partly based on real situations but complemented by the imaginative skills of the writers. Recently, the rise of disciplines such as Development Studies and to an extent Management Studies has opened a new relevance for rural concerns through selective case studies.

It is time that the strength of the intensive studies of the villages is reassessed and possible refinements introduced. For this purpose, a keynote address by Brij Raj Chauhan on 'Seven Decades of Intensive Village Studies in Uttar Pradesh' is expected to be ready soon and will form a part of the proposed seminar. Intensive studies insist on personal observations by the writer of specific events, which indicate different processes involved for the role of different actors manifested and latent, the nature of interactions taking place and the meanings that the actors give to the specific events. Then, the question may arise whether the particular event and interactions have acquired a pattern and whether the changes are ad hoc or in the process of getting institutionalised. Studies like those of Andre Beteille (1965) bring event happening in the village to the political and social movements at the state level. Srinivas (1955) and Marriott (1955) attempted serious work in studying the rural life of the village and exploring its link with the regional and the national or classical levels. Certain political changes like those of the introduction of the adult franchise at the national level and agrarian reforms like abolition of *zamindari*, consolidation of landholding and ceiling of maximum possession of landholding by families have led scholars to examine whether structural changes have occurred in substance or only formally. Community development and its later versions indicating state initiative in development have again raised a question on how far the progress reports of the macro data are indicative of the situation on the ground and whether intensive enquiries would provide answers at the grassroots levels.

The important questions before the seminar are an examination of the strength of intensive studies in the villages, the need for defining the parameters within which they have an effective role to play; and the manner in which studies in sister disciplines add further variety to the process. Secondly, as the interests in studies in rural life begins extending almost to all social services, which have the own social tools of enquiry and perspectives, how far is it possible to convince the practitioners in these disciplines to see the relevance of the intensive studies and the case materials that could to some extent be made a part of the new disciplines as well.

International experiences have been pulled together in various ways: (i) by scholars from foreign universities doing fieldwork on dissertations submitted to their respective universities but in the process interacting with their Indian counterparts, (ii) by foreign scholars getting associated with the Indian universities for supervisions of their field studies; and (iii) by scholars from India studying situations in foreign countries. Amidst these traditions it is possible to keep on assessing periodically the strength and weakness as well as prospects for the future. Such exercises have, it seems, been suspended over the last quarters of a century and need to be revived and planned through a special seminar addressed to these concerns.

References

Beteille, A. 1965, *Caste, Class and Power*, Berkeley: University of California Press.

Marriott, M. (ed.) 1955, *Village India*, Chicago: Chicago University Press.

Srinivas, M.N. 1952, *Religion and Society among the Coorgs of South India*, Oxford: Oxford University Press.

——. 1955, "Sanskritisation and Westernisation", *Far Eastern Quarterly*, 14, pp. 481–96.

6

Trends in Rural Development

A Review of Literature

Ravi S. Singh and Kavita Jaijan

Rural development, according to planner Albert Watorston, "is an integrated multi-sectoral process, incorporating agricultural development and the development of social utilities and services". Its main aim is to improve the conditions of rural population comprising mainly poor cultivators, landless persons and agricultural labourers. Rural development thus implies both the economic betterment of people as well as greater social transformation. World Bank Policy paper (1975) states that "rural development as a strategy is designed to improve the economic and social life of a specific group of people – the rural poor. It involves extending the benefits of development to the poorest among those who seek a livelihood in the rural areas. The group includes small scale farmers, tenants and the landless". Thus rural development means the development of rural economy as well as the society which attracted the attention of the social scientists in the 21st century. The present attempt is to understand the 21st century trends in rural studies as revealed by the publications in the *Economic and Political Weekly*, (*EPW*). The following survey is organised in 13 sections, beginning with a discussion on the rationale of selecting the *EPW* for the present exercise, followed by some concluding remarks.

Selection of *Economic and Political Weekly:* The Rationale

EPW bridges the academic and popular concerns, economic and development debates, and invites practitioners of all the social science disciplines as well as other allied disciplines. The *EPW* is published from

Mumbai since 1949. Its publication began as the *Economic Weekly* and since 1966 re-christened as the *Economic and Political Weekly*. Within a single issue, one finds commentaries on contemporary affairs, special articles, book reviews, etc., and it is the regular structure of the weekly which set it unique from a purely academic or popular journal/magazine. This mixing up however does not result in compromising with the quality output and seriousness of issues and discussions contained therein.

It has an apparent global character in terms of recognition, readership and also its contributors. Its reputation, as "catalyst of debates and disseminator of research output", is widely acknowledged. So while trying to understand the trends of rural studies, there is no better space to cover and navigate to discern the developments. In other words, the *EPW* becomes the natural choice while attempting a survey of the progress in rural studies, an interdisciplinary area indeed. It is difficult to deny that the major focus of this weekly is obviously economic issues. However, a serious glimpse into its coverage can reveal to the reader that it also covers other fields including that of the rural studies. Many of us would agree to the declaration available at its website, "While looking for the developments in social sciences, the *EPW* is a natural choice". The 109 references reviewed, cover papers published from 1995 to 2007 in *EPW* are selected. There were 109 contributions on development and related to rural infrastructure, the Panchayati Raj, land reforms, agricultural practices and their implications, employment, National Rural Employment Guarantee Scheme, poverty, migration, health, women in rural areas, impact of globalisation, and rural development and social justice. The distribution of these contributions along the issues of development is presented in two tables.

Table 1 shows greater concern over social justice. It needs to be highlighted that larger emphasis on social justice dimension indicates embeddedness of injustice even after the lapse of more than six decades of independence and at the same time intellectuals concern to expose it. This course of development is in every sense appreciable. Women and gender issues can also be seen in the same perspective. In the context of redistributive justice project especially in rural areas, land reforms form the basis as revealed by the scholarly works on it. Agricultural practices' environmental implication and availability, accessibility, utility of health facilities and National Rural Employment Guarantee Schemes too emerge as important. Contributors gave scant attention to migration: nature, type, cause and consequences.

Table 1

Thematic Coverage by the EPW, 1995–2007

	Theme	*Fre-quency*	*% of the total*	*Specific work*
1.	Rural development and social justice	30	20.83	Namdbi (1996), Tharu (1996), Lieten (1996), Pai, et al. (1997), Pinto (1997), Saleth (1997), Assadi (1997), Pai (1997), Desai (1995), Mahapatra (1996), Mukherjee (1996), Prashad (1996), Pai (2001), Mathew (2003), Jodhka (2002), Pai, et al. (2005), Kumar (2003), Pai (2004), Satyanarayana (1995), Morriott (2003), Kumar (2005), Kumar (2004), Chakravarthi (2001), Srinivasan, et al. (2004), Rajan (2003), Jodhka, et al. (2003), Thorat (2002), Deboshis, et al. (2006), Gupta (2005), Balakrishanan (2003).
2.	Women in rural India	19	13.19	Tharu (1996), Correa (1996), Chowdhry (1997), Rao, et al. (1997), Mathew (1997), Kulkarni (1997) Krishnaji (1995), Navlakha (1996), Rajeshwari (1996), Thakkar (1997, Kannabiran, et al. (1997), Soman (1997), Jejeebhoy (1997), Singh (1997), Kothari (1997), Bhaskar (1997), Nakkeeran (2003), Mathur, et al. (2005), Patikh, et al. (2003).
3.	Land reforms	16	11.11	Bhattacharjee (1996), Jeyaranjan (1996), Nanjundar (1996), Suryanarayana (1996), Thakkar (1997) Bandyopadhyay (1996), Radhkrishana (2002), Dev (2005), Mulji (2003), Dev (2004), Chakravarti (2001), Sekhar, et al. (2003), Sharma (2001), Hirashima (2000), Mulji, et al. (2003), Joshi et al. (2001).
4.	Health	13	9.02	Anita (1997), Krishanaji (1995), Monkodi (1996), Ghosh (1996), Rajeshwari (1996), Soman (1997), Maharate (1997), Jejeebhoy (1997), Gill, et al. (2000), Beherav, et al. (2002), Nakkeeran (2003), Mathur, et al. (2005), Patikh, et al. (2003).
5.	Agricultural practices and environmental implications	11	7.64	Chand (1996), Dev, et al. (1996), Nellithanan (1997), Behera, et al. (2002), Dev (2003), Sekhar, et al. (2003), Narayanmoorthy, et al. (2003), Boki (2003), Reddy (2003), Assadi (2000), Shetty (2004).

Cont'd...

...Cont'd

6.	Panchayati Raj	11	7.64	Mohanty (1995), Mathew (1997), Bhaskar (1997), Vaddiraju, et al. (2004), Pal (2004), Pai (2001), Rao (2003), Buch (2005), Pal (2004), Narayana (2005), Mathew (2003).
7.	Rural infrastructure	10	6.94	Rajvanshi (1995), Vora (1996), Narain (1996), Pal (1996), Bakil (2000), Narayananmoorthy, et al. (2003), Reddy (2003), Pulmate, et al. (2003), Chavan, et al. (2002), Janaiah, et al. (2000).
8.	Employment	9	6.25	Eapen (1996), Saleth (1997), Mathew (1995), Pal (1996), Matharatna (1997), Dev (2005), Radhakrishna (2002), Mulji (2003), Dev (2003).
9.	Impact of globalisation	9	6.25	Pieterse (1996), Roy (1997), Ghosh (1996), Bandhyopadhyay (1996), Assadi (2000), Shetty (2004), Balakrishanan (2003), Hirashima (2000), Murgi, et al. (2003).
10.	Poverty	9	6.25	Vohra (1996), Suryanarayana (1996), Radhakrishna (2002), Thakur, et al. (2000), Nayyar (2005), Chavan, et al. (2002), Janaiah, et al. (2000), Sundaram, et al. (2003), Refique (2003).
11.	National Rural Employment Guarantee Schemes	5	3.47	Dev (1996), Kumar, et al. (2004), Patnaik (2005), Aiyar, et al. (2006), Dogra (2005).
12.	Migration	2	1.39	Vora (1996), Refique (2003).
	Total	144	100.00	

Source: Computed on the basis of several issues of the *EPW.*

Table 2 on the regional coverage of the contributions needs to be read carefully. More than half of the contributions reviewed from *EPW* have not dealt with even a state or a group of states or a region; forget about the micro-level case study. They mostly deal with the theoretical debates. However, the desirable rigour and depth of analysis make them worthwhile to infer various insights which they provide. Nearly, a quarter of the total works deal with the Hindi-speaking region which shows the rampantness of rural challenges and also the importance of this belt in debates of national importance. The conspicuous absence of the north-eastern region as a whole is a cause of concern. Not even a single state of this region is deemed fit for academic analysis in the period of analysis. It is really a matter of serious thought. After all, there is no dearth of issues of socio-economic, cultural and political significance.

Table 2

Region-wise Coverage by the EPW, 1995–2007

India/Region/ State	*Frequency*	*% of the total*	*Specific work*
All-India level	61	51.69	Mohanty (1995), Bhattacharjee (1996), Nambissan (1996), Tharu (1996), Narjundan (1996), Narain (1996), Pal (1996), Navalkha (1996), Prashad (1996), Dev (1996), Suryanarayana (1996), Bondyopathyay (1996), Kannabiran (1997), Soman (1997), Jejeebhoy (1997), Singh (1997), Nellithanam (1997), Chowdhry (1997), Mathew (1997), Antia (1997), Roy (1997), Satyanarayana (1995), Pal (2004), Roy (2004), Nakkeeran (2003), Mulji (2003), Dev (2004), Kumar et al. (2004), Radhakrishna (2002), Dev (2005), Patnaik (2005), Aiyar, et al. (2006), Dogra (2005), Rao (2003) Buch (2005), Mathew (2003), Marriott (2003), Kumar (2005), Kumar (2004), Srinivasan et al. (2004), Rajan (2003), Thorat (2002), Gupta (2005), Deboshis, et al. (2006), Narayanamoorthy, et al. (2003), Reddy (2003), Pulamate et al. (2003), Chavan (2002), Sundaram et al. (2003), Sharma (2001), Nayyar (2005), Hirashima (2000), Joshi, et al. (2001), Krishnaji (1995), Mathew (1995), Desai (1995), Jeyaranjan (1996), Pieterse (1996), Vohra (1996), Eapen (1996).
Uttar Pradesh	12	10.16	Mukerjee (1996), Pai, et al. (1997), Pai (1997), Lieten (1996), Patikh, et al. (2003), Pai (2001), Pai et al. (2005), Kumar (2003), Pai (2004), Kumar (2005), Pai (2003), Sinha et al. (2002).
Karnataka	5	4.28	Shetty, (2004), Murgi et al. (2003), Pinto (1997), Assadi (1997), Correa (1996).
Madhya Pradesh	5	4.28	Mathur, et al. (2005), Narayana (2005), Pai (2003), Pai (2004), Kulkarni (1996).
Andhra Pradesh	4	3.39	Behera, et al. (2002), Vaddiraju, et al. (2004), Sekhar, et al. (2003), Shetty (2004).
Maharashtra	4	3.39	Shetty, (2004), Vora (1996), Dev (1996), Rajvanshi (1995).

Cont'd...

...Cont'd

Punjab	4	3.39	Gill, et al. (2000), Jodhka (2002), Jodhka, et al. (2003), Shetty (2004).
Rajasthan	4	3.39	Patikh, et al. (2003), Pai (2003), Bokil (2000), Monkodi (1996).
Bihar	3	2.54	Chakravarti (2001), Thakaur, et al. (2000), Rao, et al. (1997).
Haryana	3	2.54	Pal (2004), Ghosh (1996), Rajeshwari (1996).
Gujarat	2	1.69	Thakkar (1997), Kothari (1997).
Himachal Pradesh	2	1.69	Chand (1996), Patikh, et al. (2003)
Kerala	2	1.69	Narayana (2005), Bhaskar (1997).
Tamil Nadu	2	1.69	Narayana (2005), Saleth (1997).
West Bengal	2	1.69	Maharatna (1997), Rafique (2003).
Chhattisgarh	1	0.84	Janaiah, et al. (2000).
Delhi	1	0.84	Pai (2003).
Orissa	1	0.84	Mahapatra (1996).
Total	118	100.00	

Source: Computed on the basis of several issues of the *EPW.*

References

Aiyar, Y. and Samji, S. 2006, "Improving the Effectiveness of National Rural Employment Guarantee Act", *EPW*, 41(4): 320–26.

Antia, N.H. 1997, "Public Wealth for Private Gain: Proposal for New Institute", *EPW*, 32(32): 2019–20.

Assadi, M. 1997, "Karnataka: Changing Nature of Caste Conflict: Udbhur Incident", *EPW*, 32(32): 2017–18.

——. 2000, "Seed Tribunal: Interrogating Farmer's Suicides – Karnataka", *EPW*, 35(43–44): 3808–10.

Balakrishanan, P. 2003, "Globalisation, Growth and Justice", *EPW*, 38(30): 3166–72.

Bandyopadhyay, R. 1996, "Global Review of Land Reform: A Critical Perspective", *EPW*, 31(11): 679–90.

Behora, B. and Reddy, V.R. 2002, "Environment and Accountability Impact of Industrial Pollution on Rural Communities", *EPW*, 37(3): 257–65.

Bhaskar, M. 1997, "Women Panchayat Members in Kerala: A Profile", *EPW*, 32(17): WS13–WS21.

Bhattacharjee, A. 1996, "Economic Reforms and the External Sector", *EPW*, 31(16 and 17): 987–88.

Bokil, M. 2000, "Drought in Rajasthan: In Search of a Perspective", *EPW*, 35(48): 4171–75.

Buch, N. 2005, "Law of Two Child Norm in Panchayats: Implications, Consequences and Experiences", *EPW*, 40(24): 2421–29.

Chakravarti, A. 2001, "Caste and Agrarian Class: A View from Bihar", *EPW*, 36(17): 1449–62.

Chand, R. 1996, "Ecological and Economic Impact of Horticulture Development in the Himalayas: Evidence from Himachal Pradesh", *EPW*, 31(26): A193–A104.

Chavan, P. and Ramakumar, R. 2002, "Micro-Credit and Rural Poverty: An Analysis of Empirical Evidence", *EPW*, 37(10): 955–65.

Chowdhry, P. 1997, "Enforcing Cultural Codes: Gender and Violence in Northern India", *EPW*, 32(19): 1019–28.

Correa, M. 1996, "No Role for Women: Karnataka's Joint Management Programmes", *EPW*, 31(23): 1389–93.

Deboshis, C. et al. 2006, "Atrocities on Dalits: What the District Level Data Say on Society-State Complicity", *EPW*, 41(24): 2478–81.

Desai, B.M. 1995, "Growth with Social Justice", *EPW*, 30(47): 3019–20.

Dev, S.M. and Mungekar, B.L. 1996, "Maharashtra's Agricultural Development: A Blueprint", *EPW*, 31(13): A38–A48.

Dev, S.M. 1996, "Employment Guarantee Scheme", *EPW*, 31(9): 560–62.

——. 2003, "Agriculture, Employment and Social Sector Neglected", *EPW*, 38(14): 1353–56.

——. 2004, "How to Make Rural India Shine", *EPW*, 39(44): 4415–22.

——. 2005, "Agricultural and Rural Employment in the Budget", *EPW*, 40(14): 1410–13.

Dogra, B. 2002, "Land Reforms, Productivity and Farm Size", *EPW*, 37(6): 532–34.

——. 2005, "Rural Employment Schemes: Rhetoric and Reality", *EPW*, 40(18): 1809–10.

Eapen, M. 1996, "Rural Non-farm Employment: Some Reflections on Petty Production", *EPW*, 31(26): 1673–81.

Ghosh, A. 1996, "Health Care and Globalisation: Case for a Selective Approach", *EPW*, 31(8): 443–44.

Gill, S.S. and Ghuman, R.S. 2000, "Rural Health Proactive Role for the State: A Case Study of Punjab", *EPW*, 35(51): 4474–77.

Gupta, D. 2005, "Whither the Indian Villages: Culture and Agriculture on Rural India", *EPW*, 40: 751–58.

Hirashima, R. 2000, "Issues in Agricultural Reforms: Public Investment and Land Market Development", *EPW*, 35(43): 3879–84.

Isvilanoda, S. et al., 2000, "Recent Changes in Thailand's Rural Economy: Evidence from Six Villages", *EPW*, 35(52 and 53): 4644–49.

Jodhka, S.S. 2002, "Caste and Untouchability in Rural Punjab", *EPW*, 37(19): 1813–23.

Jejeebhoy, S.J. 1997, "Addressing Women's Reproductive Health Needs: Priorities for the Family Welfare Programme", *EPW*, 32(9 and 10): 475–84.

Jeyaranjan, J. 1996, "'Revisit' Approach to Rural Dynamics: Towards a Critique", *EPW*, 31(19): 1165–67.

Jodhka, J.S. and Louis, P. 2003, "Caste Tension in Punjab: Talhan and Beyond", *EPW*, 38(28): 2923–26.

Jonaiah, J. et al., 2000, "Poverty and Income Distribution in Rainfed and Irrigated Ecosystem: Village Studies in Chhattisgarh", *EPW*, 35(52 and 53): 4664–69.

Joshi, P.K. et al., 2001, "Impact of Agricultural Research: Some Evidences", *EPW*, 36(11): 911–13.

Kannabiran, V. and Kannabiran, K. 1997, "From Social Action to Political Action: Women and the 81st Amendment", *EPW*, 32(5): 196–97.

Kothari, U. 1997, "Women's Paid Domestic Work and Rural Transformation: A Study in South Gujarat", *EPW*, 32(17): WS5–WS12.

Krishnaji, N. 1995, "Working Mothers and Child Survival in Rural India: Insights from Spatial Patterns", *EPW*, 30(44): 2803–08.

Kulkarni, M.M. 1996, "Madhya Pradesh: Evolving a Women's Policy", *EPW*, 31(12): 713–16.

Kumar, A. et al., 2004, "Employment Guarantee for Rural India", *EPW*, 39(51): 5359–61.

Kumar, V. 2003, "Uttar Pradesh: Politics of Change", *EPW*, 38(37): 3869–71.

——. 2004, "Understanding Dalit Diaspora", *EPW*, 39(1): 115–16.

——. 2005, "Understanding the Politics of Reservation: A Perspective from Below", *EPW*, 40(9): 803–06.

Lieten, G.K. 1996, "Inclusive View of Religion and Rural Discourse in Uttar Pradesh", *EPW*, 31(23): 1411–16.

Maharatna, A. 1997, "Children's Work Activities, Surplus Labour and Fertility: Case Study of Six Villages in Birbhum", *EPW*, 32(7): 363–69.

Mankodi, K. 1996, "Political and Economic Roots of Disease: Malaria in Rajasthan", *EPW*, 31(4): PE-42–PE-48.

Mathew, E.T. 1995, "Unemployment and Self-Employment: Job Preferences and Employment Perspectives", *EPW*, 30(44): 2815–26.

Mathew, G. 2003, "Panchayat Raj Institutions and Human Rights in India", *EPW*, 38(2): 155–62.

Mathew, P.M. 1997, "Women in Panchayats: The More Relevant Question", *EPW*, 32(23): 1362–63.

Mathur, J.K. and Mathur, D. 2005, "Dark Homes and Smokey Hearths: Rural Electrification and Women", *EPW*, 40(7): 638–43.

Mohanty, B. 1995, "Panchayati Raj, 73rd Constitutional Amendment and Women", *EPW*, 30(52): 3346–49.

Mohapatra, B.N. 1996, "Orissa: Tribal-Dalit Conflict, Phulbani", *EPW*, 31(2 and 3): 160–64.

Morriott, A. 2003, "Dalit or Harijan? Self-Naming by Scheduled Caste Interviewees", *EPW*, 38(36): 3751–52.

Mukherjee, N. 1996, "Resolving People: Sanctuary Conflict in Protected Areas, Kushiara Village, Mirzapur", *EPW*, 31(4): 197–99.

Mulji, J.S. 2003, "Agriculture and Unemployment", *EPW*, 38(14): 1463–66.

Murgi, R. and Howes, S. 2003, "Karnataka Incidence of Agricultural Power Subsidies: An Estimate", *EPW*, 38(16): 1533–35.

Nakkeeran, M. 2003, "Women's Work, Status and Fertility: Land, Caste and Gender in a South Indian Village", *EPW*, 38(37): 3931–39.

Nambissan, G.B. 1996, "Equity in Education? Schooling of Dalit Children in India", *EPW*, 31(16 and 17): 1011–24.

Nanjandan, S. 1996, "Economic Reforms and Small-Scale Industry", *EPW*, 31(4): 191–92.

Narain, H. 1996, "Government Apathy to Science and Technology for Rural Development: A Case study", *EPW*, 31(4): 202–03.

Narayana, D. 2005, "Local Governance without Capacity Building: Ten Years of Panchayati Raj", *EPW*, 40(26): 2822–32.

Narayanamoorthy, A. and Deshpande, R.S. 2003, "Irrigation Development and Agricultural Wages: An Analysis Across States", *EPW*, 38(35): 3716–22.

Navlakha, G. 1996, "Women's Rights: Walking the Tight Rope", *EPW*, 31(8): 454–55.

Nayyar, G. 2005, "Growth and Poverty in Rural India: An Analysis of Inter-State Differences", *EPW*, 40(16): 1631–39.

Nellithanam, J. 1997, "Green Revolution and Subsistence Agricultural: You Reap as You Sow", *EPW*, 32(18): 930–32.

Pai, S. 2001, "Social Capital, Panchayats and Grass Root Democracy: Politics of Dalit Assertion in UP", *EPW*, 36(8): 645–54.

Pai, S. et al., 2005, "Uttar Pradesh in 1990's: Critical Perspective on Society, Politics and Economy", *EPW*, 40(21): 2144–47.

Pai, S. and Singh, J. 1997, "Politicisation of Dalits and Most Backward Castes: Study of Social Conflict and Political Preferences in Four Villages of Meerut", *EPW*, 32(23): 1356–61.

Pai, S. 1997, "Dalit Assertion in UP: Implications for Politics", *EPW*, 32(37): 2313–15.

——. 2003, "BSP's Prospects in the Assembly Elections", *EPW*, 38(30): 3135–88.

——. 2004, "Dalit Question and Political Response: Comparative Study of UP and MP", *EPW*, 39(11): 1141–50.

Pal, M. 1996, "Million Wells Schemes: Loss of Gains", *EPW*, 31(8): 447–49.

——. 2004, "Caste and Patriarchy in Panchayats, Haryana", *EPW*, 39(2): 3581–83.

——. 2004, "Panchayat Raj and Rural Governance: Experiences of a Decade", *EPW*, 39(2): 137–43.

Paliwal, D. and Paliwal, R.C. 2008, "Drudgery among Women in Rural Hill Areas in Uttarakhand", *Kurukshetra*, 56(3): 22–27.

Patikh, J. et al., 2003, "Cooking with Bio-Fuels: Risk Factors Affecting Health Impact on Rural Women", *EPW*, 38(26): 2681–92.

Patnaik, P. 2005, "On the Need for Providing Employment Guarantee", *EPW*, 40(3): 203–07.

Pinto, A. 1997, "Karnataka: Emerging Social Tensions among Dalits", *EPW*, 32(30): 1876–77.

Prashad, V. 1996, "The Untouchable Question", *EPW*, 31(9): 551–59.

Pulamte, L. and Arobal, D. 2003, "Technology Transfer for Rural Development: Managing R&D at CSIR", *EPW*, 38(31): 3315–18.

Radhakrishna, R. 2005, "Agricultural and Rural Employment and Poverty: A Policy Perspective", *EPW*, 37(3): 243–50.

Rafique, A. 2003, "Floods, Poverty and Seasonal Migration", *EPW*, 38(10): 943–45.

Rajan, N. 2003, "Left Liberalism and Caste Politics", *EPW*, 38(24): 2346–49.

Rajeshwari, 1996, "Gender Bias in Utilization of Health Care Facilities in Rural Haryana", *EPW*, 31(8): 489–94.

Rajvanshi, A.K. 1995, "Energy Self-Sufficient Talukas: A Solution to National Energy Crisis", *EPW*, 30(51): 3115–19.

Rao, M. 2003, "Two-Child Norm and Panchayat", *EPW*, 38(33): 3452–54.

Rao, N. and Rana, K. 1997, "Land Rights and Women: Case of Santhals", *EPW*, 32(23): 1307–15.

Rathore, M. and Singh, S. 2008, "Women Enterprise: A Step Towards Success", *Kurukshetra*, 56(3): 8–11.

Reddy, V.R. 2003, "Irrigation: Development and Reforms", *EPW*, 38(10): 1179–89.

Roy, S. 1997, "Globalisation, Structural Change and Poverty: Some Conceptual and Policy Issues", *EPW*, 32(33 and 34): 2117–35.

Roy, T.K. et al., 2004, "Social Inequality in Health and Nutrition in Selected States", *EPW*, 39(7): 677–83.

Saleth, R.M. 1997, "Occupational Diversification among Rural Groups: A Case Study of Rural Transformation in Tamil Nadu", *EPW*, 32(30): 1908–17.

Satyanarayana, A. 1995, "Dalit Protest Literature in Telugu: A Historical Perspective", *EPW*, 30(3): 171–75.

Sekhar, P.S. and Subrahmanyan, S. 2003, "Agricultural Growth: Pattern and Prospects", *EPW*, 38(12 and 13): 1202–11.

Sharma, P. 2001 "Agricultural Reforms: Some Unaddressed Issues", *EPW*, 36(29): 2795–96.

Shetty, P.K. 2004, "Socio-Ecological Implications of Pesticides Use in India", *EPW*, 39(49): 5261–67.

Singh, M.P. 1997, "Gender, Law and Sexual Assault", *EPW*, 32(11): 543–50.

Soman, K. 1997, "Picture of Women's Health: Three Stories", *EPW*, 32(8): 396–98.

Srinivasan, K. and Mohanty, S.K. 2004, "Deprivation of Basic Amenities by Caste and Religion: Empirical Study Using MFHS Data", *EPW*, 39(7): 728–35.

Sundaram, K. and Tendulkar, D.S. 2003, "Poverty in India in the 1990s: An Analysis of Changes in 15 Major States", *EPW*, 38(14): 1385–93.

Surganarayana, M.H. 1996, "Economic Reforms, Nature and Poverty", *EPW*, 31(10): 617–24.

Thakur, J. et al., 2000, "Rural Income Distribution and Poverty in Bihar: Insights from Village Studies", *EPW*, 35(52 and 53): 4657–63.

Thankkar, U. 1997, "Puppets on the Periphery: Women and Social Reform in 19th Century Gujarati Society", *EPW*, 32(1 and 2): 46–52.

Tharu, S. 1996, "The Impossible Subject: Caste and the Gendered Body", *EPW*, 31(22): 1311–21.

Thorat, S. 2002, "Oppression and Denial: Dalit Discrimination in the 1990's", *EPW*, 37(6): 572–78.

Tiwari, R.C. 2008, *Geography of India*, Allahabad: Prayag Pustak Bhawan.

Vaddiraju, A.K. and Mehrotra, S. 2004, "Making Panchayats Accountable: Andhra Pradesh", *EPW*, 39 (37): 4139–41.

Venkateswarlu, D. 2005, "Globalisation of When and for What Impact of Globalisation on Indian Rural Society", paper presented in *National Seminar in Changing Perspectives of Rural Development: Emerging Challenges on the Content of Globalisation*, Department of Sociology, Osmania University (Hyderabad), February17–18.

Vohra, B.B. 1996, "Better Resource Management for Poverty Alleviation", *EPW*, 31(23): 1397–404.

Vora, R. 1996, "Shift of Power from Rural to Urban Sector", *EPW*, 31(2 and 3): 171–74.

Part II

Economic Organisation and Development Administration

7

Changing Irrigation Pattern in an Indian Village

Case Studies of Two Cultivators

R. Gopinath

Indian agriculture has undergone notable changes since independence particularly with reference to sources of irrigation. The Indian State, after independence, has undertaken numerous steps to develop major and medium irrigation projects throughout the country, but the minor irrigation system traditionally managed by local people has been neglected (Narayanamoorthy, 2002; Vaidyanathan and Sivasubramaniyan, 2004). This trend has had a profound effect on the livelihoods of small and marginal cultivators in dry villages that are dependent on rain-fed agriculture, and imposed pressure on them to eke out a living outside agriculture (Balasubramanian, 2002; Sivasubramaniyan, 2000). The neglect of minor irrigation, combined with a decline in the availability of surface water, has made cultivators turn to intensive use of groundwater resources. Over exploitation of groundwater sources has resulted in a declining water table across the country. Landowners with small and medium size land have been left behind in the race for access to groundwater. Their relative inability to invest in the deepening of wells and related measures has put them at a disadvantage. While with large size of land, landowners, by and large, have been able to cope with the declining levels of the water table by appropriate investments in deepening wells. Landowners with small and marginal size of land are facing severe shortage of water over longer periods of the year. Hence, there has arisen an inevitable widening of the income gap among the farming community (Balasubramanian, 2003; Bhalla, 2007; Bhattarai et al., 2002; Dubash, 2007; Mukherji, 2007; Otsuka, 2002; Kumar, 2003; Shah, 2007).

Given this context, attempts are made in this paper to trace the changes taking place in the irrigation pattern and the coping mechanism adopted by small and medium peasants in a dry village, Naganur, of Tamil Nadu State. Naganur is in the district of Karur. This village has been studied quite intensively by researchers since 1979–80. The previous study (Athreya et al., 1990) found that agriculture in the village was mostly rainfed. The villages on the average received 800 to 900 mm rainfall in a year, mainly from north-east monsoon (October to late December) and light showers during the south-west monsoon (June–end of September). The traditional crops such as small millets, groundnut, sorghum, maize and ragi required lesser quantum of water for their cultivation and were widely cultivated, along with a limited cultivation of dry land paddy. Besides rain, tanks and dug wells were also sources of irrigation in these dry villages. The study observed deterioration in the utilisation of tank water resources in the area. As a consequence, the cultivators were found to go in for intensive well irrigation. However, no water crisis was reported, despite the sinking water table.

Men or bullock operated *mohote* (large leather pouch buckets, known as kavalai) were traditionally in use for lifting water from the wells. This practice ensured livelihood opportunities for the 'Chakkiliars' who were engaged in the fabrication of the *mohote*. As men or bullock operate the *mohote*, so the intensive use of the well water was limited as compared to the machines. Therefore, the water lifting from wells was limited and the deepening of the wells took place once in five years by hardly one or two feet.

Subsequent to the 1979–80 study, Naganur was resurveyed in 2004–05 by the same team who had done the research during 1979–80. This paper is essentially based on the recent survey of the village. The authors are part of the research team in the 2004–05 study of the village. The paper has two sections: section one deals with the irrigation pattern of the village while the second section deals with the case studies of the two cultivators in the village.

This paper attempts to understand the consequences of changes in the irrigation pattern on the livelihoods of medium sized and landowner belonging to OBC and a marginal size of landowner belonging to SC. The qualitative and quantitative information elicited from the two cultivators during frequent discussions with them, provided the basis of the analysis of the transformation that the village has undergone. Besides the details from the cultivators, information relating to changes in the cropping pattern, features of tanks, the use of tank water for irrigation and the changing pattern of water lifting were also gathered from the Village Administrative Officer (VAO) and other staff of the government departments.

I

The Transition of Irrigation Regime

In 2003–04, as per the village records, 316.87 ha of dry area were available for cultivation in Naganur. Besides this area, nine tanks in the village account for irrigation requirements of the traditional ayacut lands of 79.64 ha. The size of the tanks in the ayacut area ranges between 2.57 ha in Venkatachalam tank to 14.26 ha in Navakulam. Naganur's agriculture was essentially dependant on rains, though tanks contributed as a complementary source of irrigation. Over the years, though, there has been no perceptible decline in the overall total rainfall, i.e., 750–900 mm per year but the number of rainy days has declined. In addition to this, there has been a neglect of tanks over the years.

It is observed that, though there has not been much damage with reference to the flow of water into the tanks, but there has been substantial damage in the process of de-silting. Contrary to the proper de-silting practice, wherein the soil in the middle of the tank is lifted to strengthen the bunds, the de-silting is done by excavating the earth in the inner side of the bunds to raise them. As a result of this improper method of de-silting, the water holding capacity of the tank decreases, making it prone to overflowing even before attaining the normal full tank level (FTL). The desiltation of Navakulam tank was taken up during 2002–03 and people say that the contractors used bulldozers to strengthen the bund during that period.

Encroachment of tanks is also a reality in the village of Naganur. Navakulam is the largest tank used to provide irrigation for 14.26 ha of lands in Naganur. Today, around 6 acres of the tank has been encroached, according to VAO. This encroachment has been done by cultivators belonging to Naganur and Kambathamparai hamlets. They have converted the encroached area into cultivable lands. Further, Venkatachalam tank in Krishnampatti hamlet that had an ayacut of 2.57 ha has been converted into a pond by the quarry operators, thereby making even this tank water not available for irrigation. This private stone quarry has been operating from 1985 onwards. This quarry gives contracts of stone cutting to Self-Help Groups (SHGs) in nearby villagers. Hamlets of Nagannur village also take contracts from the quarry. It is also observed that the quarry activities have not only blocked the water inflow to the Venkatachalam tank but also lead to inundation of water in the hamlet during rainy days, affecting the normal life of people. The ayacutdars, the traditional beneficiaries entitled to the tank water, have increasingly turned to tapping groundwater, because of the non-availability of tank water. The ayacutdars and those affected by the quarry are not prepared to raise their voices against this encroachment, as they depend on the income that they get from employment in the quarry. Check dams were constructed during 1990–95 across the in-led channel to Navakulam from Veeramalai, resulting in a decline in the water flow into the tanks, leading to their disuse. As a result of factors like encroachment of tanks, diversion of tank water for non-agricultural purposes and decline in water flow into the tanks, groundwater has emerged as the chief source of irrigation in the village today.

Naganur received electrification for the purpose of agriculture in the year 1982–83. The presence of borewells was traced from 1990–91 onwards and the air compressors were first installed in the village during 2000–01. But, the electric engines used for water-lifting came into existence from 1982–83 in Naganur. The number of borewells in the village as per the records available with the Village Administrative Officer (VAO), in June 2004 were, 211 electric pumpsets (53 of these borewells used air compressors) and 68 oil motors. The water lifted from the borewells are transported to wells located even 400 feet away from the location by using PVC pipes. Such stored water is used for cultivation at appropriate time. While the traditional *mohote (kavalai)* drained the water in a gradual manner, the motors, especially those in the borewells, cause a quick decline in the water table and it requires substantial time to recoup the water level. Cultivators are forced to deepen the wells by 3–5 feet in every three years, requiring frequent investment of capital. The supply of electricity at subsidised rates by the state, which started in the early 1980s and the total free electricity for irrigation has saved the cost of water lifting for the cultivators. The facility of free electricity for irrigation has been given to the village since 1981. It has also led to indiscriminate use of power for lifting water, causing unreasonable and unwarranted exploitation of groundwater.

Thus, there has been a permanent decline in the water table which may not be revived to the desirable level in the near future.

The changes in the irrigation regime, the decline in the importance of tank irrigation and a substantial dependence on well irrigation, has brought about important changes in the cropping pattern. From the table it is clear that there is a perceptible decline in the cultivation of small millets area while market-oriented crops such as sunflower, chilies and vegetables, etc., increased in cultivation.

Table 1

Cropping Pattern: Then and Now

	Area-wise Cropping Pattern	*1979–80*	*2004–05*
1.	Tank irrigated area	One paddy crop (head-reach areas had scope of cultivating second paddy), sorghum and bajra	Single paddy crop (water scarcity during the last 10 days of the crop period), groundnut.
2.	Tank-cum-well irrigated area	Single paddy, sorghum and bajra, some persons cultivate water-intensive crops of sugarcane and banana	Paddy for two seasons, gingelly, irrigated groundnut, bengal gram, chilies, sunflowers, flowers, vegetables, such as bindi, brinjal; six cultivators having more than 3 three acres of land are cultivating sugarcane in Naganur hamlet.
3.	Well-irrigated area	Paddy for one season, sorghum and bajra	Single paddy crops, sorghum, gingelly, irrigated groundnut, tapioca and sunflower
4.	Rainfed area	Rainfed paddy, intercropping of sorghum, other crops such as, ragi, small millets, groundnut, bajra (most of the lands are kept fallow)	

The overall change in cropping pattern has a perceptible impact on the food habits of the villagers, with far-reaching consequences. The enhanced paddy cultivation and the availability of rice through the Public Distribution System (PDS), the villagers have increasingly switched over to rice consumption from small millets' consumption.

II

Impact on Two Cultivators

The above mentioned changes in the irrigation pattern over the years have a diversified effect on the cultivation practices in Naganur which affected different sections of cultivators differentially. The following case studies of a medium and another marginal cultivator is an attempt to describe the consequences of changes in irrigated cropping pattern on different classes of cultivators in the village.

- VP is an inhabitant of Naganur village. He is 58 years old and belongs to Soliya Vellala (OB) caste of Hindu religion. VP's household consists of five members: his wife, younger unmarried son, elder married son and his son's wife. His younger son has studied upto 10th standard and works as a lorry driver in Tiruchirappalli, the nearest city of the village. His eldest son is assisting his father in the cultivation of crops. VP owns eight acres of well-irrigated land. Except his second son, who works as a lorry driver, all the other members of his family are involved exclusively in agricultural activities. The second son also contributes labour off and on in their farm activities.
- In 1980, the availability of water in VP's well was at 60 feet. The availability of tank water for cultivation is hardly for 25–30 days in a normal year. He could cultivate a single paddy crop with tank water and also needed groundwater supplementation in the last 10–15 days of cultivation period. He also expressed usefulness of tank as a recharging source for the well for another one month. However, the recharge periods have declined over the years due to the declining water storage at the tank. This trend forced VP to dig borewell in 1993–94 for sustaining cultivation in his land. Presently he has deepened it to 310 feet to get assured supply of groundwater. He also has a PVC pipe network of 100 metres to effectively supply water to the entire area of his land.
- The 310-feet borewell provides him assured water supply for 2–3 hours during the March–May period. It enables him to cultivate two crops of paddy, irrigated groundnut, vegetables such as *bindy* (lady fingers) and brinjal in his lands. He also cultivates sunflower and tapioca during the drought years. It is observed that hardly two acres of his land remain fallow during 3–4 months of a year. The fallow land was located at a higher level surface than the rest of his land.

- The medium size landowner, VP, has invested in around 100 metres of 3 inch PVC pipe network to assure the maximum coverage of water supply in his land. He stated that besides the savings from agricultural activities, the income earned by his son as a lorry driver was also very useful in undertaking the above mentioned capital expenditure in his land.
- The case two is 36 years of age, belongs to Pallar (SC) community, and is educated only upto 5th standard. He is living in a lineal family, with his parents, wife and a younger son, who is studying in the local primary school at Naganur. The cultivator is residing in Kambathamparai hamlet of Naganur village and owns half an acre of well-irrigated land and four family members out of five are working as agricultural wage labourers, besides being engaged in their own agriculture. The lands of both case one and case two come under the ayacut area of Navakulam. Both are able to get the supply of tank water for around a month in a year. The wells of both have free electricity supply throughout the year. The well has 3 HP electric motor and it was installed during 1982–83 by his grandfather.
- The well used by case two for cultivation of his land is jointly owned by four marginal cultivators including the case two. Total area under the well cultivation is 4.5 acres. Today, the tank water availability is sufficient only for a single paddy crop. Even for that, according to case two the groundwater supplementation was required at the end of the cultivation period. Consequently, the case two cultivator also depends on groundwater for the cultivation of the single paddy crop. His shared well had water at 45 feet in 2004–05. They have an electric motor and benefit from free electricity supply. The cultivator under study and the other three users deepened the well during 1993–94 to 6 feet more, from the earlier level of 39 feet before 1993–94 to the present level of 45 feet. Since all the partners are wage labourers they are unable to generate resources to deepen the well further. They stated that if at all one is able to save some amount at a particular time; the others are not in a position to contribute the remaining required amount. Differences other than agriculture-related also cause difficulty in evolving a concerted effort to deepen the well. They can lift water for 2–3 hours in a day during July–November and hardly 30 minutes during lean season. It was observed that none of them get their share of water every day; they get water by rotation, thus only one gets water on a

particular day. This arrangement of water sharing creates a problem during the last stages of paddy cultivation wherein timely non-availability of water affects the productivity of crops.

- On the other hand, case two cultivator under study can get water for hardly 30 minutes during March–May. He manages to cultivate a single paddy crop followed by marigold flower in 0.20 acre. The remaining land of 0.30 acre or sixty per cent of his land area remains fallow for 6–7 months of a year.
- In contrast, case two with limited income from his own agriculture has been compelled to seek avenues of non-agricultural income for the sustenance of his family besides agricultural jobs. He thus works in other places like Erode which is more than 100 km away and Lalgudi which is more than 70 km away from the village. One of the two women in the family, either his mother or wife, goes away from the village and works in a plantation at a distance of 100 km from the village in July–September every year. They make a second visit during the harvesting period of February–March. This is entirely due to the lack of work opportunities within the village combined with an inability to cultivate their land all through the year. The men often commute from the village to nearby towns to work as casual labour.

Conclusion

The changing irrigation pattern over the last 25 years from 1979–80 to 2004–05, in a dry village with tank and groundwater sources, corroborates the widespread dimensions of irrigation transformation in many parts of the country. The case studies of two cultivators from different classes help to understand the coping mechanism made by the farming communities for sustaining the agriculture. The marginal cultivator, who lacks resources for deepening the well in order to draw the groundwater, is engaged in non-farm activities for the sustenance of his family. The medium cultivator, who has accumulated resources from both farm and non-farm activities, is able to cope by deepening his well, though he will also be in trouble if, the current water crisis continues. The findings raise twin questions of future of agriculture and the future of livelihood of the agrarian communities in India. The study also brings out the importance of using the 'correct' method for desilting tanks and restoring the significance of tank irrigation to a rainfed village economy.

References

Athreya, V., G. Djurfeldt and S. Lindberg, 1990, *Barriers Broken: Production Relations and Agrarian Change in Tamil Nadu*, New Delhi: Sage Publications.

Balasubramanian, R. 2003, "Problems of Water Resources in India: An Institutional Perspective", paper presented at All-India Conference on Agriculture and Rural Society in Contemporary India at Barddhaman during December 17–20.

Bhalla, P. 2007, "Impact of Declining Groundwater Levels on Acreage Allocation in Haryana", *Economic and Political Weekly*, June 30, pp. 2701–07.

Bhattarai, M., R. Sakthivadivel and I. Hussain, 2002, "Irrigation Impacts on Income Inequality and Poverty Alleviation: Policy Issues and Options for Improved Management of Irrigation Systems", Working Paper 39, International Water Management Institute, Colombo: Sri Lanka.

Dubash, N.K. 2007, "The Electricity-Groundwater Conundrum: Case for a Political Solution to a Political Problem", *Economic and Political Weekly*, December 29, pp. 45–55.

Kumar, M.D. 2003, "Food Security and Sustainable Agriculture in India: The Water Management Challenge", Working Paper 60, International Water Management Institute, Colombo: Sri Lanka.

Mukherji, A. 2007, "Implications of Alternative Institutional Arrangements in Groundwater Sharing: Evidence from West Bengal", *Economic and Political Weekly*, June 30, pp. 2543–51.

Narayanamoorthy, A. 2002, "Indian Irrigation: Five Decades of Development", *Water Resources Journal*, June–July, pp. 1–29.

Otsuka, K. 2002, "Poverty Reduction Issues: Village Economy Perspective", *Asian Development Review*, 19 (1), pp. 98–116.

Shah, T. 2007, "Crop per Drop of Diesel? Energy Squeeze on India's Smallholder Irrigation", *Economic and Political Weekly*, September 29, pp. 4002–09.

Vaidyanathan, A. and K. Sivasubramaniyan, 2004, "Efficiency of Water Use in Agriculture", *Economic and Political Weekly*, July 3, pp. 2989–96.

8

Development and Change in Shakrori

A Village Restudy from Himachal Pradesh

Pankaj Gupta

The Census Department of India conducted exhaustive studies in selected villages, from different parts of the country in 1961, to comprehend the landscape, bio-diversity, culture, sources of water, demographic aspects of the villages, patterns of land use and cropping pattern, indigineous institutions and knowledge. Such a study provides baseline data of the villages. An intensive restudy of a few such villages from different parts of the country will provide a better understanding of the changes and continuities in terms of their demographic aspects, bio-diversity, flora and fauna, structure of farming, cropping patterns, water sources and the impact of modernisation on the lives of the people in the villages. The village Shakrori studied in 1961 is selected for the present study from Sunni tehsil of Shimla district of Himachal Pradesh in order to comprehend the changes and continuities that took place over the last more than 40 years. The village Shakrori is selected on the basis of its rich landscape, biodiversity, flourishing agriculture and parts of the village which are delineated for the Kol dam and the construction of a cement factory. As a result of Kol dam, some areas of the village are likely to be submerged. The cement factory intensifies the pollution of water and air. In this paper endeavours are made to comprehend the impact of modernisation on the life of people and the price one has to pay for development.

Methodology

Multiple techniques were adopted for the collection of data. After selecting the village, the researcher initially spent the first few days in the village to make himself familiar with general conditions and behaviour of the villagers through observations. Special visits were made to social and religious festivals and documentation of the same was done. Interview technique was used to realise the changes that the respondents experienced in matters of lifestyles, land use pattern, cropping pattern and celebration of social and religious festivals from 1961 to 2005. Household information in terms of demographic composition, caste structure in the village, food consumption patterns and ethnic food was also documented. Biodiversity mapping was undertaken in the village to include the floral and faunal wealth in the village with particular reference to ethno-botanical information on plants. Focused group discussions were conducted to collect information on natural resource management, practices and implements used in agriculture, changes in the structure of farming and the impact of technology on agriculture practices, fairs and festivals and associated rites, folk culture, housing pattern, people's perceptions on development and change.

Village Profile

The state of Himachal Pradesh is a fascinating region of the Indian Himalayas and is located between 30°22' and 30°12' North and between 75°47' and 79°4' East. The mountainous state has altitudes ranging from 350 to 7,000 metres (1,050 ft. to 21,000 ft.) above the sea level. Shimla district lies between the longitude 77°.00" and 78°.19" East and latitude 30°.45" and 31°.44" North. The elevation of the district ranges from 300 metres to 6,000 metres. Shakrori with its picturesque landscape is located in *tehsil* Sunni of district Shimla. Shakrori falls within Shakrori Panchayat (a grassroots level organisation engaged in administrative decisions. A number of villages come under the panchayat) and Basantpur block. The nearest town, Sunni is about 3 kms from the village whereas Shimla, the district headquarter, is about 40 kms from the village. Shakrori derives its name from *Shakri* which means stones or small pebbles. Even today, the land in Shakrori is covered all over with pebbles. The village is situated at height of 1,700 ft. above the sea level on the banks of river Sutlej. The village is connected to the rest of the state and the country through Shimla. Indeed nature has tried to keep Shakrori in isolation by fencing it with hills in back and Sutlej river in front. The village Shakrori with its 95 households has a very compact settlement which is mainly confined to a single patch that presents a typical view of densely populated village. In addition to this compact settlement, there are a few independent settlements too. The central part of the village, where most of people live, is very old. The main sections of the village include *parli ber* (name of a section of village), and *gallu* (name of a section of village) Shakrori and main village.

Physical features

The river Satluj originates in the Himalayas and flows from district Kinnaur, Rampur and in front of the village. The river acts as the source of water for power generation in *Chaba* power station. Kol dam is under construction on the river. Banks of the river have hard rocks, big round stones but the river bed is narrow and deep. Where the bank has soft soil, there the river bed is wide and shallow and one can notice a few rocks emerging out of the water. Only small bushes and tress grow in the village. On the bank of this river at a distance of about 7 kms from the village, there is a pilgrimage centre, *Tattapani,* a hot water sulphur spring. People visit the centre to take a holy dip on festivals such as *Makar Sakaranti* (about transition of Sun into Capricorn on its celestial path which signifies the beginning of the harvest season for the cultivators of Indian subcontinent), *Baisakhi* (marks the beginning of a new solar year, and new harvest season), etc. Many fairs and festivals are organised on the bank of this river and people visit this place frequently whether it is for the holy dip or to attend fairs. Thus, the river has a cultural connotation for people of the village. But, with the progression of Kol dam, the hot water sulphur springs, an ancient temple of Lord Narsingh (a local deity) is likely to get submerged in the water.

Climate

Shimla, the hill station lies close to the village and it has a much cooler climate than the village. The village lies deep in the valley. Both day and night temperatures in summers are hot with a low variation between day and nights. But, the presence of greenery and Satluj river has a soothing effect on the eyes and is conducive to the health of the people. April to July is the hottest season of the year. Humidity is comparatively low. The highest temperature recorded in the month of July 2006 was 36°C. Monsoon sets in late June or in July and the temperature decreases with the monsoon showers but the humidity increases and it lasts till September. By the end of November the winter season starts.

During the winters the temperature falls up to 5–6°C. The temperature tends to rise gradually from March.

Socio-economic structure of the village

The population of Shakrori is made up of four castes, namely, the Brahmin (mainly priests), the Rajput (a former ruling caste of Northern India), the Lohars (blacksmiths) and the Chamars (traditional leather-workers and tanners). These four castes are arranged hierarchically. The Brahmins occupy the highest place in the caste hierarchy as they perform the religious ceremonies of all castes other than Chamars. There are 21 Brahmin families in the village. The Rajputs stand next to the Brahmins in caste hierarchy followed by Lohars and Chamars. There are 54 Rajput families in the village and 19 families of Lohars and Chamars. Each caste has its traditional occupation. Most of the families (95%) of the village are mainly dependent on agriculture. Most of the Rajputs are either engaged in farming activities or employed in government services. Iron-smithy is the traditional occupation of Lohars. The Rajput, Brahmins and Lohars mix up freely and also inter-dine with each other. In spite of differences in their social status, people of different castes live in harmony in the village. Only the scheduled caste people have some social and religious restrictions. But there are no restrictions on the use of land or water resources. These castes claim that they are agriculturists first, and anything else only afterwards.

Changes in land use and cropping pattern in the village

Data from the revenue records of the village, maintained by *Patwarkhana* are analysed in order to quantify and explain changes in land use over the last 44 years, i.e., from 1961 to 2005 in the village under restudy. The total geographical area of the village was 161 hectares till 2001. New land settlement was undertaken in the year 2001 which increased the geographical area of the village up to 172 héctares. Most of the village land is under cultivation and only 20 hectares are used for non-agricultural purposes till 1961. The land under non-agricultural use increased upto 29 hectares by 2005 owing to the expansion of village settlements, construction of roads and lanes. The area under permanent pastures and other grazing land has increased from 68 hectares to 87 hectares in the period of inquiry as some portion of cultivable land was converted to grazing land to meet the cattle demand for fodder. The cultivable wasteland (the land not cultivated for five years or more in succession) increased to 5 hectares in the year 1991 and then decreased to three hectares after 1991. Such decline in the cultivable wasteland was mainly due to new economic activities such as growing of vegetables from 1991. The net area sown has increased over the period 1961–1991 and later decreased marginally. This increase was mainly attributed to availability of irrigation facilities and induction of cash crops. The decrease in the net sown area is attributed to the decline in productivity and land turning barren and the decline in the availability of water for irrigation purpose. These factors contributed recently in the decline of total cropped and irrigated area. Maize, rice and wheat continue to be the major cereals grown in the village

Half of the earlier rice cultivated land is now under maize cultivation. The reasons are expressed as lack of sufficient water for irrigation and changing attitudes of people towards hard work and lesser returns in rice cultivation. Cultivation of traditional crops like *kodha* (*Paspalum serobiculatum*), barley (*Hordeum vulgare*), *koni* (*Setaria italica*), and *seul* (*Chenopodium album*) are also discarded for wheat and maize. Lesser availability of these traditional food items and their souring market prices greatly limited people's dietary pattern from rice and traditional crops to maize and wheat. Thus, not only the crop diversity declined but also the diversity in food consumption also declined.

Natural resources and their utilisation pattern

Water

There are a few springs that are the main source of drinking water in the village. The main spring, *Bain,* is near the *Patwarkhanna* (a place where panchayat land use and cropping patterns records are kept) that has cemented platform with a proper outlet. The main spring not only provides water for drinking purpose to the people residing in the central or main part of the village but also for washing clothes. The waste water is used for irrigation purposes. The spring also has a religious significance as it is worshipped by village women on different festive occasions. Another natural spring, *Paninihar* (natural spring) provides sweet and cool water used for drinking by the people residing near *parli ber.* An ancient statue of stone believed to be *Pannihar Devta* (a water body worshipped as deity) was found while digging the place. People of the village often worship the *devata* on different occasions. This spring has regular, continuous and natural supply of water throughout the year. A small spring near *Gallu* provides water for the people residing in *Gallu* locality. Besides these sources of water, there is a *kulh* (water drainage system used for irrigating fields) mainly used for bathing, washing clothes and irrigation.

Floral and faunal wealth

The village has very rich floral and faunal wealth in the form of small and big green plants, shrubs, bushes and creepers. Most of the villagers are dependent on agriculture and forest resources for their livelihood. The forest resources are used for medicine, timber and fuel. Leaves are used for fodder, and fruits and seeds are used for human consumption. The herbal practitioners with traditional knowledge and expertise collect the medicinally important parts of plants surrounding the area for the treatment of various diseases. Only a few elderly herbal practitioners in the contemporary period had knowledge about the medicinal value of plants and appropriate time for the collection of plants. However, the younger generation is either forgetting or ignorant of indigenous knowledge about the medicinal value of plants. Some of the important ones include *kachnaar* (*Bahunia variegata*), *kashmal* (*Berberies aristata*), *kakarsinghi* (*Pistacia intergerrima*), *bel* (*Aegle marmelos*), *basuti* (*Adhatoda vasica*), *arind* (*Ricinus communis*), *banna* (*Vitex negundo*), *ramban* (*Agave americana*), *kathi* (*Indigofera gerradiana*), *kadwo* (*Gentiana kurroo*), *geloyae* (*Tinospora cordifolia*), *kawarpatha* (*Aloe barbadensis*), etc. *Kakarsinghi* is used in the treatment of cough and cold while *bel*, *arind* and *kathi* are used in the treatment of digestive disorders. *Banna* is used in the treatment of joint pains and also in magico-religious practices. Extract of *ramban* is dropped in the ear to cure its ache. Gel of *kawarpatha* is applied for treating pimples. *Geloyae* is used to regulate the flow of urine and burning maturation in cattle and also in human beings. Some more plants are cultivated for their fruits and seeds that are used for human consumption. Other plants are used either for ornamental or hedge and fencing purposes, thatching, cattle sheltering sheds, and others are treated as holy plants. However, with the construction of dam on the river, some of the plants that are nearer to the river are likely to get submerged. Thus the villagers are planting trees that have a higher market value and grow fast and plants such as plum and walnuts planting have declined as they are economically less viable to the villagers. There are a number of plants like *barghad* (*Ficus bengalensis*), *gainda* (*Calendula officinalis*), *gulab* (*Rosa spp.*), *pepal* (*Ficus religiosa*), *amb* (*Mangifera indica*) in the village. People use these plants on various festive occasions and religious ceremonies. Thus, during earlier times, people had diverse cultures and land use systems. The present rate of use of the local resources will lead to the extinction of this unique biological and cultural heritage.

The fauna of the village can be put under two groups, viz., domesticated and wild. The domesticated animals of the village are cows, goats, buffalo, dogs, cats and bulls. However, some common birds including pigeon, parrots, sparrows, wild goose, and quail; mammals, such as monkey, languor, leopard, goral, wild cat, hare/rabbit, basking deer and *sambhar* (large dark brown deer), *goh (a* reptile) and snakes, frogs and lizards are seen around village. An old man narrated that there were many bats earlier in and around the village mainly on the other side of the river, hanging upside down from trees or rocks, but now their number has reduced and it is matter of chance that one can see them occasionally. Among some common animals *jungli murga (*jungle fowls), *kaw* (crow), *gidh* (a vulture), *koel* (nightingale), *titter* (name of a bird), *bater* (name of a bird) are seen around the village. But people say that now big wild animals such as leopard, jackal, sambhar and deer are seen less as a consequence of growth of population and expansion of residential area away from the main village. Still monkeys, snakes (while working fields or cutting of grass) and rats (in houses, stores and fields) create havoc in the village.

Indigenous knowledge, development and management of natural resources in the village

Traditional knowledge systems are seen as pivotal for sustainable socio-economic development and poverty alleviation in developing countries. Traditional knowledge provides the basis for local-level decision-making about many fundamental aspects of day-to-day life such as management of ecological relations with society and nature and adaptation to changes in the environment and society. In order to achieve the objective of development in villages, people's active involvement in project activities by respecting the traditional knowledge and experimental ethics in augmenting agricultural productivity is essential. Focused group discussions (FGDs) were organised to realise the various methods used in the conservation and management of natural resources in the village. Analysis of the data obtained through FGD reveals that elders pass on their traditional knowledge through practical demonstrations, folk songs and other examples to younger generations. Some of the traditional methods of management of natural resources practiced by the people in Shakrori pertaining to conservation of water, soil and natural vegetation are given in Box I.

Box I

Case Study of Indigenous Resource Management Practices

Management of water and water resources

Traditional sources of drinking water: Streams are the main sources of drinking water in the village. People pay regard to these water resources. They use the water for drinking and make efforts to keep streams clean and unpolluted. They maintain vegetation on the banks of these steams to have a clean flow without sediment and garbage. They do not allow their cattle to these places from where they collect drinking water. Thus they have their own traditional system for the management of drinking water.

Unique method of irrigation: Farmers used to carry water to their fields through small irrigation channels known as *kuhls.* These go from the source of water to the fields. In order to avoid seepage losses, farmers even use plastic pipes. By means of gravitational force they transport water from its source to the fields. Villagers clean these *khuls* regularly. Even some days, before the commencement of sowing of rabi and kharif crops, are marked for cleaning the khuls when all the villagers gather in order to clean them. There are traditional methods of weather forecasting which help the villagers to predict the rain or dry weather and accordingly they utilise their water resources for irrigation in the fields. Under rainfed conditions villagers plough their land several times before the onset of rain to conserve water and increase water retention capacity of land.

Changing cropping patterns: Keeping in mind the present scenario of water scarcity in the village, crops which require more water such as paddy are replaced by maize as the latter requires comparatively less water.

Special duties assigned to Khalhars: Khalhars, persons engaged to look after judicial distribution of irrigation water to each and every family are appointed and are paid grains for their services.

Management of soil/land resources

Practicing traditional methods of agriculture: These have not only significant environmental advantages but are also economical as irrigation is carried without the requirement of petrol or oil. The cultivators exploit the power of the river.

Use of traditional farm implements: People still use traditional farm implements such as *fail, moi, hal, ghan, phawara, khulahari, jhabal, dharati, dharat, khilana, baelcha, gainti* and *jungra* (names of traditional farm implements) in their fields. This helps in management of

Cont'd...

...Cont'd

soil and water resources. These farm implements have simplicity, efficiency, low operation and maintenance costs and are aesthetic. Thus the traditional farm implements deserve further consideration. In order to renovate them, villagers use a special type of traditional plough. Other types of 'improved' ploughs do not work in the hills as the soil is gravelly. Villagers plough their land straight for retaining moisture. Villagers prefer mixed cropping for minimising risks under rain-fed conditions and creating ground cover for checking runoff and soil erosion. They grow legumes or ginger or turmeric with maize. Now people are becoming reluctant in growing maize because of monkey menace.

Use of manure and crop rotation: In view of the texture and conditions of soil, villagers use traditional manure in the fields before sowing. For paddy they do green manure also. Use of chemical fertilisers has increased over last few years but people also retain their traditional methods. Crop rotation is done to maintain the nitrogen content of the soil and also to maintain other necessary soil nutrients.

Traditional method preparation of land before sowing: Villagers do not dig pits for the collection of cow dung for preparing manure. Instead of pits, villagers accumulate the cow dung in the open for its rapid decomposition.

Vegetative measures for natural resources management: Villagers grow plants that have an economic value and are required for their benefit. Various wild shrubs are available to meet fuel and fodder requirements. Besides depending on forest resources, people have started growing plants that can meet the demand of fodder. Villagers believe in the concept of' sacred species, sacred groves and sacred landscapes. The village institutions linked to biological resource management is often linked to religious myths and socio-cultural belief system.

Role of women and indigenous institutions in conservation

Women play an important role in the cultivation of crops, animal husbandry, dairying, child-rearing, cooking, collection of fodder and management of fuel. The village women collect fodder and fuel wood from nearby forests but they keep in mind the concept of conservation. While cutting grass for fodder, they use their sickle in such a way that the plant is not uprooted. The cultivation of rice by women is a rare display of a sustainable practice which is given in Box II. Besides this, the indigenous institutions also play a very significant role in the conservation of vegetation. Conservation and construction related decisions are taken in consultation with *Mahadev* (Shaiv order of deities) and *Bir* (name of a local deity) the two main deities in the village as mentioned in the Box III.

Box II

Rice Cultivation as a Sustainable Practice

The cultivation of rice by women is a rare demonstration of a sustainable practice. Care is taken while transplanting the rice saplings. And to do so they sing folk songs which describe how to sow a sapling properly with proper spacing without damaging the sapling. The folk song given below is like a set of instructions given by the senior experienced women to others for taking proper care during transplantation.

Gugatae-gugatae bana re dalae gugatae
Bolo lokuo gugatae-gugatae
Chaata na rubi gugatae
Chalae na pai gugatae
Dhora rumbo gugatae

Box III

Case Study of Indigenous Institutions Involved in Conservation of Vegetation

There are a few religious sites in the village where the temples of local deities are situated and are protected. People take permission of local deities in order to initiate any activity in the area. There are seven such sites in the village which are believed to be sacred and worshipped. These are: *bala ra odu* (pipal tree), *baloo* (bir devta), *dano devta* temple, *kurgan devta* temple, *jamu, panihaar* and *bhitti.* As these areas are considered sacred, so cutting trees, shrubs or grasses is prohibited. Villagers have fixed certain norms for protecting these areas like forest produce cannot be removed from such sacred land. If any bush is to be removed from such sacred places; only the people of *devta* are allowed to do so. Leather shoes or goods are not allowed to the interior part of such sacred land. Defecating or urinating in the area is strictly prohibited. Still entry of scheduled caste people into such areas is restricted. Women during their menstrual periods are prohibited from going or even passing through the land of *devta* (folk deity). Nobody is allowed to stay inside the sacred land of *devta* during the night. Use of alcohol is prohibited in the area.

Cont'd...

...Cont'd

> But domestic cattle are allowed to graze in the area. The sacrifice of a goat/sheep is not carried out regularly but only on fulfilment of the wish of any villager. The *devta* generally comes to the sacred place during the *jater* (a local fair) fair held every year in the month of June for two days. Special worship is performed by the villagers during the *jater* which is done collectively by the people of the village. The place of *devta* is considered genuine for the settlement of disputes or any other village problems. Recently during the *jater*, the villagers ask the village deity for constructing a road which is close to the temple. But two big rocks, which are believed to be of deity, were to be removed. The deity gave the permission to do so but with a condition that this has to be done properly without affecting the rocks and even surroundings. Thus the village Gods play a very significant role in the conservation of natural resources. Similarly some sacred trees are not cut and used as fuel wood or for any other purpose because of their sanctity. People also believe that the cause of excessive rains/drought at times is due to violation of the rules. To avoid such problems, people perform *chershi* (a religious occasion during which a sacrifice is made) to sanctify the area and to please the deity who would help either to stop excessive rain or to bring rainfall.

Changing lifestyle of people in the village

The villagers lead a simple but hard life. The exotic, colourful, divergent costumes and ornaments of the earlier times have been replaced by modern costumes and ornaments. The younger generations do not even know about the traditional attire and wide range of silver ornaments that people traditionally worn on festive occasions and marriages. The preference has changed from the heavy weight silver ornaments to lighter ones. Many families either exchange ancestral ornaments to get lighter modern ornaments or sell them to meet up their requirements.

Housing pattern has also changed in the village over the last 44 years. The Census report of 1961 described the general housing pattern in the village Shakrori as: "... Generally the houses in Shakrori village are kacha, having an attractive mud plaster and built on a rectangular plan using mud and stone. More than half of the houses are two storied and the rest are single storied. There are 12 houses of scheduled castes, most of which have grass roofs. The houses of the sawarnas have roofs of slate, iron sheets, bamboos and kucha stone. The cattle sheds have straw roofs".

Now, the people have converted half of the house into *pucka* and the other half as *kacha*. In modern houses the construction pattern is different. Now the rooms on the ground floor are used either for guests or as sitouts or drawing rooms. The rooms in upper storey are used as *rasoi* (kitchen) and *kothris* (smallrooms) are used as bedrooms. The upper storey is connected to the ground floor through a *pauri* (staircase). A small room under the staircase is used as a store room. The front of the house is known as *thanki*. The ground floor contains a verandah which is commonly called *bhee*. There is a small room between the roof and ceiling in the traditional pattern of housing, which is known as *chaanan. In the chaanan* harvested crop and agricultural implements are stored. The *chaanan* is not maintained in the newly constructed houses. The villagers narrated that the old houses were cool in summers and hot in winters as these houses were made of wood, mud and slate and have insulation. However the newly constructed houses are hot in summers and cold in winters as they are devoid of ventilation. After the completion of house, house warming ceremony commonly known as *griha-pravesh/ghruasani (a* religious ceremony performed before living in a new house) is performed and a feast is given to friends and relatives. The availability of resources, likes and dislikes of people and time constrains are responsible for the change in housing pattern.

Food consumption patterns determine the nutritional status and lifestyle of a community. In spite of changes in man's outlook and lifestyle over the last 44 years, villagers choose food on the basis of its nutritive and medicinal values and its "hot" and "cold" nature. In addition to this people have developed indigenous methods of food storage, preservation and food consumption. Villagers collect a number of wild fruits and vegetables like jungli chulai (*Amaranthus spp.*), ramban (*Agave armenica*), churro (*Euphorbia royleana*), kathi (*Indigofera pulchella*), karyalo (*Bafhaunia variegate*), chuch (*Nasturtium officinalis*), kawarpatha (*Aloe banbadensis*), etc. Depending upon the nature of disease, people prefer to include these items in their routine diet. The general as well as the traditional food items are *sewai, halwa, sag/wild fruit vegetable, chutney, putanday, badi, kheer, phulwari, bhalae, roat, puri, bhat, sattu, kichari, roti, dal, siddus, babru, indray, batholtu, rotkus, chausari, badana, sansay, seera, sun dried wadies (names of ethnic food items),* etc. The ethnic foods are a part of the culture and reflect the prosperity and rich cultural heritage of the village. But the food habits are changing. Earlier people used *kodha* as their staple food but now they are switching to other cereals such as maize, and wheat. Rice was a major cash crop and formed a part of staple diet of villagers earlier but now the situation has changed. Such changes not only depend on the likes or dislikes of people for a particular food but also on the relative scarcity of the item, market prices and changes in cropping pattern.

Festivals linked to fairs and festivals depict a close proximity with the agriculture, folk deities, family interactions and nature. The festivals linked with agriculture and livestock are celebrated at the community level. People cook special food on these occasions and make offerings to the folk deities. Some important festivals of the village are *Sakranti* and *Mala Purnima. Sakranti* is the moment when the sun leaves one zodiac sign and enters another. *Sakranti* takes its name from the zodiacal sign/name of the month it enters into. There are twelve *sakarantis* in a year and all are celebrated by villagers but the four main *sakarantis* come in the month of January, April, July and September. The *Sakranti* that comes in the month of January is known as *Makar Sankranti.* It is a joyous festival and marks the passage of sun from *dakshinayana* (south) to *uttarayana* (north). On this day villagers go to Tattapani (a pilgrim site frequently flocked by people from all parts of Northern India to take bath in the curative sulphur waters and pay respect at the ancient *Narsingh devta* temple to take a holy dip. The *Sakranti* in April is celebrated as *Bishu ki Sajji* (*Sakranti* celebrated during *Baisakh*) in the village. Usually on this occasion people go again to Tattapani for a holy dip. During this festival, people express their gratitude towards the Gods for good rabi crop. Married daughters and sisters are invited to the family of their origin on the occasion. Earthen pitchers filled with water are given to the daughters and priests with a symbolic manifestation of fertility (earthen pitchers to daughters) and sharing culture (earthen pitchers to priests) respectively of the area. Floor of the house is plastered with cow dung and special meals, containing *putanday* (pancakes), *shakkar* (crude sugar), *ghee* (clarified semifluid butter), rice and pulses, are prepared.

Sakranti of July is known as *jathi* (elder) *sajji* and is also called *harayali* (green) *saaji.* It marks the beginning of *Sharavan* (refers to the period of July to August in Hindu Lunar calendar) month. It is believed that this month is the most auspicious one of the year and is often called '*dharmi mahina* (sacred month)'. No animal is sacrificed in this month. This month is dedicated to Lord Shiva. Villagers visit *Narsingh Devta* (locally called *Bir,* a folk deity) in Tattapani and *Danav Maharaj* (locally called *Dhano,* a folk deity). This *Sakaranti* marks that the sowing of paddy crop has begun. The *kulh* (water source which irrigates the paddy crop) is cleaned and worshipped even before this day. Each household contributes wheat flour, jaggery, butter and *dhoop* to the priests. The priest performs *prayers* and also prepares *roat* (baked bread).

The *Sakranti* celebrated in the month of September is called *Sair.* The festival is mainly celebrated by women. They get up early in the morning and reach the *panihaar* to take bath and fill their pitcher with water. They bring the water filled pitcher to their home. They sing *Sia* (a folk song particularly sung on the occasion of *sair*) in praise of Goddess Sita. Prayers are offered and citrus fruits (*khatay*), maize cob, paddy seedling and walnuts are placed near the water source as offerings. The celebration of this *Sakranti* is linked with purity as represented by the Hindu Goddess Sita. *Mala Purnima* (full moon light) is celebrated in the month of October. The festival is celebrated to honour the cattle especially cows. The festival starts seven-eight days before *Purnima.* In the evenings women gather and sing *Mala* which is a folk song sung in series, and traces the origin and importance of festival. One day before the main event the gathered women call the names of their animals one by one and prepare garlands by using white flowers (these are specially brought from higher altitudes), *shel* (handmade rope) and *gainda* (*Calendula officinalis*) flowers. In the morning, the animals are taken out of their sheds and decorated with colours. *Dhruv (Cynodon dactylon),* sacred grass believed to be possessed by Lord Ganesh and hence considered auspicious, and walnuts are placed near the feet of the cattle. After the prayers, the cattle are left to graze in the open and villagers gather at a community place to sing and dance. Women prepare *dala* (mixture of grains) to feed the cattle. On this day women and children visit all cattle sheds in the village to distribute grains to cattle, irrespective of caste and other differences.

With the arrival of modern means of entertainment like radio and TV, all the traditional village fairs and festivals, religious ceremonies, singing and dancing in groups at a community place or homes and their frequency are declining in importance. Though such celebrations are still organised but people are getting more inclined towards the modern means of entertainment as not only they do not find time to gather at a common place but also the folk artists are no longer interested in its performance. Besides these two main reasons, there are other reasons like lack of interest among younger generation to learn these traditional folk arts and culture, and because people are less interested in the folk theatre. Thus modern music system has replaced the traditional group singing and dancing in every ceremony and function. Though modern means of entertainment is swaying the traditional forms of art among younger generation, but still the old generation has maintained the traditional culture in its pure form. Elders also feel that intergenerational relations based on traditional values like respect for elders, loyalty, mutual understanding and other warm feelings between generations are deteriorating and they believe that modernisation and media are responsible for such deterioration in the relationships.

Village Shakrori under an impending threat

Most of the villagers of Shakrori are aware and apprehensive of the affects of mining and cement factory in terms of generation of dust, solid wastes, noise, and liquid wastes that adversely affect the biodiversity, micro-flora and fauna, hydrological system, environment and agriculture in Shakrori village. Members of *Mahila Mandal* in the Panchayat Shakrori appealed the Deputy Commissioner of Shimla district to give up the plans to set up the unit in and around Shakrori Panchayat as the factory will render their lands unfit for cultivation and will dry up the water resources and will make the lives of women in particular extremely difficult and the residents of Shakrori in general. Women are fearful that there will be an increase in crime rate and violence against women besides illness among the inhabitants of the village as a result of pollution by cement factory. On the other hand, village elders have also brought the matter to the notice of Deputy Commissioner of Shimla district and expressed their serious objection to the construction of cement factory near Shakrori as it affects not only their fertile lands but also their fodder and fuel wood requirements will remain unfulfilled. On similar grounds, they objected the construction of a bridge in the vicinity of the village. They believe that cash compensations received from the factory for the loss of land get frittered away very fast but the loss of land can never be compensated. Representatives of the cement factory have approached some of the villagers to acquire their land for the construction of metalled road in order to transport cement and other materials comfortably. People firmly believe that the factory should not force them away from land with temptations of cash compensation.

The construction of Kol dam is progressing in this area. Significant changes in hydrology of the rivers, disturbance of the fragile mountain formations and soil layers, and accumulation of silt and debris are likely to be noticed in the near future. Earlier experiences of dam construction around the world in general and in India in particular, have shown that such constructions also resulted in large scale restructuring of soils and natural water springs, submergence of culturally important symbols, but also affected the habitat and livelihoods of people besides flora and fauna in the area. Landslides and earthquakes that occur naturally, threaten dams and surrounding habitations and the construction of dams and mining further intensifies this threat thus posing hazard to life. In village Shakrori nine families are affected by the construction of this dam. Though they have received the compensation and are happy with the money that they have received as compensation for their submerged land, the way the money is utilised is a matter of great concern. In two cases, the money has been utilised for wasteful practices such as drinking. In another case a sixteen year old girl was married to a seventy year old man who had got compensation in lieu of his land from Kol dam officials. This is one example of revival of *kanyasulka* (brideprice) type of marriages as observed in Andhra among Brahmins and mentioned by Gurajada in his book *Kanyasulkam*. Most of the remaining people who received compensation for the loss of land have deposited their money in banks hoping to use it appropriately in the future.

Increased employment in the government service resulted in decline of participation in agricultural activities. Both proponents and opponents of dam construction do increasingly recognise the far-reaching socio-economic impacts of dam construction. The socio-cultural impacts of dam construction and the trauma of resettlement are much more difficult to measure than the economic cost and benefits. The construction of Kol dam further affects the Tattapani, an ancient pilgrimage centre with famous hot-water sulphur springs, which along with the ancient Narsingh temple will be submerged under water of the Sutlej along with the settlement around it. People in and around Tattapani also used the riverside as cremation place will be soon lost with the construction of Kol dam. The hot sulphur springs are believed to have been originated because of the divine power and are considered the form of God. Thus, even today, at each spring site, a temple or local deity exists. This religious belief together with the therapeutic roles of sulphur springs made the people to consider these sites as pilgrimage centres. Though modern science is able to explain the origin of these springs, but the educated and the common people still consider the springs as a divine manifestation of God. As these places come under the category of sacred grooves so the government should try to protect these places before planning and implementing the development programmes. Though development is essential but it should not be made at the cost of damaging the sacred heritage. A sense of deep loss is engulfing most of the people in the area. Call it a decline of century-old culture or the price that one has to pay for development that the construction of dams is posing threats in the areas where these are constructed.

Reference

Village Shakrori, 1961, Census Department, Government of India.

9

Migration and Mobility in an Eastern Uttar Pradesh Village

P. Mishra

The process of the return of emigrants to their native lands, after staying for some years in metropolitan cities either in India or in foreign countries, and consequences of this for the social mobility of the villagers, has received scant attention in literature. What happens when adult male working persons leave behind their family members, women, children and aged parents in villages and migrate to metropolitan cities, located either in India or in foreign countries and remit their savings to the kin staying at the native place? To find out the answers to this question, data were collected through focused interviews and narrations of the experiences of migrants to metros and people of the second generation staying in a village in eastern Uttar Pradesh. This article is divided into two parts. The first part deals with the conceptual understanding of the term, migration, and its theoretical bearings. The second part focuses on a village of eastern Uttar Pradesh (UP) from where people have migrated to metropolitan cities such as Bombay in India and Singapore in Southeast Asia in the period of the British rule in India.

Migration deals with the movement of individuals, families or collectivities from one geographical area to another. It may be done within the country from rural to urban areas or from rural to rural areas or urban to rural areas. Such migration is called internal migration. If it is done between two countries, then the phenomenon is known as international migration. Such migration is classified into two types, i.e., voluntary and forced. In the voluntary type of migration, deprived sections of people in a society are inspired, on their own, to migrate either within the country or outside with a hope of getting better economic opportunities. In the forced type of migration, people feel the loss of identity in periods of revolution, war and political upheavals in the country of their birth. Under such situations, the governments, in order to safeguard its interests, imprisons its opponents or deports them forcefully from the country (Stark, 1991).

In the case of international migration, the migrants feel attached to the countries of their origin as well as the host countries (Weiner, 1990). Kinship, friendship and shared community ties are valuable components of the social capital and reduce the psychic and risk costs of migration to foreign countries (Boyd, 1989). In the host countries the migrants work on those jobs which are acceptable to their cultural values, even for a lower remuneration, which reduces the chronic unemployment in developing countries and alleviates poverty among their population. Migrants working in foreign countries remit a portion of their earnings to the country of their origin and thus enhance not only the national income but also the standard of living of people in their native lands. Many migrants, in their experiences have also talked about globalisation, which promotes transnational corporations, to invest a substantial amount of capital in the markets of developing countries. This, in turn, brings 'work to workers' as well as 'workers to work'. Theoretically, 'brain-drain' and the 'exploitation of workers' in capitalist economy will automatically be reduced to its lowest level when the development of a society will be properly organised (Todaro, 1969).

The Village and Its Migrants

The role of push and pull factors in the process of out-and return-migration in a village of eastern Uttar Pradesh is being assessed in this study. The village is unique in its composition as at least one person from each family emigrated during the British regime either to Bombay (India) or to Singapore (in Southeast Asia) (Mishra, 1996). The village under study is Oghani Gangadaspur, one of the three villages within the revenue village of Oghani under raiyatwari land tenure system. It is situated between the cities of Azamgarh and Varanasi in eastern Uttar Pradesh. Azamgarh is important to the village for administrative purpose while Varanasi is important for educational purposes. The village has 1,250 inhabitants and 750 voters. The neighbouring villagers extend *jajmani* services to the inhabitants of Oghani Gangadaspur. These villagers have cultivable land in an adjacent village, Biura as well.

Gangadaspur was a multi-caste village. There were 40 families in the village. Thakurs (Rajputs) had 20 families followed by Bhar (low-caste plowman) with nine families; Teli (oilman) had three families and Brahmin (with two families). Yadav (Ahir dependent on animal husbandry), Barai (sellers of betel leaves), Lohar (blacksmith), Kahar (well-water supplier and carry people in palanquins), *Nai* (barber), and Dhobi (washerman) castes had one family each. The families of these castes were either lineal, collateral, or various combinations of these types as classified in the writings of Kolenda (1987). Thakurs (Rajputs) owned nearly three fourths of the cultivable land of Gangadaspur while Brahmins owned less than half of the cultivatable land of Biura. Thakurs and Brahmins were traditionally restricted from direct involvement in plowing and cultivation of land and were mainly dependent on a supervisory or a tenancy form of cultivation. These castes considered plowing of land as a polluting activity and remained aloof from manual agricultural operations. The lower castes carried out all direct agricultural operations in the cultivation of crops. Under tenancy laws, some of the land was transferred from Thakurs and Brahmins to the OBCs and SCs. They also invested a portion of the remittances received from their migrant kin in the purchase of more land. Water reservoirs like tanks (3), ponds (4) and river (1) were available for irrigation. Major crops cultivated in the village were paddy, wheat, and pulses for the fulfilment of subsistence needs of the households. Sugarcane and potato crops were also cultivated, mainly to cope with household requirements.

The crop diversity once observed is now declining and at present, crops are mainly confined to high yielding varieties of wheat and paddy. These crops are under tubewell irrigation and tractors have replaced wooden plows. All the upper (general) castes are now involved in plowing the land with modern technology, indicating a change in values related to manual work for the plowing of land.

All the houses of the village are made of bricks and cement and are called *pucca* houses. People within the village use these materials though the village is 10 km away from the market place, tehsil and block. The socio-economic life of the village under study is mostly traditional. The *jajmani* system still prevails in the village without a clear-cut demarcation in the custom and contract-based relations between the service providers and receivers. Such situations occasionally lead to conflicts between the 'jajman' and the 'kamkarne waale'. The village, till a decade ago, had one government-sponsored primary school. Two people, one belonging to Brahmin and another to Thakur caste, voluntarily initiated primary education in the village in the last phase of the British rule in India.

Information on the immigration of the villagers, along with causes, positive and negative reference groups of migrants, the direction of mobility and its consequences was collected from the household heads of the village through interviews and narrations. The analysis of the data revealed that severe droughts and famines in Bengal (1943) and eastern Uttar Pradesh (in the late 1930s and early 1940s) during the British regime in India resulted in the deterioration of the socio-economic conditions of the inhabitants of the province. World War II (1938–42) further aggravated the problems of villagers. Under these deteriorating living conditions, the villagers under study mostly migrated in order to cope with the subsistence needs of their families. Instead of providing relief to the famine and drought affected people, British authorities encouraged people from the area to migrate to Far East countries under their governance and to Indian metros.

People from the village participated in the Indian nationalist movement under the banner of the Congress party for independence from British rule. Thus, the Congress as well as freedom fighters became the positive reference group and the British authorities became the negative reference group to the villagers. In order to get rid of the local pressure from the movement, the British government not only encouraged the emigration of people but also transported some of the villagers to Southeast Asian countries with monetary incentives. But, this policy of the British government facilitated the organisation of such emigrants under the banner of the Congress party in India and Azad Hind Fauj in Southeast Asia. Migrants from Uttar Pradesh, living in Singapore, Kuala Lumpur (Malaysia) and Bangkok (Thailand), joined the voluntary army and met the 'call' of Subhash Chandra Bose for 'blood' and 'money' for overthrowing the British Raj in India. The Japanese government in Southeast Asia extended support to Azad Hind Fauj. Emigrants of the village under study were mostly settled in Singapore. They mainly belonged to upper castes (twice born) and were unskilled. So, they started dairy work on business lines and later established 'dairy farms with cows', which were not only culturally acceptable, without the stigma of pollution, but also profitable. Other migrants joined the Azad Hind Fauj. In the period of Japanese occupation of Singapore (1942–45), some of the emigrants shifted their occupation from business to public and private sector jobs.

Consequences of Migration

The present study (Luhmann, 1982) assumes that money is a neutral medium of communication. The remittances of a portion of earnings by the migrants to their families in the native village provide additional cash which the family members use for different purposes.

Facts were collected through the survey method from the household heads of families staying in the village about the patterns of spending money remitted by their migrant kin. The survey method of data collection is supplemented with observations and narrations. Analysis of data indicates that emigrants to Indian metros remitted less money than the emigrants to foreign metros, as the value of one rupee of Singapore was equal to one rupee and fifty paise of Indian currency. The villagers, in general, spent the received money from the emigrants for the fulfilment of the basic needs of their family members in the village. A portion of the remaining amount of remittances was spent on the education of the younger generation up to junior high school levels. However, a variation in the pattern of use of the remaining cash was observed along caste lines. For instance, OBC families invested the major portion of the remaining cash in the purchase of non–irrigated land at cheap prices. On the other hand, the families of higher castes spent proportionally more money on the higher education of their off-spring. Most of the educated youth of this group are now settled in Indian cities.

Almost all educational achievements mentioned below belong to second generation of the emigrant families. They took their primary and middle education from the schools located in the village and nearby areas, except one who graduated from the Military school, Dehradun. Others graduated from the colleges or universities located in Eastern Uttar Pradesh, namely Banaras Hindu University, Varanasi; Gorakhpur University, Gorakhpur; Panth Nagar Agricultural University, Pantnagar; Allahabad University, Allahabad and Kashi Vidyapith, Varanasi. They were regular students of the above mentioned educational institutions. Mostly the household heads met the educational expenditures of their children. Facts indicated that there was moral trust between the first and second generation as the second generation availed the resources mostly remitted by the emigrants to the foreign metros. The message of the first generation to the second generation, repeated reminders to devote time and energy to achieve the goals set for life, acted as controllers and guides for the behaviour of the second generation. The first-generation emigrants perceived a desired change in the second generation, which worked as a pull factor for return migration. The third generation perceived persons living abroad as a kind of resource or money or status symbol. Occasionally, such perceptions reflected differences between the first and the third generation indicating that the money received from the migrants acted as a medium in the acquisition of power, status and property.

From this study, it can be safely concluded that there is a link between the metropolitan centres and villages and power is generated through money received from emigrants. Middle-ranking castes have strengthened their position horizontally through the purchase of more non-irrigated agricultural land while upper castes strengthened their position vertically through higher education, entering the new middle class of Indian society in the form of Professors and Readers (5), Managers (4), Lecturers (3), A-grade Contractors (3), Engineers (3), Commissioner (1 IAS), S.P. (1 IPS), Brigadier (1), apart from others working in different professions and jobs. These personnel belong to the second generation of upper caste families and are settled in different cities in Uttar Pradesh and its adjoining states. The contemporary situation of the village is that persons who emigrated during the British period to the metros of India and abroad came back to the village but most of them are deceased. Members of the second and third generations living in the village are almost equal in number to the first generation. In this village, the population of upper caste has remained static as a result of 'orderly' migration while the number of OBCs, and their landownership, increased. Landholding and population growth have a direct bearing on power politics, in shifting power from Thakurs to OBCs in the region, in the context of adult suffrage. Traditional inter-caste relations are still maintained through the *jajmani* system in some specific services where ceremonies and the repair of tools are concerned. The findings of this study highlight that money is not merely a neutral medium of communication, contrary to the assumptions of Luhmann (1982) but when combined with other factors like education, it generates new conditions for social development (Chauhan, 1990) that are communicative in nature.

References

Boyd, M. 1989, "Family and Personal Networks in International Migration: Recent Developments and New Agenda", *International Migration Review*, 23: 638–70.

Chauhan, B.R. 1990, *Rural Urban Articulation*, Udaipur: A.C. Brothers.

Kolenda, P. 1987, *Regional Differences in Family Structures in India*, Jaipur: Rawat Publications.

Luhmann, N. 1982, *The Differentiation of Society*, New York: Columbia University Press.

Mishra, P. 1994, *Ethnicity, Communication and Nation Building*, Udaipur: A.C. Brothers.

Stark, O. 1991, *The Migration of Labour*, Cambridge: Basil Blackwell.

Todaro, M. 1969, "A Model of Labour Migration and Urban Unemployment in Less-developed Countries", *The American Economic Review*, 59: 138–48.

Weiner, M. 1990, *Stability and International Migration*, Cambridge: M.I.T. Centre for International Studies.

10

Development Administration in North and South Indian States Compared

R. Shankar

Mukherjee (2005) indicated the importance of studying the development aspects from sociological point of view. The phenomenon of development involves structural differentiation and changing patterns of institutional integration (Smelser, 1958) and it is an important area to be comprehended from the sociological point of view. Three stakeholders, administrators, leaders and villagers are involved in the process of planned development. The earlier studies on development have made concerted endeavours to comprehend the role of stakeholders at the village level (Dube, 1958), the elite and villagers (Sirsikar, 1970) but not the role of all the three stakeholders in development. So, the present study focuses its attention on the interrelations among the administrators, the leaders and the villagers involved in developmental activities and observes the same from the grassroots level through the block to the district level in a comparative framework between two districts of UP and Tamil Nadu. In a nutshell, the study makes an effort to comprehend the following questions: What happens to central and state directives by the time they reach the grassroots level in implementation and how does the local structure respond to the developmental programmes? How far are the historical experiences of the two states relevant to the present day development administration? What are the main differences in the nature of development administration and the people's response to the same in the two states and what are the possible explanations for these differences?

Method and Unit of Study

The present study compares development administration in two districts drawn from Uttar Pradesh and Tamil Nadu. The comparative method has long been considered appropriate for studying variations. Durkheim (1895) insisted that the units in the comparative method must be similar. He analysed the sociological causes for the variation in the rates of suicide among different social groups. Later, Weber (1930) used the method in his study of the growth of spirit of capitalistic tendencies among different religious communities. Bendix (1958) has studied Indian society in comparison with others in nation building and citizenship. Brass (1966) studied the factional politics within five districts of UP. The present study tries to understand the interaction between development administration and the people's response in two districts of two states of India with different cultural and historical experiences.

In the collection of data from the two districts and their regions under reference, a combination of multiple techniques has been used in the study. Data have been collected from office records, government handouts and publications related to the programmes of development involving all the three groups. Focused and open interviews are conducted with all the three groups involved in the developmental programmes, in order to get information about their experiences in the process. Observations have been carried out to understand the significance of the data collected. Finally, data have been collected through case studies for understanding the processes of development administration with illustrations.

The investigator belongs to one of the chosen state (Tamil Nadu) with a fair working knowledge of the district in the other state, acquired by living in the aforesaid district for four years before undertaking the investigation. This experience has helped a lot in understanding the significance of events involved in this study. Some major similarities between the two districts are as follows: Both the regions under reference have perennial river water resources for agricultural cultivation. The population involved in agriculture is about 55 per cent in both the districts. The scheduled caste population in the two districts is around 17 per cent. The major developmental programmes introduced in the two districts are also the same. Some major differences can be observed among cropping patterns, land tenure system and agrarian structure, political events, marriage preferences, and mechanisation of agriculture.

The major crops cultivated in Meerut (UP) are wheat and sugarcane. Sugarcane is the main cash crop. In Tirunelveli (Tamil Nadu) paddy is the major food crop. Cotton, coconut, banana, groundnut are the main cash crops. A sugar mill in Meerut and a fertiliser factory in Tirunelveli play crucial roles in cash crop cultivation. The sugarcane varieties cultivated in Meerut are generally prepared from the seeds brought from Coimbatore, a part of Tamil Nadu. The major agricultural communities in Meerut district are the Jats (agriculturists), Gujars (pastoralists), Rajputs (cultivators in western UP) and Ahirs (animal husbandry and agriculture). In Tirunelveli, the Nadar community (once upon a time they were toddy tappers) is most industrious in agriculture, like the Jats of Meerut. The other agricultural communities include Vellala (traditional cultivating caste), Konar (a traditional milk vending community now involved in agriculture as well), and Thevars (traditionally, the territory protectors and mostly land owners, with watch and vigil duties). The modernisation of Meerut, like railway and road construction, started from the First War of independence, 1857 (Stokes, 1980). Though the land tenure pattern followed the *zamindari* system in many parts of UP, Meerut had a 'Bhaiya Chara system' in a predominant form over Pattidary and *zamindari* systems. It has been reflected in the agrarian structure of the Meerut district which has a larger proportion of owner cultivators than Tirunelveli district. Thus Meerut district shows an egalitarian agricultural structure. In Tirunelveli the land tenure system was 'ryotwari' in general but the 'mirasdari' system of land prevailed with the concentration of land in fewer hands and the presence of a large proportion of households without ownership of land. The proportion of agricultural labourers in Tirunelveli district is almost double the proportion of agricultural labourers in Meerut district. The despotism of higher castes over other castes led to the birth of the self-respect movement in Tamil Nadu. The movement forged an alliance among non-Brahmin castes and politicised the people. The Arya Samaj Movement has influenced the people of Meerut region with a large proportion of Jats joining the same, protesting against the elaborate Brahminical rituals. Meerut district remained in the fold of the national party from the beginning till now except for a brief period (Brass, 1966), where as in Tirunelveli, since the national party was dominated by Brahmins, the regional party taking the anti-Brahminical stand has been favoured for the past three and half decades.

Marriage patterns in northern and southern regions of India vary greatly (Karve, 1965). Meerut follows the pattern of extension of kinship relations by adopting 'seema seema Bhaichara rule' (fraternity settlement) whereas in Tirunelveli the marriage relations further consolidate the already existing kinship relations by multiple bonds. This is the social setting which is reflected in Mawana block from Meerut and Srivaikuntam from Tirunelveli respectively. Both the Blocks are located at almost the same distance from the district headquarters, with educational facilities available up to the graduation level. The villages in these two blocks are 100 per cent electrified. Institutional structures like bank branches are available in 3:2 ratios in Mawana and Srivaikuntam. The density of the population is in a 7: 9 ratio with post offices in a 2:5 ratio respectively. The number of tractors available is in a 22:1 ratio.

Developmental processes have been carried out in the villages for the rural inhabitants. Hence, for study, two villages have been chosen where sufficient development has occurred. The villages selected for study have significant community facilities and people have adopted several developmental measures. Records for all the villages of the block have been processed and the villages with more infrastructural facilities, like school, agricultural cooperative society, hospital, communication facilities like post office, link roads, electricity and mechanisation of farming, identified on the basis of the number of pumpsets, tractors, fertiliser consumption and crop pattern have been selected for study from the two districts of these states.

History of Development Administration in the Blocks

Development administration in the two blocks was introduced as a new phenomenon from the first 5–year plan period in the form of community development programmes as a philosophy, method and as an agency. The programme, after three years of inception in 1955, became the National Extension Service Scheme. At the second phase, democratic institutions at different levels were introduced in 1959. This was known as the Statutory Panchayati Raj system. It was conceived as a three-tier system from the grassroots Gram Panchayat to Block Samiti and Zila Parishad to secure people's participation in the developmental programme. However, the panchayat elections were irregular. The leaders could exploit this situation to promote their interests and acted as middlemen between the bureaucracy and the villagers. The emphasis was on growing more food with the help of Intensive Agriculture Development Programme in 1960–61, IAAP in 1964–65, High Yielding Variety Programme in 1966 and multiple cropping patterns in 1971. Elaborate arrangements were made to provide training and education in new agricultural technology along with demonstration to the cultivators but most of the benefit went to a well-off section of landowners. So, the government evolved programmes meant for weaker sections in 1974. Even the Community Development Department was changed and named as Rural Development Department in 1974. Development of Backward Areas Programmes was mooted, and for weaker sections, the Small Cultivators Development Agency (SFDA), and Marginal cultivators and land less labourers (MFAL) were introduced from 1974. Different systems administering rural development schemes have emerged in different states and districts as the various programmes were developed over the past decades. The Central Government also sponsored schemes such as Minimum Nutrition Programme (MNP) in 1972–73 and Food for Work Programme in April 1977; also the Whole Village Development Programme was developed in 1952. Tirunelveli district has overlapping programmes such as Small Cultivators Development Agency (SFDA) Drought Prone Areas Programme (DPAP) and so on, while Meerut has a lesser number of programmes to suit its specific conditions. All these programmes have been consolidated into Integrated Rural Development Programme (IRDP).

Inter-departmental coordination

Administration of development programme is under the control of the district collector in both the districts. Next to him there is a chief development officer (CDO) co-coordinating heads of all district level technical departments like co-operative, animal husbandry, panchayat, engineering and so on. Whereas in Tirunelveli the district is divided into two developmental districts – North and South – and further they are divided into divisions with Divisional Development Officer as its head to actively implement the scheme. There are separate agencies such as the District Rural Development Agency (DRDA). But, the agencies are more in Tirunelveli than in Meerut. Agriculture is a major aspect of development. Training and visit programmes have been established with a separate line of command separating it from the grassroots Rural Welfare Officer to the district level in July 1982 in Tirunelveli. In Meerut the older pattern is retained. The designations of the officials in Meerut are changed as Assistant Development Officer at the block, the cadre below Block Development Officer (BDO) in the hierarchy, but they remain as Extension Officers in Tirunelveli. The official at the village level is named Rural Welfare Officer in Tirunelveli and is known as Village Development Officer in Meerut. But for these kinds of variations, generally the two administrative patterns mostly resemble each other. Though the programmes have passed through several stages, the multipurpose character of the co-coordinated approach remains unchanged and it requires the development administration to attain the following qualities to carry out their functions effectively. It is a fixed series of purely administrative goals with well-defined principal functions. The administrative authority has a clear and detailed job and office specification, with suitable internal communication, with effective and flexible controls to take decisions as what has to be done. The establishment has a clear system of incentives. The administration should not have any unnecessary and paralysing controls.

The functioning of the development administration in the field reveals the following similarities: Inter-departmental co-ordination is poor in both the districts and it has been observed over a number of occasions. The DRDA officials have to attend Gram Sabha meetings and supervise whether the selection of the weaker section families on a poorest among the poor basis is proper, for the implementation of aid programmes. But, the Block Development Officers did not intimate the date and time of the programmes in time to DRDA. At the district level, also, the officials did not attend meetings organised at the District Magistrate's house in time. A few of them came in the evening when the meeting was over. In Tirunelveli, the Collector postponed the meeting of the District Consultative Committee for want of quorum, and the striking feature was that the MLA belonging to the region turned up but the officials could not attend because the information did not reach them in time. There were occasions when finance institutional officials (banks) purposely avoided the Interview Board Meeting for Self-Employment Scheme of the District Industries Centre. People in the revenue or normal administration were given more weightage than the people in development administration. The Chief Development Officer was not provided official quarters till the time he was transferred after a year, whereas a revenue official in a lower cadre was provided quarters at once. The most important and awkward situation is that many departments function without heads and some are officiated by people from the lower cadre. Hence, the morale of the agency dips down and it may not function efficiently. The head of the district industries centre is General Manager and the post has been lying vacant for nine months. Transfer has been used as a weapon to force the officials to toe the line drawn by the high-ups. It is told and observed that the lower cadres frequently visit the higher cadre's house everyday in the evening as a ritual even without any purpose or work in order to be in their good books. For instance, a department was asked to explain by a higher state level department, its failure to spend money on a specific budget head programme. However, the approval of the budget, which should have been done first, was pending at the state level office. Meetings are held very often at all levels. The BDO conducts weekly meetings of village level officials at block level. At the district level, the Collector arranges it. In a week's time one cannot expect much progress to be achieved in any programme and the weekly review becomes an embarrassment. So many departments' depot delegates attend such meetings at the last minute; they go to attend it without having done their home work and with little knowledge about the projects' background. So, the participation in the meetings cannot make substantial contribution. If the number of meetings can be reduced, with sufficient intervals in between, then it may give substance and meaning to further steps in implementation.

Inter-group relations

The administrators and the leaders come together and tend to neglect the villagers. The administrators give undue importance to rules and, in order to get away from troubles like loan recovery problem. They sanction the loans to the leaders who are normally well-off or to others who are close to the leaders and can pay back the loan. As the budget amount needs to be spent, administrators save their skin by being hand in glove with the leaders, and the real needy villagers continue to suffer for ever. The leaders, in return, protect the administrators from public wrath.

In one village at Tirunelveli, the loan transactions were done only on paper and only the subsidy amount was given to the beneficiaries. In Meerut district also, loans for motor pump sets were given by getting a cash memo from private dealers. The amount of subsidy is given and the loan amount remains in the bank in the savings account of the beneficiary. There is an instance in which a village leader got a loan in his farm worker's name. Later on, the landlord sold the engine bought against the loan received in the name of his farm worker. The poor worker had to pay the loan by disposing off the small hut he owned. The officials are also aware of such events. Generally, the owners of large-sized lands and the landless get some benefits from the development programme but the real small cultivators do not benefit.

Bureaucratic dynamism

Development administration in the two states seems to be dynamic in nature. It is adjusted and modified to suit the surrounding social conditions. Bank, development and revenue administration adjust with the local leaders and develop personal contacts and interactions, which emerge as 'informal organisations' within the formal structures for the sake of smooth operations and add substance to Blau's (1955) view of bureaucracy.

In one block a local villager quoted a higher price in an auction of the peeled skins of dead animals. However, it was denied to him and given to another local leader of the village at a lower quoted price. The matter has been reported to the District Collector and further action is awaited. Ruling political party office bearers at local level were treated with high regards and they dictated to the BDO to include their proposed names in the list for recommendation to the TRYSEM scheme. Later on it was found that the BDO obliged them. Bank Managers of Meerut visit district level heads of development administration and compliment their work and also request them to send loan applications of economically viable people for the target coverage. In another instance, the Assistant Engineer was given a big presentation and asked to give the government borewell contract order to one particular contractor to whom the bank will sanction a loan. These networks revolve around the groups of administrators and the leaders. If the administration pools together the streamlining of procedures relating to sanctions, supplies and implementation in the field and these are taken over by the government, efficiency may improve and the underhand dealings may come-down.

Some of the significant differences among the two districts are related to the importance given either to primordial or formal relations in developmental administration. In Uttar Pradesh introduction of new phenomena such as tractor, TV, HYV seeds, fertilisers, pumpsets and new practices such as cultivation methods and institutional structure such as hospital, school, agricultural cooperative societies are carried out mostly through caste, kinship and other primordial ties and not by the formal administrative set up. For example, a hospital in one village in Meerut was established at the behest of the divisional health officer who hailed from the same village and who offered his own house as the building to run the hospital immediately. The certificate seed programme was carried on in the house of one of the leaders in the village, because his son happened to be a seed-certifying officer. Tractor purchase and sales are mostly carried out on the basis of caste and kinship relations, and not on the basis of market relations. To have an individual recruited in the army, one villager approached the leader of the village to influence the leader's brother's 'sambandhi' (leader's brother's son's father-in-law) and get things done. A primary school was set up in one of the villages 100 years ago because a member of the District Board at that time was from that village.

However, in Tamil Nadu, such kinds of caste alliances are weak. Here, a different kind of quasi-social organisation emerges on a cooperative basis, cutting across caste boundaries. It can be noticed in Kottarakurichi's betel wine cultivation in which one individual takes a huge area of land, around 5 acres, on lease and then takes 10 to 15 people belonging to different castes and religion as his partners, allocating land for each person in the team. They work together as a unit for three or four years till the yield becomes low. The same way is followed in the dry land area, called 'Punjai' in Siruthondanallur, where villagers have been growing banana plantain by carrying the water up to 5 kms through pipes for the past 12 years. It is one of the main sources for the economic prosperity of the villagers. It is carried out on a co-operative basis among different caste members. In Kottarakurichi village, the high caste people who once lived in the village, are now in high official positions, but they have not done anything for the village and it is on a down hill path now. Even when people approached the high-ups for favour, their appeals were not entertained as in the case of a person who tried to get into the SPIC fertiliser factory as an employee. The Chief Engineer who was a recruiting personnel hailed from this village, but declined to help the prospective employee though they were of the same caste.

The findings of the present study not only indicate that there are inter-departmental complexities but also that the relations between the administration and local leaders are more intense than their relations with the rural population. The relations between middlemen, the administration and the villagers are strong. Primordial ties are more significant in Meerut and have yielded results. In the case of Triunelveli, the cooperative movement which has a long history (Chauhan, 1968) along with the British formal administration cuts across caste boundaries and bears fruit. In both cases the people's initiative for development is greater than that of the administration.

The relations among the administrators, the leaders and the villagers in the context of development, are complex. Some possible explanations are suggested in this study. The historical experiences of Tamil Nadu under British colonial rule and the success attained in the cooperative movement in the early 20th century, along with the self-respect movement, all have a bearing upon the formal nature of bureaucratic development and the success of co-operative efforts in bringing development to rural areas. Normally officials do not talk about the programmes and their implementation procedures until they get the permission from the higher authorities to do so. If some official is on long leave, others will not attend to his work. The very formal nature of administration even delays the budget preparation. On the other hand, 'Punjai' banana cultivators run an unregistered co-operative society quite efficiently with different caste and community members in it.

The western districts of UP had the 'Bhaiya Chara' (brotherhood) system of agrarian relations, a strong work ethic in relation to agriculture even among the higher groups and an Arya Samaj movement, which helped in the formation of a league among various sections, particularly among the Jats from the rural areas. These factors provided suitable conditions for the continuation of primordial ties even in politics and administration. One of the Jat leaders from this area has been elected repeatedly since the provincial government elections. He has rarely visited or nursed the constituency. The major consideration of success is the caste factor (Brass, 1966, 1997). Electric posts for the villages were brought in through the villager's own conveyance and costs. In the absence of the Agriculture Co-operative Society Secretary, the Pradhan and few villagers took charge of the fertiliser bags, and later, they were disbursed by the clerk, without the Secretary coming into the picture. Such a mix-up of formal and informal relations among the officials and people's representatives is a marked feature of the western UP block.

Intra-country comparative studies are important in a vast country like India, where a rich variety of political and administrative practices exists. The method of studying social phenomena in their current form, through data collection and case studies, enriched by the historical contexts of the two states, has shown some promise and can be extended to other areas too. It is hoped that the understanding of different regions will lead to informed discussions of the issues involved, which will become instructive for further policy implications. The discipline of Sociology itself stands to gain substance in extending its frontiers to inter-regional comparisons.

References

Ashley, C. and Maxwell, S. 2001, "Rethinking Rural Development", *Development Policy Review*, Vol. 19, No. 4, December.

Banerjee, A. 2006, "Economic Growth and Sustainability of North Eastern States", in P.M. Passah (ed.), *In Defense of Regional Economic Development in India: A Case for the North East*, New Delhi: Akansha Publishing House.

Baishya, P. et al., 1997, *Developmental Issues of North East India*, Prof. P C Goswami Memorial Volume, Guwahati: Lawyers' Book.

Bendix, R. 1969, *Nation Building and Citizenship*, New Delhi: Wiley, Eastern Private Ltd.

Blau, P.M. 1955, *The Dynamics of Bureaucracy*, Chicago: Chicago University Press.

Brass, P.R. 1966, *Factional Politics in an Indian State*, Bombay: Oxford University Press.

——. 1997, "General Elections 1996 in Uttar Pradesh: Divisive Struggles Influence Outcome", *Economic and Political Weekly*, Vol. 32, No. 38, pp. 36–67.

Chauhan, B.R. 1968, "Panchayat Raj and Democratic Policy", *Sociological Bulletin*, Vol. 17, No. 1, pp. 315–54.

——. 1970, *Towns in Tribal Setting*, Delhi: National Publisher House.

Dube, S.C. 1958, *India's Changing Villages*, Bombay: Allied Publishers Pvt. Ltd.

Durkheim, E. 1966, *Suicide*, New York: Free Press.

Frieiro, M. 1966, "Development Administration: A Few Sociological, Economic, Political and Technical Aspects", *Development Administration Summaries of Selected Articles*, No. 2, pp. 9–12.

Hardgrave, R.L. 1965, *The Dravidian Movement*, Bombay: Popular Prakashan.

ICSSR, 1973, *A Survey of Research in Public Administration - Vol. I*, New Delhi: Allied Publishers.

——. 1974, *A Survey of Research in Sociology and Social Anthropology - Vol. I and II*, Bombay: Popular Prakashan.

Iqbal, N. 1970, *Rural Development Administration in India*, Bombay: Popular Prakashan.

Irschick, F.E. 1969, *Politics and Social Conflict in South India: The Non-Brahmin Movement and Tamil Seperatism, 1916–1929*, Berkeley: University of California Press.

Karve, I. 1965, *Kinship Organisation in India*, Bombay: Asia Publishing House.

Meera, S.N. 2004, *Information and Communication Technology in Agricultural Development: A Comparative Analysis of Three Projects from India*, Aglen Network Paper No. 135, ODI, January, p. 20.

Mukherjee, A. 2005, *Central Police Organisations*, Kolkata: Allied Publishers.

Pai, P.V.A. 1978, *Bureaucracy and Development Administration*, New Delhi: Centre for Policy Research.

Rao, C.H.H. 2000, "Declining Demand for Grains in Rural India: Causes and Implications", *Economic and Political Weekly*, January 2.

Ravi, C. 2000, *Complete Demand Systems, Welfare and Nutrition: An Application to Indian Consumption Data*, Hyderabad: Centre for Economic and Social Studies.

Sharma, O.P. 1983, *Development Bureaucracy*, New Delhi: Oxford & IBH.

Sirsikar, V.M. 1970, *The Rural Elite in a Developing Society*, Bombay: Orient Longman.

Smelser, N.J. 1959, *Social Change in Industrial Revolution*, Chicago: University of Chicago Press.

Stokes, E. 1980, *The Peasant and the Raj*, New Delhi: S. Chand and Co. Ltd.

Weber, M. 1930, *The Protestant Ethic and the Spirit of Capitalism*, London: Allen and Unwin Ltd.

11

Commercial Banking, Peasants and Workers in a Western UP Village

Jagdish Kumar Pundir

New economic plans for the development of weaker sections of society have been implemented in the villages in India for quite sometime. The existing social structure of the village community provides the field for the operation of new measures like land distribution among landless labourers, new methods of agriculture and loan through commercial banks for various schemes. A commercial bank is a bureaucratic rational organisation and its facilitates were extended for the first time to the rural illiterate poor. For credit requirements the poor cultivators and the landless villagers were traditionally dependent on money-lenders, and Jagirdars (Mahabal, 1975) rich peasants-cum-moneylenders Jagirdars (Chauhan, 1967). These moneylenders used to charge exorbitant rates of interest from the borrowers. Such interest rates acted as hindrants in the development projects of the weaker sections of society and they remained in debt-bondage to the money-lenders. As a state policy banks were nationalised in order to extend the formal institutional lending at subsidised rates to the development of weaker sections of the society. It is considered that these formal lending institutions will act as functional alternatives (Merton, 1968) to the traditional moneylenders and fulfil the indispensable credit requirements of the poor cultivators and the weaker sections of society for their self employment schemes. How the existing traditional social structural components and the new institutional arrangements will work together, i.e., who will negotiate between the formal money lending institution and the illiterate poor in fulfilling the requisite formalities and who will act as mediators and with what interests? What are the earlier experiences of the people relating to credit and organisation of public activities in the village? How far the loans from commercial banks are complimentary to the existing traditional pattern and how far they act at cross purposes? To whom do the banks actually provide loans and what are its consequences on the economic status of the beneficiaries? These questions need a systematic study by the students of social sciences. The present paper makes an endeavour to comprehend these questions with reference to the loans given to the poor peasants and workers in village Kotana (district Meerut) by a commercial bank in 1976 for the first time in the history of banking in India. The paper, hereafter has been divided into three parts: (i) introduction to the village with some earlier experiences, (ii) new credit institutions (banks) and the process of lending, and (iii) analytical questions involved in it.

The Village

Village Kotana is situated on the eastern bank of river Yamuna in Meerut district, about 60 km west of Meerut city and some 50 km north of Delhi. The village is approachable through a link road from a nearby town, Baraut, which is 10 km from the village in the east, situated on the Delhi-Saharanpur Road. It is a multi-caste village which consists of 35 different Hindu and Muslim castes. All of them have them have their own traditional status in the caste hierarchy in the village social structure.

Since the emergence of Statutory Village Panchayat, the *Pradhans* have always been drawn from the upper social strata. In the first election in 1952, a Tyagi became *Pradhan* (is a local terminology for President of Statutory Village Panchayat) of the Village Panchayat, from 1957, he was succeeded by a Jain from 1957–1962. In 1962, a Rohella (Pathan) became the President of the Village Panchayat and continued till 1972. Again, in 1972, the Jain who worked as *Pradhan* till 1962 won the Village Panchayat election and became its President. The village could also participate in the block level politics as the first Tyagi *Pradhan* became *Up-Pramukh* of Baraut block. One person from scheduled castes was elected to the position of *Up-Pradhan*

(Vice-President) for two years. This person contacted the police and the leaders outside in order to resolve a dispute between the Harijans and the lower castes' persons from Muslims. Thus, his activities also indicate village outward contacts.

A few villagers migrated to the nearby towns, a little more than fifty years ago in the developing stage of the village. Three sons of the present *Pradhan* migrated to Kanpur, Delhi and Baraut, in order to pursue their business activities. The son, who has work in Baraut, commutes daily from the village to Baraut to look after his business activities and the other two sons visit the village occasionally. A few others commute for small business and services to the nearby villages, towns and cities. The village is located at the border of Haryana and the villagers have business contacts, kinship ties and exposure to events in the nearby villages located in the state of Haryana. Of the seven doctors extending medical facilities to the village, six belong to the villages located at a distance of three to twenty three km from the village under study. Only one doctor is a resident of the village, but he has also migrated with his family to Baraut. He visits the village daily and extends medical services to the inhabitants of the village. Thus, the village is connected with the nearby villages, towns and cities in day to day life.

Land consolidation was carried out in 1962 in the village. Land consolidation has promoted intensive double cropping and mechanisation and created a need for more capital investment in agriculture. Along with agriculture, 'Palej' (vegetables grown in the river basin) has also created a need for credit. Earlier, in the village, professional moneylenders, agriculturists and traders provided some credit facilities to the needy villagers. The villagers in need of credit also approached the rich peasants-cum-moneylenders of the neighbouring villages. Among the new institutional arrangements in the village, loans are being provided through CDP since 1958. The Credit Cooperative Society worked from 1964, as did the Land Development Bank. The Credit Cooperative Society worked upto 1974 and then lapsed. In the mean time, the commercial banks issued two big loans of ₹ 20,000 and ₹ 1,50,000 for the purchase of tractors in 1969 and 1972 and both the loans were repaid by 1976.

Since 1976, a commercial bank, under the state directive, has extended its credit facilities on easy terms with a lower rate of interest, with subsidy to the marginal cultivators, landless labourers and scheduled castes, not only for their self-employment but also to relieve them apparently from the clutches of moneylenders.

New Credit Institution and Process of Lending

A commercial bank, the 'lead bank' in Meerut district, namely, the Syndicate Bank established its branch office at Baraut in 1976 in order to serve, on priority, seven villages in Baraut development block with the consensus of the Block Development Officer (BDO). Kotana was one among the selected seven villages by the bank branch at Baraut. The bank started giving loans for dairy farming (purchase of buffaloes), and self-employment projects in 1976 on priority under the Central Government directives. This was known as priority sector as directed by the state policy. The process of commercial bank officials reaching the landless poor for the first time is comprehended in the next para.

With the help of its branch field officer the bank officials invited potential beneficiaries from the weaker sections of the village and also contacted these people in the village itself in an open meeting. On the other hand, the villagers also received information about loans through the mass media as well as from the leading persons of the village. The whole process of getting a loan from the bank involved a number of formalities that could be translated into action at the village level, through the steps observed and narrated by recipients and other knowledgeable persons. It may now be visualised as follows:

(i) Information reached the villagers through the elite, consisting of scheduled castes and non-scheduled castes.

(ii) The field officer of the bank branch visited the village and told the villagers about the purpose of holding an open meeting in the village in which the Branch Manager of the bank was also present, along with the BDO (the meeting was held in the last week of June 1976).

(iii) Aggregation of the demands of the people from among the weaker sections of society was put in place and the filling of application forms for loan was also carried out in June 1976.

(iv) Savings accounts were opened, for the persons selected in the programme in the bank's branch at Baraut.

(v) Collection of clearance certificates of "no loans to be paid to the other formal credit agencies existing in the area" and submission of these to the bank officer.

(vi) The bank authorities sanctioned the loan amount promptly (under state pressure).
(vii) The bank issued cheques to villagers on 1 July 1976 for the purchase of pigs, buffaloes and cycle rickshaws.
(viii) The recipients of the loans deposited the cheques against the savings accounts and received cash from the bank.
(ix) The recipients were given two weeks time to use the money for the purchase of the demanded productive asset.
(x) The "purchase of asset" receipt was to be submitted in July 1976.
(xi) The field officer of the bank cross-checked at the residence of each one of the recipients, whether the recipient actually purchased item, or not, in July 1976.
(xii) In the presence of the field officer, the veterinary doctor working at the development block level, counted and certified the number of animals purchased.

Later on, in a longitudinal study, these 12 steps were found to be 14 in completing a cycle of the loan from getting information about the facility of the loan to its repayment and getting benefits of subsidy and claiming a differential rate of interest in between the cycle (Pundir, 1998).

The details of the recipients of loans and purpose of borrowing along with their social categories are presented in a tabular form below:

Table 1

Loans Provided to Different Social Categories and the Purposes by the Syndicate Bank (Baraut Branch) in Village Kotana in 1976

Social Group	*Purpose*					
	Rickshaw	*Piggery*	*Milch Cattle*	*Fertilisers*	*Others*	*Total*
Harijans (Chamar and Valmiki)	—	3	38	—	—	41
Lower Muslim	1	—	3	—	—	4
Lower Hindu	—	—	1	—	—	1
Other Farmers (Hindu and Muslim)	—	—	—	4	3	7
Total	1	3	42	4	3	53
Loan/item (₹)	1,000	1,000	2,000	1,500	3,300	—
Total Sum (₹)	1,000	3,000	84,000	6,000	9,900	1,03,900

*The number of cases in each category (purpose) were specified from the ledger of bank's branch office at Baraut.

Analysis of data in the Table 1 reveals that 53 recipients received loans from formal lending agency, for the purchase of milch cattle (42), fertilisers (4), pigs (3), installation of *gobar* gas plants (3) and purchase of cycle rickshaw (1). Most of the beneficiaries belonged to the categories of Harijans (Valmiki and Chamar) (41), followed by marginal landowners of OBC (7), lower category persons from Muslims (4) and finally lower caste Hindu (1). These 53 recipients received a total sum of ₹ 1,03,900. The highest loan amount per item was given for the installation of *gobar* gas plant (₹ 3,300 per unit), followed by the purchase of milch cattle (₹ 2,000 per cattle), purchase of fertilisers (₹ 1,500 per recipient) and for cycle rickshaw and pigs (₹ 1,000 per unit). In addition to the above loan cases earlier some loans for *gobar* gas plants had been given before June 1976 and for fertilisers to farmers with good landholding in July and November 1976.

The recipients of loans have different sizes of landholdings that have been depicted in the Table 2.

Table 2

Landholdings of the Recipients of Loan by Syndicate Bank in Village Kotana in 1976

Land Holding (bighas)	*Social Group*				
	Harijans (Chamar and Valmiki)	*Lower Muslim*	*Lower Hindu*	*Higher Hindus and Muslims*	*Total*
Nil	21	1	—	—	22
0 to 7.5*	6	—	1	—	7
8 to 15	12	—	—	—	12
16 to 30	2	3	—	—	5
More than 30	—	—	—	7	7
Total	41	4	1	7	53

*Bigha is a local unit for measurement of land. One acre consists of 5.45 bighas, i.e., 4,840 square yards.

The table reveals that most of the beneficiaries from each caste or social category are differentiated in terms of ownership of land. Most of the beneficiaries are either landless (22) followed by owners of less than 2.75 acres (19) and owners of more than 2.75 acres (12). The landless beneficiaries mainly belonged to the categories of Harijan (22) and lower Muslim (1). Owners of less than 2.75 acres mainly belonged to Harijans (18) and lower Hindu caste (1). Owners of more than 2.75

acres mainly belonged to the categories of higher caste Hindus and Muslims (7) lower Muslims (3) and Harijans (2).

Every recipient of loan, according to bank rules, had to arrange two guarantors. In the case of identifying the caste identity of guarantors, at the first names of the guarantors were noted from the ledger of the bank office. Then, castes were identified during interviews with a dozen persons from the village (recipients and non-recipients) and with the help of the village level worker (VLW). The caste background of the guarantors is presented in Table 3.

Table 3

The Guarantors of the Recipients of Loan Among Different Social Groups (two in each case) in Village Kotana in 1976

Recipients	*Guarantors*							
	Brahmin	*Tyagi*	*Jain*	*Pathan*	*Shekh*	*Harijans (Chamar and Valmiki)*	*Other*	*Total*
Harijan (41)	4	22	16	6	3	30	1	82
Lower Hindu (1)	—	—	1	—	—	—	1	2
Lower Muslim (4)	—	2	1	1	1	1	2	8
Other farmers (7)	—	8	—	1	1	—	4	14
Total (53)	4	32	18	8	5	31	8	106

Analysis of the above table reveals that the Harijans received large segment of guarantors from their own caste members (30), Tyagis (22) and Jain (16). A few Brahmins (4) also provided guarantee for Harijans. Other beneficiaries received guarantors from a mixed lot of castes.

The names of the persons came to light frequently as guarantors. The village school Headmaster, a Tyagi, in 14 cases, the Jain present *Pradhan* of the Statutory Village Panchayat *Pradhan's* son guaranteed in 11 cases, his father (the present *Pradhan*) and the first former *Pradhan* of the village the Tyagi acted as guarantor in nine cases each, the former *Pradhans*, Pathan and Tyagi in seven cases each, one Brahmin and another Tyagi in four cases each. A Chamar in four cases and another in three cases provided guarantee to the beneficiaries. These persons extended their help as guarantors to the beneficiaries from the new institution and they are part of the process of taking loan.

There are 150 households of Harijans (Chamar and Valmiki) in the village, out of them 41 could avail loans from the formal lending agency, the bank. Persons from other lower castes like Jinwar (waterman), Khateek and Kasai (butcher), Teli (oil presser), Mallah (boat man), etc., are also poor but they did not receive credit from the new institution. They constitute hundreds of households. All these have been untouched so far from the facilities of credit extended by the new institution for the weaker sections of society.

Analytical Questions Involved in the Process

The social structure of the village along with the historical experiences, particularly of the political and economic aspects of rural life, provide the setting within which the new institution operates in the village scene. This raises some issues for analytical treatment.

Among the Harijans (Chamar and Valmiki) very few could get benefits from the new institution. Households of other weaker sections of the village, e.g., Jhinwar, Khateek, Kasai, Mallah and others also could not receive credit from the bank. Besides this, the benefits were limited to a fewer households as, at least in three cases two members of a family got separate loans, and three members in one household benefitted from the programme. Thus, the total number of households that received benefits from the bank is only 36, though the beneficiaries are 41 in the case of scheduled castes. On the basis of the available facts some of the causes for the limited success of the programme may be identified as follows:

1. Some of them did not feel the necessity of a loan at all.
2. Some might have lagged behind in getting appropriate information well in time and thus failed in completing the formalities in availing loan.
3. Some failed to have two ensured guarantors.
4. Some others could not get the certificates verified within the stipulated time.
5. Some others might have been afraid of their earlier experiences with the credit cooperative society that failed. Another instance of an informal organisation in which two leading men from the scheduled castes collected money to deposit the shares for getting further loan from a new society but they did not get anything, not even their own deposited share of money, could have been one of the reasons.
6. Some of the villagers could have been afraid of getting a large amount of money because it was the first agency in their life time

providing such a large amount as loan, much above their standard of living and expectations and past experiences.

7. Taking a loan from a formal lending agency is a public event, involving many formalities in a written form while borrowing money from a traditional money lender is a private and personal matter. The borrowing loan as a public event reduces the honour, prestige and status of the borrower in the village.

Taking loans from a commercial bank is a complex process that results in discomfort to the illiterate borrowers at some stage. So, they may quit the borrowing process. To avail loans at lower rates of interest and also get a subsidy certain formalities are required such as taking an application form from the District Harijan Social Welfare Office, getting it certified by the Tahsildar, and submitting to the bank office every month paying of the instalments. Both the places the bank office and the revenue office, are located far away from the village. This involves time, knowledge and the experience of contacting officials. Nobody had done it up to November 1976 that is even after five months after the launching of the scheme. In the entire process, they are required to leave their work and this also has its own cost. So, if all this is counted, then the earlier informal arrangements might have been compared with the new one which might have led to their decision not to enter the new complex process till November 1976.

The process of taking loans from traditional moneylenders has been compared with the process of taking loans from the formal lending agencies such as banks. The comparison reveals that:

1. In both the situations the peasants and labourers seek help from economically dominant social groups mainly belonging to the upper castes. Out of 106 guarantors for 53 beneficiaries from the bank, 68 guarantors belong to economically and socially well-to-do category revealing that the beneficiaries are dependent on the goodwill of the dominant category.
2. A new social group of leaders has emerged from among lower castes peasants and labourers which has received more benefits than the ordinary rural poor of their own caste category.
3. The new facilities involve not only a very long procedure but also structural constraints. To overcome the constraints, the lower group seeks help from the higher social groups and pay the price for it, whether formal or informal, economic or political. Besides this, the process of taking a loan goes on for a long duration and so

is expensive in terms of time and travel to the offices located in the towns. So the recipient has to evaluate the relative cost of taking loans from banks and traditional moneylenders.

These are some of the salient features that emerge from the empirical experiences at the very first phase of the entry of a new credit institution under state policy. More intensive village studies are needed in this area to indicate the quality and direction of change. Though it is difficult to get the information from the moneylenders about the amount of money lent and the rates of interest (Srinivas, 1976; Dube, 1955), fresh efforts by the recipients may be attempted and social relations involved in economic activities may be identified. Such further research would partly contribute to an understanding of socio-economic processes involved in the new economic activities being implemented in the rural areas through formal agencies.

References

Chauhan, B.R. 1967, *A Rajasthan Village*, Delhi: Veer Publishing House.

Dube, S.C. 1955, *Indian Village*, London: Kegan Paul and Routledge.

Mahabal, S.B. 1975, "Cooperation", in *A Survey of Research in Economics, ICSSR*, Bombay: Allied.

Mandelbaum, D.G. 1969, "Technology Credit and Culture Change in a Niligiri Village", in M.N. Srinivas (ed.), *India's Villages*, Calcutta: Asia Publishing House.

Merton, R.K. 1968, *Social Theory and Social Structure*, New Delhi: Amerind.

Srinivas, M.N. 1976, *The Remembered Village*, Bombay: Oxford University Press.

12

Nirmal Gram in Rajasthan

A Successful Intervention in a Low Priority Area of Development

Arun Chauhan

The need and feasibility of planned programmes for sanitation have national and international dimensions and their execution at the rural level in Rajasthan can best be gauged through a look at the macro picture of sanitation – access to toilet facilities. A majority of India's population not only does not have access to toilet facilities in its dwelling but also lacks sanitation facilities for the disposal of waste water. Apart from the non-availability of safe drinking water, lack of sanitation, particularly the absence sewage and disposal of solid waste, including night soil, have been observed as the main reasons for prevailing ill-health and high morbidity levels in the country. As per the 1991 Census, less than one-fourth of the households in the country had toilet facilities within the premises of their residence; the proportion was less than 10 per cent for rural households and around 64 per cent for urban households. There are significant inter-state variations in access to toilet facilities. Among the major states, at one end, in Kerala, 51 per cent of the households had access to toilet facilities and at the other end less than 10 per cent in Orissa had such an access. The percentage was higher in Delhi, Tripura, Mizoram, Chandigarh and Lakshadweep. For the most populated states in the country, including, Bihar, Uttar Pradesh, Madhya Pradesh and Rajasthan, the proportion was well below 20 per cent. Even in relatively developed states such as

Gujarat and Maharashtra, the proportion of households with access to toilet facilities was around 30 per cent. In all states, the proportion was significantly lower for rural areas in comparison to urban areas. Among the various population segments, access to toilet facilities for scheduled castes and scheduled tribes households was lower than that of other households in almost all the states. NFHS-II also provides data on access to toilet facilities. As per the survey, 64 per cent of the households in the country had no access to toilet facilities in 1998–99 in comparison to 76 per cent in 1991 as reported by the Census. Less than one-fifth of rural households and over four-fifth of urban households had access to such facilities. At the state level, the data indicate that the proportion of households having access to toilet facilities, in less than national average in larger, more populated and poorer states, such as Bihar, Madhya Pradesh, Orissa, Rajasthan and Uttar Pradesh. Among the smaller states only Himachal Pradesh followed this pattern. In Kerala, the proportion of households with access to such facilities was at 85 per cent, which was much above the national average of 36 per cent. For the majority, the problem of sanitation, at the household level, is essentially of awareness and education and not really dependent on the resources. The resources, technology and management aspects of the problem are important, and more so in the context of urban sanitation and solid waste management. Many cities and small towns generate more solid wastes than they can be possibly collected or disposed of under present institutional arrangements.

A major problem in urban solid waste management relates to sewage disposal as a large number of towns is without sewage system and others have inadequate and often malfunctioning systems. The threat to the availability of safe drinking water is quite serious in most urban areas in the country. The Government of India has drawn up a scheme for making a few villages models of cleanliness. It has laid down guidelines for the states for the villages that are to be selected. The schools in these villages need to have public facilities, like arrangements for clean water; streets and lanes have to be clean and not used for defecation. Water resources, in the form of handpumps, have to be managed in such a way that there is no waterlogging. Drainage has to be provided. The greatest stress is on every household having its own lavatory. A village able to develop to such an extent is subject to monitoring by the State Government which is under scrutiny by the

Central Government in order to be declared a 'Nirmal Gram Panchayat'. The unit of action has to be the Gram Panchayat (GP) which may cover a number of villages.

The guidelines have been received by the State Government of Rajasthan, which has selected a few districts, newly created, for putting the scheme into practice. Rajsamand district has been selected as one of them. The district is partly hilly and partly plain. The hilly region has the famous fort of Kumbhalgarh situated above 1,000 metres from the sea level. The development block of Kumbhalgarh has been selected for implementing the scheme. The total number of households in Kumbhalgarh block (as per 2001 Census) is 28,884; households having sanitation facilities are 2,158 in number and the number of households not having sanitation facilities is 26,726. A search has been carried on for the village where the new programme can be concentrated upon. Village Taladari happens to have caught the attention of the district authorities. The nature of the GP and its initial experiences need to be reviewed. The village is what sociologists call a dispersed village as distinguished from a nucleated village. The GP is composed of five revenue villages located in the hilly region. The actual households are further dispersed in the smaller hamlets. The position of the GP chairperson has been reserved for an OBC woman. The OBC have a limited number of households. The GP is preponderantly populated by the Bhil tribe, which comes under the category of scheduled tribes. As many as six out of 11 ward *Panchas* come from this group, with one each from the SC and OBC categories and the remaining three from the general section. The agricultural section is represented by people from a comparatively lower status group among the Rajputs, who cultivate the land themselves. The population of the village selected for the purpose of development has been classified into two categories: the BPL (below poverty line) having 318 households and the APL (above poverty line) having 383 households. In social terms, it is convenient to classify the population into the categories of the Scheduled Tribes (STs), the Scheduled Castes (SCs), Other Backward Classes (OBCs) and the general population. The GP has five primary schools that had started as Rajiv Gandhi Pathshalas for promoting literacy and later promoted to the status of regular primary schools. The GP with limited OBC population made it easy for the villagers to unanimously elect one female as *Sarpanch* and ward panchas were also similarly chosen. This achievement of the villagers caught the attention of the district authorities, who began to view it as a possible candidate for promoting the

'Nirmal Gram' project. Secondly, the Gram Panchayat took an initiative in making some of the BPL families willing to construct lavatories in their houses facilitated by some grant for Total Sanitation Campaign (TSC) project for the purpose. At the block level, a mini Secretariat was formed through which different departments of the district operated. The initial success of the first phase of the development was also noticed and needs some attention in a separate section.

UNICEF has initiated a pilot scheme in the district in seventy Gram Panchayats in the seven blocks of the district, i.e., ten Gram Panchayats in every block. At district level, a committee was formed, the *Pramukh* of the Zila Parishad being the Chairman. The committee consists of the District Collector, the Chief Executive Officer, Zila Parishad, a UNICEF representative, the Additional Chief Executive Officer, Zila Parishad, the Chief Medical and Health Officer, the Executive Engineer of Public Health and Engineering Department, the District Education Officer, the Deputy Director ICDS, the District Support Unit (District Coordinator, computer assistant) and all implementing partners and block coordinators. Regular monthly meetings were held at the district level. At the block level, regular monthly meetings with the implementing partners and grassroot level workers called animators or motivators was organised by the implementing agency. The members of the district support unit participated at these meetings. A monitoring format was developed through which information followed from each household to village and from village to panchayat and from panchayat to block and from block to district. Thus, it created a regular framework for monitoring the project. Here, it may be noted that the *Zila Pramukh* (women) attended all the district level meetings, except one or two. Regular field visits were undertaken by various officials from the district and block level officials, reviewing other development programmes, and water and sanitation programme too became a routine agenda along with others. The district showed a way where a low priority programme became a part of the regular monitoring process and acquired a position in the agenda of regular development progress meetings.

The Zila Parishad took a decision in the general house meeting that the water and sanitation programme would be implemented together; by this time the district was selected to implement Sector

Reform Pilot Scheme and Total Sanitation Campaign (TSC). The earlier framework formed during the implementing of a UNICEF supported project, showed a further way to implement the two pilot schemes in the district. Thus, the district was much ahead of other districts in the state as it had a structured framework for implementation, a strong committed will of public representatives at the district, and trained professionals available in the district to help in the timely implementation of the pilot schemes. It is important to note these aspects because it took two to three years during the UNICEF supported project to create a suitable environment to implement the water and sanitation project. It is a combination of various departments, at the district and block levels, which generates an environment to initiate the low priority programme in villages. An atmosphere was created at all levels of the Panchayati Raj system where villagers, public representatives, NGOs and government officials started a dialogue on these issues and began implementing them at the grassroots level.

At the second stage the non-government organisations (NGOs) and its advisors stepped in, the advisor has the experience of working at the district level and had practical knowledge of how funds allocated for one programme could, under certain conditions, be transferred to the other departments. The initial programme was run by the PHED, the adviser and the NGO prevailed on the administration that basically the programme was one of the changes in human behaviour and this broader goal was a part of the literacy mission. So, it should be possible for the literacy mission to adopt the programme as its own. Looking at the possibilities of realising its objective at the ground level, the literacy mission agreed and all the schools were taken up for proper sanitation and water facilities, along with stress on clean campus. All the teachers became part of the programme and students carried the message to their homes.

A week-long census of all houses was conducted in December 2005 to assess the status of the work done in the first phase and three classifications emerged: (i) households that had accepted the sanitation programme fully, (ii) households that had begun construction partly, and (iii) households that remained beyond this programme. The first two categories represented the section of the population that had been approached by the programme. It is interesting to note that nearly two-thirds of the below poverty line (BPL) families, had been covered by December 2005 and only one sixth of the above poverty line (APL) families had responded to it. Initially, three difficulties had to be overcome. The GP mainly consisted of the tribal population; literacy among women was nominal, the project involved a change in attitudes and behaviour; and the sanitary programme was a low priority item in planning for development. These roadblocks needed special efforts to overcome through some thoughtful planning in which the villagers and the NGOs were assisted by the state representatives of the UNICEF, the Panchayati Raj Department, and the PHED.

The new players and stakeholders

The next step was to convince the elected members of the GP to instal sanitary facilities in their households so that they could become a positive reference group for others. At this stage intensive contacts with the villagers were organised through meetings and enactment of short plays in the night in every part of the village. A drama unit with five actors was set up in the village. Boys from among the tribals were added to the group so that they could carry the message forward in peoples' own dialect and local idioms to great effect. This drama unit wholly consisted of tribal BPL members. The musical equipments and the sound system plus others accessories were funded by the DPIP programme. The unit received quite a few invitations to perform in different districts of the state. The technical and human aspects of the problem were clarified at these meetings by persons who had district level experiences; once again the main thrust was given to the remaining BPL families. When the BPL families adopted the scheme, it was simpler to convince the APL families to join it as well. Thus, by stages, the entire GP was covered by the programme, by the end of October 2006. The district authorities informed the State Government of the progress. The GP became a strong candidate for Nirmala Gram Panchayat (NGP), the state in its turn informed the ministry in Government of India and its visiting team confirmed the award. The GP was formally declared a NGP and awarded a prize of ₹ 2 lakh from the Central Government besides ₹ 1 lakh from the State Government. These would be further used for development of sanitation related activities. The continuity of an innovation in the health sector had its own problems. Two steps were devised for the same: (i) should any family be found defecating in the open, it could be subjected to social pressure; and social relations with the family are curtailed. Secondly, a rule was adopted that anyone breaking the norm could be fined upto

₹ 250. Such public pressure and regulations provided norms for ensuring that the change in behaviour continued among the members of the GP. The GP, by now, had acquired the name at the state and national level and begun to receive a number of visitors. These visits added to the prestige of the village as the villagers were keen to maintain that honour.

Part III

Changing Political Scenario

13

Nature of Power Transfer through Panchayat

A Study of Four Panchayats in Rajasthan

Shashi Bhushan Singh

In sociological enquiries most of the intensive studies have neglected the comprehension of functioning of panchayats as, in most cases, the Statutory Village Panchayat is comprised of more than one village. Wherever sociologists studied panchayat, it was by default, as the *Sarpanch* (president) was from the same village, which has been studied by anthropologists or their village had been selected in such a way that the locus of traditional and modern bases of power can be compared and the former's impact on the power relations in the village can be comprehended. Besides this, in the everyday life of the villages, traditional institutions continue to be relevant, and their presence has been more visible than that of the modern political institutions. Moreover, sociology as a discipline is interested in what holds society together, and what persists over time. This brings a more intense focus on the relevance of traditional institutions in the modern order. There is also a question of prestige in which, for a group of sociologists, talking about state and political parties is considered more prestigious than talking about panchayats.

In recent times, most of the literature on Panchayati Raj has been about its role in empowerment and development, in general, and the inclusion of traditionally excluded communities such as SCs, STs, and women, in the local power structure, in particular. Though there is a bourgeoning literature on the exclusion of those who are marginalised from the Panchayati Raj system, the complex processes that are responsible for the exclusion and marginalisation have not been properly captured. A panchayat operates in a very complex social, economic and political environment. The relations between various institutions can only be comprehended by staying within a community for a longer period of time. Moreover, as Foucault says, the real nature of power can be understood only at the micro-level and an intensive study of a panchayat provides the ideal site to understand the nature of social power. Thus, the intensive study of a village contributes in more than one way in understanding various aspects of a panchayat and the complex nature of power relations. The data for this study has been collected through participant observation method by staying within a community for over a year. The paper heavily banks upon the events occurring in one particular panchayat – Sakroda. In order to understand the complex relations, of the panchayat with numerous other institutions, data from other three panchayats, Zilla Parishad, and Panchayat Samiti have been collected and analysed.

General Characteristics of the Area

Ecology and Economy

The study area covers the Rajsamand tehsil of Rajsamand district in Rajasthan. The area is mountainous, so human settlement is dispersed. The villages are named after the *bhagals* (hamlets) which are small and generally inhabited by single castes. The main settlement is the centre of social, economic, political and cultural activities. All the government buildings; schools, hospitals, and panchayat headquarters are located in the main settlement. This gives the main settlement a decisive say in panchayat affairs. The general nature of the main village is that it has control over most of the arable land. This brings the labour class into the main village to work on the agricultural fields. Other castes provide secular as well as ritual services to the inhabitants of the main village. Thus, the dominant caste of the village has the maximum number of votes in its hand as it also controls the votes of the non-dominant segments of population. The region is predominantly dependent on agricultural occupations. In course of time, agriculture has not been able to support the economic needs of the people. People migrated to other places, particularly to urban areas, in search for livelihood. This has implications for economic dominance and power.

Social Structure

In the social structure, caste plays an important role in social interaction among different castes. Even in most of the state's development schemes, caste plays an important role in the selection of beneficiaries and allocation of developmental schemes. There are other elements of social structure, such as gender and class that still operate within the framework of the caste structure. Broadly, the society is divided into four caste categories: upper castes, backward castes, scheduled castes, and scheduled tribes.

Upper Castes

(a) Brahmins: Brahmins constitute a sizeable section of the population. Paliwals are the most dominant Brahmins in the area. They are educated and also have government jobs. Though they are politically with the Congress party as a whole, some of them are also with the BJP due to local compulsion and rivalry. The longest serving Chief Minister of Rajasthan, Mohanlal Sukhadia, a Brahmin, hailed from the area. Even now two important Congress activists C.P. Joshi and Girija Vyas (both Brahmins) are from this area. This has made the Brahmins very powerful in the political circle.

(b) Rajputs: The Rajputs are categorised in to her main categories on the basis of status, power and wealth. Chauhan, Sisodia and Rathore lineages are higher in status, whereas Kharwar and Bhatti lineages are lower in status. The Rajputs control the majority of land in some villages. Politically they are with the opposition BJP, but again due to local level political compulsions some are with the Congress Party. Their power is basically derived from the fact that they were the erstwhile rulers in the state, and lower castes still respect them.

(c) Mahajans: They are of two categories: Hindu and Jain. Since they are engaged in similar occupations, they are treated as one by others. Earlier, most of them were with the Congress but now almost half of them are supporting BJP. A very important Congressman, Gunsagar Karnawat, a Mahajan, is from the area.

Other Backward Castes

(a) Gurjars: Among the OBCs the Gurjars are numerically preponderant in this area. They are mostly involved in agricultural and pastoral work; a few of them are also involved in trade and business. They are well-represented in local level political institutions, but in spite of being numerically dominant; they are conspicuously absent in the tehsil level politics.

(b) Jats: They are numerically in a minority in this area and are present only in Piparda Gram Panchayat. They are mainly dependent on agriculture and support the Congress party.

(c) MBCs: There are many castes where the poor and weak have been clubbed with the OBCs for government welfare schemes. These MBCs, have not been categorised in the constitution, but within OBCs these castes are not on par with the dominant OBC in almost all spheres.

Scheduled Castes

(a) Khatiks: Khatiks are the most dominant among the SCs. Their main occupation is trading in goats. With the increase in urban population, the business has become profitable in recent times and some of them have become very rich. They have used their newly acquired wealth to enhance their political power. However, in social affairs, their status has not improved in correspondence to their economic and political clout. This has led to a mismatch between their enhanced economic status and stigmatised social status and also between their status and role. This has made them frustrated and politics has become the only arena for them to vent their anger against other communities.

(b) Other SCs: Bhambi, Balai and Bunkar are poor and they do not count much in the power structure, except when a seat is reserved for the SCs.

The Scheduled Tribes

Bhils: They are the main scheduled tribe (ST) community in the area. They comprise around 25 per cent of the population. They are landless and poor, and earn their livelihood by working as labourers. But, they are numerically preponderant. When a particular seat in the panchayat is reserved for STs, Bhils become the natural beneficiaries of the state's measures.

Political Structure

It is important to give a brief description of the Panchayati Raj structures. Technically, the Panchayati Raj Institutions (PRIs) are a part of the state but they have a different meaning for the local people. There are various reasons for this. These institutions are directly managed by the local people, whereas, the other organs of the state are indirectly controlled by them through their representatives. PRIs are related to the community as well as political parties in deeper ways. Many times, PRIs are seen in opposition to indirect democracy and as institution of participatory development. In the state, the Panchayati Raj has a three-tier structure. The lowest level is called

Gram Panchayat, which is composed of one village or more depending upon the population of the villages. The Gram Panchayat is divided into wards and every ward has one ward *Panch*. The Gram Panchayat is headed by a *Sarpanch* who is directly elected by the people. The secretary of the Gram Panchayat is a government official and is called Gram Sevak, also known as 'Sathiji' among people. The local level developmental programmes are handled by the Gram Panchayat. The Gram Sabha passes a proposal and it is sent to Panchayat Samiti for approval. There are many other institutions which function in the village, such as the watershed developmental programme, but the Gram Panchayat can call the committee members and ask for any information. In Gram Sabha meetings, all the officials have to be present. The important thing is that, due to reservation policy, people from weaker sections of society, including women, have got a voice in public places. Another important thing is that there is rotation for the reservation of seats in Gram Panchayat, where a seat is reserved for a particular social group, and the next time it passes to another social group. The Gram Panchayat members meet twice in a month at the Gram Panchayat headquarters to take stock of the situation. Anybody from the Gram Panchayat can go there with his or her grievances.

The nature of political process in the area is being examined, since it has bearing upon panchayat politics. There are two main political groupings in the area – Congress and the BJP, other parties either have marginal presence or are non-existent. To understand the dynamics of local politics, which is now tightly integrated with the higher level political processes, some general observations are necessary. First, from the 1970s onwards, more and more castes have experienced horizontal mobilisation in political affairs, leading to the breakdown of patron-client relations which were hallmarks of local village politics. The most important institution through which the lower castes have fulfiled their political ambition of capturing local level political institutions has been through Panchayati Raj. Thus, almost all the panchayats have seen the rise and fall of different social classes and castes. Secondly, depending upon the context and local political configurations, each political party has its supporters from all castes. Still the majority of Brahmins is with Congress and that of Rajputs with BJP. This has implications for both party and panchayat in the region. In the majority of cases the panchayat faction in the village follows the party faction, but in many other cases the panchayat factions have defied the party faction. This relation has upset both the higher level party as well as panchayat politics. Thirdly, before the 73rd amendment to the Constitution, the

Table 1

Gram Panchayats in History

Panchayat	Village	Upper Castes			OBCs		SCs		STs	
		Brahmins	Mahajans	Rajputs	Gurjars	Other	Khatiks	Others	Bhils	Others
Sakroda	Sakroda	4	10	41	140	—	25	28	40	—
	Poonawali	35	—	—	—	—	—	10	25	—
	Tarot	5	—	—	10	—	—	10	15	—
	Nada	—	—	25	—	—	—	10	5	—
	Total	44	10	66	150	—	25	58	85	
Sundarcha	Sundarcha	95	—	—	56	—	—	—	100	
	D-Kheda	—	—	—	96	—	—	—	—	
	Depty	46	—	—	—	—	—	—	26	
	Dewathari	10	—	—	—	45	—	—	22	
	T-Khurd	12	—	—	—	—	—	—	25	
	Dobar	—	12	16	—	—	—	—	55	
	Total	163	12	16	152	45	—	—	228	
Farara	Farara	4	—	220	20	17		60	75	
	K-Guda	25	10	5	—	—	—	—	—	

Cont'd...

...Cont'd

	Dhanmal	15	—	—	50	2	—	—	—
	Total	44	10	225	70	19		60	75
Piparda	Piparda	35	—	154	72	76	97	54	76
	Shankarpura	—	—	20	—	—	—	—	—
	Total	35	—	174	72	76	97	54	76

(The table gives a description of the different caste groups in Panchayats. Those castes whose numerical strength is small, and who do not matter much in the panchayat politics, have been clubbed under 'others'. The number of households of different castes is not the representative of their votes, as the households of lower castes contain fewer members than those of the upper castes. It is true that all the members of a particular caste do not vote for a single candidate, but most of the times they vote for a candidate of their caste, if the candidate is capable of winning. Because of moral pressure from the caste, men force their rivals to come to some compromise formula. Then even if some members of a caste 'cross over' to other groups, a similar thing happens in the rival caste also, and this neutralises former advantage).

Sarpanch used to play an important role in the election of the *Pradhan*. In the Congress party, there are two groups vying for the post of *Pradhan* – Gunsagar Karnawat, and Raghubir Singh Rathore. Both have been trying to bring as many of their supporters as possible to the Panchayat Samiti level. This has implications for panchayat politics at the village level as well.

Sakroda Panchayat

Sakroda and Poonawali are the two villages in the Sakroda Panchayat. Sakroda is a bigger village. Immediately after independence, the dominance of the Rajputs in the village affairs of Sakroda continued. In the panchayat elections, the villagers supported NS, a Rajput. After independence, the main challengers of Rajputs traditional power came from Brahmins and Mahajans who were mainly represented in the Congress party. So, the opposition to the candidature of NS came from S, a Brahmin from another village, Poonawali. But a compromise reached, in which people supported NS for the post of *Sarpanch* and S was elected to Nyaya Panchayat. The voting was conducted through the raising of hands and no one opposed NS. Though one Gurjar did contest against NS, he could not muster the support of even his own caste men. Owing to the compulsions of higher level political processes, this arrangement could not be questioned. The Congress party actively encouraged the horizontal mobilisation of OBCs (Gurjars) and other lower castes by 1960s, not only to break the hold of Rajputs on the lower castes but also, to secure a majority among the Gurjars from Sakroda. For this purpose, the party called B, a rich businessman belonging to the Gurjar community from Surat, to contest panchayat elections on the request of the party leadership, as other Gurjars were economically weak and unwilling to contest against NS. From Sakroda, NS, S and B contested the next elections to the panchayat, leading to division of votes within the village. Both NS and B lost and candidate S won as *Sarpanch*. There was no panchayat election for thirteen years and S continued to work as *Sarpanch*. The contestant B went back to Surat and NS who was not well versed in competitive politics withdrew from active politics. The *Sarpanch* S took away most the developmental projects like school, telephone exchange and water dam to his own village Poonawali, and neglected the developmental activities in Sakroda. This was one of the factors that brought unity among the Sakroda villagers. Thereafter, in the next elections, the villagers decided to support B, as the Gurjars were in a majority in the village, and thus the candidate B won the panchayat elections as *Sarpanch*. After the elections the struggle continued between contestants S and B, in which both continued to win and lose. But during the 1980s, contestant B became the undisputed leader in the panchayat and S withdrew from panchayat politics.

A scheduled caste Khatik became economically dominant in Sakroda village in the 1980s. Though the rich among Khatiks have left their traditional degrading occupations of trading in, as well as sacrificing goats, they have still not been to achieve the social status compatible with their economic and political clout. They always resent this exclusion from the village social sphere and keep doing something that the villagers resent. There is rivalry between Gurjars and Khatiks in village for political supremacy. The post of *Sarpanch* was reserved for OBC in the 2000 panchayat elections and the candidate B withdrew from politics owing to poor health. He sided with his son while his son-in-law withdrew from the contest. Contestant B succeeded NS on the principle of a new legal order. But now he wanted the principle of succession and the principle of inheritance to merge. Gurjars did not like the closeness of B with Khatiks, who were not able to get the desired social recognition. So they were always trying to take revenge in other spheres. The Gurjars thought that B was also responsible for the rise of Khatik power and they would become more powerful if B's son became *Sarpanch*. The opponents of B, including BJP supporters who had been supporting B for a long time, were now waiting to settle scores. The respondent R had problems not only with Khatiks but also with B, because one of the sons of B had abused R's brother. Finally, a bitter electoral contest took place in which, though overwhelming number of Gurjars were with B. R won the elections, as a minority of Gurjars supported R. For the Gurjars the election was tied to the honour of their caste, since B an icon of the Gurjars, had left his thriving business and fought a bitter electoral battle, initially with Rajputs, and later with Brahmins, which led to supremacy of Gurjars in the local power structure. After the panchayat election in 2000, Bharulal died. Right now the seat is reserved for SCs women, mother of the respondent N, who is economically and politically the most dominant Khatik and an active Congressman of the area, is *Sarpanch*. The important thing is that Naresh had problem with Rajputs as well as Gurjars, but the villagers supported his mother's candidature. This happened since the villagers wanted someone from Sakroda to become *Sarpanch*. Secondly, it was also a consideration that a *Sarpanch* who was from the village was better for the villagers than an outsider. Respondent N, the son of the Sarpanch looks after the panchayat works.

Sundarcha Panchayat

In Sundarcha Panchayat, the politics of the panchayat has to be seen in a historical perspective. The Brahmins and Gurjars in the village were once political allies not only at the panchayat level but also at the state level and initially the politics of the panchayat was in harmony with the higher-level politics. The first *Sarpanch* was a Brahmin, SP, from Sundarcha. A Nai, G, contested the elections, but Brahmins threatened him and G lost the elections. SP remained as *Sarpanch* for 13 years. Thereafter, a Mahajan, R, from Dobar, became Sarpanch but the Brahmins, did not allow him to function. He resigned without completing his term. But the development at Panchayat Samiti level influenced the politics of the panchayat. A candidate, GK, was aspiring to become the *Pradhan*, so, in the next election he supported a young Gurjar, S, against the Brahmins, Paliwals. The contestant, S, won and remained *Sarpanch* till 2000. This phase saw an intense struggle between Paliwals and Gurjars in every area. The candidate S, a Gurjar, remained *Sarpanch* for 20 years by creating a permanent support base among the marginalised lower castes people due to the policy of reservation. In 2000 panchayat elections the post of *Sarpanch* got reserved for tribals. This divided the support base of STs, and the candidate put up by him lost the elections. With the total support of Paliwals, a tribal contestant BR won the elections. In the recent elections, the seat has been reserved for women. The mother of the dominant Paliwal caste leader has become *Sarpanch* of Sundarcha and her son looks after panchayat work.

Farara Panchayat

This panchayat presents an example of 'one family rule' for the past 50 years. The priest of Farara Mahadev temple, a Congress supporter became the first *Sarpanch* of the Statutory Village Panchayat. After that a Rajput, BS became *Sarpanch* and continued as *Sarpanch* for 40 years, as the villagers perceived him as honest where as the priest was dishonest and they had no trust in him. After the death of BS, the seat was reserved for women. BS's wife became the *Sarpanch* while her son looked after the affairs of the panchayat. When the seat was de-reserved the son of BS became the *Sarpanch*. Later the seat for *Sarpanch* was reserved for STs, the son of BS got a Bhil elected as *Sarpanch* and the son of BS became the

Deputy *Sarpanch*. After the death of the Bhil *Sarpanch*, before the completion of his tenure, the son of BS has been looking after the affairs of the panchayat. The panchayat defies the tehsil level arrangement of the political system. It is alleged that there is some form of understanding between BS, a BJP supporter, and a Congress man, who is Panchayat Samiti member. During the election both support each other, which is mostly resented by the Congressman Puri. Puri, who is also a ward *Panch* and the Panchayat Samiti member, is a Congressman. The priest is also a ward *Panch* and Congress supporter but does not get enough support to dethrone BS's family.

Piparda Panchayat

In the first phase BR, belonging to the Gurjar caste and a supporter of Congress party, dominated panchayat politics. He remained a *Sarpanch* till 1977 as he received support from the higher-level Congress leadership. Voting was conducted by rising of hands and nobody dared to contest against BR. Rajputs did not take any interest in panchayat politics since they did not like the new political arrangement. The political space was a virtual monopoly of BR. The second phase started with the coming to power of the Janata Party government at the Centre and state in 1977. The respondent NSB, a Rajpur, became *Sarpanch* and continued in the position till 1988. In 1988 the son of BR became *Sarpanch*. But in 1995, NSB became *Sarpanch* and stayed till 2000. This was the phase of struggle between Gurjars and Rajputs. The third phase started in 2000 when the seat was reserved for women. The Gurjars and Jats, predominantly found in the Congress party, supported a Khatik woman. The Rajputs, mostly in BJP, supported Salvi women. The Khatik woman received total support from the Khatiks. The Khatiks saw the election of Khatik woman as beneficial to their hamlet's development. In the recently held panchayat election the seat of *Sarpanch* was reserved for OBC and the son of BR, leader of Gurjars, became *Sarpanch*.

Nature of Power Transfer

Spatial Dimensions

A quick glimpse of the history of four panchayats shows that the biggest village of the panchayat controls the post of *Sarpanch*. Though, sometimes, a *Sarpanch* belongs to a small village, it is considered an aberration and the product of circumstances. It is considered a legitimate right of the inhabitants of the biggest village of the panchayat, to have the post of *Sarpanch* with them as they have the potential to elect the *Sarpanch* on their own strength. This benefits the dominant group of the village, and if united, they force the other castes to support their claim for the post of *Sarpanch*. Traditionally, it is the dominant group of the village, which invokes the concept of village solidarity, as this benefits it, but lately, even marginalised castes have found it beneficial to have the *Sarpanch* from their village. The reason lies in the fact that, though the villages are firmly integrated to the wider world, which has led to a decline in self-sufficiency as well as village solidarity; a different factor forces the villages to put up a united front in the panchayat elections. Thus, in spite of all types of changes that the villages are undergoing, a sense of togetherness still develops leading to different types of integration among the inhabitants and new norms and values become factors in social solidarity. Moreover, as more and more people need some favour from the state, and the *Sarpanch* has a role to play in it, people aspire that someone from their village gets elected as *Sarpanch*, so that things become easy for them vis-à-vis the state as well as the market-related institutions. During the panchayat elections, the post of *Sarpanch* is the most prized one, and people are willing to do all sort of trade off with other villages and caste groups for capturing the post of *Sarpanch*. If a group or village wins the post of *Sarpanch* and loses all other posts in the electoral process, it is still called the winner of the panchayat elections. If a village has the potential to elect a *Sarpanch* but loses the post due to infighting; people from surrounding villages, politicians, bureaucrats and even relatives, ridicule the members of the defeated village. Thus solidarity is considered a virtue and disunity a vice. The castigation of the people of a defeated village goes on till the next election, particularly when the inhabitants face some problem or the village as a whole suffers, and it is thought that had the *Sarpanch* been from the village, it would have been easier to solve the problem. "If you cannot remain united and elect even a *Sarpanch* you should not blame others for your misery", is the general refrain of the government officials as well as higher level politicians. Those who are considered spoilers are ridiculed by the villagers. After every loss in panchayat elections, every group tries to blame other groups for the defeat. This is an irony that, though the posts of Panchayat Samiti and Zilla Parishad members are more crucial and have more power in the Panchayati Raj structures, their election is not a priority for people. It is the chance factor, which plays an important role in the elections to these posts.

The small villages of panchayat are relevant only for voting or supporting a candidate from the big village in lieu of some minor posts. Even if somebody from a small village wants to contest elections for

Sarpanch, all the political activities are centred in the big village of the panchayat, as he can win either by taking the support of a segment of the population or by dividing the big village. In Sakroda Panchayat, Sundarlal used to devote more time in Sakroda than his own village Poonawali. Thus, the territorial and democratic principles operate simultaneously. In the Panchayati Raj structures, it is accepted that the candidate who has more votes in the overall panchayat, will be elected for the post of *Sarpanch*. But during the election the notion of territorial solidarity plays an important role in orienting the choice of the people. Thus, a conflict arises between the modern political unit, represented by the panchayat and the traditional political unit represented by the village. One example, will give some idea about the importance of the big village in panchayat elections. In Sakroda Panchayat, in the 2000 election, when the opponents of B were looking for a candidate, they were aware that the candidate needed to be a Gurjar, otherwise the Gurjars of the village would unite and Bharulal's son would win. But, suddenly, there was a realisation among the opponents of B that the candidate should be from Sakroda, otherwise the villagers would not accept a candidate from other village. Ultimately, contestant R was elected. What were the implications of this? The Gurjars constituted only 30 per cent of population in the panchayat, and they could not win if the other castes voted for a non-Gurjar candidate. But, the notion of village solidarity forced Sakroda village to unite. In the village the Gurjars claimed that they had more votes, so they deserved to be given the post of *Sarpanch*. Thus, in spite of being in a minority, the Gurjars had control over the post of the *Sarpanch*.

Another factor, which gives the transfer of power through the panchayat a spatial shape, is the location of panchayat headquarters. In all the four panchayats, the panchayat headquarters are located in the biggest village. The panchayats have been named after the biggest village. The village where the panchayat headquarters are located has an upper hand vis-à-vis other villages of the panchayat. In any Gram Sabha meeting, the attendance is already very low, but even here the maximum representation is from the village where panchayat headquarters are located. When the *Sarpanch* is from the village where the panchayat headquarters are located, then such a village has a decisive say in any Gram Sabha meeting, and it seems that the boundary of the panchayat is coterminous with the boundary of the of the *Sarpanch's* village. People from other villages, including the *Panchs*, do not have much of a say in the panchayat affairs. But, when the *Sarpanch* has won after defeating a candidate from the village where the panchayat headquarters are located, the *Sarpanch* is even afraid of going to the panchayat headquarters. This happened in the first term of SH as Sundarcha Panchayat *Sarpanch*. This was one of the reasons that when SU became *Sarpanch* of Sakroda Panchayat. He wanted the panchayat headquarters to be shifted to his village Poonawali, leading to tension with Sakroda village, which ultimately resulted in Sakroda being united and Sundarlal getting defeated as Sarpanch. Even the state's measure of protective discrimination policy for marginalised sections has not been able to bring the marginalised into the power structure, but it is always the weaker sections of the bigger multi-caste villages that get elected as panchayat functionaries, as the dominant groups want somebody from their own village to remain in power. In Piparda as well as in Sundarcha panchayats, the *Sarpanchas* are from the scheduled caste and scheduled tribe communities, but both are from the biggest villages of the respective panchayats.

What naturally follows from the above description is that the personality and authority of *Sarpanch* is not uniform all over the panchayats. In the village where he belongs, he is not only the legal head of panchayat; but is also supposed to be the traditional head of the village. He is supposed to work in a 'partisan' manner and bring the maximum benefit to his village. He has to help in organising traditional festivals. He needs to protect people against the police and state and also guard the honour of the village. The *Sarpanch* has also to get involved in the affair that is located outside the panchayat or village but that event has a bearing on the honour of the village. He has to help the villagers in the market and government office even if the work does not fall in his domain. Whenever his opponents from the village attack him, it is on these grounds, that the *Sarpanch* has not been able to fulfil his duty – legal as well as social. Once in Sakroda a *Ramlila* was being played and the *Sarpanch* R could not even put in an appearance. Most of his opponents concluded on that basis that *Sarpanch* R did not deserve to be *Sarpanch*. In a village from where there is no opposition during the elections, the *Sarpanch* is only the legal head and cannot interfere in the social aspects, though sometimes, if relations are harmonious, people approach the *Sarpanch* for help. But in a village from where the main opponents come, it becomes difficult for a *Sarpanch* to have even legal authority. For instance in Sundarcha Panchayat, tensions emerged in the panchayat from the time Gurjars wrested control of the panchayat from the Brahmins. In 1990s, the government started a pasture development programme, and a separate committee was formed to oversee the management of pastures. While the Gurjars claimed that, under the law, the pasture was panchayat property, and even traditionally it had remained opened for grazing, the Brahmins claimed that the village had customary rights over the pasture land leading to a conflict between state's demarcation of territory as a revenue village and the traditional notion of the village. Thus, the tensions resulted in court cases, and the lower castes stopped using the pasture as it was 'legally managed' by a committee composed of people from Sundarcha. As the lower castes had the most animals, they were the worst sufferers. The department of watershed made this pasture a 'model' and every week people from other organisations and institutions went there for an 'exposure trip' to see this 'successful' project. However, the 'successful experimentation' was not owing to the fact that people loved it, but that had become a site for struggle, where the supremacy of Brahmins could be confirmed by not getting the pasture opened for grazing.

Social Dimensions

Panchayats have provided channels for the manifestation of the rise and fall in power of different castes. In these four panchayats, such a trend is observed. In Sakroda and Sundarcha, it is the Gurjars who have benefited, in Farara it is the Rajputs that have come into power after displacing a Brahmin priest and in Piparda it has been moving back and forth between Rajputs and Gurjars. Thus the power transfer has taken place along caste lines, and those castes whose number is below threshold, or who have not acquired a certain level of social, economic and political development, have been ejected from the panchayat power structure. It is not the overall population of a community in a panchayat that is important, but its spatial distribution, which plays an important role in putting the community into the regime. If the members of a social group are dispersed and living with relatively powerful groups, they will not be able to capture any post in the Panchayati Raj structure. This happens due to the fact that the notion of village solidarity forces a particular caste in a village to support another caste of its village rather than its own caste from another village of the panchayat. This unity among the dominant caste of the village may not be achieved so easily, but if it is united, all other castes have to fall in line. Though, now, with the election of ward *Panch*, many castes have got their representatives at the *Panch* level; those castes whose population is less and who are also placed lower in the economic and social hierarchy, have not benefited that much. Power has moved across those groups who have achieved a certain level of economic development. Women have not found representation due to cultural factors. It is also a fact that that more and more people from weaker sections now vote in the panchayat elections and this is the only election where the most marginalised feels his political importance. In a village where there are factions, this election provides a chance to settle scores with dominants groups. In Sakroda, till Gurjar B was *Sarpanch*, there was no place for the marginalised. But, in the 2000 panchayat election the social groups that were neglected by B, all voted for R. However, it is also a fact that they can never win the post of *Sarpanch* and continue to play second fiddle to the dominant groups.

The Rajasthan government has extended reservation facilities to scheduled castes, scheduled tribes, OBCs and women, in order to facilitate the proper representation of these marginalised in the PRIs. It provides the marginalised a space to engage in public life. Instrumentally, these may not matter much for these groups, but it has a huge symbolic value, as these modern political spheres provide an 'ideal type' of condition for these groups to move in future and relate with others. For instance in Piparda, the *Sarpanch* is an SC woman. She cannot do much in the village as she is facing a double disadvantage as a woman and also belongs to SC. Still, she has brought some sort of revolution among the women. She has got many projects sanctioned in her area. On Independence Day she was seated at the front of the podium in the school where the main village function was being held. She was the only SC and the woman there, and all other powerful people of the village were sitting behind and around her. Though she was in *ghunghat*, the message was very clear for women in particular and for the masses in general. But the efficacy of such figure is also limited, owing to the environment in which they have to work, and in many cases they have been co-opted into already existing structures. Three types of co-option, viz., political co-option, factional co-option and personal co-option are found. For example, *Sarpanch* R has been co-opted into existing political structure; BR has been co-opted in existing village faction and CB in to the existing political as well as personal co-option (Singh, 2008). The most important reason for this lies in the fact that there is only 'partial exclusion' of dominants from the political processes, whereas, though they cannot contest elections for *Sarpanch*, they can participate in all other formal as well as informal political processes. As the population of SCs and STs in not much, as compared to others, and since there are many candidates from amongst them contesting against a post, one can win elections only with the support of the dominant groups. This difference in the efficacy of the *Sarpanch* can be observed when one makes a comparison between the *Sarpanch* elected against an unreserved post and one elected against a reserved post. The *Sarpanch* of Farara, BS, belonging to Gurjars has control over everything in the panchayat and get the maximum fund allocated for his panchayat in the block (65 lakhs in five years). He has a Robin Hood image in the panchayat. In all the three panchayats, people are highly critical of the 'in-efficiency' of their *Sarpanchs* (who are elected against reserved posts) and compare them with the Sarpanch of Farara, BS. People of Farara like the *Sarpanch* as he can do all that is possible within the rules for them.

However, the difference in efficiency of *Sarpanchas* cannot be solely explained by comparing the *Sarpanchas* elected against reserved posts with *Sarpanchas* elected against unreserved posts. It has also to do with the manner in which legitimacy is conferred in society. In theory those elected in the Panchayati Raj system should have enough authority to take decision, but the truth is that they need to have more than just electoral victory to acquire authority. For example the *Sarpanch* of Sakroda Panchayat, R, has been elected in a more or less competitive manner. Though the post has been reserved for OBCs, it does not make any difference in Sakroda Panchayat since Gurjars have a majority in it. B continued as *Sarpanch* for a long time. Though R was elected *Sarpanch* of Sakroda after contest, he does not command respect even within his community, as he is seen as someone who has broken the unity of Gurjars by taking the help of those who were against the Gurjars that led to the defeat of B's son. Though Ramlal has won, the Gurjars have lost. When it comes to the honour of the caste, Gurjars say that one of their caste men is *Sarpanch*, but that is the end of the acceptability of *Sarpanch* R among the Gurjars. He does not have the support of his caste men for running the panchayat, which is necessary to be an effective *Sarpanch*. Those who had supported him during elections have already used him and have no such compulsion to support R on every forum. Even R's position is ambivalent as he claims that he is from the Congress party as most of the Gurjars in the village are with the Congress. In the Gram Sabha meetings the defeated group does not attend the Gram Sabha as it can get its work done through connections in the Congress circle. The defeated group accepts the democratic principle that the candidate who gets the maximum vote among all the contestants should be elected, but they do not accept the outcome in spirit. Now, the bureaucrats do not accept the authority of *Sarpanch* as they know that the *Sarpanch* R has no support within his community. *Sarpanch* R goes to the Panchayat Samiti everyday and nobody knows what he is does there. Though he is the *Sarpanch* of the panchayat, he has no control on the affairs of the panchayat. The officials from different departments, like, watershed or health visits the respective heads of these institutions in the village. Being a Sarpanch, R can call all these officials but he does not want to do it.

Institutional Dimensions

The most important institutional arrangement for taking decision in Panchayati Raj structure is the Statutory Gram Sabha. Traditionally, the affairs of the villages have been managed by the Gram Sabha. Though the traditional Gram Sabha has proved effective in decision-making, it excludes some of the weaker sections of the society from the decision-making process, SCs, STs and women in particular. The state has tried to make the new Statutory Gram Sabha more inclusive. But one form of inclusion has generated other forms of exclusion that have reduced the efficacy of the Statutory Gram Sabha as the panchayat generally consists of more than one village. The villages exist in relation with other villages in terms of social and economic dimensions. Traditionally, and it is true even today, there cannot be one Gram Sabha for more than one village, as every village behaves as an autonomous political unit. People from two or more villages may unite for some common purpose, but such unity is highly contextual and ad hoc. As people are not accustomed to this new arrangement, where people from more than one village sit and take political decisions, the Statutory Gram Sabha does not become a cohesive entity. Secondly, the way the modern Gram Sabha functions is alien to the customary decision-making process to which the villagers have been accustomed. Unlike the traditional Gram Sabha, the new Statutory Gram Sabha has no scope for re-negotiation among different groups, as everything has to be decided on the spot. This is not possible as the villagers are not accustomed to taking decisions in this manner. Thirdly, in Panchayati Raj schemes, the cluster of villages is treated like a community. But, the notion of community has always been contested, and with the development of society there is more differentiation among different social groups in terms of ideas, values and material interest. Then, even the state, in practice, does not treat the villages which compose a panchayat as community, partly because it understands inter- and intra-village cleavages, and partly owing to the fact that if there is tension between the national direction of development and the aspirations of the local community, the former gets precedence. All these complications force the state to direct everything to the panchayat, including the time when the Gram Sabha has to be held. In the developmental programmes all the components have been fixed. Thus panchayats have been told not only what to do, but also how to do it. But this, as Fesler (1968) says, is nothing but 'pseudo-decentralisation' as the genuine decentralisation means autonomy in decision-making.

Once everything has been directed from above, and the rules are rigid, the 'subversion' of rules becomes an in-built part of Panchayat Raj structures and functioning. Under these circumstances, many informal organisations develop to deal with the situation. How and why the informal organisations develop can be demonstrated through an example. It is obligatory for the panchayats to provide drinking water during the summer season. The procedures for getting approval for providing water are complex and it takes months to complete the formality. So, without taking formal sanction, but with informal consent from officials, the panchayat provides water, and later on, money is disbursed. There are informal arrangements through which most of the panchayat works are handled, which may enhance the efficiency of the panchayat, but sometimes also lead to corruption and goal displacement.

Now, let us see the power transfer within the formal political system. All the political parties, and factions within them, try to control the panchayat by putting up their supporters in it, and if it is not possible they try to co-opt the independent panchayat functionaries in to their fold. This is required since panchayats control vast resources of the state, which are used to provide patronage to the supporters of political parties as well as create a political base. In this process, the existence of the panchayat gets a new meaning for all these stakeholders. Here the panchayat does not remain a unit for development and empowerment, but a political unit to create a support base and to extend patronage. The panchayat does not remain a local level political unit, but becomes a part of the wider political processes. It not only takes a toll on the efficacy of the panchayat, but also complicates matters for the political parties. An example will make the things clear. There are two groups in the Congress party at the block level and both try to have more of their supporters in PRIs. In the 2000 panchayat election, the Congress party got a majority in the Panchayat Samiti, but the faction of Congress headed by RS split the party. RS became Panchayat Samiti *Pradhan* with the help of BJP members. The party expelled him. Its impact can be seen in Sakroda Panchayat. In that panchayat, the defeated lobby of B and some Khatiks are close to the official Congress. It has forced R, the new *Sarpanch* to side with the expelled member from the Congress, RS. The local Congress MLA, BG has to keep the *Sarpanch* and the *Pradhan* on his side as they control the panchayat. This has created complications in the local Congress party and the official Congress headed by GK resents this. It has taken a heavy toll on the development programmes as well. A hospital was constructed in Sakroda but was not functioning because both the factions wanted their respective leaders to inaugurate the hospital and to exclude other faction leader from the inauguration function. The official Congress wanted to exclude RS, but R, the *Sarpanch* of Sakroda Panchayat was adamant about bringing RS to the inauguration of the hospital, as the *Sarpanch* R needed RS support in running the panchayat. The hospital could not function for two years even though it was ready. Ultimately, owing to local political compulsions and pressure from the villagers, a compromise was arrived at, and leaders from both the factions came for inauguration as the higher-level Congress bosses wanted unity for the sake of the party.

However, there is a limit to co-option as the 'institutionalisation of any system usually creates new collectivities and organisations. These organisations (Eisenstadt, 1968) develop needs, interests, and orientations of their own, which may impinge on various other groups and institutional spheres, thus creating their attitude towards the premises of the system.' In spite of all the measures, the higher level politicians take to integrate the panchayat into the wider political process, the panchayat keeps a certain level of autonomy. This becomes possible because in a small political unit where face-to-face relations matter a lot, the grammar of local level politics becomes different from that of the higher-level political process. But it is also a compulsion on the part of higher level representatives to bring the panchayat into its fold. When it does not happen, they try to neutralise its efficacy through other methods. In these situations there is an attempt to bypass panchayats. There are different methods. One of the important means through which it is done is the existence of various committees, which deal with village developmental programmes. These committees separately manage their account and have the power to frame rules about the election and selection of its members. The watershed committee of the Rajasthan government is the one such example. Those who are in these committees do not like any interference from panchayats. This, in many ways, curtails the power of panchayats.

But there is another side to the whole phenomenon. The panchayat is part of the overall democratic structure of the nation. Democracy is not only about empowerment and development, but also an institution for power sharing. It respects plurality. These various committees are also used to share power among the contending groups in the villages. When different contending social groups have to come to a compromise during panchayat elections or for power sharing, they achieve it by dividing among themselves the headship of these committees. In Sakroda Panchayat, when B was *Sarpanch* and different castes groups and individuals were looking for a place in the village power structure, he made the policy of dividing various posts among the contending parties in the village to manufacture consensus. The Khatiks were given the post of Deputy *Sarpanch*, the Rajput nominee was made the head of the Pasture Development Programme, and B himself became *Sarpanch*. The existence of committees also includes those who are not included through the normal democratic processes or are excluded due to state intervention (due to reservation of seats for a particular caste or community). Thus, they do not create much trouble for the *Sarpanchas*, and ultimately the head of the panchayat remains free from many of the tensions which would have haunted him otherwise. The problem is that once the seats have been divided, all the posts become autonomous in the sense that all these committees though technically under the jurisdiction of panchayat, work independently in practice. They do not recognise the authority of the *Sarpanch*.

Conclusions

The working of the panchayat can be understood within the framework of the 'interplay between the traditional social and modern legal order'. Since both orders continue to be relevant in social and political life, it leads to tension, accommodation, negotiation and compromise for political space. Which order gets a more prominent place depends upon the context. There are laws of politics, but also laws of society and both are encapsulated in the functioning of the panchayat. Thus, the panchayat has to negotiate with many other institutions, and in the process, it acquires different meanings for different stakeholders. In the course of its journey, the panchayat has got transformed to some extent, but it has also changed the character of the social and political institutions with which it is interacting.

The statutory panchayat, in most cases, does not take the boundary of the traditional village as a unit for empowerment and development. It is composed of more than one village, unless the village is too large, which is more an exception than a rule. But, the traditional notion of a village becomes more important in the life of people. This generates spatial inequality in the transfer of power through the panchayat, in which big villages have a greater say in the affairs of panchayat. There is difference between the concept of the self-sufficiency of the village and the notion of village solidarity. Villages were never self-sufficient, but village solidarity was always a part of village life. Today, villages are more and more integrated with the wider world, and it is also true that it has affected social solidarity; still it is the 'compulsion of living together' which forces the villages to unite. On the other level, there is tension between the notions of the revenue village, which is a unit for revenue collection, and the proper village, the unit of settlement which is considered a village by the people. Whenever some development project is granted in the name of a village, the main village grabs it and the other parts of that revenue village are left out of the development process. There is also a contradiction in the way that decisions are being taken at the traditional village council and the decision-making processes followed in statutory panchayat.

Socially, the panchayat has played the most radical role in power transfer, but it is the dominant castes and groups of the biggest village who have mostly benefited from it. The small villages are marginalised, irrespective of whether they are inhibited by dominant castes or the weaker sections. Power transfer takes place along caste lines. The policy of reservation has helped the marginalised in many ways, but its success is also limited. There is no case where, after a seat is de-reserved, the previous *Sarpanch*, who was elected against the reserved seat, has been re-elected against the open seat. The moment the seat is de-reserved it has again gone back to the dominant community. The power of the marginalised has also gone down due to the policy of rotation of reserved seats. Once an incumbent knows that the seat will go to some other reserved category next time, or will become open, he never takes any interest in nurturing the constituency and looking for a permanent alliance with like-minded social groups.

The politics of panchayat has been influenced by both local as well as higher level political processes. In the political system, the power transfer has been more radical and this has led to the co-option of the panchayat in the wider political system. In this scenario, the panchayat has moved away from community life, and has become closer to the wider political system. Still, the panchayat has kept some form of autonomy, and this has led to the emergence of many parallel institutions leading to the marginalisation of the panchayat. But these institutions also play a role of power sharing, which sometimes helps the weaker section incumbents by insulating the panchayat affairs from other dominant groups and individuals.

The success and failure of a development programme has links with many factors. There is a chain reaction and one event is closely tied to another event. There is 'exchange of conflict' where a conflict at the social level finds expression at the political level. There are many projects which are considered 'failed' but have provided a channel for social mobility. Thus, the institution may not be serving the purpose for which it has been created, but it may play a much larger role in the structure as well as functioning of society. It is true that the panchayats have led to factionalism in villages, but most of the social conflicts of the villages are channelled through the political route owing to the existence of panchayats. Rather than fighting on social issues in everyday life, people wait to settle scores through politics and for the village community the panchayat provides the most important forum.

The most important conclusion is that there is a need to see the place of panchayat in society. There is place for other political institutions – traditional as well as modern – in society, and the panchayat cannot displace all these institutions. If it tries to do so it will be culturally alien, technically unsound, economically inefficient and politically unacceptable to the villagers. While trying to expand its sphere, it must respect the existence of other institutions, otherwise the holders of these institutions will retaliate and it will only weaken the panchayat. Writing in the 1970s about the crisis of democracy in the United States, Huntington (1975: 115) opines that the threat to democracy in United States comes 'from the internal dynamics of democracy itself in a highly educated, mobilised, and participant society … . A value, which normally is good in it, is not necessarily optimised when it is maximised. We have come to recognise that there are potentially desirable limits to economic growth. There are also potentially desirable limits to the indefinite extension of political democracy. Democracy will have a longer life if it has a more balanced existence'. Perhaps this also holds true for the panchayat.

References

Baviskar, B.S. and Mathew, J. (eds.) 2008, *Inclusion and Exclusion in Local Governance: Field Studies from Rural India*, Delhi: Sage Publications.

Beteille, A. 1965, *Caste, Class and Power: Changing Social Stratification in a Tanjore Village*, Berkeley: University of California Press.

Blau, P.M. and Scott, W.R. 1962, *Formal Organizations*, San Francisco: Chandler Publishing House.

Chauhan, B.R. 2003, "Village Community", in Veena Das (ed.), *The Oxford India Companion to Sociology and Social Anthropology*, Delhi: Oxford University Press, 409–57.

Eisenstadt, S.N. 1968, "Social Institution: Concept", in D.L. Sills (ed.), *International Encyclopedia of Social Sciences*, New York: Macmillan.

Escobar, A. 1995, *Encountering Development: The Making and Unmaking of the Third World*, Vol. 14, New Jersey: Princeton University Press.

Fesler, J.W. 1968, "Centralisation and Decentralisation", in D.L. Sills (ed.), *International Encyclopedia of Social Sciences*, Vol. 2, New York: Macmillan.

Huntington, Samuel P. 1975, "The United States", in Michel Crozier et al. (eds.), *The Crisis of Democracy*, New York: New York University Press.

Kripa, Ananthpur, 2006, "Selection by Custom Election by Statute: Interfaces in Local Governance in Karnataka", in N.G. Jayal, A. Prakash and P.K. Sharma (eds.), *Local Governance in India: Decentralisation and Beyond*, Delhi: Oxford University Press.

Lijphart, A. 1996, "The Puzzle of Indian Democracy: A Constitutional Interpretation", *American Political Science Review*, Vol. 90, No. 2, June.

Luhman, N. 1982, *The Differentiation of Society*, New York: Columbia University Press.

Manor, J. 1999, *The Political Economy of Democratic Decentralisation*, Washington, DC: World Bank.

Ratzlalf, Ralph H. 1962, *Village Government in India*, Bombay: Asia Publishing House.

Singh, S.B. 2008, "Devolution of Power through Panchayat", in B.S. Baviskar and J. Mathew (eds.), *Inclusion of Exclusion in Local Governance: Field Studies from Rural India*, Delhi: Sage Publications.

14

Empowering the Rural Poor

Panchayat Representation, Party Representation and Political Empowerment of the Poor

Atanu Sengupta and Md. Salauddin Khan

The political empowerment of the poor is one of the most important concerns of democratic Indian polity in general and of the Left government in West Bengal, in particular. Empowerment refers to the process where the powerless gain greater control over the circumstances of their lives. Political empowerment necessitates both institutional representation as well as party representation. Representation of the socially backward classes in Statutory Village Panchayats (SVPs) is a necessary condition for the empowerment of the poor but not a sufficient condition. The sufficient condition is that along with panchayat representation, the poor must hold political power or have greater control over the political party to which they belong. In West Bengal's panchayat system, different committees are constituted under the guidelines of the party and decisions are primarily taken in internal party meetings. These committees are the decision making units. The decision regarding the allocation of development funds among different villages under a Gram Panchayat is primarily taken by the Panchayat Guide Committee. Then, the Gram Committee (constituted at the village level with active party supporters) immediately calls a meeting as it receives the development fund in order to distribute these funds in different development projects and also among poor and needy households belonging to the target group. Thus, the decision about the distribution of the development fund is percolated from the party organisation to the formal panchayat system and then to the beneficiaries in the villages of SVP. The SVP members are mostly party members as much as they are the party's people. The poorest of the poor in the backward classes will be benefited, if their representation in the party organisation is at a satisfactory level. So has long as SCs, STs and other socially and economically backward classes lack proper representation in the party's decision making units, they will not be able to implement the development projects which benefit the target groups.

A study has been conducted in Shyampur SVP in order to comprehend the political empowerment of the rural poor in West Bengal. A sample of 960 families out of 6,430 families has been selected from nine villages of Shyampur SVP. Data have been collected from the elected families of the SVP for the period of 1978–83 and 1998–2003 through interviews, observations, panchayat records and the survey method to realise the level of literacy, education, enrolment and drop-out from schools and the class and caste composition of guide committees. The SVP under study has a total population of 38,416, with nearly six persons per family and with a gender ratio of 1,122 men per 1,000 women. The SVP is preponderantly populated by general caste Hindus followed by Muslims.

Williams (1999) has categorised peasants on the basis of the size of landholdings into rich (with more than 7.5 acres), middle (5–7.5 acres of landholdings), poor (3–5 acres of holdings) and marginal peasants (with less than 3 acres of landholdings). This classification of peasants has been used throughout our analysis. The analysis of data, on the basis of size of landholdings as mentioned above, reveals that poor and marginal peasants are numerically in preponderance followed by agricultural labourers.

Analysis of the data on the basis of population in the selected sample families from the Shyampur SVP reveals that 32.73 per cent of the respondents are general caste Hindus, followed by 16.72 per cent SCs, 1.2 per cent ST members and 49.38 per cent are Muslims. Analysis of data on the basis of number of families selected for the study reveals that they predominantly belong to general Hindu caste category (46%), followed by Muslims (9%), SCs (19%) and STs (6%) out of the selected families for the study. On the basis of size of landholdings, out of these families 49 per cent are in the poor and marginal peasant category, followed by poor peasants (26% of the families), middle peasants (16% of the families) and only (9%) of the families belong to rich peasants' category. Among SCs, STs and Muslims, most of the respondents belong to the age group of 6–20 years.

Elementary Education: Literacy, Enrolment vs. Drop-out

Dynamics of Literacy

In order to understand the dynamics of literacy, gender and caste-wise educational achievement of the family members aged more than six years is analysed. The analysis reveals that general caste Hindu men have nearly total literacy (98%) followed by Muslim men with 87 per cent, scheduled caste men with 80 per cent, and ST men with 79 per cent. The analysis further reveals that both caste Hindu and Muslim women have 95 per cent literacy, followed by SCs with 54 per cent and STs with 33 per cent. Comparison of literacy on the basis of gender reveals that women literacy among the Muslims (95%) is higher than that of male literacy (87%). The literacy gap on the basis of gender is very less among general caste Hindus but it is more visible in the case of SCs and STs. Literacy of SC (54%) and ST women (33%) is lagging far behind than that of the general caste Hindu and Muslim women (95%). At least in terms of literacy achievements, among women of GCHs and Muslims, the gap has disappeared. In almost all cases (except Muslims), female literacy is lower than that of male literacy. Thus literacy-based inequalities can be comprehended on the basis of gender and caste in rural West Bengal.

Figure 1

Literacy Levels by Gender and Caste (aged 6 years and above)

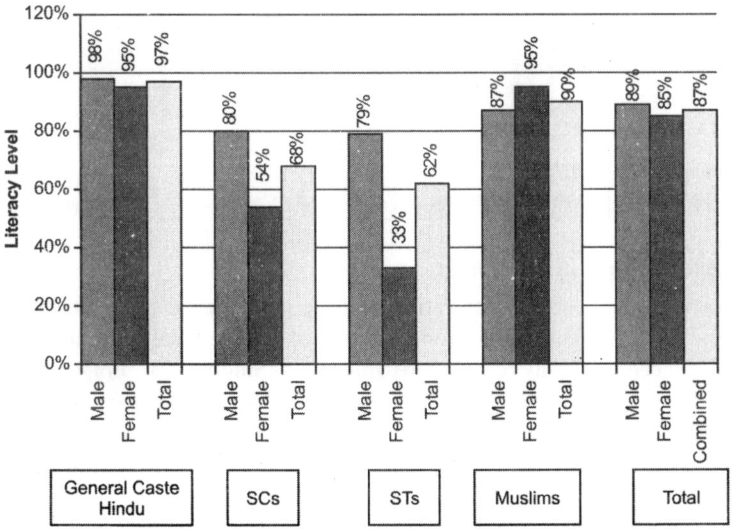

Enrolment vis-à-vis Drop-outs

In order to know the position of enrolment, drop-out ratios and reasons for drop-out/enrolment among the students in the age group of 5–9 years, data from the sample families under study have been analysed along caste lines. The analysis reveals that the drop-out ratios among SCs is the highest (27%) followed by STs with 24 per cent and Muslims with 22 per cent. However the drop-out ratio is nominal among general caste Hindus (2.2%). In terms of effective enrolment ratio, the general caste Hindus occupy the first position (82.77%), followed by SCs with 62.47 per cent and STs with 58.50 per cent. Muslims have the lowest effective enrolment ratio (52.10%) among all social groups.

Figure 2

Caste-wise Enrolment and Drop-out Ratios

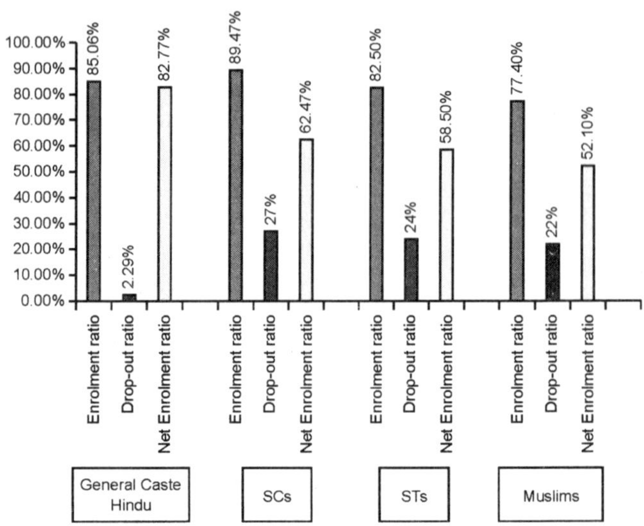

Determinants of Enrolment

Variations in enrolment ratios in different villages of West Bengal under study are observed along the lines of economic development. The three economically developed villages – Singhapara, Bolgana and Biskopa – have high enrolment ratios in comparison to other backward villages. Access to schooling in terms of increasing the number of schools, especially in remote areas, would help in achieving the targets of enrolment. In the absence of requisite facilities it is resulting in fictitious enrolment. This clearly brings out the point that the policies to improve literacy ought to integrate the demand and supply of assets as the supply factors ensure higher enrolment, while the demand factors help in reducing the drop-out rates.

Poverty and participation in economic activities in the form of wage-labour as well as unpaid labour such as working on one's own farm and supporting the parents in their activities are found as the most important reasons for drop-out/non-enrolment among male as well as female children. Poverty played greater influence (in 43% of the sample) in the drop-out/non-enrolment rates in the backward regions. Participation in economic activities (44% of the sample) followed by poverty (37%) constituted the main reasons in the drop-out/non-enrolment rates in the developed regions. The greater labour demand in developed regions, especially during the peak seasons, acts as a pull factor in the lower rates of enrolment or higher rates of drop-outs. Lack of interest among parents (33%), poverty (23%) and involvement in domestic activity are found as determinants for the drop-outs and non-enrolment, especially in the case of females. On the other hand, school problems seem to play a less important role in the drop-out/non-enrolment of children both in backward and developed regions.

Table 1

Guide Committee Representation of Different Parties at Shyampur Gram Panchayat, 2003

Caste/ Community	*Members of Guide Committee*	*Male*	*Female*	*Class Composition*		
				Middle Peasants	*Poor and Marginal Peasants*	*Landless as Labourers*
General Caste Hindus (GCHs)	38 (73%)	33 (87.5%)	5 (12.5%)	19	19	NIL
Scheduled Castes (SCs)	5 (9%)	5 (100%)	NIL	—	5	NIL

The SVP is an institution which helps to increase the political empowerment of the rural poor. In order to the increase the capacity of SVPs in improving political and social power amongst the less privileged sections of society, data are collected from the Shyampur SVP. The Guide Committee functions at the grassroots level through their political party representatives. Five political parties, namely, CPI (M), Forward Bloc, Indian National Congress, Trinamul Congress and BJP were observed as functioning in Shyampur SVP area.

Analysis of the data related to political party affiliation of the Guide Committee members in 2003 reveals that there are 52 members affiliated to different political parties at Shyampur SVP area. Out of the 52 members, 38 are general caste Hindus (GCHs) and among GCHs, male representation is predominant with 87.5 per cent. Muslim representation in the Panchayat Guide Committee is only 18 per cent, i.e., nine members out of 52. In the party's Panchayat Guide Committee, the decision making unit, SC representation is only 9 per cent. There is no representation from the ST category. Panchayat Guide Committee is dominated by male representation (91%) while female representation is found to be only 9 per cent. No female representation from SCs, STs and Muslims is found here. Analysis of data along class lines reveals that 44 per cent members are middle peasants and 56 per cent are poor and marginal farmers. Panchayat Guide Committee of different parties at Shyampur SVP has no member from among landless agricultural labourers.

It should be noted from the above observations that one of the decision making bodies of any political organisation, i.e., guide committee, has no representation of the landless agricultural labourers. It indicates the powerlessness of the landless agricultural labourers at the grassroots level democratic set-up. It is also noticed that female representation is also low. On an average, only 9 per cent of the total members of the Guide Committee of different parties are women of the middle class and general upper caste Hindu categories. With all these findings, it may be concluded that the rural poor are not as empowered as they are expected to be.

The SVP of Shyampur, in 1978–83, had only 19 members. The SVP members were mainly dominated by the upper caste Hindus and Muslims like Brahmins, Augris and Seikh-Syed (14 members out of 19) and by rich (10 out of 19 members) and middle peasants (4 out of 19 members). The lower caste representation in the Shyampur SVP, in 1978–83, was only five out of 19 members and they were either share croppers or landless agricultural labourers.

However, in the panchayat elections of 1998–2003, the SVP had 23 seats. Out of 23 panchayat members, 17 members were from the lower castes like Bagdi, Muchi, Dobha, Duley and low category Muslims (recently included in OBC list in West Bengal) and the remaining six members were from Brahmins, aguris, Seikh-Syed Muslims. Analysis of data of these members along class lines reveals that only five members were rich peasants, 10 were middle peasants and eight were landless agricultural labourers. Here, it is to be noted that the 73rd and 74th constitutional amendments, reserved 33 per cent seats for SCs, and STs, but not for lower caste Muslims. Thus, we see that the present panchayat (1998–2003) is dominated by lower caste and middle peasants and landless agricultural labourers. In the SVP of 1998–2003, lower caste representation to the panchayat has increased significantly as compared to the composition of members of 1978–83 SVP.

A comparative analysis of the panchayat representation in the SVP at two time periods 1978/1983 and 1998/2003, reveals that there has been a shift of power from upper caste to lower caste and also from rich and middle peasants to middle peasants and landless agricultural labourers in all political parties. With the passage of time, there is a radical change in the distribution of power in the panchayat institution. This can be seen as a good symptom for empowerment of the poor and backward classes.

What is the relationship between caste, class and politics in Shyampur SVP under Pursurah block in Hooghly district of West Bengal? In order to comprehend the relationship, data were collected from peasant, youth, village level committees and women wings of different political parties. The data were analysed along caste and class lines. Finally, these findings were compared with the findings of the Shyampur SVP members' class and caste status. Analysis of data relating to class and caste status of 430 members of the peasant wing of different parties reveals that only 39 per cent members were from the category of lower castes, while their representation in the Shyampur SVP in 1998–2003 was 73 per cent. Thus, lower caste group had a better representation in the panchayat under study (73%) but their representation in party/organisation was relatively weak (39%).

In the peasant wing of different parties, only 39 per cent represent landless agricultural labourers, 21 per cent marginal and poor peasants, while the remaining 40 per cent middle peasants. Thus, lower class and lower castes were represented in a moderate way in the peasant wings of different political parties. However, the panchayat representation of lower caste people in Shyampur SVP indicates a radical change in the distribution of power in favour of the poor and the ex-untouchables/lower castes in the period of 1978–83 and 1998–2003.

In the youth wings of different parties, the majority of the members (65%) out of 350 members belonged to upper castes like Brahmin, Aguri, Seikh Muslims, and middle peasants (47%). Only 35 per cent members represent the lower caste group in the youth wings of different political parties. In terms of their landholdings, 17 per cent members are from poor and marginal peasant families, 47 per cent members are from middle peasant families and 36 per cent members are landless agricultural labourers.

Table 2

Caste and Class Composition of Members of Women Wing of Different Parties

Total Number of Members	*Caste*				*Class*
	SCs	*STs*	*Lower Caste Muslim*	*Upper Caste*	
225	124 (55%)	36 (16%) = 80%	20 (9%)	45 (20%)	Rich Peasants = 45 (20%) Middle Peasants = 90 (40%) Poor and Marginal Peasants = 90 (40%)

Source: Party office, different parties.

Data were collected from 225 members representing the women wing of different parties. No member from landless agricultural labourers' households represents the women's wing. The lower caste people have the largest representation (80%) in the women's wings of different political parties. Upper castes have the lowest representation (20%). This shows that the upper caste people have a general tendency not to allow their women to become members of women's wings. It may be owing to psychological barriers, although it is a subject of testing. The class of poor and marginal peasants is represented in significant proportion (40%) in the women's wings of different political parties. This is a significant change.

Table 3

Reasons for Not Taking Membership of Women Wing of Any Political Party by the Upper Caste Women

Reasons	*Number of Women*	*Percentage*
Psychological barriers due to fear of loss of family status/husbands' disliking	98	82%
No interest at all	22	18%
Total	120	100.00%

Source: Field Survey, 2006.

Non-acceptors of membership of women, in women's wing of different parties were interviewed to find the reasons for non-acceptance.

We tried to personally contact 120 upper caste women, including housewives, who were approached by political leaders with requests to become members of their women's wings. All of them refused. The answers indicate that the fear of loss of family status (also husbands' dislike) is the most (82%) important reason for non-acceptance of membership. There are, therefore, psychological barriers which prevent them from taking membership in such party organisations. Eighteen per cent of upper caste women showed no interest in politics.

Analysis of data on the basis of caste and class composition at the village level committees of different parties reveals that they are mainly dominated by rich peasants and businessmen (47%). The representation of middle peasants, poor and marginal peasants and landless agricultural labourers is 19 per cent, 10 per cent and 24 per cent respectively. Here, upper caste representation (58%) is higher than lower caste representation (42%)

Figure 3

Panchayat Representation, Village Panchayats Income Expenditure, Government Schemes are Discussed and get Approval from the Gram Sabha and Party Representation

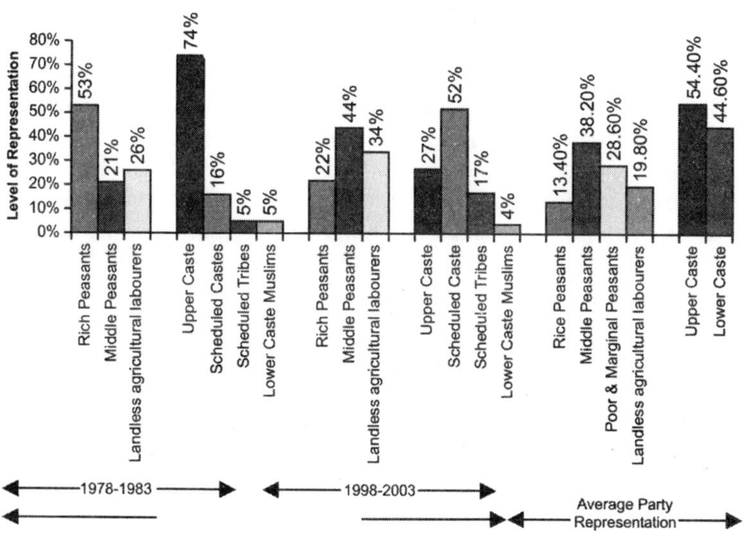

The relationship between castes, classes and politics in Shyampur Gram Panchayat under Pursurah block in the district of Hooghly in

West Bengal has been drawn both at the level of the Panchayati Raj Institutions (PRIs) and the organisational structure of different parties. Politics may be seen as power located in various structural arrangements of society. In contrast to the earlier panchayat dominated by upper caste and rich and middle peasants, the present panchayat of 1998–2003, and 2003–2008 is dominated by middle peasants and agricultural labourers. This is a major change in the distribution of power in the study area. On average, the numerical strength of lower caste and lower classes is relatively less represented at party organisation than at the panchayat level.

The above figure leads us to conclude that there has been a shift of power over time from upper castes to lower castes and also from rich and middle peasants to middle peasants and landless agricultural labourers in the panchayat representation. The poor and the ex-untouchables are found in minority in almost all political party organisations. The political party organisations are dominated by the rich and middle peasants and by upper caste.

The findings may be summed up as follows:

1. Each of the castes has its own hierarchy and for this reason, Dumont's (1955) thesis could not be applicable in our study area. We have failed to draw a 'true hierarchy' in terms of ideology because of the overlapping nature of various sub-castes. Hence we find that Gupta's concept (Gupta, 1992) of continuous hierarchies and discrete classes is applicable in our study area.
2. The lower castes and lower classes have been found to be numerically dominant at the level of panchayat and other organisations. But, at the leadership level, power is concentrated in the hands of middle peasantry. The economic and social positions of agricultural labourers and lower castes would not be changed radically if the decision-making powers remain in the hands of the middle peasantry at the leadership level. Power should be handed down to the rural proletariat if the responsible political parties intend to realise the basic principle of 'people's democracy'.
3. At the level of the elected body one would expect to have a higher percentage of agricultural labourers and poor peasants. Findings of the study indicate that the absence of this group in the party level signifies no radical restructuring of the rural power structure. All political parties have to take note of this if they want to make any breakthrough in agrarian mobilisation.

The last panchayat election in West Bengal was held in 2008. Similar trends as found in the earlier panchayats were observed in the 2008 elections. Though representation from the poor and agricultural labour families in the formal panchayat system has improved in proportion but they are represented either very less or are absent in the decision-making units, i.e., in party organisations.

References

Dumont, L. 1955, *Homo Hierarchicus*, Chicago: University of Chicago Press.

Gupta, D. (ed.) 1992, *Social Stratification*, New Delhi: Oxford University Press.

15

Changing Patterns of Power Structure in Village Panchayats

A Study of Four Village Panchayats in Andhra Pradesh

A. Nageswara Rao

The Indian State after independence introduced three-tier Panchayati Raj system in 1960s with a motto of democratic decentralisation of power based on adult suffrage and with a provision of reservation of positions for SCs and STs in these statutory panchayats at village, block and district levels. Such reserved positions for SCs and STs were filled through co-option and nomination. Studies (Narain, 1967, 1969; Sirsikar, 1974; Carter, 1974; Sharma, 1979) on the consequences of the statutory village panchayats (SVPs) based on adult suffrage and reservation of positions to SCs and STs on the distribution of power in villages reveal that upper castes dominated SVPs (Ramreddy, 1970). Thus, an overlap between well-to-do sections of upper caste landowners and power exercisers emerged in the SVPs. Though SCs got some positions reserved for them constitutionally in the panchayats but remained more or less as name sake representatives (Mishra, 1977). Srinivas (1959) tried to comprehend distribution of power in the villages through dominant caste. Hirway (1986) observed that the SVPs served mainly the interests of larger size of land owners and rich traders who usually belong to the upper castes. Secondly, the elites of the village selected from SC/ST members to the panchayat through co-option/nomination have practically no say in the decision-making process in the panchayat, with the result that the activities of the panchayat do not serve the interests of the poor in development activities including the special programmes for the poor. Gurumurthy

(1987) also made more or less similar observations in his study. Study conducted in the villages of UP and AP reveal that 'power structure captured and controlled by the powerful and land owned class in the villages do not want to bring change in the status quo' and 'the existing rural power structure cannot be easily transformed without any constitutional/mandatory provisions. Given the entrenched caste system in villages, the possibility of SC men and women heading the SVP was almost impossible to imagine. In those panchayats the marginalised groups like women, SCs and STs had no voice at all (Mathew, 2000). Several other studies also clearly show that the socio-economic power structure in rural areas does not allow the benefits of Panchayati Raj system to flow down towards the weaker sections of society.

But contrary to this, there were studies to prove that the Panchayati Raj Institutions (PRIs) contributed to change in the rural power structure in favour of the weaker sections. Beteille (1965) found that the rural social stratification was changing from cumulative to dispersed inequalities in the context of adult suffrage. Singh and Rahim (1989) observed a major shift in the rural leadership pattern and authority structure in the SVPs of West Bengal, Andhra Pradesh, Rajasthan and Gujarat. Shivaiah (1986) argued that the reservation/co-option facility for the SCs/STs in the PRIs made it possible for the weaker sections to get into elective offices and to get into the pace of further development. In the same line of argument, Chaudhary (1987), too, observed that the concentration of power in the upper castes was slowly weakening and new bases of power were emerging.

In order to hasten the pace of decentralisation of power in rural India, the 73rd constitutional amendment was passed through which not only were *Sarpanch* (President) positions reserved for SCs, STs, OBCs and women in the Village Panchayats but a certain proportion of positions was also reserved for them. One-third of the positions were reserved for women belonging to these categories. On a similar pattern, positions in the panchayats were reserved for OBCs too. These reserved positions were allocated on rotation basis. Such provisions of reservation for SCs and STs and OBCs increased their numerical strength in the panchayat positions.

The present paper makes an endeavour to comprehend the impact of such an increase in the numerical strength of SCs, OBCs and women in the VSPs on the rural power structure and constrains emerging in such a transfer of power. Four Village Panchayats have been chosen from Andhra Pradesh, one each from the agriculturally prosperous coastal area, economically backward Rayalaseema with intensive factional feuds, and a prosperous Village Panchayat from Telengana, a semi-dry region with intensive violence between castes. One more Village Panchayat, exclusively dominated by SCs has been selected from the coastal area in order to realise the causes for the formation of a separate panchayat for SCs and its impact on the power structure.

Andhra Pradesh Case

Andhra Pradesh, a South Indian State, lies between 12° 41' and 22°N latitude and 77° and 84° 40'E longitude. It is bounded by Maharashtra, Chhattisgarh and Orissa in the north, the Bay of Bengal in the east, Tamil Nadu in the south and Karnataka to the west. It is the fifth largest state in the Indian nation and forms the major link between the northern and the southern states of the nation. The state has three distinct regions. Firstly, the Telengana region is semi-dry and backward area in terms of infrastructure, educational facilities and the advancement of women, etc. Secondly, the coastal delta area that is very similar to the parts of northern India influenced by the green revolution, with relatively more secure canal irrigational facilities for the cultivation of high yielding paddy and sugarcane. Many of the cultivators from this region are typical capitalist farmers who have diversified their surplus into non-agricultural activities (Satyanarayana, 1985). The area is relatively more developed in terms of female literacy, per capita income, and infrastructure. The third region is Rayalaseema which is drought prone, with intensive violent feuds between factions. The state of Andhra Pradesh has a density of 241 persons per km^2. The state is considered the rice bowl of South India. The official language of Andhra Pradesh is Telugu and the second language is Urdu. The capital city of the state is Hyderabad. According to the 2001 census, the SC population constitutes 16.19 per cent of the total population of the state, which is very near to the percentage of SC population in the country as a whole.

In Andhra Pradesh, elections to panchayats were held in 1959, 1964, 1970, and 1981 in the pre-73rd constitutional amendment period and in 1996, 2001 and 2006 in the post-73rd constitutional amendment period. Out of the total number of panchayats in the state, 15.5 per cent of the Village Panchayats had *Sarpanch* positions reserved for SCs. In addition to the reserved positions for SCs, another 2 per cent of SC village *Sarpanchas* was elected in the 2001 elections through open category, indicating the future dynamics of the village power structure.

In the panchayat elections of 2006 too, a similar trend was observed. Let us see in detail the dynamics of the power structure in the four selected Village panchayats of Andhra Pradesh.

Case Study 1

The village Pedda Amberpet is situated 23 kms away from Secunderabad and 3 kms away from Hayatnagar Mandal headquarters. It is a multi-caste Village Panchayat. The castes inhabiting the Village Panchayat are Reddy (cultivators and entrepreneurs), Brahmin (priestly caste), Vyshya or Komati (traders), Kamsali (goldsmith), Yadava (cultivators), Gowda (toddy tappers), Kammari (ironsmith), Kurumas (a land owning local OBC), Dasari (casual labourers), Kummari (potterer), Chakali (washerman), Mangali (barber), Telaga (oil pressers), Besta/Pallekarlu (fisherman), Mudiraj (wage labourers), Pittalollu (hunters especially who drive away birds from destroying the crops), Madiga (SC, traditionally involved in tanning and leatherwork) and Mala (SC, mostly landless engaged in agricultural work), Mondollu (mendicants). On the basis of their population, Madigas were numerically preponderant (24%), out of the total population of 6,424, followed by Reddies (15%), Yadavas (15%), Gowdas (15%), Malas (14%), Muslims (5%) and Telagas (5%). The remaining castes of the panchayat combinedly have less than 7 per cent of the total population.

The Village Panchayat is preponderantly populated by Hindus (85%) followed by Christians (10%) and Muslims (5%). Hindu temples like Anjaneya Swamy (Hanuman) and Shivalayam (Shiva) are found in the central part of the village inhabited by the dominant castes. A *masjid* is also located in the central part of the village. Two churches, one for Malas and another for Madigas, have been recently constructed in the scheduled caste hamlets that are geographically segregated not only from one another but also from the main part of the village. In the hamlets of the scheduled castes (Dalit/Harijan/Mala basties) deities of little tradition are found. In almost all temples and holy places, until recently, the scheduled castes were not allowed to enter.

A considerable proportion of the arable land, out of 4,120 acres, is owned by Reddies (40%), and followed by Gowdas (20%) and Yadavas (10%). The scheduled castes are dependent on the landowners, mainly as bonded labour, daily wage labourer, contract workers, and seasonal labourers, for their livelihood. They take loans from the landowners to cope with the contingent expenses on the occasion of their daughters' marriages and for subsistence at higher rates of interest. In the event of non-payment of debt, the borrowers are insulted/beaten up/dragged to police stations/courts. A landless respondent aged 60 years narrated, 'Few years ago we used to go to the fields early in the morning at 4'o clock and work till late hours in the fields as we were indebted to the Reddies and were treated as sub-humans'. A landless Dalit woman aged 50 years reveals her experiences in the following words, 'If we go with food for our working husbands in the landowners' fields then we were supposed to remain standing until the landowner ordered us to sit. Otherwise we were subjected to punishment. One day I went to the field with food for my husband working in the fields and sat on the field without the permission of landowner as I was suffering with fever. Then, the landowner ordered me to stand on a single leg as a punishment though I pleaded, 'I am sick'. In hotels, two glass system was in practice earlier. Even in government schools, according to a Dalit respondent aged 50 years, who pursued education in a government school till the 7th standard, 'All the Dalit students were used to siting separately from the non-Dalits. Now and then, the students of upper castes used to beat us and we could not retaliate for such actions of dominant castes' children even in the school'. The struggles for entry into temples, supported by liberal leaders of Reddy and Gowda communities, changed the situation to a certain extent.

Senior citizens of the village revealed that people of Reddy community worked as *Patels* in the police department and Patwaris in the revenue department in the period of Nizam rule in the area and received *inaams* (gifts in return for their services either in cash/land/others). After the merger of the princely state of the Nizam into independent India through police action in 1948, Reddies acquired hegemony in the area till the abolition of the Karanam and Munsabdari system in 1986. They remained in the police department as Police Patels and in the revenue department as Patwaris. They also owned large tracts of arable land and engaged in different modern urban occupations, besides contacts with political leaders. The ex-untouchables considered Yadavas and Gowdas also as dominant castes of the Village Panchayat as they, too, owned significant proportion of arable land, educated their youth, had contacts with officers and politicians, were able to take initiatives, and could spend money in the pursuit of their interests, if required.

In the pre-73rd constitutional amendment period, the Village Panchayat positions were mostly held by the Reddy, Gowda, and Yadav caste people. One or two SC representatives were either nominated or co-opted into the panchayat. The co-opted members remained as members only for name sake or just as symbols in the panchayat power structure, as their views, needs and problems related to their community were hardly taken into consideration at the time of decision-making in the Village Panchayat. They used to nod their heads in affirmation of the decisions of their patrons. Two people, CNR and SRR, from the Reddy caste, held the position of *Sarpanch* for 30 and 15 years respectively. SRR got upward mobility in political life as President of Mandal Parishad Territorial Constituency (MPTC) for the period of 2001–06 after the Village Panchayat was reserved for SCs. Villagers perceived that socio-economic status, urban contacts, modern occupations and patron client based reciprocity provided a support base to these people to control the power structure of the village.

In conformity with the 73rd constitutional amendment, the Andhra Pradesh Panchayati Act was enacted in 1994 and the Village Panchayat was under the general category in the 1996 panchayat elections. Three candidates contested for the post of *Sarpanch*. Two of the contestants belonged to the Reddy caste and the third contestant (PP) belonged to Madiga caste. PP took voluntary retirement from the Andhra Pradesh Road Transport Corporation (APSRTC) from the position of driver in the year 1995. He also owned 10 acres of cultivable land in the village. Though he did not have any previous political experience before contesting elections, he was an active member of APSRTC employee union and Madiga Reservation Porata Samiti (MRPS) which is an organisation for protecting the Madiga reservation. Though PP was defeated in the elections, he gave a tough competition to the dominant caste contestants.

In 2001, the Village Panchayat was reserved for the SCs. In this election, there were two candidates for the position of *Sarpanch* from the scheduled castes. One of the contestants was PP, supported by his own community, as well as NGOs and the Telugu Desam Party (TDP). His opponent N belonged to the Mala community and was supported by the upper castes especially by a faction of Reddy and backward classes. PP gained much sympathy in the village, as a section of the villagers perceived that his defeat in the last election was a consequence of the manipulations by the Reddy caste. His personal rapport with the local people, as a driver in APSRTC, also helped him to gain support. Finally, PP won the elections with a thumping majority in 2001.

The struggle in the Village Panchayat between the elected Vice-*Sarpanch*, SBR, belonging to the Reddy caste and the President,

PP, belonging to the Madiga caste came to light just after PP took position as the Panchayat President. Initially, the Vice-*Sarpanch* wanted to exercise power on behalf of the elected *Sarpanch* and tried to convince the *Sarpanch* about the same. PP was harassed and threatened with dire consequences many times as he declined the proposal made by SBR. Some of the obstacles created for PP in the panchayat functioning are illustrated in the paragraphs below.

An annual function of the government school in the village was organised in 2002. Officials of the education department, school teachers and PP attended the function. A Reddy boy was continuously disturbing the function. Then, the *Sarpanch* came down from the dais and told the boy, 'It is not proper to behave like this in the school function attended by officials and village elders'. Immediately the boy got up in anger, slapped the *Sarpanch* and started abusing him with his caste name, and interpreting his name derogatively as *Pandi* (pig) *Penta* (excreta) iah'(sir). It irritated the *Sarpanch* and he wanted action against the boy. Elders of the Reddy, backward classes and officials convinced the *Sarpanch* and pleaded to pardon the boy as he was a child. This shows how cultural notions are used, even by the children of the upper castes, in the exercise of their hegemony and their dominance over the lower castes with the, alleged, latent approval of their elders. Later, the dominant caste people under the influence of SBR alleged that PP was misappropriating funds allocated to the panchayat. They also influenced the higher authorities to withdraw cheque issuing powers from the *Sarpanch;* these were renewed later with a great effort. They finally contemplated introducing a no-confidence motion in order to throw him out of the position. However, they could not introduce the no-confidence motion as most of the panchayat members and villagers trusted the *Sarpanch*. Even the district level officials intervened to restore normalcy as they found no evidence in support of the allegations.

Another incident of violent conflicts between the upper castes and SCs was observed in the celebration of the Dusshera festival in 2004. In and around Hyderabad, people celebrate the Dusshera festival with pomp and show. PP assumed the position of *Sarpanch* in 2001 (August), the first three Dusshera festivals were celebrated under his leadership and non-SCs played important roles in the celebrations. But, in 2004, those who were actively involved in these celebrations were provoked by their leaders not to get involved unless PP gives more money. The *Sarpanch* denied the proposals and that was why he depended on his own community to make preparations for the event.

The youth of the SCs got such a chance for the first time in the history of the village. Working with enthusiasm day and night, they prepared a 42 and half feet effigy of Ravana to be burnt on Dusshera. The religious elders of the village fixed 4 pm as an auspicious time to burn the effigy of Ravana on Dusshera. Around 3 pm some youth of the dominant caste warned a *Dalit*, an educated *Mala* youth entrusted to act as Hanuman and to burn the effigy, with dire consequences if he burns the effigy. They said, "If a *Mala* boy burns the effigy of Ravana, it will be a bad premonition of a calamity or something worst to the whole village". Dominant caste people started throwing, stones, kerosene, matches and cigarette butts at the effigy. The Village Panchayat President observed this and contacted the Hayatnagar police station for the deployment of the police force. Only two police personnel were deployed. The Mala youth entrusted with the role of Hanuman, four other SC persons and the *Sarpanch* were severely beaten. The police personnel posted in the village witnessed the violence without interfering. At last the dominant caste persons burnt the effigy and PP, along with the victims, went to the police station in the midnight to lodge an FIR against eight people. The government of Andhra Pradesh announced a compensation for the victims at the rate of ₹ 50,000 each for the two severely injured persons and ₹ 6,250 each for the remaining four persons with minor injuries. The revenue department identified the main victims and handed over the compensation. Announcement and payment of such compensation, rather than pro-active steps to prevent such events, is a regular feature in the event of violence against cumulatively deprived sections of society in the Indian democracy.

Kula Nirmoolana Porata Samithi (the association fighting for the abolition of caste system) initiated a collective action in the form of *dharana* and petitions to the administration though the SC/ST Commission had not visited this place. Persons of the dominant caste of the Village Panchayat influenced political leaders and bureaucrats to weaken the case. They succeeded in bringing divisiveness on the basis of Mala and Madiga within SCs as Malas under the influence of the dominant castes declined to become witnesses in the court though they provided evidence in the initial stage of the violence. Higher political leaders offered the position of MPTC to the *Sarpanch* if he compromised on this issue. They also threatened to ruin his future political career if he declined for a compromise. In order to weaken this case, many local level and higher level conflict resolution process were made. The court, in the absence of evidence, finally released the imprisoned persons without sanctions.

Though there was continuous resistance from the dominant caste persons in the village, PP converted all the roads of the Village Panchayat into cement concrete roads, arranged street lights, and provided tap water to the main village and to the hamlets in the purview of the panchayat. He often supervised the functioning of Anganwadi centres and government schools in the panchayat. He was later elected District President for the Association of Scheduled Castes' Sarpanchas in Rangareddy district. Conflicts between upper and deprived castes, as well as within deprived sections, and alignments between them, are influencing either maintenance or change in the traditional power structure of the Village Panchayat.

Case Study 2

Village Krishnarayudi Pedapudi, in short K. Pedapudi, is located in Amalapuram revenue division which is one of the richest divisions within the fertile and prosperous East Godavari district of Andhra Pradesh. There are 1,190 households and 4,250 inhabitants with a gender ratio of 999 women per 1,000 men, according to the census of 2001. The inhabitants belong to 14 castes. The castes are Brahmin, (priestly caste) Kapu (OBC, cultivators or landless labourers), *Raju* (claimants of Kshatriyas status, agriculturists and entrepreneurs), Komati (traders), Devangula/Padmashalis (weavers), Gowda (toddy tappers), Kummari (potterer), Kammari (ironsmith), Kamsali (goldsmith), Chakali (washerman), Mangali (barber), Madiga (SC, traditionally involved in tanning and leatherwork) and *Mala* (SC, mostly landless and engaged as agriculture labourers). The scheduled castes (Mala and Madigas) are in numerical preponderance at 40 per cent of the total population followed by the OBCs, (Devengula, Padmashalilu, Settibalija/Eediga, Kamsali, Gowda, Kummari, Kammari, Chakali and Mangali at 38 per cent and general category castes (Brahmin, Raju, Kapu, and Komati) with just 22 per cent of the total village population. Only 20 inhabitants of the Village Panchayat belong to the scheduled tribe Erukala (plain tribes who rear pigs and are engaged in weaving baskets and mats for livelihood) which does not have representation in the panchayat.

Key informants of the village revealed that Brahmins once had substantial land under their ownership but now they have migrated to urban centres in search of jobs. Very few still own land and lease it out on tenancy to Kapus and Rajus. Some of the Brahmin families have sold off their land and settled in urban centres. Kapus, Rajus, Eedigas and

Gowdas have purchased the land that came into the market and these castes own most of the land in the village. The majority of landless labourers belong to the SCs and backward classes, while a few families from other castes too work as daily wage labourers.

The Village Panchayat elected nine people as *Sarpanchas* from 1964. Out of them, four were from the general castes, three from OBC and two from SC, even prior to the reservation in the panchayat for SCs in the 2001 elections. The village had a unique traditional method of electing the *Sarpanch*. A small boy or girl in the presence of elders would be asked to handover a *laddu* (sweet) to the person whom he/she liked the most from among the aspirants for the *Sarpanch* position. The person who received the sweet would work as *Sarpanch* for five years in general. Through this method the above mentioned nine *Sarpanchas* were elected. MVR, a Madiga by birth, too, became the *Sarpanch* through this method in 1981. But within two and half year charges of misappropriation of government funds allotted for the Village Panchayat development were levelled against him and he was forced to resign from the position as he had no supporters in the panchayat though he had constructed concrete roads in the village. After his resignation, another scheduled caste person was given a chance to function as the *Sarpanch* for the remaining period. The people of the panchayat perceived that 'though seven *Sarpanchas* from non-scheduled castes served the panchayat, none made such allegations against them though they did little work, as they were powerful individuals from within the dominant caste of the panchayat. A scheduled caste *Sarpanch* was forced to resign from the position because he was weak in several aspects such as the absence of SC members in the panchayat, contacts with politicians and officials, etc.

The panchayat was reserved for SC women in 2001 elections. From the SCs, a woman, ULK, was elected to the position of *Sarpanch* in the panchayat elections of 2001. She belongs by birth to Madiga caste. During her term, she had eleven panchayat members, four members each from OBC and general castes and three from the SCs. She pursued her studies up to the 7th class. Her family owned nine acres of fertile land under double cropping of high yielding variety of paddy. She had no previous political experience. She was proposed by her own community as well as a dominant faction of the village on the basis of her family background. Her husband was a retired employee of Andhra Pradesh State Electricity Board (APSEB, which is now AP Transco and AP Genco), and acquired a reputation in the village for solving the electricity related problems of the villagers as he served in and around the village. Thus, the family acquired a reputation and status within the village besides urban contacts. Her immediate challenger was another lady from the Mala community of the village. Villagers perceived that the 'behaviour of ULK's family was relatively better and also more non-controversial than that of her competitor for *Sarpanch* position in the village'. These perceptions facilitated the election of ULK as the *Sarpanch* of the Village Panchayat with a huge margin.

ULK was not given a proper place in several official meetings conducted outside the Gram Panchayat. Officials and political leaders did not follow a protocol in the *mandal* meetings and neglected her though her family enjoyed a reputation within the village. Once, government officials, like the Mandal Revenue Officer (MRO), Mandal Parishad Development Officer (MPDO), political leaders like Zilla Parishad Chairman and Member of Legislative Assembly of that constituency, were attending an official programme at the *mandal* level, in which the *Sarpanch* of the village was not given a seat on the dais though *Sarpanchas* from other panchayats were given a place. ULK's son used to accompany her to *mandal* level official meetings. She explained that 'to attend any official meetings at the *mandal* and district levels she needed her son's support, because her husband was a retired old person'. She attended the training programme of the government conducted at district level and considered it as 'quite useful in running the panchayat'. She conducted all the official meetings with the help of the secretary and other fellow members of the panchayat. She actively participated in the decision-making process related to the identification of potential beneficiaries for each governmental programme without hesitation.

ULK, as a woman, gave importance to solving the problems related to women in terms of providing facilities related to sanitation, drinking water through taps, and promotion of self-help groups under Development of Women and Children in Rural Areas (DWACRA) to empower women. She often supervised the Anganwadi centres and school in the village and established Anganwadi centres in all wards with the help of mandal and district authorities. She got *pucca* (brick and cement constructed) houses constructed for the poor in the village under the Indira Avas (Housing) Programme. She gave priority to education, drinking water and infrastructure in the village. All wards in the village received electricity besides cement concrete roads. She felt that 'this position is a respectable one' in the village. She contributed to the Village Panchayat's development in the above mentioned way through the knowledge acquired at the training centre and hard working nature and attitude of service towards the villagers. Of course, earlier, the dominant castes controlled the levers of power in the Village Panchayat and the development activities were mainly confined to the main village but the hamlets of the weaker sections were neglected. Now, under the 73rd constitutional amendment-based reservation provisions in the panchayats, women of deprived sections are also getting a chance not only to enter into the power structure of the Indian democracy but also to function effectively with autonomy from the influence of their husbands or others. Such an entry of the women of weaker sections into the political structure is resulting not only in their political socialisation but also their political empowerment. Such empowerment further brings the specific strategic concerns of women into the limelight. Relations between castes and factions of the panchayat are now more or less balanced in terms of power in the panchayat and so the factions need the support from both women and men of the cumulatively deprived sections of society to function in the panchayat thereby indicating symptoms of decentralisation of power.

Case Study 3

The Vadavalli Ravigunta Village Panchayat is closer to the Vadavalli Village Panchayat in which the former was a hamlet prior to 1977 and was exclusively inhabited by SCs. The panchayat was also recognised as an ideal panchayat in the Mudinepalli *mandal* of Krishna district of AP. The formation of the Village Panchayat needs a brief historical account. Prior to 1977, the hamlet, along with another one, P. Ravigunta, was in the Vadavalli Panchayat, the main village of the panchayat. Most of the developmental funds were used for the development of the main village in terms of building a panchayat office, metalled roads, school, veterinary hospital and other facilities. The two hamlets were neglected and there was not even a connecting road to reach the hamlets. Both the hamlets were also segregated geographically, not only from the main village but also from one another. Both V. Ravigunta and P. Ravigunta villagers contacted the officials and pleaded for the constitution of a separate SVP for them as the main village dominated by Kammas was discriminating against them. These two hamlets were separated from Vadavalli Panchayat and a new Village Panchayat came into existence. After just five years of this bifurcation from the Vadavalli Panchayat, there emerged a rift between the OBC-dominated P.

Ravigunta and the exclusively SC populated V. Ravigunta as the OBCs started showing discrimination towards the SC inhabited area in developmental activities. An educated youth of SC shared the same with all his fellow Dalits. However, the issue of discrimination became more manifest in 1986 when the Village Panchayat wanted to construct drainage on the side of the SC inhabited area for the disposal of waste water originating from the OBC inhabited area. SC interpreted such a decision not only as loss of land from their inhabited area, without compensation, for public purpose, but as also as the creation of unhygienic conditions in their living area. Thus, they opposed the decision and pleaded for the construction of drainage on both sides of the road so that the waste water of both the hamlets could be drained out without affecting the interests of another.

One day, the *Sarpanch* and his supporters came with labourers and started digging the drainage on the side of SC inhabited area. *Dalits* collectively opposed this and said, 'If you want to dig drainage dig it on both the sides of the road. So, the waste water that comes from your location will flow through the drainage located on your side and our waste water will flow through the drainage constructed on our side'. The Kapus were not convinced with the logic and came on the next day with weapons like rods, other digging utensils like iron bars, cycle chains, etc., to attack the Dalits if they opposed the action. All the Dalits collectively opposed the action of the upper castes and some people from both the sides received injuries and acquired inter-caste sensitivity not only in the village but also in the district. Officials responded positively towards Dalits as some of them belonged to Mala caste and promised to do justice. The Andhra Pradesh government abolished the *samiti* system and introduced the Mandal system in 1986. At that time, the villagers of Mala hamlet protested and staged *dharnas* before the District Panchayat Officer (DPO) and demanded the formation of a separate Gram Panchayat to them. The officials perceived that 'if Ravigunta Gram Panchayat contained both the hamlets of both non-Dalits and Dalits, it will result in intensive violence and conflicts between SC and OBC' any day. An IAS officer, Mala by birth, and the Commissioner for Panchayat Raj Department visited the village, realised the intensity of the problem and recommended a separate panchayat to the hamlet. On that recommendation, Ravigunta Panchayat was divided into P. Ravigunta (closer to Peddathummidi village) and V. Ravigunta (nearer to Vadavalli village). Thus, two panchayats, P. Ravigunta and V. Ravigunta, were formed in the reorganisation of the Mandal system.

The V. Ravigunta Panchayat had 314 inhabitants and exclusively belonged to SC. The village had 270 acres of fertile arable land. Out of the total land 62 acres are owned by 13 SC families and the remaining land was owned by both P. Ravigunta and Vadavalli villagers. The remaining 57 SC families were landless. On the basis of the size of landholdings, seven families owned five acres and more per family, and the remaining owned less than five acres. The landless families of SC were wage labourers and seasonally migrated to distant places like Nellore for agricultural work (Satyanarayana, 1985) and to Pune for non-agricultural work in Muthas (work groups). They used to take loans largely from the richer sections of their own community. The inhabitants of the village are affiliated to Hindu and Christian religions. Nearly half of the SC population has converted to Christianity, which liberated them from the traditional notions of purity and pollution. The SCs have their own places of worship and separate drinking water wells. Almost all the Dalits above 14 years pursue their studies beyond the 5th standard. They are affiliated politically to the Congress and they exercise their votes independently from the influence of the upper castes.

Since the inception of this panchayat, four *Sarpanchas* have been elected from scheduled caste, Mala. The first *Sarpanch* of the Village Panchayat, AVR, aged 60 years played a crucial role in the development of the village and the improvement of the living conditions of the SCs in the village. He had pursued his studies up to B.A. He spoke fluently in the English language, which facilitated effective communication with the bureaucracy. He served for sometime at Pune in the defence department. After retirement from the defence services, he started a printing press at Hyderabad for a short time and finally returned to his native village after the death of his parents. He owns eight acres of fertile arable land in the village. He is an Ambedkarist. The *Sarpanchas* elected later also take suggestions and help from AVR. These *Sarpanchas* have converted all the mud roads in the village into cement concrete roads. The village, at present, has a school, upgraded from primary to upper primary, with a committed teacher belonging to their own caste. Each house in the village is provided with individual latrines under the Central Government scheme of Nirmal Gram. All the children in the age group of 5–12 years attend the school. Out of 70 households, 45 got house under the Indira Avas Yojana along with safe drinking water and drainage facilities. Such a development has become feasible as the concerned officials, MRO, MPDO, visit the village frequently and cooperate in sharing information about the programmes and promptly resolve problems. If the officials fail to visit the village then the villagers express their concern by visiting the *mandal* and Collector's (DM) offices to covey their requirements and complaints before the officials. So, officials do not neglect this village. Let us illustrate the endeavours of AVR in making the landless into owners of half an acre of land through the collective action and cooperation of officials and lending agencies.

In order to provide land to the landless families of the SCs, AVR proposed a plan of not only identifying the vacant land in and around the village but also purchasing it through part contributions of the villagers and financial support from the lending agencies and finally distributing it among the landless SC families. After getting a nod from the administration, AVR discussed the plan with the villagers. The villagers enthusiastically approved the plan. AVR not only mobilised people but also collected a portion of the required money from them and searched for land in and around the Mudinepalli and Bantumilli *mandals*. He identified 25 acres of non-cultivable land in the area for distribution among the landless people of his community in the village. The State Scheduled Castes' Finance Corporation extended financial support for this scheme. Thus, he was successful in not only getting the land but also in distributing it. Personality factors like commitment, community support, communication skills and urban contacts all contributed to this.

Thus, centrifugal forces contributed to the emergence of a separate panchayat for the SCs from the original Vadavalli Panchayat. This resulted in the shift of the power structure from the dominant caste(s) to the cumulatively deprived sections of society. Their collective unified power, supported by the social capital and networks of their committed and motivated leaders, further reinforced the development of the village to the level of an ideal panchayat of the *mandal*.

Case Study 4

This Village Panchayat is situated in Allagadda *mandal* of Kurnool district in the Rayalaseema region of Andhra Pradesh, which is a drought-prone area with violent factional conflicts. The Village Panchayat came into existence in 1959 and eight *Sarpanchas* were elected for the panchayat. Out of them, for the first two terms, the *Sarpanch* was elected from the trading caste (Komati), followed by four times from the Reddy (agricultural) caste and once from the Kamma caste before the panchayat being reserved for SCs in 2001. In the last elections of 2001, a Mala caste person was elected to the position.

The Village Panchayat has 16 castes in all, with a population of 2,831 and a gender ratio of 987 women per 1,000 men. In the Village

Panchayat, though the Brahmins occupy the first rank in the caste hierarchy on the basis of ritual status, they are numerically in minority with 1.5 per cent of the population out of the total population of the village, and 1.2 per cent of the total land in the village. These facts indicate that the Brahmins are only superior in terms of ritual status but not in economic and political matters. They are followed by the Reddy caste with 12.36 per cent of the total population and 38 per cent of the total land of the Village Panchayat. The Komati caste occupies the third place in the caste hierarchy with 1.76 per cent of the total population and 3 per cent of landownership and is mostly dependent on trade and money lending. The Kamma is an agricultural caste with 1.5 per cent of population and 10 per cent of landownership. The other castes like Kapu (OBC, agriculturists or landless labourers), *Kamsali* (goldsmith), Boyas (hunters/archers), Gollas/Yadavas (cattle herders and agriculturists), Kummari (potterer), Kammari (ironsmith), Vadrangi (carpenter), Eedigas (toddy tappers/daily wage labourers), Padmashali (weavers) are clubbed under OBC which is a heterogeneous category created by the polity. They in total had a population of 42.38 per cent with 40 per cent of landownership in the panchayat. Among the scheduled castes, Mala (sweepers and landless labourers) constitutes 19.42 per cent of population and Madiga (traditional leather workers) comprises 19.74 per cent of population. They together own 8 per cent of the total land of the panchayat. The scheduled tribes (Chenchus) are only 0.42 per cent of population. Malas are affiliated predominantly to the Congress while Madigas are affiliated to the TDP. Most of the SCs are landless and earn their livelihood as agricultural labourers. In the lean season they migrate to the nearby urban centres for work. Both Mala and Madiga have their own welfare organisations named Ambedkar Yuvajana Sangam for Malas and Arundatiya Yuvajana Sangam for Madigas. Thus, the Reddy caste has the maximum proportion of the total landholdings in the panchayat and dominates in the village matters. However, they are not in numerical preponderance.

Elections for the Village Panchayat were held only twice, prior to the reservation of the panchayat for the SCs in 2001 elections. The SCs got a chance to occupy the position of the *Sarpanch* of the village for the first time in the history of the Village Panchayat and participated in the elections enthusiastically. OY, whi Yosebu a person belonging to the Mala caste by birth, illiterate and a Hindu was elected as the Sarpanch of the village. He had not converted to Christianity but his parents named him Yosebu. The village has 2.88 per cent of the population converted to Christianity out of the total population of the village. Yosebu is one among the landowners from the SCs. He owns 6 acres of arable land and a bullock cart, is a milk vender and leases out the bullock cart for transportation of agricultural produce to the nearby urban centres and for agricultural imports to the village. Thus, urban contacts in the process of hiring his bullock cart are established which have been further reinforced after he became the *Sarpanch* of the village. He admitted his children in the village school at the primary level.

OY had no earlier political experience and initially faced many problems in interacting with the administration and also in carrying out the functions related to the panchayat. Educated SC youth made him aware of the duties and rights of the *Sarpanch* and also helped him in carrying out the functions of the panchayat effectively. The contribution of the educated youth of the SC in the success of OY as *Sarpanch* of the Village Panchayat needs a brief mention. Whenever officials and political leaders called the Grama Sabha meetings in the absence of the elected *Sarpanch*, scheduled castes' youth used to insist on the presence of the elected *Sarpanch* in such meetings, pleading that the decisions made in his absence could not acquire legitimacy. OY in general used to feel shy, hesitant and show little interest in sitting on the chair, with officials and political leaders, on the dais in public meetings. Such behaviour of the SC *Sarpanch* not sharing the dias with officials and dominant castes is treated as a traditionally and culturally acceptable behaviour in public meetings. Having an SC person sitting with them on a chair on the dais in public meetings attracts the wrath, coercion and physical violence of the dominant castes. OY was not in a position to assert his official position and also was unaware of the protocol of Grama Sabha meetings. He used to sit on the floor away from the dais. In one of the village assembly meetings, officials and political leaders asked OY to sit on a chair along with them on the dais. He declined to sit with them on the dais on a chair and instead sat on the floor. Then, youth of the SC started shouting at the political leaders and officials sitting on chairs on the dais that 'the protocol needs to be observed. Ultimately, officials and political leaders decided to sit on the floor with OY. This instance indicates that the assertion from the youth of SC brought changes from hierarchical to egalitarian norms of interaction. OY worked for the conversion of all the mud roads in the Village Panchayat either into metal/gravel/cement concrete roads. He also worked for the construction of an overhead tank for the supply of safe drinking water to the entire Village Panchayat. Officials also helped him in the construction of houses under the Indira Housing Scheme. They also helped OY in implementing the old age pension scheme in the panchayat. This case study basically reveals the changing norms of interaction between the cumulatively deprived and dominant sections of society under the influence of the 73rd constitutional amendment.

These case studies reveal four different trends in the transfer of power to the cumulatively deprived sections under the 73rd constitutional amendment. The first trend is that the upper castes refuse to take part in the Dusshera festival celebrations for the preparation of the effigy of Ravana as the elected *Sarpanch*, who is a SC did conceding to the views of the dominant caste individuals in the village. Then, the youth of SC made preparations for the Dusshera and at the time of lighting the effigy of Ravana, the dominant caste opposed the lighting of the effigy by a Mala caste person acting as Hanuman under the instructions of the *Sarpanch*. It resulted in violent clashes. Factions, political parties and officials resisted the attempts for the promotion of the SC cause but the sheer spirit of social service and dedication to duty in the developmental activities was asserted by the elected SC *Pradhan*.

The second case reveals that when more than two villages are included under the Village Panchayat and the inhabitants of one of the villages perceives that the other village in the panchayat is devoting funds mainly to their own village but giving lesser importance to the other, it results in the separation of a village from the panchayat and the formation of a separate Village Panchayat. When such deprivations are perceived along caste category lines, the newly formed panchayat is further divided into two panchayats under the *mandal* system introduced in 1986 in place of the *samiti* system indicating centrifugal tendencies. The third case is a case of a woman *Sarpanch* from SC working again with the help of the educated youth of her community in particular for the development of the village in general and the practical and strategical concerns of women. In the fourth case, it is observed that when the elected *Sarpanch* who is a SC tries to accommodate the traditional norms of maintaining distance from the upper castes, then the youth of SC, asserting the practice of protocol ensure the acceptance of egalitarian norms in interaction. NGOs and welfare associations of SCs also played a significant role in the process of transfer of power from the dominant castes to the SCs. False allegations, luring of SC *Sarpanchas* to higher positions in the political system by the dominant castes (to avoid police cases of violence against SCs) and calling the names of the caste of SC are features frequently found among the dominant castes in these Village Panchayats.

References

Béteille, A. 1996, *Caste, Class and Power: Changing Patterns of Stratification in a Tanjore Village*, New Delhi: Oxford University Press.

Carter, A. 1974, *Elite Politics in Rural India*, Cambridge: Cambridge University Press.

Chaudhary, S.N. 1987, *Dynamics of Rural Power Structure: Case Study of an Indian Village*, Delhi: Amar Prakashan.

Gurumurthy, U. 1987, *Panchayati Raj and Weaker Sections*, New Delhi: Ashish Publishing House.

Hirway, I. 1989, "Panchayati Raj at Crossroads", *Economic and Political Weekly*, July 22, p. 1664.

Mathew, G. 2000, "Power to the People", in M.K. Santhanam (ed.), *50 Years of Indian Independence*, Publications Division, Ministry of Information and Broadcasting, Government of India, pp. 27–62.

Mishra, S.N. 1977, *Patterns of Emerging Leadership in Rural India*, Patna: Associated Book Agency.

Narain, I., K.C. Pande and M. Sharma, 1976, *The Rural Elite in an Indian State*, New Delhi: Manohar Book Service.

Ramreddy, G. 1970, "Social Composition of the Panchayati Raj: Background of Political Executives in Andhra", *Economic and Political Weekly*, June 6.

——. (ed.) 1970, *Pattern of Panchayati Raj in India*, New Delhi: Macmillan Company of India Ltd.

Satyanarayana, A. 1985, *Technology, Work and Social Relations in Agriculture*, Meerut: Sociology Workers Sangam.

Sharma, S.S. 1979, *Rural Elite in India*, New Delhi: Sterling Publishers.

Shivaiah, M. 1985, *Panchayat Raj Elections in Andhra Pradesh, 1981: A Study in Institution Building for Rural Development*, Hyderabad: National Institute of Rural Development.

Shivaiah, M. et al., 1986, *Panchayati Raj Elections in Andhra Pradesh 1981: A Study in Institution Building for Rural Development*, National Institute of Rural Development, Hyderabad.

Singh, S. and C.A. Rahim, 1989, "Evolving Panchayati Raj Leadership", *Journal of Rural Development*, Vol. 8, No. 4, pp. 415–29.

Sirsikar, V.M. 1970, *The Rural Elite in a Developing Society*, Delhi and Bombay: Orient Longmans.

Srinivas, M.N. 1959, "The Dominant Caste in Rampura", *The American Anthropologist*, Vol. 61, pp. 1–16.

16

People's Participation in Village Institutions

M. Gurusamy

After the Second World War many colonial states became independent and adopted parliamentary democracy to govern and administer society and to achieve development. A new syndrome of 'modernity in tradition' and 'tradition in modernity' was operating in the socio-political processes of these countries. Decentralisation of power and authority at grassroots was seen as being effective in the achievement of local development and social construction to address the issues of social justice and local institutions. The 73rd constitutional amendment in India provided reservation to women, SCs, STs and OBCs in the constitutionally established panchayats that interact with the traditional panchayats working in the villages. The caste/community leaders are members of such traditional panchayats and one among these members is selected as the President or leader of such traditional panchayat. These community organisations are vibrant in involving the people in local activities. In a few places, a small group of persons in the traditional panchayat chooses the individual to be the leader of the panchayat. In many places, even in a modern society, traditional institutions still look after the affairs of the community such as temples, community properties and more particularly, water and local disputes. They also operate a huge corpus fund. It is now widely accepted that pluralistic and widespread governance will be effective in managing the affairs of the society and hence authority and power should be spread at different levels and multiple centres of power have to be established.

The researchers studied both these panchayats working for the welfare of the people in their respective areas with regard to the participation of the people in these activities. The researchers tried to study the interrelationships among the village institutions (traditional panchayats and Statutory Village Panchayats) and participation of people in village developmental activities.

Methodology

In two Village panchayats, the formal panchayat leaders and the traditional functionaries were contacted with the objective of eliciting their opinion of the success of the formal panchayat in the context of the presence of the traditional panchayat. Formal panchayat leaders, traditional community leaders and leaders of social and cultural institutions were asked questions related to people's participation. Their reactions and observations are presented in this work. Both primary and secondary data have been used for the paper.

Nallukottai Village

The total area of Nallukottai Panchayat is 3.5 square km. There are 5 acres of *poramboke* (common village) land divided under various heads like grazing land, threshing floor and pathway. The village has 460 households in which 3,024 people live. The gender ratio is 909 per thousand males. There are 10 castes in the village like Thevars (territory guards), Kallars (whose traditional occupation is stealing), Pillaimars (industrial agricultural community), Kullalars (potters), Chettiar (trading community), Barbers, Dhobi (washerman), carpenters and scheduled castes (SCs). Agriculture is the main occupation in the village. Agricultural landless workers (coolies) do not get adequate work throughout the year. Their employment is seasonal. Among the total 460 households, 216 belong to BPL category (below poverty line). The village has one anganwadi. One primary and another middle school are located in the panchayat. There is no discrimination between caste groups. The SC community is now empowered. Earlier they called the upper caste land owners Ejaman (i.e., Lord), but nowadays they sit as equals with other castes and fearlessly share their opinions. There is no practice of untouchability. For instance, every year, in the month of September, the villagers, irrespective of caste, worship the village boundary God named Lord Ayyanar. At that time they arrange for a community dinner for all the villagers. Another significant instance of maintaining harmony in the panchayat is the provision of a common burial ground *(samathuva mayanam)* for all caste groups. All the people, including the scheduled castes, bury their communal differences and come here to bury or burn the corpses (interview with the Nallukottai Traditional Panchayat Leader, March 2007).

Women play a significant role in maintaining a clean environment and personal hygiene in the village. The Oorsabhai (place where the elders sit, discuss and take decisions on important matters of the village development, particularly common property resources) and the Gram Sabha Statutory Village Panchayat council meetings motivate the women SHG members to maintain a clean environment and personal hygiene. Thirty self-help groups (SHGs) of women are functioning in the village. One fair price shop is run very effectively and profitably by a self-help group. They earn a net profit of ₹ 25,000 per annum. One grocery shop is also run by another SHG with the help of a subsidy linked credit. Well trained and service minded members of the SHGs involve themselves voluntarily in every aspect of the sanitation of the village. Most of them get subsidised loans from nationalised banks at the minimum rate of interest to carry on some small trades and small business in the village (interview with the SHG president, Nallukottai, March 2007).

There are three village temples, namely, Angalamman temple (equal to territorial ancestor Goddess temple), Mariamman temple (Goddess of small pox and measles) and Adikunda Ayyanar temple (territory protecting God). Freedom is given to the SC people to worship and to have celebrations in these temples. The Ayyanar temple of the village is also known as Grama Deivam (village deity). At the time of the festival the *Oorsabhai* members, youth group members, panchayat ward members, women and SHG members are involved in the law and order maintenance activities and render their services voluntarily. They conduct several competitions during the festival (interview with a traditional panchayat elder member, May 2007).

Local Community Organisation (LCO)

The *kudi* (community settlement) system is the basis of the *Oorsabhai*. The persons who are permanently settled in the village, own land and use the tank water for irrigation are considered as *kudi* members. SC families owing land are also members in the *kudi*. The frequency of the *Oorsabhai* meeting depends upon the needs of the *kudis*. Normally, a minimum of 10 meetings and a maximum of 40 *Oorsabhai* meetings are conducted in a year. The *Oorsabhai* constitutes an Executive Committee of six members headed by the *Oorsabhai* leader for tenure of one year. The Executive Committee convenes *Oorsabhai* meetings, maintains control over the staff, implements the decisions of the *Oorsabhai*, collects contributions from the members, maintains the accounts, receives representations from the villagers, attends the emergency functions of the villagers, looks after the general welfare of the villagers, represents the village to the government and other agencies, prepares yearly accounts statements and finally gets them approved in the *Oorsabhai*.

Participation in Oorsabhai

All the *kudi* members are informed through the public address system and tom-tom to attend the *Oorsabhai* meetings. The meetings are conducted in front of the Amman Kovil from 7 p.m. when people return from work activities to the hamlet. Punishment in the form of fine is levied on the persons who do not attend the meetings. The meeting of the *Oorsabhai* on 1 September, specifically decides upon the date for the bullock – setting festival (a traditional festival). Before a decision is taken in the meeting of the *Oorsabhai*, the opinions of all segments of the community are solicited and only with their unanimous approval the *Oorsabhai* leaders announce the decisions. In case funding from the village is required, the *Oorsabhai* discusses and decides upon the quantum of monetary contribution from each household. For example, in the erection of a drama stage, the *Oorsabhai* decided to collect contributions from the villagers rather than seeking assistance from the government. Accordingly ₹ 3 lakh were collected and finally a drama stage was erected. The details of the income and expenditure of the village are read out and presented in the *Oorsabhai*. If any member present in the meeting requires any clarification, it is provided to the member and after that the accounts are approved. The balance amount is retained in the *Oorsabhai* account and the signatures or thumb impressions of the members of *Oorsabhai* are obtained.

Executive Committee

The Executive Committee of the *Oorsabhai* constitutes six members headed by the *Oorsabhai* leader for tenure of one year. Continuation of the Executive Committee for more than one year seeks concurrence from the *Oorsabhai*. *Oorsabhai* usually changes the Executive Committee in the month of September. Normally, the Executive Committee members are selected, not elected. Though the Executive Committee and the leader of the Oorsabhai have the powers to make decisions, all the decisions are taken collectively in the *Oorsabhai* meeting only. The Executive Committee and the leader of the *Oorsabhai* implement the collective decisions taken in the *Oorsabhai* meeting.

Role of Oorsabhai in Elections

The *Oorsbhai* plays a pivotal role in the elections at different levels of the democratic institutions such as Lok Sabha, State Assembly and local statutory panachayats. The *Oorsabhai* collectively makes decisions regarding the candidates to be supported in the Lok Sabha elections and State Assembly elections. They decide upon the candidates for the post of the Village Panchayat President and Village Panchayat ward members. They also fix the candidates for panchayat union councilor as well as district panchayat ward member. In the Statutory Village Panchayat elections, the *Oorsabahi* decided candidates for Village Panchayat ward membership and the Village Panchayat President were successfully elected for the last three elections (1996, 2001 and 2006).

Participation in Gram Sabha Meetings

All the eligible voters are also eligible to attend the Gram Sabha meetings. They receive information about the Gram Sabha meetings through circulation of pamplet, tom-tom. The Village Panchayat President and the ward members also personally inform and invite the members of the Gram Sabha to attend the meetings. There is no punishment for absence in the Gram Sabha meetings.

Relations between *Oorsabhai* and Village Panchayat

Oorsabhai members regularly attend the Gram Sabha meetings organised by the Village Panchayat. Before attending the Gram Sabha meetings, the *Oorsabhai* members decide upon the items to be discussed in the Gram Sabha and gets quorum through these *Oorsabhai* members in the Gram Sabha. The demands of the *Oorsabhai* are discussed and resolutions are passed thereon in the Gram Sabha. Then the resolutions are implemented. Gram Sabha carried out some important resolutions at the urging of the *Oorsabhai*. They are: (1) ban on plastic use, (2) cleaning houses and streets, (3) imposition of penalty for open defecation, (4) 100 per cent rainwater harvesting, (5) 100 per cent coverage of individual household latrines, (6) small savings, (7) solid waste management, (8) the total sanitation campaign, (9) school and anganwadi sanitation, (10) water and sanitation, (11) health and sanitation, (12) tree plantation, (13) women empowerment, (14) bathing facilities provided for the public to encourage personal hygiene,

(15) creation of a *Samathuvamayanam* (common burial ground for all communities) in the village, (16) creation of a gym-cum-recreation centre in the panchayat for the benefit of the youth, (17) construction of drama stage *kalaiarangam* with 100 per cent contribution from the villagers, (18) arranging a weekly market, and (19) vermin compost made from bio-degradable waste.

Before the Village Panchayat's approval, the above mentioned issues were first discussed thoroughly in the *Oorsabhai*. So, the villagers themselves not only participated in the implementation of these decisions but also extended cooperation to the Village Panchayat President in the implementation of these decisions. Mr Ramanathan as President of the *Oorsabhai* and Statutory Village Panchayat President played a pivotal role for the recognition of the panchayat as the best panchayat by the state government and also received the best panchayat award for two consequent years, i.e., 1998–99 and 1999–2000.

Karisalpatti Village

In the Karisalpatti village, Vanniar caste converted to Christianity is numerically preponderant and owning significant proportion of the cultivable land of the village. Out of the 500 families in the village, Hindu Vellalar caste has 150 families followed by scheduled castes with 100 families and *Chettiyar* caste with 10 families. Karisalpatti has been a Christian Parish since 1976. A primary school was started in 1885 and run by the Parish. In the year 1960, the village community donated four acres of land and ₹ 10, 000 cash for the high school.

Role of Traditional Panchayats

The traditional Panchayat Committee of the Christian Vanniars consists of three members. The *Nattanmai* is the head and the *Maniam* and the *Chinna Nattanmai* are his deputies. The traditional Panchayat Committee is consulted for any social or religious activity in the village. In villages traditional Panchayat Committee members are mostly drawn from influential families. It is observed that through the traditional Panchayat Committee social control is imposed on the people of *Karisalpatti*. Among the Hindus caste-wise traditional Panchayat communities are also functioning. Any unresolved dispute in these panchayats is brought to the traditional Panchayat Committee of the Christian Vanniars for its resolution. The decision of this committee over the dispute between the members of other castes is final and accepted in general by all. The committee also decides the candidates for statutory panchayat elections. The candidates proposed by the committee have succeeded in the last three elections of the statutory panchayat.

Common Property Resources

Drinking water resources

Karisalpatti and Kasavanampatti villages have a joint water supply scheme and the villagers share water in the ratio of 5:3. Nearly 130 households have safe drinking water connections, partly satisfying the drinking water requirements of the villagers. A deposit of ₹ 1,000 and monthly water tax of ₹ 30 per household is collected from these 170 households and partly contributes to the income of the panchayat.

Street light maintenance

There are eighty tubelights in Karisalpatti village. The Government of Tamil Nadu allowed the panchayats to replace the tubelights with sodium vapour lamps which resulted in higher electricity bills. So, the Karisalpatti Panchayat President consulted the traditional panchayat leaders. After that the President declined to replace the tubelights with sodium vapour lamps. Besides this the panchayat used the tubelights between 7 p.m. and 5.30 a.m. and to save electricity and money.

Community tanks and maintenance

A tank under the category of *Manthai* remained unutilised for several years. Villagers used to take their cattle to the tank for washing whenever water was available. After discussions in the traditional and Statutory Village Panchayats, the villagers planted coconut trees, silk cotton trees, bamboo trees, tamarind trees and vaagai trees on the banks of the tank. The community cooperated with the panchayat in the maintenance of this tank. Two years after planting the trees on the bank, the panchayat auctioned these fruit trees and earned ₹ 10, 000.

Community initiative in digging a new tank

Due to the scarcity of water, landowners faced problems in irrigating their land and expressed the need for constructing a new tank in their area during the Gram Sabha meetings. The President of the Statutory Village Panchayat informed the community that the village had no common land to spare for digging a new tank. Then, a few landowners suggested that the parish of Karisalpatti had 4 acres of spare land. They also suggested that the land could be the fittest site for the construction of a new tank. They observed not only that the topography of the land was suited to serve as a catchment area but also that a channel running on the other side of the land could be used as an outlet of water in the monsoon. An eleven-member Anthoniar Tank Renovation Committee was constituted to take up this assignment with the Parish. The Statutory Village Panchayat President served as an advisor to the committee.

The committee, along with the President, met not only the parish priest but also the traditional panchayat Committee members and shared the idea of constructing of a new tank for the benefit of the villagers, in general, and the farming community, in particular. After considering the plea of the villagers, the parish came forward to spare four acres of land for the construction of the tank. The value of the land was ₹ 1.5 lakh. The church authorities permitted the villagers to dig a new tank there. The committee appealed to the potential beneficiaries of the tank, the cultivators whose lands were located around the land earmarked for the tank, to join in this endeavour. ₹ 1 lakh was collected and the tank and the check-dam-cum-outlet-sluice arrangement were constructed at a cost of ₹ 70 thousand. The Anthoniar Tank Renovation Committee and the Village Panchayat organised a ceremony in which the member of the State Legislative Assembly took part in order to show appreciation of the efforts of the community during 2001–02. The committee declared that the tank could be utilised by all the people though the parish owned the legal title to the land. The panchayat leaders facilitated the interaction between the Tank Committee and the Church Parish in getting the land and digging the tank. For the second time the panchayat got a state-level prize and cash amount of ₹ 5 lakh. It constructed community-cum-marriage hall near the panchayat office. An old building was renovated and a part time library is now functioning in it. The Annai Velankanni Pilgrimage Association donated folding chairs to the library. The villagers are using the library.

Major Findings

1. In both the villages the traditional panchayats attracted more participants to the meetings, in the decision-making process and in implementation of the decisions.
2. In case of traditional panchayat meetings, the community decides the date, time, place, rules and regulations as well as agenda for the meetings and in case of Village Panchayats, except the venue, all things are decided by the government and its officers.

3. The Statutory Village Panchayat, with the support of the committees and traditional panchayat, maintains common village properties like tanks, roads and burial ground.
4. People felt that the traditional panchayats implement all decisions taken in the *Oorsabhai* meetings but in the case of Statutory Village Panchayats the decisions taken in meetings need approval and finance from the government.
5. The participation of people in village development activities undertaken by both types of panchayats is in the form of labour, materials and contribution of money.

Conclusions

In recent years it has been found that the convergence between traditional and modern institutions provides an opportunity to use the expertise of the elder members of the traditional panchayat and their indigenous knowledge in not only planning but also implementing village development plans in collaboration with the modern institutions.

Reference

Kudi Register, 2004, Nallukottai: Local Community Organisation.

Part IV

Socio-psychological Probings into Village Life

17

Education, Development and Happiness in the Villages of Western Uttar Pradesh

Prachi Ghildiyal-Dwivedi and R.C. Tripathi

The concept of development in the contemporary period includes factors beyond economic life such as education, health, gender parity, political participation, etc. It is now prefixed with, either social or human, which incorporates the new facets of development. This does not mean that economic development has been relegated to the background. There is no denying the fact that economic growth is a prerequisite for social and human development. But an equally important condition is whether such economic advantages reach/percolate down to the neediest. This approach views poverty as 'capability deprivation' and development as an 'expansion of human capabilities' (Sen, 1999). Economic growth can thus be seen as only one aspect of development that in turn is instrumental in enhancing human and social development. Aristotle too had viewed economic development as 'merely useful and for the sake of something else'. This something else is viewed by Drèze and Sen (2005) as enabling and freedom. Freedom is postulated by them as an essential means as well as the most important end for development. Thus, they view that education and health can play an important role in enhancing freedoms and expanding choices (Drèze and Sen, 2002). Some analysts even make a case for positing these as fundamental rights. Freedoms of different types complement each other and help in building various capabilities which in important ways contribute to the enhancement of quality of life.

Objective data on economic, social, political and health indicators provided guidance to the discourses on development besides the social indicators' research of Ogburn (1946). This approach is considered as 'vulgar' (Canoy and Lerais, 2008) as subjective factors impose limits on the human judgments. It resulted in the development of the concept of bounded rationality (March and Simon, 1958). Thus objective indicators based comprehension of development has shifted to indicators based on the quality of life and subjective well-being in 1970s (Andrews and Withey, 1976; Campbell, 1981). They got attracted to this notion only after they were exhausted of assessing development in terms of so-called 'objective' economic indicators of development. True, the ranking of countries with respect to happiness levels are relatively recent but the concern with the meaning of life is age old and occurs repeatedly in all cultural and religious traditions, particularly in Greek and Indian traditions. Roy (2006) argues that the pursuit of developmental needs of man can not be attained without subjugating it to higher values which sustain life. Kosaka (2007) points out that happiness has remained on the margins of development studies. Studies earlier conducted in relatively wealthier conditions revealed that the level of happiness declined with increased affluence. This is called 'Easterlin paradox' named after an economist (Easterlin, 1974). There is now a world database of happiness and also world maps of happiness based on physical, mental and spiritual health, time balance, social and community vitality, cultural vitality, education, living standards, good governance and ecological vitality. The nations are arranged hierarchically on this basis to comprehend social progress. It is based on the empirical research literature on happiness, positive psychology and well-being.

It is in this context that the issue of correlates and associates of happiness becomes important. Education has long been seen as the cure for all problems that detract a nation from its path towards progress or development. Education also appears to be correlated to psychological well-being as it is conceptualised in Veenhoven's happiness scale (Kirkcaldy et al., 2004). Drèze and Sen (2002) posit five kinds of roles that education has for the freedom of the individual. First, education provides an opportunity for self improvement and growth. Second, it leads to employment and mobility on socio-economic ladder. Third, the educated people are seen as demanding accountability not only from the public servants but also from their political leaders. Education liberates the marginalised sections of society from various oppressive conditions and empowers them to oppose the oppressive conditions.

Finally, education liberates the individual. Hayward, Pannazo and Colman (2005) found that education as primary source of human capital is associated with high paying jobs, better health, personal and political efficacy, capability for better utilisation of resources all of which lead to higher levels of happiness.

However, Michalos (2009) points out that this relationship may not be so direct. Whether people are going to view themselves as residing in paradise or hell is a function of their objective living conditions, accuracy of perceptions, appropriateness of actions they take and nature of outcomes. There are four logical outcomes of interactions among these variables. People see themselves as living in *Real Paradise*, if their living conditions are good and are perceived as such and people take appropriate actions which lead to positive results. They may be living in *Real Hell*, if living conditions are bad and people perceive them as so and their actions result in negative outcomes. Similarly, people may be living in *Fool's Paradise*, if their living conditions are bad but people perceive them as good and their actions yield negative consequences. *Fool's Hell* is described as one where living conditions are good but people inaccurately perceive them as bad and they do inappropriate actions which lead to negative results. The relationship between education and happiness in our case is likely to be governed by the villagers' perception of their living conditions which may differ considerably from the perceptions of living conditions, needs and values of urban people. In the case of village studies, social scientists assessed development more in terms of the needs of villagers and less in terms of their life goals and aspirations. Thus the paper explores the meaning of happiness, its magnitude and relationship with education in the eleven selected villages of western Uttar Pradesh, from Mawana tehsil.

Context of the Present Study

The study is conducted to understand the relationship between education and happiness in the western UP as this region became prosperous as a result of green revolution, as agricultural production has been 22 quintals of wheat/acre compared to 18 and 12 quintals per acre in eastern UP and Bundelkhand, respectively besides more quantum of fertiliser use and mechanised farming. The region has a much higher population density and also greater degree of urbanisation. However, this relative affluence of farmers does not reflect in similar ways in various social indicators like female literacy levels, the gender ratio, gender development index, employment of farm labour, health status of women and children. This region has higher rates of crime as compared to other regions of UP. The rural society continues to be organised hierarchically and along the traditional lines based on caste. Caste panchayats continue to be very strong in governing social relationships and in maintaining them, particularly, relating to marriages. Marriages within the same 'gotra', and within the same village, are found totally unacceptable. The dominant social values support patriarchy and feudalism. The culture of honour is the characteristic feature of these villages. The dominant caste of the region is Jat and the culture of the region has largely evolved around their values. Jats are a group of very proud people and trace their ancestry to the ancient kings who have ruled this Gangetic *doab* belt for a very long period of time. The following Hindi couplet aptly describes the manner in which Jats construct their identity:

Load kar ke rifle, jab Jeep par sawar hote,
Baandh saafa, jab gabaroo taiyyar hote,
Dekhati hai duniya chhat par chadh kar,
Kahti hai kaash, hum bhi Jat hote

(When they load their rifles and ride their jeeps; when the handsome hunks dress up by tying their turbans; the entire world looks at them from their rooftops and says 'Wish, we too were born a Jat!).This couplet provides an excellent social representation of *Jats* which is based around power (represented symbolically by rifle), economic well off-ness (jeep), social prestige or honour (turban or head gear), and physical strength (*gabaroo*). These also happen to be the core values of the people of this region which underline social transactions and inter-personal behaviour.

Objectives of the Study

The purpose of the study was to understand how education relates with various indicators of development. The current state of educational development of the sampled villages is assessed along with other indicators of human development. Data, collected from various households, are analysed to find out the relationship between educational development and happiness levels, their hopes and aspirations within and across villages.

Method

In the first phase of the study, 20 villages of Meerut district of Mawana tehsil were selected. Mawana, one of the three tehsils of Meerut district, provided an excellent contrast for answering the research questions raised in this study in comparison to other two tehsils of the district. It houses the famous Mawana Sugar Factory which had contributed to its development in a significant manner and also covers within it the *Khader* area which gets flooded almost every year during the monsoon season and remains waterlogged. Cultivators of the tehsil were rather affluent while others were either landless or very poor. The population of the Tehsil as per 2001 Census was 69,199 with a gender ratio of nearly 900 women per thousand men. Secondary data, collected from various offices and available village records, were used for assessing human development. Employing similar procedures, Human Development Index (HDI) was computed for each village. Based on HDIs and other indices, 11 out of the twenty villages originally selected were finally chosen for a further in-depth study. The following indicators were used to assess social-human development in the study:

- Overall literacy rate
- Female literacy rate
- Overall sex ratio of population
- Sex ratio of 0–6 population
- Overall infant mortality rate
- Female infant mortality rate (IMR)
- Female work participation ratio(WPR)
- Overall WPR
- Per cent of households below poverty line (BPL)
- Number of civil litigations

The selected eleven villages for the in-depth study were Bahorupur, Alipur Morna, Pali, Makhan Nagar, Bhandaura, Mubarikpur, Maqboolpur, Assa, Kohla, Jhunjhunee and Dudli Khadar.

Data were collected from these villages using three sets of interview schedules aimed to get information from the head of the household, whether male (660 respondents) or female (213 respondents); a woman member of the selected family (806 respondents); and a child; boys (236) and girls (199) from the selected family. Thus the total number of respondents in the study was 2,114. The schedule for the head of the household was framed in a way so as to seek information on demographic variables, economic status, quality of basic amenities, education, health, hopes and aspirations, values and social questions.

The schedule for women mainly focused on issues like aspirations for their children, child rearing practices they use, health related questions, issues related to female foeticides, sonography, family responsibilities and role in decision making as well as questions relating to their desire to learn skills and participate and contribute in efforts aimed at providing education.

The schedule for children included questions related to the activities in which they were engaged in and the time spent on, their aspirations, and educational needs, as well as their liking for the school and the teacher. Besides, the interview schedules, investigators conducted focus group discussions to supplement data collected through interviews. All interviewers also maintained field diaries during their stay in the villages. Thus, both quantitative and qualitative data were collected to answer the research questions.

Children, in the age group of 10–14 years were only included in the sample so that they could respond to the schedule. The sample, thus drawn was purposive. In order to make the sample caste representative, the entire village was divided into *majras*. These *majras* are generally organised around caste lines. Respondents from different *majras* were selected in proportion to a *majra's* size. Thus, in our sample, 47.2 per cent respondents belonged to Other Backward Castes (OBCs), 29.9 per cent to scheduled castes (SCs), 17.3 per cent to minority community and 5.6 per cent respondents to the general caste. This kind of distribution was fairly representative of the demographic distribution based on caste lines in the Mawana tehsil.

Data Analysis

The responses to close-ended questions were coded on the basis of obtained responses on the scales. Appropriate codes were developed for response to open-ended questions and data were analysed in terms of various dimensions of development such as economic, education, health, gender, political participation and social. Infrastructure was taken as another dimension of development. On the basis of correlations, all variables that were significantly correlated to one dimension were selected as components of an index of that dimension, e.g., educational development. However, since all the variables were on different scales that were not comparable, the raw scores for the selected components were transformed into Z-scores. The Z-scores thus obtained for each component of one dimension of development were then added up to get the composite score of that index of development. In this way, indices of economic, education, health, gender, and political participation, social and infrastructure development were computed, which were then summated to get an overall development index for each village. In all, nine indices were developed which included economic well-being, educational development, happiness, social capital, social values, village governance, gender parity, health and infrastructure. These were combined together to form the overall development index. Since this paper focuses on the relationship between education and happiness, the component indices are given below:

Educational Development Index (EDI) was composed of the following dimensions:

- *Educational attainment:* It included the monthly expenditure on education, average educational level of the family and highest educational level in the household.
- *Educational and career aspiration for boys:* It assessed the aspiration of the head of the household for the highest level of education for boys in the family as well as the nature of career desired for them.
- *Educational and career aspirations for girls:* It included the highest level of education and the career desired for girls by the head of the household.

Based on the educational development index, the villages were categorised in to low (mean EDI = 45.4); medium (mean EDI = 51.1); and high (mean EDI = 54.4) levels of educational development. The villages which were categorised as low on educational development were: Bahorupur, Maqboolpur, Dudli Khadar and Assa. The ones which fell in the medium category were – Makhan Nagar, Alipur Morna, Kohla, and Mubarikpur. Similarly, villages with high EDIs were Bhandaura, Jhunjhunee and Pali.

Happiness Index contained the following dimensions:

The extent of family happiness: It included items on the extent to which family members were happy and maintained harmonious relations.

- Engagement in creative work covered items relating to the nature of work a respondent was engaged in and the satisfaction she/he derived from it.
- Social capital included family status, expectations of help from others in times of need, conflicts with other families in the village and the manner in which conflicts are resolved.
- Optimism about the future included items that reflected the hopes of villagers relating to what kind-future they visualised for their family, children and themselves as also for the village community.

The demographic profiles of the villages reveal that there is no systematic relationship between education and other development indicators. Clearly, there is much more to development in the rural areas that need to be accounted for in terms of variables other than education. One of the most surprising findings of this study was that in the high EDI group of villages, the gender ratio was found to be the lowest. The work participation rate of the females also declined with increasing EDI indicating the impact of affluence on sanskritisation process.

General Results

Educational Attainments

Though a lot of efforts have been made to enlarge the scope and accessibility of quality education to all, still the population that has traditionally been marginalised – the SCs, minorities and females – are still lagging behind in most cases. Thus, a caste-wise analysis of the educational attainments reveals that the villages with low educational status still continue to have the highest percentage of illiterates mostly from the deprived groups like minorities (44.4%), SCs (31.9%), OBC (23%), as compared to General Castes (9%). Though OBCs of the region are relatively better off economically but they are relatively disadvantaged in terms of education than the general castes. The proportion of minorities and SCs population is more in the educationally less developed villages. Analysis of correlation between the infrastructure index and the educational index reveals that educational achievement was positively correlated with the average distance of government and private schools from the village (primary, middle and secondary combined), 0.80** and 0.64* respectively. This suggests that physical proximity of schools is associated with greater educational development as it provides educational facilities relatively easily to the villagers. Aspirations of heads of households to provide higher than secondary level of education to their children are negatively correlated with the average distance of the government senior secondary schooling facility from the village (–0.69*) and career of their boys was negatively associated. Thus the aspirations for higher education appear to be the function of not only easy accessibility of government schooling facilities in terms of both physical proximity and financial affordability.

Literacy and Educational Level

Literacy is a fundamental need of an individual or society just like food, habitat, clothes and health. It is also an essential component of self-sustaining human development. Assessment of literacy level of the households in the villages reveals that 26.4 per cent of children in the age group of above seven years were illiterate. The highest percentage of these illiterates was found in the educationally less developed group of villages followed by middle level of educationally developed villages (23.9%) and in highly developed group of villages it was 24.5 per cent.

Caste-wise the highest percentage of illiterate population was among SCs (32.8%) and minorities (31.3%). Analysis of data along caste-wise and gender-wise distribution of illiterate population reveals that SC females are experiencing the greatest disadvantage with about 47 per cent illiteracy followed by females of minority communities with 40.3 per cent illiteracy. These facts indicate that the gap between men and women illiterate population appears significantly high across the villages and caste groups.

Educational development was also seen in terms of the educational level of the households by assigning numeric weights equal to the level of education that he/she pursued in a school per each member in the family, to get the educational level of the households and then averaging the scores gender-wise. The overall education level of the entire sample households so worked out was found upto upper primary level (numerically denoted as 2.4). Again caste-wise analysis reveals that, only the upper castes had an above average educational level, with an index of 3.4. This was equivalent to high school level. Educational levels of minorities and SCs were found to be far below the average education level as their indices are 1.7 and 1.9 respectively. This showed that their level of education was on an average, only up to primary level. This reflected their disadvantageous position in terms of education. In the villages with low educational index, the educational level of villagers was on an average at the primary level followed by medium and high educational index category of villages with upper primary level and high school level respectively.

Apart from the average educational level of the households, an effort was made to find out the highest educational level achieved by people in the village. Our assumption was that those with higher educational levels will serve as reference models and stimulate similar desire for higher education among the children of the village. On the whole, only in 3 per cent of the sampled households, all the household members were found to be illiterate, while only in 2.1 per cent of the households all the members were just literate without formal education. About 35 per cent of the households were educated up to 8th class, 38.4 per cent up to secondary level and 21.6 per cent possessed higher educational degrees. The percentage of those who were just literate without any formal schooling fell down with an increase in the educational development of the villages. The combined percentage of illiterates and those with barely literate status without formal education has declined with an increase in the educational level of the villages.

Schooling Status

School going status of the 5–14 years age group of children reveals that 92.2 per cent of them were attending schools. The lowest proportion of children attending school was 86.7 per cent in educationally less developed villages followed by 93.5 per cent in medium and 96.7 per cent in the educationally highly developed group of villages. This shows that children out of school were mainly concentrated in the less educationally developed villages. Girl children were suffering the maximum disadvantage across all categories of villages. The children of SCs and minorities are the most disadvantaged in terms of their schooling status and their drop out rates from primary to secondary and from secondary to college were the highest.

Access to School

In terms of access to schooling the national norm of access to schools within a distance of 1.5 kms is denied for about 21 per cent of children in the study. However, one noteworthy finding of the study is that the less educationally developed villages have access to school facilities either within the village or within a distance of 1 km at the most. Amongst those who had never attended school, nearly 70 per cent of the children were from less economically developed villages. Interestingly, more boys were found in the category of never attended school than girls while in the case of drop-outs, the reverse was true.

Expenditure on Education

On an average each family was spending an amount of ₹ 222 per month including the expenditure on fee, books, copies, dresses and contingencies for the education of their children. The average monthly amount of expenditure increased from ₹ 163.1 in case of villages with lower level of education index to ₹ 222 per month for medium and ₹ 253.6 per month for higher ED group of villages. The households were willing to incur higher monthly expenditure for the pursuit of higher education to their children in the future from the present to ₹ 229.6, ₹ 331.2 and ₹ 337.5 in the villages of low, medium and higher educational development respectively. On an average each household spent 15.5 per cent of their monthly total expenditure on children's education. Caste-wise analysis of expenditure on education reveals that the general castes spend the highest proportion of their total monthly expenditure on education (20.2%) followed by the OBCs (16.6%) and SCs (14%). Minorities spent only 10 per cent of their monthly expenditure on education. Interestingly the share of monthly expenditure of all caste categories is the least in the high educationally developed villages except in the case of OBCs. The probable explanations for such a scenario may be that either the government schooling facilities provided in high educationally developed villages may be better, thereby, requiring less expenditure by these families or the interest of these people on education of their children is not much, probably due to the prevailing unemployment scenario.

Table 1

Caste-wise Expenditure on Children's Education as Percentage of Total Monthly Expenditure of the Family

Level	*Village Name*	*EDI*	*SCs*	*OBCs*	*Minority*	*General*	*Total*
Low	Bahorupur	43.4	22.5	—	11.0	—	11.6
	Maqboolpur	45.1	8.4	28.6	—	13.9	10.6
	Dudli Khadar	45.5	8.3	13.3	12.7	8.7	10.1
	Assa	47.7	11.9	17.3	11.6	31.3	16.9
	Mean	**45.4**	**12.8**	**19.7**	**11.8**	**18.0**	**12.3**
Medium	Mubarikpur	50.5	13.4	17.7	6.3	34.1	16.3
	Alipur Morna	50.8	22.3	10.5	8.0	14.0	14.2
	Kohla	51.2	10.1	17.1	2.7	45.5	15.2
	Makhan Nagar	51.7	19.3	12.1	10.5	10.6	15.0
	Mean	**51.1**	**16.3**	**14.4**	**6.9**	**26.0**	**15.2**
High	Bhandaura	53.1	0.0	12.9	—	—	13.2
	Jhunjhunee	54.1	7.1	18.4	5.0	7.4	16.3
	Pali	56.1	9.4	20.2	0.6	—	19.1
	High Mean	**54.4**	**5.5**	**17.2**	**2.8**	**7.4**	**16.2**
Total Average		50.3	14.0	16.6	10.0	20.2	15.5

Note: The percentage calculated on total expenditure within the caste group.

Source: Field Survey, October 2005.

Aspirations for Future Education

Both heads of the households and their counterparts (women) wanted their boys to be educated on an average up to graduation (average years of education being 13.8 and 13.5 respectively) and on an average up to intermediate level for their daughters. The gap in the educational level aspirations for the boys and girls by the household heads and their counterparts declined with educational development of the villages. The analysis of profile of educational development and its relationship with other indicators of human development reveals that education was significantly associated with economic development but not with other indicators of human development. This is not to suggest that education plays no role in human development but to explore the necessary conditions under which education plays an efficient role in the human development. This leads us to comprehend the effect of education on the levels of happiness experienced by the villagers in their lives.

Education, Happiness and the Good Life

In the previous discussion it was observed that education was significantly associated with many of the indicators of economic well-being. Data dealing with the relationship between education and the respondents' subjective perceptions about the extent of their family's happiness are presented in the Table 2. Majority of the respondents (46.5%) reported that they are neither very happy nor less happy. Only 26.3 per cent reported being very happy and 18.4 per cent as less happy. About 8.1 per cent of the respondents even reported not being happy at all. The study reveals that respondents who were very happy inversely increased with lower levels of educational development and the respondents who were 'not at all happy' decreased when respondents were found relatively backward on certain indicators of economic and social development. Thus the bettering objective conditions of life (income or wealth) have no effect on personal well-being of urbanised population in the west (Brickman and Campbell, 1991; Bruni and Porta, 2005). Such is also observed 'paradox of happiness' for the present villages under study.

The following reasons were mentioned by the respondents for their being happy with life: Though economic prosperity and a debt free life (24.2%) was the most cited reason for their happiness with life in all the three levels of educationally developed clusters but the largest percentage of the respondents came from the less educationally developed group. In higher educationally developed group of villages' family and children are frequently mentioned as sources of happiness but these facts do not find a place in the less educationally developed group of villages. Amity and accord is perceived as more important in less educationally developed group of villages than in higher educationally developed group of villages. The paradox is that relatively affluent villagers, reported lower happiness levels.

Table 2

Extent of Family's Happiness (percentage)

Levels	*Village Name*	*EDII*	*Very Happy*	*Neither Very Happy Nor Less*	*Less Happy*	*Not at all Happy*	*No Response*	*Total Households*
Low	Bahorupur	43.4	28.7	56.3	13.8	1.1	0.0	87
	Maqboolpur	45.1	26.6	46.8	15.2	11.4	0.0	40
	Dudli Khadar	45.5	32.5	47.5	17.5	2.5	0.0	33
	Assa	47.7	27.8	46.8	20.3	5.1	0.0	115
	Mean	45.4	28.9	49.4	16.7	5.0	0.0	275
Medium	Mubarikpur	50.5	33.3	42.2	20.0	2.2	2.2	140
	Alipur Morna	50.8	22.9	47.9	20.7	7.9	0.7	79
	Kohla	51.2	20.0	45.0	22.5	12.5	0.0	60
	Makhan Nagar	51.7	25.2	42.6	15.7	15.7	0.9	79
	Mean	51.1	25.4	44.4	19.7	9.6	1.0	358
High	Bhandaura	53.1	26.7	53.3	10.0	10.0	0.0	45
	Jhunjhunee	54.1	24.3	41.7	23.5	9.6	0.9	115
	Pali	56.1	24.2	36.4	27.3	9.1	3.0	80
	Mean	54.4	25.1	43.8	20.3	9.6	1.3	240
	Total Average	50.3	26.3	46.5	18.4	8.1	0.5	873

Note: Percentage figures denote row percentage.

Analysis of data on the requirement for a good life reveals that educationally less developed group of villages' perceived economic prosperity as the most important requirement for a good life. However, the medium and higher educationally developed group of village respondents felt that employment is required for a good life.

Clear-cut gender differences were found in the perceived necessary conditions for leading a happy life. Education and a good character (values, discipline, conduct) were endorsed as most important for boys, and housekeeping skills were emphasised more for girls. Though people in the high educationally developed villages acknowledged the importance of education for girls but they were not yet, prepared to relinquish the traditional views of what a girl should be like and should be competent at.

Caste is an important basis for social identity in India, so the participants in the study were asked to enumerate the reasons for being happy and for being sad with their caste. Close to 81 per cent were somewhat happy with their caste. The proportion of not happy respondents' among the total unhappier ones was found in the medium educational development group, while the lowest percentages were found in case of the high educational development group. Amongst those who were happy, 43.9 per cent said they were so because of the cohesiveness of their caste.

Hopes and Aspirations

An important aspect of the happiness of persons is their optimism when they contemplate about their future. Amongst low and medium educational development group of villages, jobs were the main aspiration while for those in the high educational development group, education was the primary aspiration. Job was the choice of most parents for boys. In the case of girls, the largest percentage (36.7%) aspired to get their daughters married. Education was the second most aspired thing for their daughters (23.1%) as against 30.5 per cent for their boys. Interestingly, education appears to have a regressive influence in attitudes towards girls as the highest percentage of those desiring marriage for their daughters was in the high educational development group and the lowest in the low educational development group. Nevertheless, the desire for jobs for their daughters (including wanting them to become professional) increased with an increase in the educational levels. It seems that with high educational development, respondents desire girls also to be involved in economic activities like jobs. In the low educational development group however, more focus is on education alone but not for employment.

Economic prosperity and progress-related aspirations were most frequently found with regard to the expectations of self. A relatively small number had no hope of a better future (6.5%). The most frequent expectation regarding the self in the low and medium educational development groups was of economic prosperity whereas with increase in educational development, most of the respondents became more optimistic about overall progress. But the percentage, from the respondents who were not optimistic about their future, was the highest among the educationally most developed.

Most of the respondents were optimistic about the future and the hopes of a large percentage of them were anchored in their children's welfare (children's success, 31.7%; daughter's marriage 4.4%). About 27.6 per cent believed their family would be happy, prosperous and united. The highest percentage in both low and high educational development group hoped for a happy, prosperous and united family while in the medium educational development group higher proportion of respondents hoped for their children's success. Compared to hopes for the self, a reverse trend of negative hopes for family was observed with the development of education.

Seen on the basis of educational level, the most optimistic hopes were held by those in the medium level followed by high and low educational development groups. Interestingly, the most negative hopes also were held by persons in the high educational development group followed by those in the low and medium level of educational development. Thus, on the whole, it appears that those at the medium level of educational development are the most optimistic followed by those at the high level of educational development. Those having low educational development were the least optimistic about the country's future.

Relationship between Happiness Index and EDI

The three villages where people seemed to be relatively less happy were Maqboolpur, Bahorupur and Alipur Morna while the happiest people were in Bhandaura. Looking at educational development and state of happiness of villages, the least happy persons were in the low educationally developed group and the happiest ones were in the high educationally developed group. Thus higher level of education was associated with a higher level of happiness. However, the happiness index of Maqboolpur, Bahorupur and Alipur Morna were lower relative to the rest of the sample, but it did not indicate unhappiness or dissatisfaction with life. The people here were also happy though somewhat lesser than the rest of the sample. On the whole, high levels of happiness coexisted with higher educational achievement (0.364**), higher educational and career aspirations for boys (0.220**), and girls (0.146**) and higher overall educational development (0.375**). Also, high levels of EDI were associated with engagement in more creative occupations, higher levels of family happiness and more optimism. The correlations between EDI and happiness index at the three levels of EDI are given in the Table 3.

Table 3

Correlation between Happiness Index and EDI

Correlated Variables	*High EDI*	*Medium EDI*	*Low EDI*
Happiness Index and Educational Attainment	0.264**	0.394**	0.324**
Happiness Index and Educational and Career Aspiration for Boys	0.202**	0.182**	0.257**
Happiness Index and Educational and Career Aspiration for Girls	—	0.231**	—
Happiness Index and EDI	0.267**	0.417**	0.339**
EDI and Engagement in Creative work	0.331**	0.495**	0.320**
EDI and Family Happiness	0.245**	0.289**	0.121*
EDI and Optimism	—	0.201**	0.227*
	N = 240	N = 358	N = 275

Conclusion

We found that the villages with less educational development were characterised by a higher percentage of the deprived and marginalised groups like SCs and minorities while higher levels of educational development is associated strongly with the population of OBCs and general castes. At a very broad level, this would also imply that most of the ill effects of illiteracy are being suffered by those groups who have always been at the marginalised position. The less educational development is associated with higher proportion of illiterate population, more out of school children, less average education, highest number of landless persons, least per capita income, and most of BPL households – in short less economic well-being. It is the people belonging to the SC or minority groups who are again found to be the most deprived ones in these matters. Especially in this region, the OBCs are financially sound and the few general castes are also not in a bad situation.

However, despite low education and poor economic conditions, the less educationally deprived villagers did not rate low on subjective well-being. They, of course, have relatively less interest in the future of their state and the country and might be less optimistic about them but they do have strong social networks and are optimistic about their own future. They are happier than those who are relatively more educated and prosperous. They may be living in what Michalos (2009) may term as *Fool's Paradise* because they evaluate their bad living conditions inaccurately as good or tolerable. The relationship between EDI and happiness index is found to vary according to the level of educational development of the villages. Correlations between these two are generally found to be some what higher for the medium group of villages and some what lower for the high EDI villages. One surprising result is with respect to close to zero correlations between indicators of girl child's education and happiness in the villages with High and Low EDI. This is another paradox which one needs to understand. On the surface, the result may appear to be due to the general feeling of insecurity felt with respect to the girl child which prevents parents from having educational aspirations for them. Findings with respect to relationship between education and happiness levels have been rather equivocal. Veenhoven (2003) has reviewed the findings on the association between happiness and education over a period and across the countries. They range between close to zero to around 0.65. Cantril's (1965) study done in the sixties also showed similar results. The correlation between education and happiness was as low as 0.07 for West Germany and as high as 0.72 for Panama. It was found to be 0.31 for India. Our study also shows that there are no secular trends and there are a lot of local factors and conditions which mediate the relationship between level of education and happiness. This may also explain the need to look for the socio-cultural factors in formulating government policies in order to have desired transformations and development across villages in different regions.

Thus, education might not have a very clear-cut influence on one's subjective well-being or happiness. Could this be true because of the so-called collectivistic culture of India and the premium which is placed on going beyond the materialistic acquisitive attitude towards life, although in most villages one finds that a good life is defined in terms of fulfilment of basic needs? A more acceptable explanation could be that the villages in India today are in the midst of a transition where ascription and achievement are valued in the same degree. This is evident from the fact that education is found positively correlated with economic well-being and also predicts it but in the case of happiness, social capital is the main predictor with economic well-being and education entering in the second and third steps of stepwise regression equation. This is to be expected in a culture where life satisfaction and life purpose are derived from one's relationships – not only with the world around but also that which is beyond.

References

Andrews, F. and Withey, S. 1976, *Social Indicators of Well-being: American Perceptions of Life Quality*, New York: Plenum Press.

Brickman, P. and Campbell, D.T. 1991, "Hedonic Relativism and the Good Society", in M.H. Appley (ed.), *Adaptation-Level Theory: A Symposium*, New York: Academic Press.

Bruni, L. and Porta, L. (eds.) 2005, *Economics and Happiness: Framing the Analysis*, New Delhi: Oxford University Press.

Campbell, A. 1981, *The Sense of Well-Being in America*, New York: McGraw Hill.

Canoy, M. and Lerais, F. 2008, *Beyond GDP*. http//www. Beyond-gdp.eu

Cantril, H. 1965, *The Pattern of Human Concerns*, USA: Rutgers University Press.

Drèze, J. and Sen, A.K. (eds.), 2002, *India: Development and Participation*, New Delhi: Oxford University Press.

Easterlin, Richard A. 1974, "Does Economic Growth Improve the Human Lot?", in Paul A. David and Melvin W. Reder (eds.), *Nations and Households in Economic Growth: Essays in Honour of Moses Abramovitz*, New York: Academic Press, Inc.

Hayward, K., Pannozzo, L. and Colman, R. 2005, *Draft: Developing Indicators for the Educated Populace Domain of the Canadian Index of Well-being, Interim Report*, GPI Atlantic, Halifax.

Kirkcaldy, B., Furnham, A. and Siefen, G. 2004, "The Relationship between Health Efficacy, Educational Attainment and Well-Being among 30 Nations", *European Psychologist*, Vol. 9, No. 2, June, pp. 107–19.

Kosaka, K. 2007, "Sociology for Happiness: Beyond Western versus Non-Western Perspectives", *Sociological Bulletin*, Vol. 56, No. 3, pp. 369–82.

March, J.G. and Simon, H.A. 1958, *Organisations*, New York: Wiley.

Michalos, A.C. 2009, "The Good Life: Eighth Century to fourth Century BCE", in K.C. Land (ed.), *Handbook of Social Indicators and Quality of Life Research*, Netherlands, Dordrecht: Springer.

Ogburn, William F. 1946, *A Study of Rural Society*, Cambridge: Riverside Press.

Sen, A. 1999, *Development as Freedom*, New York: A.A. Knopf.

Veenhoven, R. 2003, "Happiness", *The Psychologist*, 16 (3), p. 128.

18

Psychological Status of Suicide Victim Cultivators of Sangrur in Punjab

Sanjay and A. Satyanarayana

The phenomenon of suicide among cultivators in the states of Andhra Pradesh, Karnataka, Kerala, Punjab and Maharashtra in India has attracted the attention of social scientists and public policy makers in recent times. This phenomenon is mostly prevalent among cultivators of commercial crops with high yielding varieties of seeds like cotton, groundnut, chilli, soyabean, etc. Such commercialisation (AWARE, 1998; Assadi, 1998; Vasavi, 1999; Iyer and Manick, 2000; Deshpande, 2002; Mishra, 2006; Jodhka, 2006; Rao and Suri, 2006; Sridhar, 2006) of agriculture with high cost of production, crop failures, and price fluctuations has resulted in greater intensity of indebtedness among cultivators of such crops. The studies (Iyer and Manick, 2000) conducted on suicides among cultivators reveals that high intensity of indebtedness and crop failures, are found as the most important reasons for the phenomenon. Besides, these two factors domestic discord, and drug abuse are also found as contributing to the suicides mostly among poor peasants (Kumar and Sharma, 1998). Various surveys (MASR, 1998; Iyer and Manick, 2000; Kumar and Sharma, 1998; Association for Democratic Rights, 1998) conducted in Punjab reveal that crop failure and high intensity of indebtedness are the main causes for suicides. Mohanty (2005) tried to comprehend the phenomenon of suicides among cultivators in Maharashtra. He found that the rate of suicides among small size of landholders is more as they devote more than 60 per cent of their total land for cotton cultivation. Even though different size of landholders are cultivating high yielding varieties of crops that requires more capital, differential consequences are observed on the basis of size of landholdings. Most of the small size landholders fail to recover the production cost and thus fail to repay the borrowed loan either from formal or informal agencies or both. However, larger size of landholders experienced more intensity of family quarrels, business failures, degradation of social status and power that seems to have contributed to suicides among rich peasants. Sharma and Mohankumar (2006) further support these findings on the basis of their study in Kerala. Jodhka (2006) observed that drought leads to differential consequences on the basis of size of landholdings. It affected more intensely the small cultivators and resulted in downward social mobility in terms of landholdings leading to loss of status in rural life. Narasimha and Suri (2006) found supportive evidence to the earlier studies from their study in Andhra Pradesh. Mishra (2006) compared the normal cultivators with the suicide victim cultivators and found that indebtedness in proportion to the asset what the suicide victims owned is very high than the normal cultivators. In addition to this, the suicide victims' households have a larger size of family with more women and non-workers. Sridhar (2006) observed that the suicides are concomitantly related to the shift in cropping pattern from traditional rain-fed cereal crops to commercial crops in the recent past in Andhra Pradesh.

Though indebtedness and crop failures are chronic in the traditional Indian agriculture but suicides among cultivators were never reported earlier to 1988. The observations of Darling and Darling (1927) on peasants in Punjab are insightful. According to them "The Indian peasant takes birth in debt, lives in debt and dies in debt", but they found no suicides among cultivators. The traditional agriculture dependent on rainfall with significant crop diversity and traditional variety of seeds fulfiled at least minimum subsistence requirements of cultivators at times of partial crop failures due to drought/heavy rainfall. In case of total crop failure, family labour was the only loss the cultivators incurred. Other inputs are available at local level in terms of farm tools, cattle and fertilisers. In the case of commercialised and mechanised agriculture, the high yielding varieties of seeds are vulnerable to insecure irrigational facilities. Besides this, cultivation of HYV crops requires use of fertiliser at proper time to have optimal produce. This vulnerability further intensifies with market fluctuations and disparity in agricultural produce price and agricultural input prices. This disparity in prices and price fluctuations will lead to chronic indebtedness among cultivators. Besides this the consumption pattern of the cultivators too changed towards adoption of urban cultural symbols that seem to contribute to the enhancement of their status in the rural society and also the intensity of debt.

However, these above-mentioned studies have given scant attention to the following issues: first, the integration of the individual with institutions such as family, economy and culture needs to be comprehended more systematically. Second, the use of loans and its recovery process by formal and informal lending agencies also needs to be understood that affects the family and individual in terms of social isolation, feelings of degradation of status, disintegration of joint household and drop-out of the children from schools. Third, the occupational diversification of the family and the urban support system to the rural kin also needs to be looked into in order to comprehend this phenomenon more holistically in a comparative framework. Fourth, the households with suicides and the households without the incident but with similar intensity of indebtedness are compared in order to realise the significant differences between these two types of households. These four questions are addressed in this study conducted in district Sangrur, Punjab. Sangrur district has been chosen for the study as the percentage share of total suicides in the district is up to 50 per cent of the total suicides in Punjab and the rate was 12.08 per lakh population (Kumar, 1988).

II

The study was conducted in 10 villages belonging to three blocks, of Sangrur district. In these villages, sixty-two cases of suicide victims' households were identified through multiple techniques. For instance, these cases are identified from the police records (only 5 suicides), the study of Institute of Development and Communication (53 suicides), the study of Punjabi University (79 cases), the study of Iyer and Manick (2000) (80 cases) and movement against state repression (120 cases). For the purpose of comparison, a representative sample of 50 indebted cultivators was selected at the rate of five households from these ten villages in consultation with Nayab Tehsildars and village Pradhans. Thus, the sample of the study comprised 62 suicide victims' households, a control group of 50 indebted normal cultivators.

Close relatives (mainly victim's husband/wife and parents) and friends of suicide committers, normal cultivators' family members were interviewed with an unstructured interview schedule in order to identify the processes and structural conditions that caused the suicides. Interviews were recorded in the form of narratives. From these narratives case studies were developed. These cases will provide substantial evidence to realise various causes of suicides beyond indebtedness.

Besides narratives, a Depression Level Examination Scale (DLES) was developed to access the depression level of the suicide victims and normal cultivators to the mechanisms adopted by the formal and informal lending agencies for recovery of the debt. The formal lending agencies issue and paste recovery certificate notices on the walls and doors of the indebted cultivators while the informal lending agencies issue threats and humiliate the debtor even in the public places such as market. Such mechanisms have an impact on the behavioural pattern of debtors. Such changes in behavioural pattern were collected from the close relatives of the suiciders, i.e., husband/wife/parents, etc. Some items of the DLES were related to the standard depression scales developed by Hamilton Rating Scale for Depression (Hamilton, 1960; Radloff, 1977).

III

Analysis of data of suicide victim and normal cultivator households reveals that both belong to middle age group (26–55 years), followed by younger age (below 25 years) mostly, were illiterate (more than two-fifth), married, with less than four hectares of land. Households were larger in size (7–8 members per household) and mostly belonged to upper castes like Jat and Brahmin. In terms of consumption pattern both normal and suicide victims have more similarities. Both the categories belonging to rich cultivators purchase two wheelers like scooters and motorcycles, colour televisions, air-conditioners and refrigerators while the middle peasantry purchases mostly colour televisions, coolers, two wheelers and jeeps. More suicide victims belonging to poor peasant category had music system, black and white TV sets, coolers and two-wheelers than normal cultivators. Thus, both the cultivators adopted those cultural items that enhance their status. These facts indicate that cultivators in general are diverting a portion of their borrowed loans in purchasing status enhancement oriented cultural items and remain indebted. Both the suicide victims and normal cultivators mostly adopted the high yielding varieties (HYV) of seeds of paddy and wheat that requires both short and long term loans to cope up with the crop-cycle requirements and they borrow loans from informal lending agencies like commission agents, arathiyas, dealers and sub-dealers of pesticides and moneylenders besides the formal lending agencies after mortgaging their land and farm tools like tractor.

The landless labourer and the normal cultivators with smaller sizes of landholdings, in general, had marginally higher intensity of indebtedness to the tune of 1.02 of the total assets where as the suicide victim cultivators had intensity of indebtedness to the tune of 0.98 to the total assets they owned. It indicates that both the sample categories had more or less the same intensity of indebtedness in proportion to their assets. As the intensity of indebtedness is more or less same in both the categories of the sample, so it can be assumed that indebtedness may be a necessary condition but not a sufficient condition to explain the phenomenon of suicides. These are only fewer similarities between suicides victims and normal cultivators.

However, both the categories of the sample differ on the following points. The normal cultivator households have a higher average size of landholdings (2.04 hectares) than suicide victims (1.22 hectares) at the time of repayment of loan though they had similar average size of landholdings. The members of normal cultivator households had a higher degree of occupational diversity, as 11 members of the normal cultivator households are involved either in government/private service or in shopkeeping in urban centres. The suicide victim households are mostly dependent on agriculture either as cultivators or as landless labours and occupational diversification is very less as only three members are involved as salesperson: one in shoe shop and two in tailoring in urban centres. This occupational diversity possibly provides some support system to the indebted normal cultivators' kin dependent on agriculture in rural areas but the possibility seems to be less in the case of suicide victim households as their three kin members are engaged in low paid jobs. These observations would be clearly visible in case study data.

Both normal and suicide victim cultivator households devoted their land mostly for wheat and paddy crops but the proportion of land allotted to cotton, vegetables and maize is relatively more by the suicide victim households than the normal indebted cultivator households. The intensity of cropping before receiving the receipt of recovery notice is more or less same in both the cases of suicide victims and normal cultivators. However, after the receipt of recovery notice and imprisonment, the intensity of cropping in the case of suicide victim households has declined nominally while the normal cultivator households continued and maintained the earlier intensity of cropping. This indicates that the interest of suicide victims in activities prior to committing suicide has declined though nominally in comparison to the normal cultivators. Most of the suicide victims are partial owners of farm tools such as bullock carts, tractors, tubewells and threshers. If we analyse ownership of tools according to size of landholdings then 13 households with less than 2 hectares of land had a tractor and 18 households had a tubewell and three households owned threshers from the sample of suicide victim cultivators. More proportion of suicide victim households (20/62) had no farm tools and only nine out of 50 normal cultivators had no farm tools and they hired agricultural tools on rent. Thus the normal cultivators have more farm implements than suicide victims. Owners of less than 2 hectares of land used tractors mostly for transporting people and visiting religious places rather than hiring it out in the case of suicide victim cultivators whereas the normal indebted cultivators besides using their tractor for religious functions and ceremonies, also leased it for income generating activities such as plowing, transporting and other activities to certain extent. So the normal cultivators could generate additional income from hiring the tractor whereas the suicide victims used the tractor more or less as a status symbol and source of prestige in society.

Analysis of data on the patterns of using the borrowed loans revealed that most of the suicide victims spent the loans borrowed from informal agencies on renovation of the residence, giving dowry, social ceremonies like *mundan* (hair shaving of the children), birthday celebrations and purchasing non-consumable goods such as coolers, television sets, tractors, two-wheelers. Nearly three-fourth to two-third of borrowed loans are spent on these items. The same pattern has also been observed in the case of normal cultivator households though the proportion of borrowed loan has been around less than 50 per cent on average. Thus, both failed to repay the loan instalments in time.

In the context of non-payment of regular instalments to the lending agencies in time, both the agencies initiate steps for the recovery of loan. The formal lending agencies allow the accumulation of dues in general for one-year and such accumulated dues lead to penal interest in addition to the normally specified interest rate. Delay in repayment of regular instalments to formal lending agencies, results in the issue of recovery notices, which are pasted on the walls of the indebted person's residence. If the indebted person fails to respond to the recovery notice in the form of depositing a portion of the accumulated interest, second recovery notice gets issued just after two weeks along with a warning of police arrest and finally auctioning of property. Even after the second recovery notice, if the indebted person fails to pay a portion of the debt, then the third recovery notice will be dispatched through registered post. These recovery steps of formal lending agencies will result in stress and prolonged anxiety to the indebted person for repayment of loan. Non-compliance of recovery notices will force the formal lending agencies to take further harsher measures like actual arrest and imprisonment for two weeks and finally auctioning his property. Thus indebtedness converts the personal problem of an indebted person into a public concern and arouses anxiety and injects a feeling of status deterioration within their rural community.

In the crises of repayment of debt, the indebted person expects financial and social support from primordial relations like family, kin, and friends. Instead, his siblings take steps to partition the unmortgaged land among them, leaving the mortgaged land with the indebted person. Such an action results in unpleasant feelings, sadness and reduction in the integration of the indebted person with his family and kin. The final act of arrest and imprisonment further leads to social isolation and stigma. The debtors' economic and social status further deteriorates when patrimony is auctioned, which provided him social status and power in the community and fulfiled subsistence needs of his family. These processes of loan recovery are generally followed in the case of suicide victims and normal cultivators. However, both the samples under study differed in coping with such situations, i.e., the normal indebted cultivator households paid the loan first and later partitioned the patrimony among siblings or remained to live jointly while in the case of the suicide victim households the younger siblings partitioned the unmortgaged land leaving the mortgaged one with the borrower of the loan. These facts indicate that priority of values differed in terms of collectively or individually coping with the crisis.

In the case of suicide victims, out of cultivators indebted to formal lending agencies (10), four-committed suicide just after receiving the recovery notices and six after police arrest and imprisonment. The remaining suicide victims borrowed loans from informal lending agencies (41) and (11) from both formal and informal lending agencies, faced humiliation in public places like market and village. Beside this humiliation, they also received threats of dire consequences in the event of non-payment of loan in time. In the case of suicide victims these processes of recovery and lack of social and financial support from the primordial relations led to loss of self-respect, honour, and status, and resulted in social isolation, shame and guilt. This is revealed in the content analysis of the narratives provided by the kin of suicide victims.

Though the normal cultivators too experienced the same recovery processes of loan recovery from formal and informal lending agencies, but their well-to-do primordial relatives like brothers, uncles and brother-in-laws engaged in both agricultural and non-agricultural activities extended financial support. Eleven collateral households paid their loans after selling the mortgaged land. After the repayment of loans only few of them partitioned the un-mortgaged land among them equally (13/50) or borrowed another loan from *arthiyas* after mortgaging other piece of land (26/50) and retained the collateral household structure. However, the wife of the suicide victim households insisted not to sell the land but to find alternative ways for the payment of loan as it yields power and status in the community not only for the present generation but also to the next generation. Auctioning of property is treated as a loss of status and power in the village community by both respondents but alternative life chances were searched more by the normal indebted households while the suicide victim households could not visualise alternative life chances for survival after the loss of patrimony. These interpretations are supplemented with case studies of cultivators belonging to normal cultivators and victims of suicide in the last section.

IV

The content analysis of narratives given by the close friends and family members of suicide victim and normal cultivator households reveals that the suicide victim households were interacting less with family members and friends, i.e., socially isolated/alienated with family/kin and friends, used to look sad, expressed feelings of hopelessness, feelings of worthlessness in their talks with the family members, decline of livestock care, crops and farm tools, sleep disorders and headaches more intensively than the sample of normal indebted households. The above items are categorised into social, psychological, economic, and physical health and are presented in Table 1.

Table 1

Frequency, Mean Score and Standard Deviation of Contents of Different Items of Narratives of Suicide Victim and Normal Cultivators

Content Items	*Suiciders Cultivators (62)*			*Normal Cultivators (50)*		
	Freq.	*Mean score*	*SD*	*Freq.*	*Mean score*	*SD*
1. Social Dimension						
A Socially isolated/ alienated with family and friends	193	3.02	2.16	00	00	00
B Interacting less with family members and friends	104	1.76	2.50	00	0.54	0.76
2. Psychological Dimension						
A Feelings of helplessness	219	3.39	2.34	01	0.02	0.14
B Looking sad	195	3.15	2.24	27	0.54	0.68
C Worthlessness feelings	91	1.47	1.85	00	0.00	0.00
3. Economic Dimension						
A Decline of interest in livestock, crops and farm tools care	87	1.37	2.04	27	0.54	0.73
4. Physical health Dimension						
A Sleep disorder	135	2.13	0.00	27	0.54	0.76
B Headache	41	0.61	1.14	22	0.42	0.61

The above table shows that the suicide victim cultivators had higher mean scores on all these items in their narratives than that of the normal cultivators. The chi-square analysis of data revealed that on the above mentioned dimensions there was a significant difference between the two categories of cultivators along each dimension, i.e., social (χ^2 (1)= 307**, p<.01), psychological (χ^2 (1)= 426.88**, p<.01), economic (χ^2 (1)= 31.58**, p<.01), and physical health (χ^2 (1)= 35.94**, p<.01). It can be safely concluded on the basis of these results that suicide victim households' social interaction declined more with family members, kin and friends as compared to the normal indebted households. The suicide victim households expressed feelings of hopelessness, helplessness and worthlessness more frequently in their talks with their kin and friends and were looking sad frequently than the comparative sample of households. In economic activities too, the family members observed that the suicide victim did not show interest in their livestock, crops and farm tools care. Besides this, the family members of suicide victims reported that the suicide victims used to tell now-and-then, about their daily sleep disorders and headache related problems 15 to 30 days before committing suicide.

V

The DLES, containing five points, was used in order to rate the behavioural patterns as observed, 15 to 30 days before committing suicide or payment of loan, by close friends, kin and family members of the suicide victim and normal indebted cultivators. In the administration of DLE scale, only 50 suicide victim cultivator households out of 62 could be contacted as the remaining families emigrated from the villages. DLES consists of four dimensions – unhappy feelings (feelings of sadness, hopeless, discouraged, isolation and restless/lacking energy), reduced activities (decline in livestock care, taking no care of ones health, less talk, meeting no friends, withdrawal from others), physical changes (sleep disorder, headaches, frequent feelings of irritation for smaller and smaller issues), negative thoughts ("I am a failure", "I am not good", "No one cares", helplessness, "May be my family would be better off without me"). Variation in the intensity of depression states of suicide victims and normal cultivators was statistically analysed through t-test.

Table 2

Variational Intensity of Depression States of Normal and Suicide Victim Cultivators

Dimensions	*Sample*	*Mean Scores*	*Std. Deviation*	*T-value (df = 49)*
Unhappy feelings	Suicide victim cultivators	6.44	1.30	16.92**
	Normal cultivators	2.72	0.86	
Reduced activities	Suicide victim cultivators	22.36	2.71	27.90**
	Normal cultivators	9.48	1.82	
Physical changes	Suicide victim cultivators	6.56	2.21	9.66**
	Normal cultivators	3.24	1.02	
Negative thoughts	Suicide victim cultivators	14.62	2.55	25.32**
	Normal cultivators	4.82	1.00	
Overall depression level	Suicide victim cultivators	49.98	5.02	33.90**
	Normal cultivators	20.26	3.63	

**p< (2.01), *p< (2.68)

Suicide victim and normal indebted cultivators differed significantly in the overall depression level (t = 33.90**), unhappy feelings (t = 16.92**), reduced activities (t = 27.90**), physical changes (t = 9.66**) and negative changes (t = 25.32**).

The item-wise mean scores and t-test on DLES have been calculated corresponding to normal and suicide victim cultivators (Table 3). An inspection of the mean scores reveals a greater variation between suicide victim and normal cultivators' scores on the five-point rating scale.

Table 3

Mean Score and t-score of the Items of DLES between Suicide Victims and Normal Cultivators

Item Content	*Suicide Victim Cultivators (50)*		*Normal Cultivators (50)*		*t-score*
	Mean score	*Std. Deviation*	*Mean score*	*Std. Deviation*	
Looking sad	3.66	1.10	1.50	0.68	11.83**
Not caring for health	3.48	0.79	1.74	0.88	10.44**
Loneliness (isolation)	3.74	0.83	1.56	0.67	14.43**
Lesser talks	4.16	0.79	1.36	0.48	21.33**
Sleep disorder	3.10	1.31	1.50	0.68	7.66**
Not meeting friends	3.88	0.85	1.74	0.88	12.41**
Feelings of failure	3.30	1.16	1.02	0.14	13.74**
Frequent expression of irritation	2.78	0.91	1.22	0.42	11.01**
Feelings of 'I am not good'	3.64	0.96	1.76	0.89	10.12**
Feelings of 'May be my family would be better off without me'	3.68	1.27	1.02	0.14	14.73**
Decline in the livestock care	3.12	1.38	1.56	0.97	6.54**
Sense of complete powerlessness (helpless)	4.00	0.95	1.02	0.14	21.99**
Headaches	3.46	1.42	1.74	0.88	7.30**
Withdrawing from interaction with others (staying in house)	3.98	1.20	1.52	0.61	12.87**

**p< (2.01), *p< (2.68)

The analysis of the data obtained on the DLES from the respondents, on the basis of mean scores, reveals that the suicide victims and normal cultivators differ significantly on every item of DLES. Mean score of every item of DLES also suggests that suicide victims had more negative symptoms and feelings than normal cultivators.

The analyses of the scores obtained on DLES along dimensions are categorised into low, medium, and higher levels of depression. The comparison was based on mean scores and significance was tested using χ^2 – value.

Table 4

Frequency and Percentage of Suicide Victim Cultivators and Normal Cultivators on Three Levels; High, Medium, and Low Level on basis of Different Dimensions of DLES

		Unhappy Feelings	*Reduced Activity*	*Physical Changes*	*Negative Thoughts*	*Overall Depression*
Suicide victim cultivators	High	11(22%)	31(62%)	14(28%)	26(52%)	17(34%)
	Medium	38(76%)	19(38%)	24(48%)	24(48%)	33(66%)
	Low	1(2%)	0(0%)	12(24%)	0(0%)	0(0%)
Normal cultivators	High	0(0%)	0(0%)	0(0%)	0(0%)	0(0%)
	Medium	6(12%)	5(10%)	15(30%)	7(14%)	4(8%)
	Low	44(88%)	45(90%)	35(70%)	43(86%)	46(92%)

The above table shows that the suicide victims' cultivators were suffering from either high or medium levels of depression while most of the normal cultivator households experienced low level of depression. Thus the study reveals that indebtedness *per se* may be a necessary cause of suicides but not a sufficient cause. The non-extension of normatively expected support in crisis by the close kin and breakdown of families into nuclear type at the time of repayment of loan and downward social mobility of the cultivators from the marginal and small size of landowners to landless category led to helplessness, isolation and depression that cumulatively contributed to the suicides. This point can further be elaborated with case material.

VI

Case of Suicide Victim: A Middle Peasant

The cultivator was a Sikh-Jat, 45 years old, and illiterate. He had two sons aged 8 and 10 years and attending class 2nd and 3rd respectively in the government primary school located in the village. He jointly owned six acres of land along with his two younger brothers. His two younger brothers were aged 37, and 35, married and educated up to 5th standard. The collateral household used to cultivate wheat on the total land and paddy on almost total (5.9 acres) land. Vegetables were also cultivated for household consumption on a small piece of land. They hired the farm tools for plowing, and household members contributed labour in the cultivation of crops. They irrigated the land by leasing in the services of tubewell from neighbourous landowners. To cope up with the plowing and transportation requirements, the three brothers jointly decided to purchase a second hand tractor from their own saving and bought one in 1988 with the help of a broker. The river Ghaggar overflew the banks in the rainy season and damaged the kharif crop (paddy) severely for two successive years from 1990 to 1991. The severe damage of kharif crop forced the household to borrow agricultural loans, as he had no more saving after the purchase of tractor, to the tune of ₹ 1 lakh from the cooperative bank after mortgaging two acres of their cultivable land in 1992. In the process of receiving loan, the household received help from a broker who took a total of ₹ 9,000 as commission along with the bank staff. Thus, the household head received only ₹ 91,000 out of the total sanctioned amount of ₹ 1,00,000. He invested 33 per cent of the borrowed loan in purchasing seeds, fertilisers and pesticides. He spent the remaining 66 per cent of the loan on renovation and painting of the house and purchased a colour TV (in place of a black and white TV), cooler and arranged a party for his kin and friends on the eve of receiving the loan amount. In 1992, the kharif crop was once again damaged for the third consecutive year due to floods. The household was not able to repay even the instalments in the period of 1992–93. In June 1993, the household head received recovery notice from the cooperative bank. He contacted the bank officials and pleaded for relief but in vain. Then he contacted the broker, who was instrumental earlier in getting the loan, to pursue the bank officials for relief. The broker assured to get the instalment amount deducted but informed the cultivator that the number of instalments would increase. He also told the cultivator that the coming new government in the state would waive the loans for all and assured the household head not to worry. For this service the broker took a sum of ₹ 8,000 from the cultivator as his service charges. The cultivator could not pay even the reduced instalment amount for six months and in addition, the loan was not waived by the state. In the meantime, the principle, interest and penal interests cumulatively increased up to ₹ 1,30,000. In addition to this he had to pay a sum of ₹ 8,000 to the broker. In order to cope with these demands, the cultivator sold the tractor for ₹ 40,000 and paid the broker's commission (₹ 8,000) and ₹ 32,000 to the bank against the loan. After this, the cultivator was unable to pay even the reduced amount per instalment for six more months. After six months, the cultivator again received a recovery notice. Even under these crises, he still continued his sons' education. To overcome this situation, he sought help from his brothers, and friends. His brothers expressed not only their inability to extend support but also parted away with their share from the non-mortgaged land.

His two younger brothers outrightly said, "*Asi twadi koi madad nahi kar sakde, karza twade naam he, tusi chukao, tusi apna hissa bech kar karza chukka sakde ho. Asi kuchh nahi kar sakde hai. Sada hissa saanu de do*". [We can't help you. The loan is in your name and you are responsible for its payment too. We have no role in the payment of the loan. You pay the loan by selling your share of property (mortgaged land). We cannot help you in this. Give us our share of land]. After refusal of cooperation from his younger brothers, the respondent approached his friends for help.

His friends said, "*Tere per to bahut jayada karza hai, aur sadi kol itte paise nahi ki teri koi madad kar sakoo. Waise sade bhi itte kharche hai ki itni kamai se hamara hi kharch pura nahi honda. Tu aisa kyo nahi karta ki apni zameen bech kar apne saare karze chukda kar de. Asi to chah kar bhi teri koi madad nahi kar pa raha hoon. Asi nu maaf kariyo mitra, aur kisi chij di zaroorat hove to zaroor bataiyo.*" [You are highly indebted. We do not have so much money that we can help you. Anyway, we have so many expenses and we are unable to meet out our own expenses from our own earnings. Why do not you sell off your property to repay the loan? We cannot help you even if we want to. Forgive us friend. If you need any other thing, please tell us.]

Thus, the friends, who took part in the party arranged by the respondent after receiving loan, also showed their helplessness to the indebted cultivator. The two brothers parted with two acres each from the non-mortgaged land. They also partitioned the house into three portions and got one room and a kitchen each. In addition to this, the eldest brother got a cooler and TV which he purchased from the loan. The eldest brother received the mortgaged land of two acres. As the cultivator was unable to pay the loan instalment, police arrested him and the children were withdrawn from the school.

At the time of arrest, the wife of the cultivator overheard, according to her, the whispers of the villagers in the following manner,

"*Aamdani atthanni kharcha rupiya, logo nu dekh-dekh kar karza leke itta kharcha bada litta ki ab karza nu chukane ke lale pad gaye, ab iske pichhe iske bibi-bachcho ki ki hovenga. Aadmi ki jitni badi chadar hove hai utte hi pair pasarne chahinde*". [Income is only 50 paise and expenses one rupee. People increase their expenses by borrowing loans and also change their lifestyles. Now people are unable to repay their loans. 'Cut your coat according to the size of your cloth'.]

The police imprisoned the cultivator in the *Tehsil* jail for six days. His wife took food to the jail for her husband for all the six days traveling a distance of 20 km by bus. She borrowed a sum of ₹ 120 to meet the travel expenses from her neighbours. Neither his brothers, nor his wife's relatives nor friends visited him in the prison.

The cultivator in jail told his wife, "*Sadi karan tum logo ki itni paresaani badh gayi hai, tu yahan roz-roz mat aaya kar, ek din ghar nu khana nahi khaoonga to mar thode na jaaoonga*". [Your problems have increased because of me. Don't come here every day. If I will not eat home made food for a day, will I die?].

His wife told, "*Persani ki ki baat hai, tusi sahi-salamat ghar aa jao bus, phir sab apne – aap thik ho jayega, Asi kuchh na kuchh zaroor kar hi levenge, upar wala hamari zaroor madad karega*". [What problem? You come back home, that is all, then everything will be fine on its own. We will certainly be able to do something. God will definitely help us.] Thus, the wife of the respondent expressed optimism.

During her visit to the prison, the children lived in the home alone and her cousins refused to give them a company. After six days in prison, the cultivator was released from the jail. Ever since his return to home, he remained aloof and avoided talking to his children and wife. He refused to see anyone.

Whenever his wife asked him for food, he used to yell at her and once said, "*Are ek din khana nahi khaunga to mar nahi jaoonga, tum log khane ki jagah mujhe zaher kyo nahi de dete, roz-roz nu jhanjhat khatam ho jayengi, tujhe bhi mujhse chhutkara mil jayega*". [If I won't eat for one day I won't die. Why do not you give me poison instead of food and every day's problems would be solved. You would also get rid of me].

He kept aloof in a single room in darkness while the other members used to be in the kitchen. He used to wake up late in the morning. He used to get irritated on every small issue. He also avoided visiting the fields to see the crop and rather remained silent and sad at home.

After observing her husband, for over a week, his wife told him one day, "*Tusi thoda bahar ghum phir aaya karo, dil bahal jayega.*"[You should go for a stroll, you will feel better.]

He said, "*Mainu kahin nahi jaana, keh to ekdum se chala jaanoo, tum logo ki musibat door ho jayengi.*" [I do not want to go anywhere. If you say, I will go forever (die), all your problems would end.]

Wife said, "*Logo naal tusi nahi miloge to kaise paise nu intezaam hovenga. Logo naal milo unko sadi gal sunauo, shayad kuchh rasta nikal aawe*" [If you will not meet people how can you manage the money for repayment of loan? Meet people, tell them your woes. May be, we could get a way out].

The cultivator said, "*Sub se to mil liya, kisi ne kuchh kitta? Sub hasenge mere per, paise da intezam nahi honda hai to kya mainu apni jaan de doo. Mujhe Kisi se kuchh nahi kehna hai, tujhe jo samajh me aaye kar, mai to haar gaya hoon. Asi aisi zindgi naal ub gaya hoon.* [I met them all, did they do any favour. Everyone would laugh at me. If I couldn't arrange money should I give up my life? I have nothing to say to anyone. Do what ever you want. I am a loser. I am fed of such life.]

His wife said,"*Aisi zillat di zindagi se to marna behter hai*". [It is better to die than to live a life of such disgrace].

The cultivator said, "*Are tu kahe maregi, sare fasad nu jad to asi hai, asi he mar jande hai, kush rahiyo sub!*" [Oye! Why will you die? I am the root of all troubles, I am going to die, you all will be happy after my death.]

On the eighth day, one of his friends, who were also indebted and facing similar problem, came to meet the respondent.

The friend told, "*Aaj ghar me sada bhi dil nahi lag raha tha, socha tere yahan chal kar lassi-wassi pi jaye, chal yaar thoda baher ghoom aaye,*" [Today, I was also not feeling well at home, so thought of having sweet curd (*lassi*) at your home. Come friend; let's go out for a stroll.]

He went out with his friend for the first time after his release from the jail. He returned home after consuming alcohol for the first time in his life. He mortgaged his watch for the drinks. The watch had an emotional value for hit to his wife as her parents had given him at the time of their marriage. On his return home his wife inquired about the watch.

He said, "*Bech ke daaroo pi gaya*". [Sold it and consumed liquor.]

His wife said, "*Bus yehi ek kami reh gayee thi, wo bhi aaj puri kar ditta. Ab daaroo bhi pini suru kar di, aaj ghadi bech di, kal ghar nu saare saman, bertan bhi bech ke daroo pi jaaoge, fir ek din mainu aur mundo ko bhi bech dalna*". [This was the only thing left and that too you have fulfiled today. Now you have started drinking liquor too; today you sold off watch; tomorrow you will sell all our household belongings. You will sell off utensils as well as to drink liquor; then one day you sell me off and the children too].

The cultivator said, "*Haan saara ghar bech daaloonga, tujhse kya matlab, Asi sada saman bechta hoo, tere baap nu ki janda hai, mujhse jyada jaban ladai to yahi jaan se maar daloonga, meri aakhon ke samne se hath ja warna thik nahi hoga*". [Yes, I will sell the entire house; it is none of your business. I am selling off my own belongings; what loss I am incurring to your father. If you will argue too much with me, I will kill you here itself. Go away from my eyes or else it will not be good for you.]

Under these conditions he quarrelled with his wife the entire night and beat her up and drove her out of the house. His wife reached her parents' home along with her two children in the early morning. Thus, the cultivator became further socially alienated. Under such conditions of accentuated alienation and lack of support from the close kin, friends and brothers, he consumed sulphas, available at home for agricultural purpose and committed suicide in February 1994.

The family became very desperate after the cultivator's suicide. There was no earning member in the family. Subsequent to his suicide, his wife sold one-acre out of the two acres of land, which the family inherited, for ₹ 1,10,000 to clear the outstanding debt. The family now consists of the widow of the suicide victim, and her two children. Her two children started working at the *paan* (beatle) shop. The children were compelled to drop out from the school and rather start earning as the question now was that of very survival.

Analysis of this case reveals that the person's interaction with family, friends and kin declined. At the same time, his children were withdrawn from educational institutions. His economic position had significantly deteriorated in terms of landownership, i.e., downward mobility to landless position, and ownership of farm tools and his involvement in economic activities too had deteriorated. The imprisonment shattered his social status in the village. The family got divided in crises instead of facing the crises jointly. Thus, the person's integration with primordial relations as well as with formal lending financial institutions became weak. Thus, the reduced integration of the individual with different institutions like family and economic institutions resulted in depressive tendencies at psychological level that led to suicide. The process of recovery of loans itself is very humiliating to the cultivators in the rural community where private (personal) worries are made public. Conversion of such personal worries into public ones lead to status degradation in rural society, as status concerns are of prime importance in the rural society. These processes at social, economic, cultural and psychological level cumulatively seem to have resulted in such fatal events besides indebtedness and crop failures. The conditions of indebtedness and crop failure may be necessary ones but sufficient ones seems to be linked with reduction of integration of individual with family and economic institutions that might have led to depressive psychological state and finally suicide.

Case of Normal Cultivator: A Poor Peasant

The cultivator was a Hindu-Harijan, aged 32 and studied up to class 4th. His mother owned two acres of land and the respondent cultivated the land. He had only a wooden plough and no farm cattle. His elder brother aged 35 lived in city with his family; wife and three children. His brother's wife aged 30 years is illiterate. They had three children aged 14, 12 and 10 years and were studying in class 6, 4 and 3 respectively. He had a shoe shop in the city Sangrur near the bus stand. He sold and repaired the country made shoes. The respondent lived along with his mother aged 60 years, his wife and four children. The respondent's family was a supplement nuclear type. The respondent's wife aged 27 is illiterate. His mother used to help the respondent's wife in daily household work. Among their four children, two were boys aged 8 and 6 years and two girls aged 11 and 9 years. The boys were studying in class 3rd and 2nd in the government primary school located in the village. Both the girl children never went to the school. Girl children had been extending help to her mother in the household work, weeding, harvesting, transplantations, and threshing of the crops in their field. The respondent used to cultivate wheat, paddy and vegetable crops on the land. The production was mainly oriented for subsistence. Elder brother did not take share from the agricultural produce and did not extend regular financial assistance to his younger brother's family. They used to plough the land on the basis of reciprocal exchange of farm cattle and labour and leased in the tubewell services from neighbouring landowners to irrigate the crops.

His wife was a patient of chronic jaundice from 1990. She had to visit the city hospital located 20 kms away from the village at a daily frequency of once in 15 days. He was gradually finding it difficult to meet both ends. In order to overcome these problems he borrowed a loan of ₹ 20,000 at a rate of 40 per cent interest per annum from a local commission agent in 1993. He spent a large proportion of the loan in providing medical facilities to his wife (about ₹ 18,000) and very less in agriculture (to purchase seeds, pesticides and for irrigation). Six months after borrowing the loan, he could not pay even a single instalment. Village moneylender made efforts to recover the loan and interest. The moneylender abused him in the weekly market.

Moneylender told the debtor, "*Jab chukda nahi sakde to karza kis waste lende ho, char-char munda paida kar ke baith gaya hai aur unko khilane nu jimmedari sadi hai kya? Jab khila nahi sakde to paida hi kahe kitta hai! Mere paise chukka aur jitney chahe munde paida karta reh*". [When you can't repay loan, then why did you borrow it? You have delivered four children. And is it my responsibility to feed them? When you can't feed them then why delivered so many children? Return my money and deliver as many children as you wish.]

The respondent felt, bad, humiliated and insulted, because it happened in a public place, the market. When he narrated this to his wife, she too felt very bad and humiliated. His wife felt herself as the root cause of this problem and felt guilty. Her feelings of guilt could be comprehended through the conversation she had with her husband.

She told her husband, "*Dekho jee tusi ab sadi bimari naal koi karja na lo. Asi ab jeena nahi chahnde hai. Mainu tusi mar jaane do. Ab aur jayda karza mat lo.*" [See, don't borrow more loans for my illness. I don't want to live more. Please, let me die. Don't borrow more loans.]

Hearing these statements from his wife he lost his hope and felt helpless. He met his elder brother in the city and discussed this incident. His feelings of helplessness were visible in his conversation with his elder brother.

The indebted younger brother told to his elder brother, "*Pra Ji, sadi halat bahut kharab hai, idhar bachche di ma nu bimari thik honde hi na aave hai. Sanu sara paisa uski bimaari naal kharch ho jaandi hai. Kheti naal aamdani se kharcha poora na honda hai. Isi waste asi khet girvi rakh ke Mahajan nu karza litta hai. Sara paisa bimaari nu, kheti nu aur ghar kharch nu khatm ho jatti hai. Is waste asi Mahajan nu biyaj bhi nahi chukka sakde, Mahajan ab sadi jameen kabja karne nu dhamki de raha hai. Asi ki kitta? Asi mann karda hai ki zahar pi ke so jaun.* [Brother, my financial condition is very bad. My wife is not recovering from illness. I spent all the money on her illness. The income from agriculture is not sufficient to meet out the family expenses. To meet out the medical and agricultural expenses I borrowed loan from money-lender after mortgaging the land and spent the total amount on the treatment of her illness, cultivation of land and household expenses and failed to pay the interest to the moneylender. Now, the *Mahajan* is threatening to auction our landed property. What should I do? I feel that I should take poison and commit suicide.]

After listening to the woes of his younger brother, the elder brother assured help and said, "*Chhote dekh, waise to sade naal bhi utni kamai nahi hai ki tusi kuch madad kar saku. Tusi aisa kar pind vich sada mitra naal kuch paise le udhar le kar apna kuch karza kam kar aur patni nu ilaaz kara. Phir aage dekha javega. Tu dekh aisa vaisa kuchh mat kar lio.* ["See, my younger brother I too do not have much money to help you as my earnings are very meagre. I will borrow some money from a village friend of mine. Repay a portion of your loan to the moneylender and provide medical treatment to your wife. Let us see in future. See, don't commit anything wrong.]

His elder brother's friend provided a sum of ₹ 15,000 as loan to the respondent in 1993 at the rate of 24 per cent interest per annum. The respondent paid a sum of ₹ 10,000 out of the total loan to the village moneylender and provided medical treatment to his wife and purchased seeds, pesticides and paid rental charges to the irrigational facilities. Still a loan of ₹ 14,000 has remained unpaid to the moneylender. He couldn't repay the interest and instalments borrowed from his elder brother's friend. He also failed to repay the debt to the *arathiya* for six months after paying ₹ 10,000. The moneylender demanded for the repayment of the next instalment as early as possible. He had ₹ 37,000 debt including interest. Again he approached his elder brother. His elder brother suggested him to sell the total land and clear the loans first and begin to work with him. He sold one-acre land for ₹ 60,000 out of the two acres and clear the loans of the moneylender and brother's friend. His elder brother kept the respondent's family with him in the city for about 6 months and trained him in the repair and sale of shoes. The elder brother helped his younger brother to start a shoe shop in the village from the balance amount of the land sale in 1995. He sold the remaining cultivable land (one acre) and expanded the shoe shop in the village. Now, he works in his shop. The family thanked his brother and God.

This case reveals that the normal cultivator received social and financial support from primordial relations to cope with the problem of indebtedness. Secondly, alternative life chances are opened with the training of alternative skills for survival from the urban kin. Thirdly, in the crisis period though he had the ideas of committing suicide as a solution to the problem of overcoming the debt, but the support received from the kin restored integration of the respondent with other social units. Thus the support of urban kin and generation of awareness about the existence of alternative life chances in this case, even under severe crisis of humiliation, and status degradation, led to the continuity of his life whereas non-fulfilment of normative expectations, egoistic tendencies (Durkheim, 1938) within family and weak integration with social units like siblings, friends, kin and financial institutions led to suicide in the case of suicide victim.

References

Assadi, M. 1998, "Farmers' Suicides: Signs of Distress in Rural Economy", *Economic and Political Weekly*, Vol. 33, No. 14, pp. 747–48.

AWARE, 1998, *Report on Farmers' Suicides in Andhra Pradesh*, Development Research Advisory Group, Hyderabad.

Darling, M.L. 1927, 1977, *The Punjab Peasant in Prosperity and Debt* (Reprinted), New York: Oxford University Press.

Deshpande, R.S. 2002, "Suicide by Farmers in Karnataka: Agrarian Distress and Possible Alleviatory Steps", *Economic and Political Weekly*, Vol. 37, No. 25, pp. 2601–10.

Hamilton, M. 1960, "A Rating Scale for Depression", *Journal of Neurology, Neurosurgery and Psychiatry*, Vol. 23, pp. 56–52.

Iyer, K.G. and M.S. Manick, 2000, *Indebtedness, Impoverishment and Suicides in Rural Punjab*, Delhi: Indian Publishers and Distributors.

Jodhka, S. 2006, "Beyond 'Crises' Rethinking Contemporary Punjab Agriculture", *Economic and Political Weekly*, Vol. 16, No. 4, pp. 1530–37.

Kumar, P. and S.L. Sharma, 1998, *Suicides in Rural Punjab*, Chandigarh: Institute for Development and Communication.

Mishra, S. 2006, "Farmers' Suicides in Maharashtra", *Economic and Political Weekly*, Vol. 16, No. 4, pp. 1538–45.

Mohankumar, S. and R.K. Sharma, 2006, "Analysis of Farmer Suicides in Kerela", *Economic and Political Weekly*, Vol. 16, No. 4, pp. 1553–58.

Mohanty, B.B. 2001, "Suicides of Farmers in Maharashtra", *Review of Development and Change*, Vol. 6, No. 2, pp. 146–88.

——. 2005, "We are Like the Living Dead: Farmer Suicides in Maharashtra", *Journal of Peasant Studies*, Vol. 32, No. 2, pp. 243–76.

Radloff, L.S. 1977, "The CES-D Scale: A Self Report Depression Scale for Research in the General Population", *Applied Psychological Measurement*, Vol. I, pp. 385–401.

Rao, P.N. and K.C. Suri, 2006, "Dimensions of Agrarian Distress in Andhra Pradesh", *Economic and Political Weekly*, Vol. 16, No. 4, pp. 1546–52.

Sridhar, V. 2006, "Why Do Farmers Commit Suicides? The Case of Andhra Pradesh", *Economic and Political Weekly*, Vol. 16, No. 4, pp. 1559–65.

Suri, K.C. 2006, "Political Economy of Agrarian Distress", *Economic and Political Weekly*, Vol. 16, No. 4, pp. 1523–29.

Vasavi, A.R. 1999, "Agrarian Distress in Bidar: Market, State and Suicides", *Economic and Political Weekly*, Vol. 34, No. 32, pp. 2263–68.

http://www.chcr.brown.edu/pcoc/cesdscale.pdf

http://healthnet.umassmed.edu/mhealth/HAMD.pdf

19

Intergenerational Relations in the Reotipur Village Families of Eastern Uttar Pradesh

Sunil Kumar Verma and A. Satyanarayana

In this paper an effort has been made to comprehend the pattern of intergenerational relations in rural joint families belonging to upper, middle and lower socio-economic status as most of the earlier studies were conducted not only in urban areas but were concentrated in Western countries. These studies used either surveys or questionnaires or scaling methods to collect data related to intergenerational relations which mostly gives us normatively expected answers. Thus the study makes an endeavour to understand the pattern of intergenerational relations in rural joint families through behavioural perspective and the socio-economic statuses of the selected families are derived on the basis of consumption pattern.

Family is a primary universal social institution that performs various functions like adding new members to the society, socialising the children and providing affection and social bonding in life-cycle events among its members. It also provides emotional, social, economic and health support to the older members in the family, besides looking after the children. Family is also analysed as an association with interdependence, reciprocity and common identity among its members. Murdock (1949) defined the family as a "social group characterised by common residence, economic cooperation and reproduction" and Kolenda (1968) identified twelve types of families in India, i.e., single person household, sub-nuclear family, supplemented sub-nuclear family, nuclear family, supplemented nuclear family, collateral joint family, supplemented collateral joint family, lineal joint family, supplemented lineal joint family, lineal collateral joint family, supplemented lineal collateral joint family and other types. Kapadia (1958) observed that joint family system has a considerable importance in both Hindus and non-Hindus. Wadley and Derr (1997) analysed changes in family types on the basis of data of Karimpur village from 1925 to 1984, and found that both single, sub-nuclear and supplemented nuclear families have declined in their proportion out of the total families in the period. The proportion of nuclear families has increased from 22 per cent to 44 per cent. The joint families in their proportion increased from nearly 16 per cent to 33 per cent by 1975 but later declined to 28 per cent. These facts reveal that the proportion of families with more than two generations is increasing in the rural areas. In such families father is generally perceived as a breadwinner and mother as responsible for the up bringing of the children along with taking care of their needs in the form of love, care and protection. Grandparents have a very important role to play in the family as the custodian of culture and conventions. They take care of the grandchildren in the absence of their parents, and socialise them. Children in the family are expected to respect their elders and provide care for the younger ones and offer a helping hand at home when necessary (Pandey, 2007).

Urbanisation, mechanisation and commercialisation of the economy affect not only the rural social structure but also the functions of family in terms of reciprocity and support between the generations within the family. It also brings change in priority of attitudes and values between generations within family. Mishra and Tiwari (1980) analysed differences in attitudes and values between generations in rural and urban families and found intergenerational gap in terms of attitudes and values. The gap is more pronounced between older and younger generation in urban families than in rural families. The study also found more homogeneity of values and attitudes between older and younger generations of rural families than in urban families. Bhingradiya and Kamla (1997) conducted a study on intergenerational relations in rural Saurashtra. They found that increase in experience enhanced the status within family and enabled the older generation to give advice to the younger generation and also to take decisions. On the other hand, very few older generation family members perceived a decline in their status owing to their dependency on younger generation. These findings indicate that the respondents transmitted knowledge orally in the socialisation process of their younger generation. Versa-Sanso

(2004) reviewed studies on intergenerational relations and found that families with two generations received greater attention in the studies on intergenerational relations than the families with three or four generations. Versa-Sanso's (2007) study of neighbourhoods in Tamil Nadu reveals that post-liberalisation, privatisation and globalisation, after 1991, besides long term changes in the rural economy and state policies, have significantly widened the customary need gap between the older and younger generations. The needs and aspirations of the younger generation have expanded rapidly than the perceived needs of older generation. However, the means to meet the expanding needs are severely destabilised as the demand for agriculture labour has been declining and has reduced the sons' capacity to meet the needs of not only their conjugal and natal families but also the older generations.

Most of the family studies are conducted in southern, central and western India. These parts of India have a preponderance of nuclear families with individualistic tendencies. In the North India, joint families are in more preponderance (Kolenda, 1968). Secondly, most of the studies on intergenerational relations were conducted in urban areas than in the village settings. Thirdly, they emphasised more on the changing structure and functions of the family but could not depict a clear-cut picture about intergenerational relations in rural families.

Thus, the present study aims to comprehend the predominant patterns of intergenerational relations in rural families and the factors influencing these patterns. The study is also concerned with explaining the variational patterns of intergenerational relations with the help of socio-economic status of the rural families.

Method

Sample

A sample of 46 old aged members (23 men and 23 women) was selected on the basis of random purposive sampling from the joint families of Reotipur village in order to understand their day-to-day perceived significant behavioural manifestations with their married children. Nearly three-fourths of the sample was living in lineal collateral families, followed by lineal families. The sample mainly belonged to Hindu religion. The mean age of the old aged respondents was 62 years. On the basis of level of education one-third of the sample was illiterate, followed by one-fifth of the sample with intermediate level of education, one-seventh up to high school, one-tenth graduates, only one post-graduate, four middle school, three primary and one literate without formal education. On the basis of caste affiliation of the sample, mostly belonged to general castes (23) followed by scheduled castes (SCs, 18) and OBCs (5). The sample was occupationally diversified as 18 respondents were involved in household work, followed by 14 labourers, four petty shop keepers, three cultivators, two retired Class III employees of the government, one in Class II job, and others were unemployed.

Location

The sample was drawn from the village Reotipur located in between Gahazipur city of UP and Baksar city of Bihar state. The village is inhabited with 23,307 people. Nearly 20 per cent of the total population belongs to scheduled castes. The gender ratio is 930 women per 1,000 men. Nearly 63 per cent of the villagers are literate. The average size of the household is 7.3 members. Nearly 28 per cent of the total population belongs to the category of workers.

The Measures

Narrative method was used to explore the nature of intergenerational relations. Narratives of the respondents' day-to-day perceived significant experiences in terms of behavioural manifestations while interacting with their sons and daughter-in-laws in the family were collected on the following points.

- Description about the family members.
- About his/her occupation and behaviour in the family.
- What are the differences and similarities in the priority of values that the respondents perceived with the other generation? The perceived significant differences in behavioural manifestations are illustrated with the experiences of the respondents.
- Narrations related to the pattern of behavioural manifestations as experienced in their interaction (tensions or conflicts or harmony) with the next generation and the coping mechanisms adopted by the respondents with illustrations from their own experiences.
- Decision makers and the processes involved in decision making. If any conflict arises in the process of decision-making, what are the mechanisms used to resolve the conflict. Illustrations from the experiences of respondents within their family.

  Some issues relating to women probed were:

- What are the differences and similarities in the behavioural pattern related between the place of origin and the husband's house?
- Who looks after the children and prepares them for school?
- Socio-economic status is identified on the basis of consumption pattern.

Table 1

Consumption Pattern and Socio-Economic Status

Consumption	*Rural*		
	Upper SES	*Middle SES*	*Lower SES*
Air conditioner			
Car/tractor	√√		
Television	√√	√	√
Music system			
Tape/radio	√√	√	√
Scooter/motorcycle	√	√	
Refrigerator	√	√	
Washing machine	√	√	
Computer			
Generator/invertors	√		
Telephone	√	√	
Gas	√	√	
Tubewell/boring	√	√	
Thresher	√	√	
Diesel engine	√	√	
Bicycle	√	√	√
Animal	√	√	√
Agricultural land	√	√	

On the basis of consumption pattern of goods, the market value and name of the company that produced the goods; the respondents were differentiated into upper, medium and lower socio-economic status. The higher SES respondents owned a car and generator/inverter in addition to the items owned by middle socio-economic status respondents. The lower SES respondents owned a black and white TV, radio, bicycle, and goat/animal only but no scooter/motor cycle, refrigerator, washing machine, telephone, LPG fuel, tubewell, thresher, diesel engine, and agricultural land. The middle socio-economic status respondents had most of the items owned by the upper socio-economic status respondents but not the car/tractor and refrigerator.

Results

Table 2 reveals that the older generation respondents while interacting with the younger generation within their family experienced three patterns of intergenerational relations. These are solidarity, ambivalent and conflict patterns. These elderly respondents while interacting with the younger generation in family experienced mostly solidarity pattern (53.46%) than the ambivalent (37.20%) and conflict patterns. Similar trend is observed on the basis of gender between generations within family. On the basis of socio-economic status 32.54 per cent of upper class, and nearly 21 per cent of lower class respondents had experienced solidarity type of relationship. However, in the case of middle class families' ambivalent pattern of intergenerational relations was found. Only four respondents of lower class families' respondents experienced conflict pattern of intergenerational relations.

Table 2

Patterns of Intergenerational Relations Along Gender and Socio-Economic Status

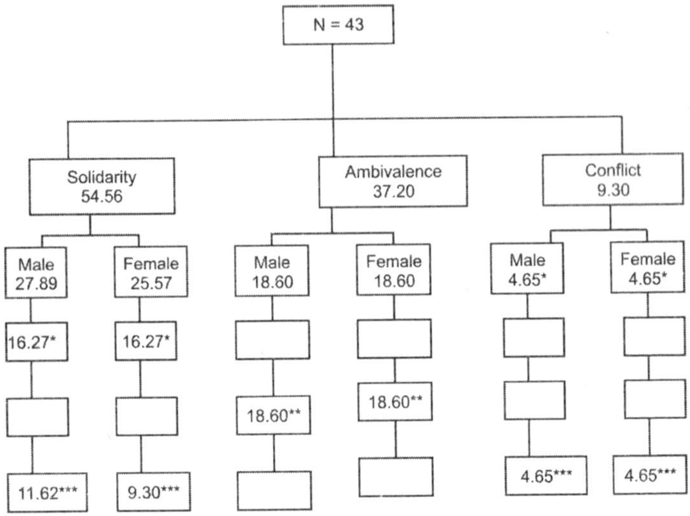

* denotes upper socio-economic status families.
** denotes middle socio-economic status families.
***denotes lower socio-economic status families.

Thus, the narratives of the respondents are analysed at perceptual and manifested behavioural levels. They perceive differences in intergeneration relations in terms of priorities of values given either to collectivism or individualism, traditional versus modern values, saving versus consumption, education versus orientation to earn money, disciplined life versus autonomy, and strict discipline in childrearing practices versus liberal ones. The respondents experienced differences or similarities at behavioural level in terms of fulfilment of obligations, roles and responsibilities. These are observed in the form of perceived level of economic, physical and emotional support that the younger generation (YG) extended to the older generation (OG), besides the OGs perceived loss of authority, power and autonomy in making decisions. Besides the manifested behaviour, the perceived differences in behaviour between generations also resulted in stress and strain. Such stresses and strains are coped through either problem-focused/emotional-focused/reaction-focused behaviours that resulted in the solidarity/ambivalent/conflict pattern of intergenerational relations respectively (see Table 3).

Table 3

Differences in Priority of Values between Generations at Perceptual and Behavioural Level

Category	*Factors*
Perceptual level (consensual)	• Individualisms vs. collectivism • Traditional vs. modern values • Lifestyle (importance to comfortable goods, laziness, lack of interest in household work, dressing style, food habit, etc.). • Education vs. income • Consumption vs. saving • Discipline vs. autonomy • Child rearing practices
Behavioural level	• Fulfilment of role, responsibility and obligations • Support (economic, physical and emotional) • Parental authority (loss of power and authority, autonomy in decision making) • Subjective experiences (stress and strain in relationship, abuse) • Coping pattern (problem-focused/emotional-focused/reactionary behaviour)

The above mentioned influencing factors are operationally defined as in the following way:

Individualism vs. collectivism

Individualism refers to the concern mainly for self and own family (wife, son, daughter) while collectivism indicates concern about all the members living in the household (brother, sister-in-law, father, mother, uncle, aunty, nephew and niece, unmarried sisters and brothers, etc.).

Traditional or older values

Traditional values refer to the concern in following religious norms, showing respect towards OGs, observance of *Ghunghat* before in-laws, etc.

Daily routine

Behaviour in everyday life in terms of sleeping early/late hours in nights, food habit in terms of vegetarian/non-vegetarian, going to bed early/watching TV at late night, spending free time at home with family members or outside home with friends and partners in business.

House-hold work

It refers mainly to the division of labour in the performance of household duties between women of OG and YG in terms of preparing breakfast, preparing children to school, etc.

Occupational preferences

It refers to selection of occupations in agriculture and government service/private service and business.

Consumption vs. saving

Consumption deals with priority of obtaining and using goods, services, new technology, money and resources for the enhancement of status in place of giving priority in conserving a portion of earned money and resources for future use rather than using it for immediate/expressive status considerations.

Child rearing practices

These deal with practices that are adopted in the socialisation of children. The practices may be either through strict discipline through caning or refraining from the caning behaviour.

Lifestyle

It refers to the individual priorities as expressed in matters of food habits vegetarian/-nonvegetarian, preparation of food with/without onion and garlic, preference in the pattern of dress wearing *sari/salwar kurta*, use/non-use of cosmetics like soap, detergent, *mitti* (soil), etc., and style of hair dressing, etc. Differences in the pattern of showing respect by the daughter in-laws towards their father-in-laws symbolically as they rarely faced their father in laws directly, but now they don't mind doing it.

Education vs. income

It can be defined in terms of preferences either for income or the pursuit of higher education.

Differences of preferences are observed in terms of either to move geographically away from the village in search of better life chances or preferring to stay back within the village.

Differences in role expectancy

This concerns with rigid or flexible role expectations of mother-in-laws and father-in-laws from their daughter-in-laws.

Household skill

Inculcation of skills that are required to run the day-to-day activities in the household like sieving the flour, cooking and serving meals, hospitality to the guests and the lack of such skills.

Familial roles are concerned with preferences either to the fulfil the familial norms or to give priority to individual comforts.

Obligations

With reference to appropriate behaviour that is perceived within the context of specific personal relationship with the kin and family members, like caring and fulfiling the needs of the family.

Parental authority

This deals with preferences of the OG either to hold/share/yield autonomy, power and authority to the YG in the decision making process within family.

Subjective experience

It refers to the experiences that are subjectively felt in terms of stress/strain; solidarity/ambivalence/conflict in the intergenerational relations.

Coping pattern

It refers to the pattern of coping with stress and strain in relations between generations in family in terms of problem-focused (avoid the situation, talk to each other and maintain the communication), emotional-focused (avoid the person block the communication) or reactionary behaviour (abuse in terms of physical and verbal nature). The variations in the coping patterns will finally influence the intergenerational relations.

Discussion

Relations between generations in the family are based on interdependence and reciprocity but the perceived priority of values differ between generations. Generally, the OG perceive that their YG in the family are emphasising more on individualism, modern values, with emphasis on consumption that enhances social status, opting for non-vegetarian food, going to bed at late hours, and asserting autonomy and liberal patterns of child rearing practices. On the other hand, the OG feels that they are giving priority to collectivism, traditional values, less importance to consumption but more for savings, sleeping at early hours, vegetarianism, more interest in household work and the pursuit of higher education, and disciplined life with rigid child rearing practices. Though the OG perceives that the younger ones are fulfilling their responsibilities, obligations and support in the matters of economic, physical and emotional aspects, but they experience loss of power and authority in decision making that results in stress and strain in intergenerational relations which is coped through either problem-focused or emotional-focused or reactionary behaviours. These coping patterns of stress further influence patterns of intergenerational relations in the direction of solidarity/ambivalent/conflict type.

Table 2 shows that most of the families with solidarity type of relations belong to the category of upper socio-economic status (32.5%) followed by lower socio-economic status (20.92%). Mostly ambivalent pattern of intergenerational relations (37.20%) were observed in the case of middle socio-economic status families and conflict pattern in the case of lower socio-economic status families. Thus the study reveals that solidarity pattern of intergenerational relations was predominantly observed. On the basis of gender too similar pattern was observed.

In the case of solidarity pattern of intergenerational relations, it is observed that preferences on consensual factors differed along generations in terms of values and attitudes. The older generation emphasises more on collectivism, education, hard work, discipline, canning in the socialisation of children, avoidance of modern lifestyle of consumerism, saving of resources, lesser importance to luxurious goods, sleeping at early hours, vegetarianism, simple dressing style, more interest in household work and prefer government jobs more than private jobs as it provides security in life. On the other hand, the older generation perceives that the younger generation is giving more importance to consensual factors like individualism, more earnings as a goal rather than looking about the appropriateness of means, laziness, indisciplined life, liberal socialisation of children, conspicuous consumption, more importance to consumerist style of living, less interest in household work, sleeping at late hours, viewing TV at late hours, preferring non-vegetarian food, dressing style, and mostly prefer private service, business, contracts, politically ambitious and gets higher income in short time though their jobs were less secured. Though the OG experience support from the YG in terms of physical, emotional and economic matters besides fulfilment of familial obligations and responsibilities, they but do not consider these upto their satisfaction. Generally in higher socio-economic status families if the dependent YG makes heavy economic demands on the OG, then generally the OG avoids meeting such demands. Such situations occasionally lead to tension and stress between OG and YG in their interactions. The OG with such stresses and strains through sharing their experiences with the YG, rationalise the situation as a consequence of the wider level social change and avoids the situation to make efforts to maintain solidarity pattern of intergenerational relations. This pattern of intergenerational relations can be comprehended through case study material.

Case 1

He is a retired degree college lecturer and lives with his wife, married son and two unmarried daughters. The eldest daughter is a graduate. The son after completing post graduation is pursuing B.Ed. The son also looks after the agriculture work. Younger daughter and daughter-in-law are educated up to 10+2 standard.

"*AAA ... differences are timely, we have our own thoughts. Differences in views are there but conflicts occur only when the distances between hearts increase but these differences are an issue of mind not heart. That is why even after these differences we sit together, talk, eat and still love each other*".

Generally older generation perceives that the younger generation prefers leisure and takes lesser interest to work that further leads to economic scarcity and insecurity. Such a situation results in tension between generations. But both the generations perceive extension of support in terms of physical, emotional and economic matters reciprocally in general. When undue demands are made by one of the generations then the tension of such situation is met with either sharing their viewpoint and experiences or by avoidance of such stress situations and making efforts to promote fulfilment of familial responsibilities and obligations on other issues. Let us illustrate with case 2.

Case 2

He is a graduate and works as a class three employee in Hydroelectricity Department in Jharkhand. His wife is a school teacher and his two married sons are unemployed after post graduation. "*The parents report that their children demand expensive consumerisitic items. Then the children are made to understand the situation by informing them about the situations that the parents faced in their young age. So we feel tense in the situations that are incompatible with the children's demands and the financial condition and future economic security*".

Some differences are observed in the context of priority of values and attitudes, in terms of collectivism vs. individualism and pursuit of higher education vs. taking a job just after graduation, between the generations. In the case of OG, collectivism is preferred or given priority while the YG emphasised on individualism. Under such conditions, the OG subjectively experienced loss of their power, autonomy and authority and the YG experienced an increase in taking decisions autonomously. For example:

Case 1: "*Individualism is increasing with the increase in consumerism. I and my family, children and wife, should eat well and drink well. Inclination to help others has declined. Earlier we used to live with limited resources but now the YG thinks more about their selves and less about their brothers, parents and society. Even with better resources at present, the YG is not satisfied. People are becoming more and more selfish*". Thus, the OG perceives that the YG is becoming more individualistic in their behaviour. However, decisions in their families are taken either collectively or in consultation with the YG and experience solidarity pattern of intergenerational relations.

Case 17: The family belongs to lower socio-economic status where the YG gives priority to geographical mobility in search of jobs but OG prefers their younger ones to stay back at the place of origin. The weak economic position forces the YG to become mobile geographically and the OG finally accepts the migration of YG. Thus, the YG's decision to migrate gets the consent of the OG. "*There are many differences between me and my children. Nowadays whoever is a bit educated wants to migrate to other places for earning but they maintain relations with the family by retaining their wives and children at the village to be looked after by the OG. The eldest son migrated first and the younger one followed the eldest one. I tried to stop the younger son but he did not listen to me. He is doing business. I was forced to accept the decisions though I differed. Though the differences exist, but maintain relations of cordiality ones the decision is taken and accepted*".

Differences in priority of values, in matters of lifestyle, agricultural practices, and responsibilities, interest in household activities, consumption and saving between generations are also observed. The OG does not emphasise on modern facilities and they perceive that the younger generation gives importance to luxurious life. Also they consider that the YG is a bit lazy and shows lack of interest in household work and savings and feel themselves to be independent and autonomous. The YG do not share the investments and expenditure of their income with the OG. These differences in the priority of lifestyles between generations lead to stress and both adopt the coping strategy of avoiding the situation and maintain solidarity type of intergenerational relations. Let us see the cases 17 and 3.

Case 18: is an illiterate married woman with four sons. Out of those four sons, three sons are married. Elder two sons have migrated while the younger son is pursuing intermediate level of education. The head of the household's wife and her two daughter in-laws are agriculture labourers and live jointly. The mother-in-law expresses her perceptions about differences in the matters of lifestyle between generations in the following words in the family, "*There are differences between the present and the past in terms of style of living. Earlier people used to have one sari on their body and another was washed and that was sufficient. But now even though they have more than a dozen saris of different kinds but still they keep on demanding for more*".

Case 3: AQ woman belongs to the higher socio-economic status family and pursued studies up to intermediate. She has one married daughter. Her three married sons are graduates and her husband is educated up to intermediate. The father and sons are engaged in business. The woman respondent reports, "*There are differences in the way they talk and behave. How much is the difference, I cannot say but there is difference. I try to control my behaviour thinking that if I lose my control, the prestige of the family will be at stake. It means tolerating the differences by taking into account the family and its status*".

From these cases it can be derived that though generally the OG perceived differences in priority of values and lifestyle with their YG but they try to make their points understood, avoid the issues on which the generations differ and make decisions on other issues either collectively or in consultation with the YG within the family and the perceived solidarity pattern of intergenerational relations in their families.

Ambivalence

The OG of the middle socio-economic status families, perceived ambivalence pattern of relations with their YG as the latter though fulfil the familial obligations, responsibilities and support the OG in the family but the OG feels that the support received from the YG is not up to the mark. The OG perceives that the YG is giving priority to individualism, modern values, lifestyle in terms of consumerism, and food habits of non-vegetarianism while the OG gives priority to collectivism, saving resources, disciplined life style, respect pattern, and strict child rearing practices. On the basis of these differences, OG experiences stress and strain and some time low intensity of conflicts in the family but they cope with the situation through emotional-focused approach/accept the situation/avoid the person, and avoid communication. The OG subjectively experience insecurity towards future and experience a mix up of solidarity and conflict patterns of intergenerational relations as the OG though pushes the YG towards independence but is not willing to relinquish their authority and control on the YG. Such a situation leads to ambivalence type of intergenerational relations. The ambivalent pattern can be exemplified through the following case studies.

Case 5: A retired school headmaster has five sons. Four of them are married. The eldest son is in private job in Gurgaon and his family lives with his father. The second son is in Army and posted at Assam and lives with his wife while his son lives with his grandfather. The third son lives in Delhi with his family. The fourth son is living in the village with his father and looks after the agricultural work while the fifth son is doing Bachelor of Ayurvedic Medical Sciences (BAMS). The youngest son doing BAMS reports, "*I completed my higher secondary examination from UP board with 78 per cent marks and after that I took admission in 11th class with Mathematics group. I wished to prepare for Civil Service examination, after my graduation. But after three months after my admission in class 11th with Maths group (Maths, Physics and Chemistry) my father and the eldest brother pressurised me to take admission in Biology group and to prepare for premedical entrance examination in order to have admission in MBBS. I opposed it, but they did not concede to my view point, so I left regularly attending the classes and gave the examination of class 12th directly and passed in second division. After this incidence my father gave autonomy to me to do what I want. I took admission in B.Sc. in BHU in Physics, Chemistry and Zoology group. After six months in BHU, once again my father pressurised me for preparation of the medical entrance examination and admitted me at Lucknow for medical coaching. After four attempts, I was selected for BAMS and took admission. Presently I am dissatisfied with my father's decisions because he gave freedom to me, nominally, to choose my profession but interrupted me repeatedly. Such a situation is not freedom*". Thus, the OG though nominally gives autonomy but still holds their authority in the selection of professions, on the YG. In order to cope up with it they avoid or withdraw for sometime or develop hostile feelings along with affection and after sometime the relations become normal.

Case 14: He is retired from the post of *Subedar* in Army. He had two sons. The eldest one is in service at Calcutta. The son's wife and three unmarried daughters live with his parents. His second son is still pursuing LLB. The retired *Subedar* subjectively experiences differences with his sons in terms of discipline vs. autonomy. According to him, "*We as military men go by strict rules and follow a strict (routine) life style. Being a villager you can't have strict rules and lifestyle. After retirement I was, working in a coal mine for six months. Now, I think that I should do as my sons say. I accept blindly whatever my sons say in order to avoid confrontation*".

He also *reports differences on the consumption and saving between* OG and YG women, "*Earlier people used to be very simple. Now they have all the desire of the world like wearing extravagant clothes, using surf, shampoo and soaps, but we used to wear simpler and less costly clothes and used to wash without surf, shampoo and soap*".

On the basis of these experiences, the OG and YG reports maintenance of distance reciprocally out of respect. Along with this they acknowledge changes in decision making within the family in terms of giving autonomy and maintaining control on YG and resulting in ambivalent relationship.

Conflicts

Among the lower socio-economic status families under study, only a few families experienced intergenerational conflicts. The OG attributed the conflicts mainly to the poor socio-economic conditions, and dependency of the YG on OG as the former are unemployed. In the context of scarcity of resources, the OG fails to fulfil the expectations of the dependent YG and the YG abuses the older ones for the non-fulfilment of their demands. The elderly under such circumstances experience not only stress and strain latently but conflicts are also manifested with their dependent children and contribute to the disorganisation of families. In the second sub-type, the OG with disability experience power shift to the YG besides non-fulfilment of economic, physical and emotional support and face abuses from their younger ones. To cope with such situations, the OG tries to convince the YG to understand about the scarcity of resources, try to negotiate with them on the contentious issues but the younger ones refuse to yield to the logic at all or react and abuse the OG that leads to conflict between generations. Let us illustrate this with case 18.

Case 19: A is a lower socio-economic status family with a disabled, old age person dependent on his son. The son has five unmarried sons. The grandchildren of the respondent work as wage labours in an unorganised sector and do not contribute their earnings to the common pool of the family income and do not support the family. The elderly narrates, "*In earlier times, one person used to earn and the rest of family used to carry out their livelihood. Now-a-days when six people are earning, one older person is not getting food. How can one survive by earning 50 rupees as labour per day? Five (grandsons) would earn and waste their earnings in gambling and drinking but do not contribute a single penny to the family. Expenditure of 8 members has to be managed, the children do not care how it is done/howsoever it may be done, they do not care*". When the OG tries to share the problems of livelihood and seeks their contribution to the maintenance of the family, then the YG not only abuses the older ones but occasionally also exercises physical coercion on the OG.

Differences are also observed between generations in terms of values and attitudes. OG gives priority to collectivism and stresses more on liability and perceives that the YG is gives more priority to individualism and treats liabilities as a burden. The YG spends more on the maintenance of social status and thus remains indebted. Such differences result in higher levels of dissatisfaction between generations.

Case 20: Older generation of lower socio-economic status family performing manual labour in unorganised sector, narrates his past experiences of what he did for his children and his social prestige. "*Nothing to eat but abuses ... Fights always, would demand money that they be given immediately and wouldn't give a single penny back to us. How will we be able to provide money? We organised their marriage by borrowing money. Had they been contributing ₹ 10, at least we could clear out the debt ... could construct a house or engage in some business or employment? They won't give, would ask from us instead. Ask us to bring money and give it to them, from where are we going to get the money in order to give it to them? Got both the sons married by working as labourers. If we hadn't got those married, then the community people would have blamed us.* "Under such differences the OG subjectively experience that the YG as showing disrespect to them and also distrusting and involved in conflict with them".

Thus, the elderly experience difficulties as the YG declines not only support but also remains economically dependent on OG. Such a situation creates stress and strain in the relationship between generations which is manifested in the form of hurling abuses at each other to exchange of blows.

In the entire upper and some lower socio-economic status families, the OG subjectively experienced solidarity pattern of IGR while interacting with the YG in the families of the village under study. Here, both the generations fulfilled the complimentarity of role expectations in terms of fulfilment of normative expectations and physical, emotional and economical support. In upper socio-economic status families, generally both the generations are economically independent and physically fit and extend timely support mutually and maintain affection and association. Thus fulfilment of normative expectations and functional reciprocity between generations promotes solidarity pattern of IGR even in the village families of a developing country with priority on affiliation. Similar findings were observed in the studies of Bengtson et al. (1991), Luescher and Pillemer (1998), and Chaddha and Malik (2004).

In the urban studies of IGR, it was observed that the OG was perceived negatively as it leads to feelings of helplessness, loneliness and lack of assistance or support at the time of serious health problems (Rabindranathan, 2006). But, in this study, many of the lower socio-economic status families, the OG perceived their relations with YG as positive as the YG left their dependent wife and children with their parents in the village and migrated to urban centres in search of sources of livelihood. The YG extended monetary support and fulfiled needs and expectations of the total family in the village while the OG provided security and support to the wife and children of his emigrant son. This lead to fruitful and satisfactory relationship between the generations. Similar pattern of findings are observed in the works of Gulati (1983), and Rawat and Rawat (1986).

The YG objectively fulfils reciprocity of familial obligations, support and normative processes with the OG which the OG acknowledges but perceives subjective dissatisfaction with the extent of role performance of the YG. Such situations result in an ambivalent pattern of IGR that incorporates both love and hatred to the other generation. On other instances, the older generation would like to see their children autonomous and independent from them, but they would like to retain authority with them. Such a situation also leads to ambivalence pattern of intergenerational relations. Similar findings are reached in the studies of Cohler and Geyer (1982) and Kwak (2003).

In some of the lower socio-economic status families, both the younger and older generations are seasonal manual labours in unorganised sector, working and staying at the same place and experiencing paucity of resources. In the context of paucity of resources, both the generations feel overstressed in the fulfilment of reciprocity of role expectations and obligations. Though the OG extends support to the YG, the YG fails to reciprocate it through fulfilment of physical, emotional and economic support to the OG. Besides this, the pattern of conspicuous consumption of YG further reduces the availability of resources that could be extended to the OG. It leads to manifested conflict between generations. Raju (2002) and Versa-Sanso (2007) too observed similar findings in their studies.

So, the study of families in Reotipur village reveals predominance of solidarity pattern of IGR than the ambivalent and conflict patterns. In the agrarian economy of developing societies, the child contributes to the family well-being through working in the field and providing security to the parents while the OG fulfils complimentarity of role expectations and support. These processes promote solidarity pattern of relations between generations. In situations where the YG extends support to the OG, the OG also acknowledges but feels dissatisfied with the extent and nature of support from the YG that results in ambivalence pattern of IGR. The paucity of resources in the case of a few lower socio-economic status families contribute to the emergence of abuses and conflicts between generations.

References

Bengtson, V.L. and Robert, R.E.L. 1991, "Intergenerational Solidarity in Aging Family: An Example of Formal Theory Construction", *Journal of Marriage and Family*, pp. 856–69.

Bhingradiya, P. and Kamla, R. 1997, "An Intergenerational Study on the Situation of the Elderly in Rural Saurashtra", *Indian Journal of Gerontology*, Vol. 11, No. 3 and 4, pp. 78–84.

Chaddha, N.K. and Malik, N. 2004, "Intergenerational Relations: A Futuristic Framework", *Indian Journal of Gerontology*, Vol. 18, No. 3 and 4, pp. 318–47.

Cohler, B.J. and Geyer, S. 1982, "Psychological Autonomy and Interdependence within the Family", in F. Wals (ed.), *Normal Family Process*, New York: Gilford Process.

Gulati, L. 1983, Impact of Development Process in Indian Family, Unpublished Manuscript, Centre for Development Studies, Trivandrum.

Kapadia, K.M. 1958, *Marriage and Family in India*, 2nd edition, New Delhi: Oxford University Press.

Kolenda, P. 1968, *Regional Differences in Family Structure in India*, Jaipur: Rawat Publications.

Lal, A.K. 1989, *The Urban Family: A Study of Hindu Social System*, New Delhi: Concept Publications.

Luescher, K. and Pillemer, K. 1998, "Intergenerational Ambivalence: A New Approach to Study of Parent-Child Relations in Later Life", *Journal of Marriage and Family*, Vol. 60, pp. 413–25.

Murdock, G.P. 1949, *Social Structure*, New York: Free Press.

Pandey, J. 2007, "India", in Georgas et al. (eds.), *Family across Culture: A 30 Nations Study*, Cambridge, UK: Cambridge University Press.

Rabindranathan, S. 2006, *The Elderly in Urban Indian Families: Conflict in Solidarity*, New Delhi: B.R. Publications.

Raju, S.S. 2002, "Meeting the Needs of the Older Poor and Excluded in India, Situation and Voices: The Older Poor and Excluded in South Africa and India", *UNFPA Population and Development Strategies*, No. 2, pp. 93–110.

Tiwari, B.B. and Mishra, R.C. 1979, "An Intergenerational Study of Value Orientation", *Journal of Psychological Research*, Vol. 23, No. 3, pp. 198–99.

Mishra, R.C. and Tiwari, B.R. 1980, "Intergenerational Attitudes: A Psychological Analysis", *Psychologia: An International Journal of Psychology in the Orient*, Vol. XXIII, No. 3, October.

Verma, S.K. and Satyanarayana, A. 2007, "Influencing Factors of Intergenerational Relations in Indian Family: A Narrative Approach", *Journal of Research and Development*, Help Age India.

Versa-Sanso, P. 2004, "They Don't Need It and Can't Give It: Familial Support in South India", in P. Kreager and E. Schoeder-Butterfill (eds.), *The Elderly Without Children: European and Asian Perspectives*, Oxford, UK: Berghahn.

——. 2007, "Increasing Consumption, Decreasing Support: A Multigenerational Study of Family Relations among South Indian Chakkliyars", *Contribution to Indian Sociology (n.s.)*, Vol. 41, No. 2, pp. 225–48.

Wadley, S.R. and Derr, B. 1993, "Karimpur Village over Sixty Years", in Patricia Uberoi (ed.), *Family, Kinship and Marriage in India*, New Delhi: Oxford Press.

20

Conception of Self, Values and Perceptions of Rural Women

D. Punetha, A. Satyanarayana, Sanjay and Atul Singh

A person while interacting with other people in their environment develops a tendency to understand oneself, imagine about oneself and construe a conception of self (Kelly, 1959). Thus individuals construe conception of self on the basis of their own experiences, ideal ambitions and imaginations as well as the way others perceive their existence meaningfully. According to Rogers (1951), the interaction of the organism with the environment and with significant others results in the gradual emergence of a concept of 'Who am I'. In the process of actualisation, children interact with others and acquire ideas about themselves, their relationship to significant others, the things they like or dislike, and the things they can or cannot control. The concept of self is composed of those conscious perceptions and values of 'Me' or 'I'. Some of these perceptions are the result of the evaluation of an organism's own experiences with others. Though these experiences seem to be personal but the social and cultural contexts of the individuals will not only affect their ideas and conceptions of self but also guide the future ambitions and actions of individuals. Social values, preference for certain states of affairs over others (Hofstede, 1980), of a person will influence the person's self-image; positive or negative, his behavioural orientations (Rokeach, 1973), culture of an individual and society (Rokeach, 1973; Zavolloni, 1980) and his mental health. A positive conception of self-image will result in the meaningful development of individuals with a better mental health than those with a negative conception of self (Maslow, 1970; Rogers, 1980). These studies conducted mostly in the western developed societies reveal that the conception of self and value structure are interrelated. However lesser attention is given to the comprehension of relationship between self-image and changing social milieu in the developing societies in general and specifically focusing on women living in the villages. So, the present study makes an endeavour to understand differences in the perception of self-images of women as members and non-members of self-help groups (SHGs) in the context of changes and programmes introduced by the Indian State.

Indian State through its policies is promoting the active participation of women in the economic activities through SHGs. Thus village women are coming more in interaction with personnel working in the developmental administration as members of SHGs. Such interactions may affect the self-images of self-help group women members and also their perceptions about women after becoming members of self-help groups. The Field Work Manual-3 (2002) described that the SHGs are informal groups in which the members display an urge for collective action to meet their emergent economic needs. The members pool their savings on a regular monthly basis to generate a common fund which is deposited in the bank in the name of the group. In multiples of the saved amount, the bank lends money to the group to pursue the bank sanctioned common economic activity/project at a lower rate of interest than the interest charged by the traditional moneylenders. The requests for loans for the members of the group are decided on the basis of consensus in the monthly meetings of the group. The loan amounts are relatively small and for a shorter duration. The loan procedure is simple and flexible. Members repay their loans in time as delay in the repayment leads to penal interest. Thus, the SHGs induce time perspective, confidence, sense of independence and interdependence among its members. The non-members of self-help groups lag in these attributes and behavioural patterns to a larger extent from the members. So, the membership and non-membership in SHGs brings variation in the conception of self, perceived identity and social values, but they have received lesser attention in the earlier village studies on women. Thus, in the present research, endeavours are made to comprehend the impact of these changes on the conceptions of self, values and perceived identity of members and non-members of village women in SHGs. Are women aware of their own motives, needs, preferences and values as well as their rights and responsibilities? Do they perceive themselves as significant members of the village or they perceive themselves as dependent on their men or do they have their own independent identity?

Method

Sample

The sample consists of a total of 55 village women who are members (36) and non-members (19) of SHGs. The sample is selected randomly from Kaundhiyar block of Allahabad district. There are 78 villages in this block with a population of approximately 2.5 million in 2001. The respondents are mainly illiterates, married, Hindus and belong predominantly to Other Backward Castes (OBCs) in the category of below poverty line and to the age category of 14–55 years. The members of SHGs are closely related with one another through primordial relations such as kinship and neighbourhood. The SHG members are not only working on their small plots of land for their subsistence, but are also involved in reciprocal exchange of labour with others even before becoming members of SHGs.

Dependent Measures

Two dependent measures are used:

1. An unstructured twenty statement test (TST) for the measurement of conception of self (Kuhn and McPartland, 1954) is used in the study. The respondents are asked to make twenty statements about her on the question 'Who am I?' translated into Hindi language.
2. The revised Rokeach Value Scale of Ng and others (1982) is used in the study. It contains 40 items and each item is measured on a 9 point scale where the respondent has to choose relatively more important ones from among the alternatives in the scale. The scale is developed in Hindi language.

Procedure

The sample of women respondents was contacted through a social activist, NGO and a village primary school lady teacher. The respondents were informed about the purpose of the study. Two investigators, one male and another female, pursuing their D.Phil programme in Psychology Department collected the data. The lady teacher too assisted in the data collection. Conversations and interviews for data collection were carried out in Hindi language.

Results and Discussion

The data obtained from the respondents are analysed along the conceptions of self and value structure. The results are described in the following paragraphs:

Conception of 'Self'

Analysis of TST data of all the respondents in the study reveals that in general each respondent gave only five or six answers indicating that their conception of self was simplistic and limited to concrete and overt categories like a woman, a mother, wife of a cultivator or landless labourer, and a daughter-in-law. Thus, these women have not thought much about themselves. This indicates that the women's identity was only bounded to their external psyche. They understand themselves mainly in gender and social roles. They did not know their own inner resources and potentials and did not mention their needs, motives, and future aspirations. The respondents' self is extended only to their external self. This suggests that the lives of women respondents are mechanical and prone to conformity without self-analysis as if they were not motivated to evaluate themselves. It seems that the identity of women is extended to their bodily self only but not to their inner layers of self as suggested by Allport (1961). This also suggests that such an identity can be observed in the period of infancy but extends as child grows towards adulthood. In the present work, the respondents are in the age range of 14 to 55 years and still their self development seems to be less in comparison to their age. The respondents in general have a lower level of social and role identity indicating that they have poorly developed mental health (Maslow, 1970) with lesser stress tolerance and coping skills.

However, the members of SHGs have a higher level of tolerance and skills to cope with stress than the non members of the SHGs as the former category of respondents share their stressful situations in the regular monthly meetings, during reciprocal exchange of labour among them and extend support among them with collectivistic orientation. On the other hand, non-members of SHGs do not share their personal troubles regularly but work for their own individualistic interests and do not extend support to one another regularly. In that context, it is observed that the non-members have lower levels of tolerance and coping skills of stress than the members of SHGs. From these facts it can be safely concluded that the membership and non-membership in the SHGs does not affect the conception of self of women under study but are in general interrelated with others in the family and community. However the respondents differ on the issue of coping and tolerance of stress on the basis of membership and non-membership in SHGs. The members of SHGs have a higher intensity of social capital in terms of trust and reciprocity than the non-members. This variation might be superimposed over the membership and influence tolerance and coping to stress.

Both the categories of women respondents perceive the conception of self with reference to others in the family as mother, wife and daughter-in-law. The findings also make it clear that most of the women members of SHGs belonged either to the same clan or were neighbours, established dependency relations with other members of the SHGs, in order to find solutions to the problems related to poverty, health and education of their children, apart from close family relations. Thus the earlier social embeddedness has further strengthened through their participation in SHGs. These close relations with members of SHGs further induced more self-confidence among them than among the non-members of SHGs. It was observed that in comparison to the non-members, members of SHGs participate in their monthly meetings, where they mostly share their agonies, despair and difficulties among them in order to solve them collectively and perceive themselves in relation to others in the community. Often the SHG members organise meetings to plan future course of action, attend the meetings and extend their meetings for the next time. Sometimes they join the meetings organised by NGOs, bank, and other developmental administrative bodies. It seems that attending meetings in time, making preparations for meetings by preparing dresses, by discussing the agenda among members for a number of times, provides them an opportunity to inculcate time perspective. These women also become familiar with the men-folk who are not from their own village but are outsiders. The women do not feel hesitant with unfamiliar persons. Their speech and language is coherent in talking to outsiders. It seems that the SHG members were more skillful and presented themselves very well owing to experience of the SHG. Markus and Kitayama (1991) pointed out that interdependent construal of self is unbounded and flexible and contingent on the context. In other words, the features of the conception of self are related and inseparable from the specific social context. It seems that the 'self' is deeply embedded in the social milieu and it is hard to separate it from the cultural context.

These women living in villages have larger families (extended or joint families), make living through agricultural activities that require cooperation. Sinha and Verma (1993) state that the elements of collective culture in terms of giving priority to group, and family integrity is mostly a preferred value than individualism in the Indian social milieu. Thus women accept and prefer those values that are desired in the socio-cultural setting. It is reasonable to assume that the quality of life of the women is determined by the social context rather than by their own inner resources and inner potential which can be acquired and developed at an individual level. Thus, these findings support the earlier observations of Ng et al. (1982), Triandis and others (1993), Schwartz (1994) in the Asian nations which prefer mostly collectivistic orientations rather than individualistic ones. It is also observed that benevolence related values are found more in the case of members of SHGs than non-members and the values have motivational goals related to welfare of others in the group. This suggests that though the conception of self is related to the traditional notions of conformity and social structure but the extension of social support and collectivistic orientation in crisis is mostly found among the members of SHGs than non-members as the latter lacks frequent interactions to share their troubles in a collectivity and become more individualistic in addressing the problems.

Value Structure

The analysis of scores on value scale reveals that though both the categories of respondents preferred mostly the values of family security and its responsibilities but differed significantly on eight values. It was found that the members of SHGs gave more preference to a comfortable and exciting life, inner harmony (free from conflict), and national security in comparison to the women non-members. It seems that members of SHGs are more focused towards a comfortable life and are more aware of their surroundings such as an exciting life which is the product of the modern culture imported from the Western world than the non-members. Members of SHGs gave more importance to national security than the women non-members. It appears that SHGs women are more organised, structured, jointly share, and enjoy more information than the non-members. However, the non-member women scored high on broadminded, honest and loving (tender, affectionate) in comparison to members of SHG. The non-members of SHGs valued individualistic values more than the members of SHGs. This result makes it clear that individuals might adhere to the above values at the individual level. In order to survive in a society, each individual has to perform certain complimentarity of role expectations and obligations in general for the maintenance of stability in the society. Miller (1976), Jordan and Hartling (2002) have rightly pointed out that in the relational cultures, relationships are the central organising features in general development and more specifically to women's development. It means that people crave for connection and fostering of relationships through mutual empathy and empowerment. The cultural relational theory recognises the significance of patriarchal culture in women's lives where women have lesser power than men. Women often adapt to relationships that are unequal and essentially non-mutual in patriarchal culture. Women often feel insufficiently empowered to have an impact on important relationships in their lives.

It is clear from the study that women who are members of SHGs have acquired skills, language and are exposed to such experiences that their behaviour is more suited to express themselves in comparison to non-members. They have become more aware of their own surroundings, rights, responsibilities and enjoying their experiences as fresh and they are more self-assertive with self analysis in their village settings than the non-members.

References

Allport, G.W. 1961, *Pattern and Growth in Personality*, New York: Holt Rinehart and Winston.

Hofstede, G. 1980, *Culture's Consequences: International Differences in Work Related Values*, London: Sage.

Jordan, I.V. and Hartling, I.M. 2002, "New Developments in Relational Cultural Theory", in M. Ballon and L. Brown (eds.), *Rethinking Mental Health and Disorders: Feminist Perspective*, New York: Guilford Press.

Jung, C.G. 1968, *Analytical Psychology: Its Theory and Practice*, New York: Pantheon Books.

Kelly, G.A. 1955, *The Psychology of Personal Constructs*, New York: Norton.

Kitayama, S. and Markus, H.R. 1992, Construal of Self as Cultural Frame: Implications for Internationalising Psychology, Internationalisation and Higher Education, paper presented at Symposium in Ann Arbor, MI.

Kuhn, M.H. and McPartland, T.S. 1954, "An Empirical Investigation of Self-attitudes", *American Sociological Review*, Vol. 19, pp. 68–76.

Maslow, A.H. 1970, *Motivation and Personality*, New York: Harper and Row.

Markus, H. and Kitayama, S. 1991, "Culture and the Self: Importance for Cognition, Emotion and Motivation", *Psychological Review*, Vol. 98, pp. 224–53.

Miller, J. 1976, *Towards a New Psychology of Women*, Boston: Beacon Press.

Myers, I. 1980, *Gifts Differing*, Palo Alto, CA: Consulting Psychologists Press.

Ng, S.H. et al., 1982, "Human Values in Nine Countries", in Rath et al. (eds.), *Diversity and Unity in Cross-Cultural Psychology*, Holland, Lisse: Swets and Zeitlonger.

Rogers, C.R. 1951, *Client-Centered Therapy*, Boston: Houghton Mifflin.

——. 1980, *A Way of Being*, Boston: Houghton Mifflin.

Rokeach, M. 1973, *The Nature of Human Values*, New York: Free Press.

Schwartz, S.H. 1990, "Individualism and Collectivism; Critique and Proposed Refinements", *Journal of Cross-Cultural Psychology*, Vol. 21, pp. 139–57.

——. 1994, "Studying Human Values", in Bouvy et al. (eds.), *Journeys into Cross-cultural Psychology*, Holland, Lisse: Swets & Zeittinger.

Sinha, J.B.P. and Verma, J. 1993, Social Support as a Moderator of the Relationship between Allocentrism and Psychological Well-being. Manuscript submitted for publication.

Triandis, H.C. et al., 1993, "An Etic-Emic Analysis of Individualism and Collectivism", *Journal of Cross-cultural Psychology*, Vol. 24.

Zavolloni, M. 1980, "Values", in H.C. Triandis and R. Brislin (eds.), *Handbook of Cross-cultural Psychology, Vol. 5, Social Psychology*, Boston: Allyn & Bacon.

Part V

War and Collective Actions

21

Conflict at the International Border

Women's Narratives of 'War' and 'War-like Situations' in the Villages of Northwest India

Abha Chauhan

The northwest international border of India has witnessed a long drawn out conflict over the last six decades owing to the unsettled territorial dispute between India and Pakistan over Kashmir. Pakistan always contested the position of the princely state of Jammu & Kashmir (J&K) which was acceded to the Indian Union on 26 October 1947. As a result, India and Pakistan have fought four full-scale wars (1947, 1965, 1971 and 1999) in addition to the less intense and proxy wars. Besides this, there have been several cross-border firings, artillery duels and frequent skirmishes at the international border and the Line of Control (LoC) that led to the migration of people from the villages near the border areas to the interior safer places, temporarily or semi-permanently. These movements in most cases have been forced, sudden and recurrent. Even, when such conditions of war and conflict are not there, the people at the borders live in uncertainty, insecurity and anxiety. Mostly, in case of agriculturists, their fields are often mined and bunkers and ditches created for army personnel and patrolling becomes a normal feature. The entry to the area is restricted and people are subjected to constant checks and scrutiny. Such are 'war-like-situations' in the state of J&K today.

The impact of these conflicts during 'war' and 'war-like situations' on women in the process of migration to different places, during life in camps and houses where they take shelter are all very crucial, severe and different. The views of women do not find a mention in many studies on conflicts, though the atrocities perpetrated on them become markers of the violence that is used by the state and the people to blame the 'other'. Women's perceptions and subjectivity are subsumed under meta narratives of violence, conflict and war.

The paper attempts to bring out the lived experiences of women during 'war' and 'war-like situations' through their narratives. The women belong to villages near the line of control close to the international border in the northwestern part of India in Jammu district. They have experienced several wars, firings or skirmishes resulting in serious consequences of losing family members, being maimed, houses and property being destroyed, having to migrate all of a sudden, and living in the most difficult circumstances.

The Background

In the ancient times, several local chiefs and petty princes ruled the Kashmir region, each with a separate and distinct regime, often with no political affiliation with others for long periods of history. In the medieval period, many of these small kingdoms, like the hill states of Rajouri and Poonch, and also Baltistan and Ladakh, were incorporated under the Mughal rule till as late as Aurangzeb's reign at the end of the sixteenth century. After Timur's invasion, Maharaja Ranjit Singh brought Kashmir under the Sikh empire in 1819. He rewarded Dogra Raja (king), Gulab Singh by conferring upon him the title of *jagir* (territory to rule) for Jammu and some other neighbouring areas. Gulab Singh expanded his *jagir* soon and by 1840 brought the states of Ladakh and Baltistan under his rule.

As the British-Sikh differences arose alongside Sikh-Dogra tensions, Gulab Singh turned to the British for help for maintaining his nominal independence by promising to remain neutral if the British attacked the Sikhs. The 1846 treaty of Amritsar followed. It marked the eclipse of the Sikh empire and affirmed the establishment of the Dogra rule in Kashmir. Gulab Singh was rewarded with quite a few territories. He later extended his empire, which by 1850, included the regions of Jammu, Kashmir valley, Ladakh, Gilgit and Baltistan, and founded the Dogra State of Jammu & Kashmir (Bamzai, 1973). The Dogra dynasty ruled the state till 1947, when the Indian subcontinent was partitioned between India and Pakistan.

In 1947, J&K was among the largest of 562 princely states in the Indian subcontinent. These were nominally self-governing units, ranging in size from tiny principalities to sprawling fiefs, ruled by Hindu, Muslim and Sikh feudal potentates with pretensions to royal status. Collectively, the princely states covered 45 per cent of the land mass of the subcontinent and 99 million people were permitted to administer their holdings as personal and dynastic fiefdoms in exchange for acknowledging the 'paramount' power of the British. The British directly controlled and administered the rest of the subcontinent (Bose, 2003).

At the time of the India's independence in 1947, the ruler of Kashmir, Maharaja Hari Singh, exercising his rights under the India Independence Act (passed on 16 July 1947), chose to remain independent. India wanted the Muslim majority territory of Kashmir as an emblem of her secularism and Pakistan claimed this territory as 72 per cent of the subjects were Muslims (Samaddar, 2004). But, as this did not happen, the state of J&K saw several tribal attacks, more so since October 1947 on Kashmir supported by the Pakistan army looting and killing people. In the meanwhile, there was a general revolt by the people of Kashmir against the rule of Maharaja as was most explicit in the 'Quit Kashmir Movement' launched against the autocratic rule in 1946 which was also supported by the Congress (Samaddar, 2004). Seeing the gravity of the situation, the Maharaja approached the Indian government for help and signed the formal 'Instrument of Accession' to India on 27 October 1947 (Samaddar, 2004) by which the state of J&K became an integral part of India. This position is, however, contested by Pakistan and since then wars have been fought over Kashmir several times between the two countries.

Amidst these processes of wars and near-war situations, the boundaries of the two nations adjoining each other shifted and till today India has about 740 kilometres of the border as LoC, still not declared as the international border (ib). Before partition in 1947, the erstwhile princely state was divided into four administrative units. These provinces were Jammu, Kashmir, the Frontier Region of Ladakh and the Frontier Region of Gilgit. Since the end of the first Indo-Pakistan war over Kashmir in 1949, the territory has been divided into Indian-administered Jammu & Kashmir (IJK, comprising the regions of the Kashmir valley, Jammu and Ladakh), with approximately 10 million people, and a smaller area under Pakistan control ('Azad' Jammu & Kashmir [AJK] or Pakistan Occupied Kashmir [POK]), plus sparsely populated regions in the high Himalayas known as Pakistan's northern areas with perhaps 3 million population. The dividing line between IJK and AJK-northern areas which originated as a ceasefire line in 1949 and was marginally altered during India-Pakistan wars in

1965 and 1971. It was renewed as the LoC by India-Pakistan agreement in 1972 (Bose, 2003). Precisely, India and Pakistan share 4,010 km-long western border. In J&K, it is 1,126 km, of which 198 km is the international border extending from Kathua to Akhnoor and 740 km is the LoC extending from Akhnoor to Siachen Glacier. It is from the LoC part of Akhnoor, adjoining the international border, which this paper seeks to draw the experiences of women.

At present, there are 14 districts in J&K (India) out of which six districts fall in Jammu province, six in Kashmir province and two in Ladakh. The total area of the state is 1,00,397 square kms with a population of 1,00,69,987 as per the 2001 census (the whole state however has 2,22,246 square kms which includes 78,114 square kms under illegal occupation of Pakistan, 5,180 square kms illegally handed over by Pakistan to China and 37,555 square kms under illegal occupation of China). The situation in Indian Kashmir is further complicated by the fact that while the state has an overall Muslim majority, Jammu has a Hindu majority and Ladakh a Buddhist one (Butalia, 2002). Muslims constitute nearly 96 per cent of the population of Kashmir valley. In Jammu, the population of Muslims is 30 per cent and that of the Hindus is 66 per cent. Ladakh has 50 per cent Buddhists (majority in Leh district) and 46 per cent Muslims (mostly Shias in Kargil district).

Conflict at the Northwest International Border

Conflict is understood as a state of opposition, disagreement or incompatibility between two or more people or groups of people, which is sometimes characterised by physical violence. In political terms 'conflict' refers to an on-going state of hostility between two groups of people or two nations. This paper focuses on the armed conflict between India and Pakistan and its impact on the people living on the northwestern international border between the two countries. Though the state has seen several forms of conflicts, especially violence as a result of the terrorist and insurgent activities, the focus of this paper is on the conflict at the border during the times of 'war' and 'war-like situations'.

'War' is generally seen as a struggle between two or more countries or opposing groups within a country, involving a large number of soldiers and weapons. By 'war' here is meant the major wars between India and Pakistan like those of 1947–49, 1965, 1971 and 1999. The term 'war-like situation' is used to refer to a state when armed forces are mobilised in an apparent preparation for war. Such situations may prove to be as traumatic as a real war. During such situations there are frequent checks and patrolling by the army and police, digging of bunkers, fencing, mining, construction of ditches, etc. The mining of agricultural fields renders the fertile land useless and directly affects the livelihood of the people. The presence of troops in and around the fields and houses restrict the freedom of the people and constant checking at the fences creates unnecessary delays and other problems. Sudden orders to evacuate and subsequent displacement of people and the hardships of the camp life – all but make people experience 'war' even when there is none.

Though there has been a ceasefire between the two countries, India and Pakistan for more than a year now and then limited exchange of fire, activities like 'fencing' the border have added to the woes of the people on the border. By December 2004, approximately two-thirds of the 740 km of the LoC had been fenced. A number of villages along the LoC have been boxed in between the fence and LoC. For instance, over 40 villages in border districts of Rajouri and Poonch sectors have been fenced out. This kind of fencing has taken place all along the LoC, cutting many villages into two (*The Kashmir Times,* 26 December 2004).

Women's Narratives of Wars in the Villages at the Northwest International Border

Partition and the War of 1947–48

Pakistan launched a full-scale invasion of Kashmir on 22 October, 1947. The Indian army reciprocated this. The first major battle was fought on 7 November 1947 at Sholatana in the outskirts of Kashmir. The Indian army, carrying on a relentless offensive, defeated Pakistan on 14 November at Uri, at a distance of 65 kms from Srinagar. However, at other places all along the border like Naushera, Jhanjar, Rajouri, Bhimber, Mirpur, Kotli and Poonch the fight continued for a year or so and most of these places were taken back by the Indian Army. At last, the war ended when the UN declared a ceasefire on 1 January 1949 though one-third of Kashmir still remained under the occupation of Pakistan. The Indian stand on Kashmir is that the merger of Kashmir with India is final and irrevocable and any attack on Kashmir is an attack on India (Rajiv, 1989).

The events of partition and the discourses on it in India have been captured and interpreted by many writers like Urvashi Butalia (1998), Ritu Menon and Kamla Bhasin (1998), Veena Das and Ashish Nandy (1986). These works question the simplistic and often stereotypical portrayal of characters along particular religious lines. Das and Nandy (1986) for instance state that, 'The experience of the partition produced a large volume of literature, much of which was autobiographical in inspiration. Most of this literature remained inauthentic, because it tried to reduce the violence to the language of feud in which violence from one side was equally balanced with violence from the other'. Thus, the description of violent, inhuman acts perpetuated upon those traveling by a train coming from Lahore was matched by another description of similar gruesome acts by those going from Amritsar.

Oral narratives provide a counter-balance to these rather closed written accounts and give more space and freedom of expression. An oral narrative is one's own interpretation of events and not a justification of what 'they' have done to others and blaming what 'others' have done to them. Veena Das' (1991) research about women's stories of partition shows that the dislocation is very sudden and abrupt with no time to comprehend the situation and take decisions accordingly. The 'disruption' of the 'private' lives of women has been described by her as follows: 'The forms of representations that emphasize the disruption of everyday life and violence to the women's world for cooking and feeding and decorously covering the body are also not idiosyncratic expressions – they represent forms through which disruption of life through a sudden announcement of death is traditionally represented in personal narratives of women'. As 'normal' activities of women are terminated, they are suddenly thrown into open space.

The account of such a violent transition from the private to public space was made even more difficult by the killings all around and has been narrated by women survivors as recorded by Furrukh Khan (2006). According to him, 'Many survivors convey a sense of personal confusion (following the rupture of old life) loss of identity, and increasing focus on minutiae of life on the move, a state of alertness to the particular which alone might contribute to survival'. He further says, 'A number of subjects said that they became much more aware of their surroundings, factors like the sugarcane plantations and the direction of the wind assumed critical importance in order to escape detection. They had to be very vigilant of the water wells, for a number of them had been deliberately poisoned' (Khan, 2006). It was through the bodies of women that 'self' and 'other' were defined as diametrically opposed notions of differentiation. 'There were numerous occasions in which the interviewees had been eye-witnesses to the savagery inflicted on women from one group of men from another, which included amputation of breasts, mass rape, parading them naked through public and religious places, cutting open pregnant women, and tattooing their bodies with nationalistic and religious slogans' (Khan, 2006).

Ritu Menon and Kamla Bhasin (1988) explain it like this: 'Marking the breasts and genitalia with symbols like the crescent moon or trident makes permanent the sexual appropriation of the woman, and symbolically extends this violation to future generations who are thus metaphorically stigmatized. Amputating her breasts at once desexualizes a woman and negates her as a wife and mother, no longer a nurturer (if she survives, that is) she remains a permanently inauspicious figure, almost as undesirable as a barren'. Most of the experiences of women that they narrate do not form a part of any written history, whether the state or the individual. According to Furrukh Khan, 'This form of articulation of memory of partition has been marginalised for long enough, and has suffered because of the postcolonial nation's obsession with the colonial version of collecting and articulating a national history, which has always been in a written form. Orality demonstrates the complexities of remembering that cannot be captured in written literature and hence adds a dimension missing from the otherwise linear narrative. These collective voices need to be tapped in order to create new hybridised forms of national autobiography' (Khan, 2006).

Collection of oral narratives of 'partition' is important to understand and achieve a realistic understanding of what took place during that time. It is pertinent to avoid generalising the experience of suffering and give voice to various perspectives of those who experienced pain and sufferings. Individual narratives make connections which are totally ignored by the 'vertical', 'fact-based' discourse of the 'official' history. The women's accounts of their experiences provide a simple narration of their stories, how they experience war or partition as different from meta-narratives of the state which chooses particular leaders, religious ideology or a community to cast as the entity solely responsible for everything that went wrong during partition. It tells us how, for instance, their 'private' domesticity was suddenly shattered by the events taking place in 'public' where they exercised little or no influence. Women's narratives add a new dimension to the hitherto 'layer' of someone else describing their experiences, something more than what is usually considered to be the only or authentic version of partition.

Krishna Mehta's narrative on 'This happened in Kashmir' sheds light on the crises she had to face all of a sudden and also the help and the friendship of those designated as 'enemies'. She gives a moving account of what happened to her and her five children when she had to leave Muzzafarabad where her husband was the District Officer. This was the time of raiders attack just after partition (October 1947) in which her husband was killed (about which she came to know much later) and she had to make a long and arduous journey to safety. Her house was blown. 'It was staggering looking at that house going up in smoke. Heaven knew what I was to do. Where my husband was and what was he doing? Where could I take these children? I was tired of brooding and my mind wandered around' (Mehta, 2002). They received shelter in a Muslim house and were given food as well. 'The food remained untouched; we had lost our appetites through fear. Everyone in the house was very worried, for the raiders insisted on entering every Muslim home; they pretended to be looking for Hindu women in hiding but finally looted the homes of the co-religionists. Very often, they even kidnapped Muslim women' (Mehta, 2002). The incidents of common mass protecting and sheltering people of other religions than their own are found in personal experiences of many, despite the depiction of the opposite. This seemed to be true in this study too.

Rampyari, a widow and a resident of Pallanwalan village in Akhnoor sector, in her late seventies, is a courageous woman. She was married in 1946 at the age of 15. She describes her experience of 1947 partition as, 'It was a time of great turmoil. We had to flee away all of a sudden. I was newly married. We went to Jourian and then to Jandial across Akhnoor bridge. We stayed there for 20 days. It was a very difficult time with nothing much to eat. After this we went to another place called Jorian Chak. We heard there that some Muslims have come and they will finish us. Hari Singh (the Maharaja) sent truck full of rifles and distributed them to us for our protection.' She further talks about her days during the time of partition and the relations between the Hindus and the Muslims. Many such accounts suggest that the local people tried to help each other irrespective of their religious affiliations. But when the situation worsened, they advised them to leave. According to Rampyari, there were several Muslims in our locality – Bhatti, Teli, Lohar, Rahri .... We gave shelter to Mamnu Lohar and his wife and kept them in our house for 10 days and then sent them across the border to Pakistan safely. The relations between the Hindus and the Muslims in Pallanwalan were very good. Similar is the case at my village Kalakot (her parental house). My father was the Lambardar and I was like a daughter to everyone irrespective of caste and religion'.

Treating of women and girls as daughters in their natal places is a common feature in the villages of North India and many people protect their daughters and sisters based on fictive kinship ties as much as they kill them for their honour. In both situations, they become symbolic representations of the community and locality, but in most cases the former is less emphasised. The gender dimension to crises situation and those of war and conflict, in situations of migration and displacement, not only tells us how women are affected differently but also brings out the ease or difficulty of situations owing to gender.

Indo-Pakistan War of 1965

Before the next Indo-Pak war of 1965, Hindus and Sikhs in large numbers migrated from the areas of Muzaffarabad, Mirpur, Bagh, Rawalkot (Western Poonch), Bhimber, Kotli, Jhanger, etc. which were captured by Pakistan. The area is referred to as Pakistan Occupied Kashmir (POK) by India. In 1965, a war between India and Pakistan took place in August–September. Pakistan launched an attack and reached the outskirts of Srinagar where massive firing took place between the Pakistan armed persons and Indian Border Security Force (BSF) during the nights of 10 and 11 August. On September 1 1965, the Pakistan army launched a massive attack with 90 tanks in the Chhamb-Jourian sector of Jammu. To relieve pressure on the Kashmir front, Indian forces counter-attacked in Punjab, near the Pakistan city of Lahore, and they crossed the international border. Consequently, pressure on Chhamb-Jourian of Akhnoor sector eased. At the initiative of the United Nations Security Council, a ceasefire was called to which both sides agreed. A negotiation for settlement was followed thereafter and from both sides important territorial concessions were made.

During the 1965 war, 1,00,000 Hindus and Sikhs were forced to flee from Chhamb-Jourian area in South west Jammu when the Pakistan army overran it. During this time many people from the border villages had to migrate as the attack from this side of LoC was severe. According to Kartar Chand of village Gigriyal, 'Pakistan first resorted to firing and then the air attack. Subsequently it was tank attack and they were 70 in number. They crossed Jourian and almost reached Akhnoor. It was only when India attacked from the side of Amritsar (Punjab) that Pakistan pulled back'. Vidya Devi belongs to Pallanwalan village. She moved here from village Pallanwalan when land was allotted to her family in village Gigriyal in 1965. She was 35 years of age then. But, as the war broke out, the family had to leave the village quickly. 'We heard the firing and knew what was coming. We immediately rushed in whatever clothes we were in. We walked and walked … till Akhnoor. It was very difficult. Then we put up at Muthal and stayed there for two years. There was always a problem of food and shelter. The children were small. How long we could depend on others?

The Indo-Pak War of 1971

The Indo-Pak war of 1971 began after a civil war in the East Pakistan (now Bangladesh) province of Pakistan over the demand of regional autonomy. The Pakistan army began a crackdown on Dhaka, resulting in the large scale killing of people and raping of women. An unprecedented number of refugees began to flood from East Pakistan into the Indian state of West Bengal. As several diplomatic attempts of India to solve this problem failed, India provided a resistance move, known as *Mukti Bahini* (liberation force) which began attacking military instalations in East Pakistan. Pakistan then declared war on India on 3 December 1971. The Indian army routed the Pakistani forces and on 17 December 1971 both India and Pakistan declared ceasefire. Consequently, the 'Shimla Agreement' was signed on 2 July 1972 and it was agreed by India and Pakistan that the LoC in the state of Jammu & Kashmir should constitute the international boundary between India and Pakistan and the two should respect and not violate the agreement.

The 1971 war displaced nearly 4,900 people from 10 villages in the Chhamb area that India ceded to Pakistan. Around 2,400 families were accommodated in tented camps at Kishanpur-Manwal in Udhampur district of J&K, where they had to stay for about five years. Later, they were officially registered as displaced and scattered in different parts of Jammu region. Besides those displaced from their original homes and settled elsewhere, there were innumerable people who migrated from the border areas to interior safer places during the 1971 war. Each family has its own story to tell. On an average people stayed out of their homes for nearly two to three years. For Vidya of Pallanwalan, 'These were the three most gruesome years when we stayed in tents near Mishriwala and also on rent at Janipur'. Another respondent Santosh Singh from the same village Pallanwalan was in the state of advanced pregnancy when the war broke out and she had to leave immediately. 'My husband was in army and he was in Bangladesh then. I remember it was 3rd of December when we heard the gun shots and with my in-laws and other relatives we quickly left in whatever state we were in. With great difficulty we reached Mishriwala where tents were put up for the migrants. There were innumerable problems, there was no light, the water was dirty, medical care was negligible and there was no toilet facility. Though we used to go to open fields, but even this place was not available to us. My first child, a daughter was born there on 31 December 1971. What a tough time we had, I shrug thinking of those days!'

It was nothing new for Rampyari who had to leave suddenly with her family from Pallanwalan during 1971 war to a place called Dharam Kuan and stayed there for two-and-a half months. 'We then moved to a camp in Mishriwala and stayed there for a year. We did receive a small amount of money, which was not enough even for our survival. People there used to make fun of us and sometimes accuse us. They said you drink our water, you are not ashamed, you have enough land (the Pallanwalan area is very fertile and known for the best quality basmati rice), why do you come and trouble us? Being a woman, I had to see the arrangement of food for children, their health and my older in-laws. My husband could not see with one eye and since our livelihood depended on agriculture, here there was no work and no earning. He also fell ill and things became even more difficult. There was no time to think of my own health'. Rampyari's words reflected the pain and the trauma, for being a woman and also her capacity to move ahead in adverse circumstances. Her problems, like those of many others were also aggravated by the attitude of local people. This shows that sudden and forced migration brought problems to those who migrate as well as to those with whom they stayed with or near whom they were made to stay.

Vidya Devi's story reveals the strength of being a woman, meeting the crises situation single handedly. According to her, 'During the 1965 war when we were at Muthal, a hill place where all the migrants were put up, my husband died. My youngest daughter was then seven months old. There were three other daughters. I had to nurse my husband as he was quite unwell, my daughter used to cry, I could not even feed her properly. During that phase we had to shift from one place to another and stayed at Muthi as well. After a year or so I came back to Pallanwalan, widowed with young daughters. I realised my youngest daughter was mentally retarded. I had to take extra care of her. As I began settling down and bringing my house in order, the 1971 war started. I again left the house and this time stayed in Mishriwala for almost two years. My house broke three times and the government gave very little compensation. I could not leave this place and go, it's my husband's house, I built and rebuilt it'.

The life of a woman has many dimensions, her life as a widow in rural India is even more difficult especially in situations such as war when the crises are never ending. Yet she clings to her memories, the things attached to those memories, and that is where she derives her strength along with the support of her husband's kin, who she thinks are her own.

The 1999 Kargil War

To continue with Vidya's story, she again had to migrate when the war broke out between India and Pakistan in Kargil in 1999. By this time her three daughters were married. She stayed in Devipur camp for nearly six years with her youngest daughter who is in her late thirties and unmarried – something extremely rare in rural India. She says, 'Life in camp is extremely difficult for a widow to stay with her retarded young, unmarried daughter. The tents are open and unsafe. In the village I could just leave my daughter and go to the fields as we stayed in the same premises as my 'devar' (husband's brother). We had a joint family. Now they are also here but in different camps and that makes all the difference. In Pallanwalan, my family had 6 kanals (8 kanal = 1 acre) of land. A good variety of crops, especially rice, used to grow there. Here in the camp we have to depend on government's relief, the supply of which is erratic. There is no saving now. I cannot even buy medicines at times'.

In May 1999, India and Pakistan, in their most serious military engagement since 1971, clashed in Kashmir. A thousand or more infiltrators from POK crossed the LoC from Kargil-Leh side. They were well equipped, better acclimatised and the Indian army was unprepared due to intelligence failure and also because the relations between the two countries were moving in a cordial way. Despite earlier setbacks, India was able to resist the attack by launching 'Operation Vijay'. The intruders – a majority of whom were almost surely Pakistani soldiers, had withdrawn, though India's success came at a high cost, both financially as well as in the form of human resource with more than 400 Indian soldiers having been killed.

The Kargil war came suddenly and without warning to the local people. 'We did not have time to even wear slippers or dupatta in case we were working without them' said Sita Devi of Hamirpur village. This is no different from the situations faced by women in other areas affected by the Kargil war. Khatooni, a Shia Muslim woman in a village in Kargil district says that in May 1999 'We left behind everything, our livestock, our belongings, clothing, and food stock, everything ...' (Bhagat, 2002). And when she came back in September at the end of war 'There was just rubble, even the school building had collapsed. We had no belongings left, everything was gone. We could not find our ponies and sheep. There was no firewood, food or money to sustain us through the approaching winter' (Bhagat, 2002: 99–100).

An old widow Shanti Devi aged 74 years, from border village Gigriyal, about 5 kms from village Pallanwalan, lived in a joint family, but in Devipur camp the family was split up. She stayed with her son in a tent. Her daughter, who was also a widow, stayed in a nearby tent with her three children. The old widow's eyes swell up with tears as she recalls the time when her 25 year old son was killed during firing in 1999. 'My son, Raghuveer was a very nice boy, he did not hurt anyone. And suddenly a bomb fell in Pallanwalan market and he along with his cousin died on the spot. After one-and- a-half years of my son's death, my husband died as he could not bear the pain. In the village we had everything, land, buffaloes, a good house, but here in Devipur camp we were put in a tent that remains open and unprotected through out the year. I don't know till when I have to stay like this. We were displaced three times earlier, but we were never so unsure of our return. I do not wish to live longer, but I am alive only to see my youngest son get married. He is in army and at present posted in Srinagar' (Shanti had three sons, the middle one died in the firing and there are two daughters, one of them is a widow). How difficult it has been for Shanti, and how much worse it could be for Zaima in Drass, when her two sons, aged 14 and 12, were blown up to pieces after the bomb exploded (Bhagat, 2002) can only be imagined.

The 1999 Kargil war left a number of people dead in Pallanwalan. The sights of many houses and shops full of holes suggest a gruesome past. Shanti's son and Parsino's husband were two of the victims. According to Parsino Devi, 'It was 20 June and I was in my 'peke' (parent's house) in Mishriwala when I got the news of my husband's death. I was shell-shocked as he was just fine. It was 4 am in the morning when he was taking the milk when a bomb fell and he was hit by its splinters. It was a Sunday. He was the first victim of Kargil conflict and his death immediately forced people to flee the village. Since then I have been displaced as well. I did not stay in tents. I stayed in Akhnoor with my sister for one year, in Taroti for 2–3 months, then in a place called 'dyaran' near Mishriwala for two years with one of my sons, his wife and two daughters. We lived on relief for the last six years, but now we do not get any relief. The land is infertile and it will take time to make it cultivable after a long gap of six years'.

In the Akhnoor *tehsil* of Jammu district, where this study is based, several camps like Bomal (Ramnagar), Naiwala, Devipur and Thandi Choi were constructed to give shelter to people who migrated from the border during the Kargil war. The governmental as well as some non-governmental organisations (NGOs) worked for the 'migrants' living in the camps by providing them basic amenities like accommodation (tents), education, water, electricity, medical facility, sanitation and clothing. The government of J&K provided relief both in kind and cash to these people. The quantity of relief material was 5 kg of rice, 9 kg of wheat flour, and 2 kg of sugar per person per month and 10 litres of kerosene per family in a month. Besides this, ₹ 400 per person was given to every person with the maximum of four members in each family, i.e., ₹ 1,600 maximum to a family for a month (but this was for the unemployed persons). Even this amount was very erratically given and people did not get the relief continuously for months.

Life in the camp and living in tents was indeed a very difficult task for the villagers. According to most of the people in Devipur camp, there was no privacy as the tents were open and difficult to live in extreme weather conditions. The problem increased, when for instance, somebody fell seriously ill. Sometimes the tents caught fire as well. The words of a 60 year woman from Pallanwalan, Kamlesh Kumari, who lived in Devipur camp, reflected tremendous pain as she said, 'My husband died in the camp from a heart attack, we could not carry him to hospital due to lack of conveyance. We had 9 kanals (A little more than an acre) of land in the village. Rice and wheat of good quality were grown. Now we have to depend on government relief to eat and survive. We get nothing from the land. The land is under Army control. We got ₹ 1,000 only once. My tent was burnt twice and my whole household material burned down. I cannot see fire anymore; I do not have the capacity .... I want to construct my own house'.

Loosing house, land and husband and being forced to live in a camp like situation with tremendous uncertainty can be most difficult for any woman. For people life almost came to a stand still in Devipur camp. A male respondent, who migrated from village Pallanwalan and stayed in Devipur camp with his four children, narrates his experiences in the camp in these words, '*There was not much work for the people for they were agriculturists and could not perform any other activity. So they spent their leisure time gossiping and playing cards. Women were engaged in the household work, but owing to lack of agricultural work, their activities also declined*'.

However, some significant changes were witnessed in camp life as people stayed here for 5–6 years. A new feeling of sharing something common in a crisis situation and helping each other by forming 'Migrant Committee' and supporting each other, irrespective of caste, religion or village, was a unique experience for the people. In Devipur camp, for instance, which had about 1,350 to 1,500 families, residents of eleven villages were also staying together. Most of the people were Hindus, but some Christian and Sikh families were also staying there. Different castes were present, but the main castes were the Rajputs and the scheduled castes. One could see that, unlike in their villages, in the camp the members of different castes mixed more freely and women enjoyed greater freedom as well as more responsibility which went with it.

War-like Situations

A war-like situation is understood to be that state when there is a threat of war and armed forces are mobilised in preparedness for it. Border skirmishes, shelling and firings at the border get intensified. In such conditions, the physical movement of the people is restricted, they live in constant anxiety and insecurity, economic activities come to a halt, especially of the agricultural communities, as in the Jammu region; and social and cultural life is severely curtailed. The sight is often of soldiers moving around, tanks and trucks patrolling, bunkers and ditches constructed, constant checking and searching, lying of mines, fencing, etc. This has been happening since the last several years at the northwestern border between India and Pakistan, though more vigilance has been seen only after the Kargil war of 1999 and the attack on the Indian Parliament in 2001. Such situations are observed more by those who stay at the border and experience problems in their day-to-day lives without knowing when they will be required to run away and in whatever condition they are in; sometimes for a long duration and at other times for a few days but can never be sure of their return. The migrants of the Kargil war took six years to return, and the Kashmiri Pandit migrants still stay in several camps in Jammu, having migrated in 1990 from the Kashmir valley.

Migration

The most significant impact of war-like situations has been the migration of people from the border areas to the safer places in the interiors. People at the border areas do move out, not only during major wars but also in between when, for instance, the firing and shelling at the border increase. It is the magnitude, the intensity and frequency of migration that affect the border people much more than anyone else. The suddenness and forced nature of such migrations make the situation worse for the border migrants. Given this nature and scope of migration the choices for people, not only related to the question 'to whether to move or not to move' but also what to carry and what to leave, are highly circumscribed. In such situations, women are usually seen as dependents, largely a part of associational migration, and represented as the victims of circumstances. The narratives of women here question these assumptions of the dominant discourse and explore the space for women's agency in these situations of migration induced by war and conflict. It simultaneously highlights the suffering to which women are subjected in a conflict situation and the survival strategies they adopt.

The first migration occurred around 1947 when a large number of people from both the sides migrated – Hindus and Sikhs from Pakistan and Muslims from India after much of mayhem, murders and killings. It is estimated that presently there are as many as 1,11,067 West Pakistani refugees living in J&K, mostly in the border belt of Jammu and Kathua districts. Some others estimate the population to be more than two lakhs. These refugees are still without full citizenship rights. The second migration took place during the 1965 Indo-Pak war, when almost all the people residing along the border had to migrate to safer places loosing many of their belongings. The next biggest migration took place during the 1971 Indo-Pak war when the entire Chhamb area of Jammu district went to Pakistan. The people were accommodated in tented camps at Kishanpur-Manwal, about 50 kilometres from Jammu, where they had to stay for about five years. They faced innumerable problems and only in 1976 the government provided them relief as well as some land to lead a normal life.

The violence in 1989–90 led to the mass exodus of the minority Kashmiri Pandit community. It is reported that the population of migrants rose to about 3 lakh; most of them stayed in various camps and colonies in Jammu. In 1996, the subversive activities were extended to Doda district and the massacres there caused more than 3,000 families from Doda to move to Jammu. In June 1999, the Kargil war caused another phase of migration. People from Pallanwalan and Pargwal areas in Chhamb-Jourian sector were the worst hit. Without prior notice, about 50,000 families had to flee to safety when the Pakistan army started heavy shelling. Most of them lived in camps or schools. The attack on the Indian Parliament in December 2001 created bitterness between India and Pakistan. It was followed by heavy shelling and firing from Pakistan on the border of Jammu & Kashmir. This led to the migration of people of border villages of Kathua, Jammu, Rajouri and Poonch districts. Up to June 2002, over 1.75 lakh people had migrated from the border villages. Most of these movements were temporary, with people going back after some months to their homes, like those who came after the parliament attack of 2001. For some others it took a longer time, especially for those who came after the 1999 war and settled in camps in Akhnoor.

Thus, the number of migrants from the border villages and the LoC, according to a team of the Union Home Ministry, is estimated to be 1.75 lakh (*The Daily Excelsior*, 2002). Of the total, 1.07 lakh were displaced from Jammu, 17,692 from Kathua, 10,327 from Rajouri and 21,952 from Poonch (*The Daily Excelsior*, 2002). In the wake of the Kargil conflict from Akhnoor block, nearly 6,072 families from 21 villages were displaced. From Pallanwalan sector of Akhnoor, the total number of families displaced was 1,044. In this sector nearly 62 villages were affected, out of which 19 villages were displaced from the zero point. The number of families displaced from zero point is nearly 6,040 and the total number of deaths was 26 (*The Himalayan Mail*, 2004). In the whole of Jammu district till May 2003, the total population displaced was 3,92,081, the number of families displaced was 24,479, the number of people displaced was 1,17,007 and the number of villages deserted was 93.

Krisna Devi, a 45-year-old widow from village Gigniyal, with five children to look after, two boys and three girls, narrates her experiences in the following way, 'My husband's family is originally from Deva Batala in Pakistan. After 1971 war, the family got land from the government in village Gigriyal. We migrated three times after our marriage. After the 1971 war we settled permanently in India. We had 2 kanal (one-fourth of an acre) of land, but as it was just on the border, it came under mining. We got very little compensation, ₹ 1,500 and that too only once'. A part of the area called Chhamb which was with India prior to the 1971 war, went to Pakistan, and the Hindus in the villages of this area migrated and were given land in villages on this side of LoC, Gigriyal being one of them. This shows how porous the border between the two countries has been. The widow says emphatically that she will marry her daughter outside the conflict area.

A widow aged 59 years Sushila faced multiple problems by virtue of being a woman in a patriarchal society and belonging to a lower caste. She narrates, 'My husband was a blacksmith, he died in the market. After four years since then, my daughter got a government job which was earlier given to me. This is because of the pressure from the boy's family to which she is engaged. We do not have any land but only a small shop at Pallanwalan. When my husband used to work as blacksmith, I used to work in the fields of other people as agricultural labourer. We used to get grain for the work. Now the compensation we get is far less, but we live mainly by that only. The entire burden of the house is on me. I have to work in some private school as a helper'.

Mining

Mining has been done often at the borders in situations of war as in 1965 and 1971. Lately, it was after the 13 December 2002 parliament attack that about two lakh mines were laid in Jammu Division. For this, the army took under its control a total of 70,100 acres of land (*The Himalayan Mail*, 2004). Regarding the casualties, as per the *Landmine Monitor* collected data, 332 new mine casualties took place in 2001 alone, of which 133 people were killed and 199 injured throughout the international border and the line of control that India shares with Pakistan. Of 332 reported casualties, 225 involved military personnel or militants. Of 107 civilian casualties, 32 were children.

Besides inflicting harm to the army, civilians and animals, mining also affects the village economy by restricting agricultural activities and rendering it unfit for cultivation. Since the border migrants of Akhnoor sector stayed away from their homes and fields for six years from 1999, their fields witnessed the growth of weeds. The land will remain unproductive as long as the fields are not de-mined. The process is an ongoing one, but it has to be properly and carefully executed as even de-mining at times can claim the lives of the people. For instance, till March 2003 the de-mining process, after operation *Parakaran*, claimed 14 lives and injured 39 others (*The Hindustan Times*, 2003). Also, the mines that remain undetected and un-defused also lead to heavy casualties. It was reported that more than 2000 victims of land mines had been recorded in one of the belts of Jammu division (Rajouri-Poonch) between 1947 and 1989 (*The Kashmir Times,* 2003).

A 70 year old widow, Sharda Devi, who originally came from Mirpur and stayed in Devipur camp after the 1999 Kargil war, said that before this migration, which was unexpectedly long, she had to leave her home five times (1947, 1965, 1971, 1987, 1992). Each time, according to her, the loss was tremendous. While in Devipur camp she said, 'We had 10 kanals (almost 1.25 acres) of land and on it was grown rice, wheat, millet .... We used to grow good quality of rice on our land but here we have to eat low quality things which government provides us. We actually had 50 kanals (more than 6 acres) of land but some got drowned in flood, some went under army control and only some 10 (nearly 1.25 acres) kanals remained with us'.

Similarly, a 50 year old woman, Radha Kumari regrets leaving her fertile land in village Pallanwalan while staying in miserable conditions in the camp. According to her, 'We had 24 (3 acres) kanals of land in which rice, wheat, mustard were grown and we used to sell grains. A considerable portion of my land has come under mining area and we got very little compensation for that. But I managed with my three children as my husband is a bank employee and gets good salary'. About recalling her days of migration Sharda Devi said that this is the six time she had migrated and was forced to stay in Devipur camp where there were innumerable problems like – waterlogging, lack of medicines, inadequate electricity, fuel supply, educational matters, etc. According to her, 'In 1947 we stayed in a camp for nine months, in 1965 for three months in a school, again in school for 8 months in 1971, for three weeks in 1987 in school and in 1992 for a week in a relative's house'.

Firing and Shelling

The border people, living at a distance of 5–10 km from the border, suffer because of frequent firings, since they come in its direct range. The intermittent firing, directly targeting the civilians, further adds to the suffering of people at the border. Firing in the border villages is a regular feature. As per a report, between January 2003 and May 15, 2003, firing took place as many as 1,007 times, claiming the lives of 29 people, 29 cattle and damaging 49 houses (*The Daily Excelsior*, 2003). People consider these shellings as a sign of war and they immediately move out from their villages.

According to a resident of village S.M. Pur in Ramgarh sector, he was on his way to government high school Ramgarh on a bullock cart loaded with household goods and family members inform, 'It is the twelfth time after 1971 that we are leaving our houses and searching for shelter for ourselves and cattle. I have lost five members of my family in the cross-fire between the two countries and now, I want that I should purchase land far from borders so that my coming generations at least would not suffer like me in future' (*The View Today*, 2003).

The children of retired army personnel in village Pallanwalan had to remain under the bed with hardly any food for three days during the shelling at the time of Kargil war of 1999. Any such instance or even a rumour makes them take recourse to these acts and they shrug at the very thought of going through such traumatic experiences. Nearly all the people and all women interviewed talked about *lundi pan* (mockery war) in 1989 that forced people to migrate to nearby safer places and stay there for some days. Kaushalya Devi, a 65-year-old woman from village Guda Mahla (3 kms from LoC) who lost her husband in 2000, while in Devipur camp, had to bear all the hardships of being a widow and taking care of her young children. According to her, 'I came back to my village only one year after staying in Devipur camp. I kept on going back to the camp in the next 5 years as the bomb shelling never stopped completely. But I had no fear; the fear went away with the death of my husband'.

Fencing

The fencing of the North western border between India and Pakistan took place at a greater speed in 2004, perhaps for the first time the borders between the two neighbouring countries became more or less permanent and less porous and flexible. By December 2004, approximately two-thirds of the 740 km LoC had been fenced (*The Kashmir Times*, 2004). The ceasefire announced by India and reciprocated by Pakistan, coupled with the completion of the border fence, reduced the violence along the LoC and IB but the same proved to be a nightmare for the people living all along the international border and the line of control. According to a villager of Gigriyal, which is just at the border, 'Earlier there was no checking and we could go easily to collect grass. But now since the fencing has been done there are many restrictions. We have to show passes, we can go only at a prescribed time, sometimes we are refused entry … .' Not only this, many people have lost their fertile lands because of fencing and some of them have got no compensation. The villagers of Gigriyal migrated from the Chhamb area that went to Pakistan, lost their land in fencing and received no compensation. This was because they had no proprietary rights on the land that they cultivated.

A number of villages along LoC have been boxed in between the fence and the LoC. For instance, over 40 villages in thin border district of Rajouri and Poonch sectors have been fenced out (*The Kashmir Times*, 2004). There are thus a number of people caught between the ceasefire line and the fencing. In cases of labour pains, snake bites or any other health hazard, the families are the worst hit. In the Kupwara sector of Kashmir Division, 300 km long, 12 feet tall, barbed-wire fence has not only divided nearly a dozen villages along the Uri into two but has also cut into half as many villages along the LoC in Keran Karnah sector. In this sector fencing has been constructed 10 kms inside the Indian territory due to impending fear of Pakistani shelling that has resulted in the partition of the villages. According to a resident of Silkot (Uri), 'To prevent a few militants from crossing over to this side of the border they have cut a line through our hearts' (*The Greater Kashmir*, 2004). Such situations bring distress in the lives of the people as well as questioning their very identity. A resident of Tilwari (Uri) lamented, 'Every Kashmiri has a predicament about his identity, but the people living in these villages face a peculiar situation. We do not know whether we are Indians, Pakistanis or belong to no man's land' (*The Greater Kashmir*, 2004).

A villager of Silkot, Uri has to walk seven km up and down the mountains to seek permission from soldiers at PP Post in Uri to meet his daughter on the other side of the barbed fence (*The Greater Kashmir*, 2004). The schooling of the children, too, is severely affected. As per the official sources at least nine government schools of middle and primary standard have been left out on the other side of the fence near zero line on the LoC on the south of the border at Poonch district. More than any one else, it is the farmers who have badly suffered. The people of Mandi and Swajian tehsil of Haveli and Balakot and Balnoi sector of Mendhar tehsil failed to sow maize and *Rajma* crop in the fenced out areas due to several security restrictions. Animals also become victims of the barbed fencing. According to Nazir Ahmad, 'I could not help but watch helplessly as my cow along with her calf was blown to pieces when she came into accidental contact with the barbed wire' (*The Greater Kashmir*, 2004).

Conclusion

Narratives, mainly in the oral form, provide much more authentic data of events of war and war-like situations that women face. They are accounts of women's lived experiences and give rare insights into the situations they have gone through. Such narratives provide a counter-point to the closed, written meta-accounts which often support stereotypical simplistic notions of events related to wars and conflicts. Women's narratives of these events bring to light often ignored and marginalised issues of the differential impact and responses to the conflict situations, a variation from those in the recorded history of the state and the people, thus adding a missing dimension to the linear narratives. Women's narratives provide a different version to the accumulation of knowledge hitherto produced by someone else describing their experiences, and to what is considered as the only authentic version of wars and conflicts.

Such differences are brought out through the oral narratives of women living in the villages on northwestern border of India in the Jammu region of Jammu & Kashmir state. The differential impact was seen in the ways women experienced each war and each migration. This was visible in cases where they happened to be pregnant, gave birth to a child in camp, carried children alone, nursed an ill husband or experienced his death, single-handedly managed the entire household work at the cost of their own health, coped with a young son's death, faced the wrath of the local people ... besides, becoming widows, living in the situation of missing men, being landless or of low caste ...

Studies with feminist perspectives highlight similar problems of women, but also their agency that comes out best in such adverse conditions. Women do not give up, commit suicide, run away or take to drugs to avoid such situations, but face problems and take them as challenges. This was seen in many narratives of women, some of them quite old and widows as well. They adopt new strategies of survival, develop networks of support, take on non-traditional roles and get elected in decision-making bodies, among other things. Living with a heterogeneous population, as happened with the people in Devipur camp, had a liberating effect on women. It was seen how camp consciousness, cutting across caste, community and village lines, developed in the course of living for five to six years together. It certainly brought in more egalitarian values and provided greater opportunity for women to articulate their views and take decisions.

The study also provides a critique of feminist writings by bringing out the significance of women in crises situation, like war and war-like-situations, and their conception of events as different from women in the normal condition. The migrant women attach much importance to their village life, their fields, their 'home' – *ghar, watan, desh* – as expressed by most of the women in their narratives. Also the significance of being married, having a husband and children, is often felt and their support considered desirable.

References

Bamzai, P.N.K. 1973, *A History of Kashmir*, New Delhi: Metropolitan.

Bhagat, P. 2002, "Reclaiming Lives: The Health of Women in Kargil District", in Urvashi Butalia (ed.), *Speaking Peace: Women's Voices from Kashmir*, New Delhi: Kali for Women.

Bose, S. 2003, *Kashmir: Roots of Conflict, Paths to Peace*, New Delhi: Vistaar Publications.

Butalia, U. 1998, *The Other Side of Silence: Voices from the Partition of India*, New Delhi: Penguin Books India (P) Ltd.

——. (ed.) 2002, *Speaking Peace: Women's Voices from Kashmir*, New Delhi: Kali for Women.

Das, V. 1991, "Composition of the Personal Voice: Violence and Migration", *Studies in History*, 7 (1): 65–77.

Das, V. and Nandy, Ashis 1986, "Violence, Victimhood, and the Language of Silence", in Veena Das (ed.), *The Word and the World: Fantasy, Symbol and Record*, Delhi: Sage Publications.

Hussain, S. 2002, "Will Peace Return? Trauma and Health-related Work in Kashmir", in Urvashi Butalia (ed.), *Speaking Peace: Women's Voices from Kashmir*, New Delhi: Kali for Women.

Khan, F.A. 2006, "Speaking Violence: Pakistani Women's Narratives of Partition", in Navnita Chadha Behera (ed.), *Gender, Conflict and Migration*, New Delhi: Sage Publications.

Manchanda, R. (ed.) 2001, *Women, War and Peace in South Asia*, New Delhi: Sage Publications.

Mehta, K. 2002, "This Happened in Kashmir", in Urvashi Butalia (ed.), *Speaking Peace: Women's Voices from Kashmir*, New Delhi: Kali for Women.

Menon, R. and Kamala, B. 1998, *Borders and Boundaries: Women in India's Partition*, New Delhi: Kali for Women.

Rajiv, R.K. 1989, *World Famous Wars and Battles*, New Delhi: Family Books Pvt. Ltd. Publishers.

Samaddar, R. (ed.) 2004, *Peace Studies: An Introduction to the Concept, Scope and Themes*, New Delhi: Sage Publications.

The Daily Excelsior, 22 March 2002, 7 July 2002, 10 May 2003.

The Greater Kashmir, 22 July 2004, 23 July 2004.

The Himalayan Mail, 27 August 2004, 4 November 2004.

The Hindustan Times, 15 April 2003.

The Kashmir Times, 13 January 2003, 22 August 2004, 29 December 2004.

The Kashmir Times, 26 December 2004.

The View Today, 1 June 2003.

22

The Impacts of Conflict and Tsunami on the Rural Social Structure in East Coast of Sri Lanka

Shahul Hameed Hasbullah

Villages in Asia have undergone significant changes in the recent decades. The degree, nature, quality and factors associated with the changes vary across different Asian communities. The paper looks at the nature, causes and agents of change in the village life of the east coast of Sri Lanka. The east coast of Sri Lanka is rural and less developed as compared to the rest of the country. The resource rich eastern region was long neglected by the Kandyan kings and the colonial powers. Governments that ruled the country after independence developed the interior parts of the eastern region with irrigation and land development for the benefit of the landless people of the wet zone of Sri Lanka, in order to ease population pressure there. The post-independence governments of Sri Lanka settled poor and landless rural Sinhalese in the eastern region. Prior to the resettlement of the rural Sinhalese on the east coast, the coastal eastern region was predominantly populated by minority communities like Tamils and Muslims and was excluded from the government's development initiatives. This led to disparity in economic development between the people of different communities and was one of the root causes of ethnic conflict in the eastern region of Sri Lanka. The conflict continued for more than two decades and destabilised the communities in many respects. Death and displacement due to war and conflict have had the most devastating effects on their lives. The livelihood of people has got disturbed and communities have disputed over land, the scarce prime source of livelihood, in the region. The tsunami has added another layer of suffering to the people of the eastern region. Both ethnic war and tsunami have contributed to the reduction in the rigidity of the caste system because people have been forced to adapt to the changed situation.

The paper addresses the following issues. First, it overviews the overall changes in the villages of Sri Lanka and compares them with the changes observed particularly in South Asia. Second, it introduces the eastern coastal communities of Sri Lanka and tries to comprehend the effect of war and tsunami on them. Third, the paper illustrates the changes through three case studies drawn from different geographical regions and ethno-social settings of the east coast. Fourth, the paper synthesises the impact of war and tsunami on the east coast communities and provides suggestions on how to address these problems for the better future of the communities of the east. Finally, the paper synthesises the changes observed and suggests what is expected in the future as positive and progressive changes in the east coast communities as well as conflict affected Sri Lanka. Though war and conflict did interrupt data collection, the researcher collected both qualitative and quantitative information in the northern and eastern parts of Sri Lanka through direct field experiences by interviews and observations in order to assess the nature of changes and the impact on village communities in the East as systematic data were not available for the period of war and tsunami.

Studies of Village Changes in Sri Lanka

The village-level studies in Sri Lanka date back to the colonial period. A survey of literature on village studies reveals that the research in this area covered a wide range of themes. These aspects of study have changed gradually over the years. Studies of the pre-independence period had the specific purpose of acquiring useful information that could be used effectively for administrative and other needs of the colonial government (Dasgupta, 1937; Casie, 1934 and Colonial Government of Ceylon, 1937, 1937, 1938, 1938, 1939, 1944 and 1944). In the years immediately following independence, especially in the fifties and sixties, research interests were directed largely towards the understanding of the changes in the land tenure, social structure and related changes in Sri Lankan villages. For example, Obeyesekere's

(1966) and Leach's (1961) studies were outstanding contributions in the comprehension of land tenures and the social organisation of rural areas. While Ryan (1958) and Peiris (1956) were concerned with caste and the social organisation of villages, Robinson (1975) studied village political structures and changes in it.

Village studies after 1970s have emphasised on the analysis of crucial current political and economic problems related to the socio-economic development of village settlements in the dry zone. For example, Weeramunda (1982) and Wanigaratne (1979) studied the socio-economic developments relating to village settlements in the dry zone. Moore and Wickramasinghe (1980) made efforts to comprehend similar problems in the wet zone villages. In addition, other village studies have attempted to examine the politicisation of rural inhabitants (Hetige, 1984; Warnapala and Woodsworth, 1987); agricultural modernisation (Hameed et al., 1977); and employment generation in the rural areas (Wickramasekara, 1980 and 1981). In the recent decades, village studies in southern Sri Lanka have focused on aspects of increasing unemployment and poverty in the rural areas, while the village studies of northern and eastern Sri Lanka have focused more on the impact of conflict and war on the lives of people of the area.

East Coast Communities

Trincomalee, Batticaloa and Amparai districts are administratively included in the east coast province of Sri Lanka. Geographically, the East coast is different from other areas of Sri Lanka in many respects. It is a long and narrow coastal region with a low rank among the less developed areas of Sri Lanka. It falls in the dry climatic zone with a lower density of population (98 persons) than the state average (226 persons) per square km (Census, 1981). The coastal belt in the eastern region had a higher density of population while a vast area of the interior is sparsely populated. People in this area are predominantly dependent on fishing and rain-fed rice cultivation for their livelihood. The region also ranks among the less developed areas of Sri Lanka.

Though the region contains all the major ethnic groups of the country, a clear geographical segregation between Tamil and Sinhalese speaking population can be observed. The Sinhalese live in the interior of the region while Tamil-speaking Tamils and Muslims live along the coast. Though Muslims of Sri Lanka and particularly those who live in the north and east consider Tamil as their mother tongue, they assert that they wish to be considered as a separate ethno-cultural community within the nation. Such an assertion is an outcome of politicisation of communities on the ethnic lines. The rift between Tamils and Muslims of the north and eastern parts, in the recent past, has further driven these two communities apart. The *purana* (ancient) Sinhala villages trace their roots for several generations in Ampara. It is evident from the local tradition that the Sinhala, Tamil and Muslim village settlements co-existed for centuries. The state policy of settling the Sinhala population in the interior areas of the east by way of agricultural colonisation after independence, has drastically changed the demography of the east in favour of the Sinhalese. The roots of conflict between the ethnic communities lie in the above developments.

The Tamil-speaking population comprises two distinct ethno-cultural communities, Tamil Hindus and Muslims, and preponderantly inhabits the east coastal belt. Both the ethno-religious communities have been living intermixed for centuries along the coastal stretch and exhibit a distinct pattern. There is a colloquial term *pittu* to describe their settlement pattens. *Pittu* is a local food item prepared by placing the flour mix and coconut fluff in layers, one after the other. In the same manner, Muslim and Tamil settlements are located next to the other in layers, which indicates ethnic cordiality between Muslims and Tamil Hindus of the eastern province. However, such cordiality waned away because of the increasing mistrust and misunderstanding between these two communities in recent times.

The population of the coastal belt has increased significantly since independence. Besides natural causes, the increase in population can be attributed to the in migration of population from the interior part of the eastern region during the war in the last two decades to avoid the difficulties related to war, recruitment of children as soldiers into rebel forces and the day-to-day difficulties experienced in rebel controlled areas. In the mean time, national minorities such as Tamils and Muslims living in Ampara and Trincomalee districts in the eastern province migrated to the coastal areas due to frequent incidents of ethnic tensions between them. The minority population mostly migrated to the coastal belt as the Sinhala ethnic majority predominantly populated the interior areas. Ever since the escalation of ethnic conflict in the mid-1980s in Sri Lanka, between the government forces and the LTTE, the eastern area has remained politically unstable. By the early 1990s, more than one-third of the population of the region had been subject to internal displacement, partly due to the prevailing war situation in the region at that time.

The proportion of men to women in the region drastically declined as men either lost their lives in the war or disappeared from the area and took asylum overseas, and many men were recruited into the militant struggle as soldiers. On the other hand, the proportion of war widows and unmarried women increased in this region. Mostly, this population inhabited the non-military controlled areas which had high areas of malnutrition and little or no access to health and other services. The local economy was seriously affected and unemployment increased significantly. Traditional family life and livelihoods were deeply affected. The ethnic co-existence prevailing between different communities prior to 1990 was seriously affected and communities became suspicious about each other.

At the time of the tsunami, war in the north and east between warring factions, the state and the rebels (LTTE), was stopped and the area acquired normalcy after signing a ceasefire agreement (CFA) between the state and the rebels (LTTE) in February 2002. After the CFA, a number of resettlement and developmental activities took place, especially in the coastal belt of the east, which was the target of tsunami waves of 24 December 2004.

The tsunami affected the east coast badly because it was the first landmass that obstructed the powerful waves but the sea was also very deep closer to the coast. About 71 per cent of the total deaths as well as much of the destruction of property and houses, occurred in the east coast as a consequence of the tsunami in 2004. The state and non-governmental organisations carried out rehabilitation activities in an ad-hoc manner which further aggravated the situation of tsunami victims as the tsunami victims were settled in locations where employment facilities and other basic amenities were non-existent. In most cases, houses meant for settlement of tsunami affected people were poorly planned. The consequences of the tsunami were then forgotten as fighting between the state forces and rebels began from early 2006 and continued intensively till 2009. Thus, the sufferings of the eastern coast people continued without an end.

Rural Changes in Selected Regions of the East Coast

Changes in the rural areas of the east coast have been further illustrated through three case studies drawn from Trincomalee (ethnically mixed) Batticaloa Tamil dominant) and Ampara (Muslim and Sinhala dominated) districts. The study attempts to illustrate the complexity of the changes that occurred in the case study locations, besides the life stories of some families affected by the changes in the study areas.

Case Studies from Muthur

Muthur is located on the coast of strategically important Trincomalee bay. It has long been isolated by the sea on the northern side and farm land in the southern direction. Further, this area is located in the delta of river Mahaweli. So, internal transport is often interrupted during the floods. Isolation did not hinder the peaceful rural living in Muthur for a long time. Resource-wise, Muthur was rich enough to survive without much outside assistance. In Muthur, different linguistic, religious and cultural groups co-existed in peace and amity. After independence, the state renovated an ancient Buddhist temple, which not only attracted pilgrims from different parts of the country but also promoted economic activities. The state gave land to Sinhalese people, after settling them in the area, and also developed irrigation schemes. Gradually, proportion of Sinhala settlers has increased in Muthur. Initially, it was not seen as a negative development. However, ethnicised national and regional politics transformed peaceful Muthur into a conflict and confrontation ridden area.

Muthur was ethnically and strategically an important place for Tamil rebels who were operating between the northern and eastern parts of Sri Lanka. Several battles occurred between the state and the Tamil rebels in Muthur. Initially, the armed conflict between the state and militants had driven out many Sinhala people from the isolated areas of Muthur. Later, vested interest groups instigated tensions between the Muslims and Tamils of Muthur, which resulted in the repeated displacement of these communities in the last two decades. The agricultural economy was significantly affected as the farming lands were located in mixed ethnic community areas. Fishing activities were severely affected because of the state's restriction on fishing in the strategically important Trincomalee bay. The tsunami hit Muthur coast very severely in 2004 and caused immense loss in the form of human life, cattle and property. The latest round of war in Muthur in early 2006 was fought for the capture of strategically important Trincomalee bay costal areas from the LTTE. The state succeeded in the war against LTTE and brought the area (Muthur) under its control. The recent war also displaced an immense number of people in Muthur. While most of the Muslims and Sinhala people were able to return to their homes, Tamils could not do so as the government declared strategically important coastal belt of Trincomalee bay, where Tamil people were predominantly living, as High Security Zone. Conflict in Muthur affected the social and economic aspects of lives of the villagers. It is very difficult to say whether normalcy will ever return to war-torn Muthur in the near future or not.

The experiences of two families are being illustrated in order to understand the impact of the war on individuals and families in Muthur. The LTTE asked Muslims to vacate Muthur without delay in mid-June 2006. The Muslims of the area did not expect such action from the Tamilians (LTTE). Nearly 40,000 Muslims left the area in a hurry as they had no alternative. Out of these Muslim families, one was contacted in order to understand its experiences. The family walked several miles through LTTE controlled areas while seeing some of their fellow escapees killed either by LTTE or by the shelling of the Sri Lankan armed forces. The family lived for several months in a refugee camp located almost outside the conflict area. The family had undergone sufferings due to the lack of food, clothes and other essentials. The author visited them during their displacement and observed the hardships that they were facing. After LTTE was defeated in the Trincomalee district, the government forced this family and the others to return to Muthur. Though people were not willing to return to Muthur at that time, as the war between the government and LTTE was not fully over in the east, they had no option when the government forced them. When the sample family returned home, it found that most of its household items were stolen during its displacement. It had to start life again. When the author visited it in January 2008, the family felt secure because it was rehabilitated in the same area that it was living earlier.

The second family of Muthur was Tamil and the author met it in a refugee camp of Annamalai (closer to Chennai), when visiting India in December 2007. This family came to the refugee camp three days before the author visited the camp. Earlier it was hosted at the Mandapam refugee camp in Ramanathapuram. In fact, the family fled Muthur even before Muslims fled the town. First, this family came to Trincomalee town and from there it came along with others to the west coast of Sri Lanka (Mannar). From there, it came to the Indian coast. The family will not have a home in Sri Lanka, if it returns in the near feature. During the last visit to Muthur, the author felt that Muthur town was not yet conducive for Tamil people to return.

Case Study from Vahri

The second case study is from Vahari area. It is located in the northern part of Batticaloa district which is predominantly rural, remote and underdeveloped. The population is thinly distributed along a costal road which connects Batticaloa and Trincomalee districts. On the eastern side of the road is deep sea (Indian Ocean) and on the western side is thick forest (jungle). Unlike most of the other areas of the East coast, Vahari consists of only one ethnic and religious group, i.e., Tamil Hindus. The development of this area has long been neglected for the reasons explained earlier. People are mainly dependent on forest related economic activities, slash and burn agriculture and coastal fishing for their livelihood.

Thick forest cover of Vahari had given an ideal cover for Tamil rebels who were using this area as one of the eastern base in their fight against the state. The government forces were not able to penetrate into the interior areas of the region. As this has been a rebel territory for a long time, the state is not extending developmental and welfare assistance to this area. Those who lived here felt almost like living in an open prison. They survived on coastal fishing and some farming activities. Tsunami came and destroyed everything they had. Tsunami recovery activities were allowed in rebel territory as well. Some people benefited by getting help from organisations that built houses for them while others continued to live in temporary shelters which were built by NGOs and waited for permanent houses. In the mean time, renewed hostilities erupted between the government forces and LTTE and the place of rebel hiding was targeted by the armed forces. People fled from the area and sought refuge in the adjoining administrative division, Valachenai. The victory of government forces in wiping out rebels from the strategically important Trincomalee area had given them an advantage of taking back the Vahari areas as well. People were allowed to return back to their homes. When people returned, they found that the houses built under tsunami recovery programme had been destroyed by the shelling. Also all the belongings left behind were missing. Now, people were neither allowed to go for coastal fishing nor for forest related activities for the reason of security by the state's armed forces. Also people were searched and questioned constantly by the armed forces in order to capture the rebels.

Vahari is an area still not accessible to all especially for researchers and NGOs because the government suspects them as LTTE informers and sympathisers. Family stories of Vahari are from the last field observation done in the early part of this year. People of Vahari were met at different locations. Some of them are still living in welfare centres (refugee camps) and others in the villages. One of the families met in a refugee camp was affected by not only war but also tsunami in their life.

The household head of this particular family was almost in a state of depression as he lost two of his sons while fishing in the sea and the father had not seen them afterwards. Loss of two bread winners severely affected the family and the father was in a state of depression when the researcher met him. The second family consisted of a young lady whose husband was killed by LTTE because of his association with the government forces. The widow was waiting at the local government office to seek assistance from the office for the loss. Government recognises the services of such families and some times it assists the victims of LTTE. But it is not sure that she would surely be assisted and also she was not sure how to cope with three young children after the loss of the bread winner to the family. She was waiting along with her children to see the official for assistance.

Case Study from Puttuvil

The third case study is from Puttuvil area. It is located in Amparai district. Puttuvil is rural, under developed and preponderantly populated by Muslims. Tamils and Sinhalese were also living in this coastal belt but were numerically in a minority. Like in other places, the Sinhala population gradually increased not only in the interior part of Puttuvil but also in the coastal area. It must be mentioned that Puttuvil is one of the best places for sea surfacing (e.g., Arugambay). Tourism still attracts many outsiders. Confrontations between communities are now noted in Puttuvil on land issues, on ancient Buddhist temples and many other areas of resource sharing and allocation. The rural landscape has changed significantly. The state is supportive of the Sinhala population. The minorities are left with no protection.

Two families with different experiences have been selected for illustrating rural change in Puttuvil. The first family, whose economic livelihood used to be cultivation of land with paddy, has been changing in the recent past due to the growth of tourism in the neighbourhood. This particular farmer was located in the interior area where he was not able to go and do his cultivation because of the war situation. Sometime ago, he sold his land to a Sinhala cultivator and found employment in the tourist sector which was closer to his home. The income earned by him from the tourist sector was good. After the tsunami, he was not able to get regular employment in the tourist sector because of fewer tourists coming for the famous sea surfacing at Arugambay coast. The head of the second family was a Sinhalese and he was living in a village which now had a mixed population of Sinhalese and Tamilians. In fact, this village was one of the oldest settlements in the east coast. His family is also ethnically mixed. Before the ethnic conflict, having an ethnically mixed family was considered good; but now it is not only considered bad as families with mixed marriages also suffer at the hands of both the government forces and LTTE owing to the association or non-association with these armed groups.

Rural Change in Sri Lanka: Summing up

The legacy of the plight of present day Sri Lanka has roots in the colonial past. But many of the negative changes of the day were the results of post-colonial policies that were adopted. Among others, three major post-independent changes were important in driving Sri Lanka to the present state of conflict.

Firstly, at the time of independence in Sri Lanka, the cultivation of rice was the main economic activity of the rural plains, while well-developed plantation crops in the hill areas of the country earned foreign income. It is evident in the last 60 years that the economy of the country has not developed and progressed but experienced a negative economic growth.

Secondly, significant social and demographic changes occurred after independence. Sri Lanka was known as a model country for achieving better social indicators in the developing world. The welfare policies promoted the well-being of the people in general, but contributed directly or indirectly to the unprecedented rapid growth of population. In the context of stagnated and negative economic growth, open and hidden unemployment, especially that of educated youth, has increased.

Thirdly, the nature of policies pursued and the impact of post-independent politics was also significant. The post-independence governments of Sri Lanka focused in particular on the development of domestic agriculture and the promotion of social services. The lack of adequate political representation of Tamils in the central government after independence resulted in the neglect of Tamil interests in the national agenda. As Appathurai (1983) indicates, the post-independence state policies related to state language, employment in civil service, education, electoral and resource allocation policies was against the interests of Tamilians and it alienated them from the mainstream of Sri Lankan society. Radical elements grew among the Tamil youth as a result of limited higher educational opportunities and increasing unemployment. In 1977 and 1983 ethnic riots against Tamilians further aggravated their frustration. This led to a civil war situation and a demand for a separate homeland for Tamilians – the Tamil Eelam.

War was concentrated in the north and east of Sri Lanka where Tamilians were predominant. The neglect of post-independence economic policies in the early years of independence, and the war in the recent decades, have affected the north and east badly and resulted in further worsening of problems. The tsunami has simply added another layer of problems to the already existing problems in the north and east. Rural areas have been affected most in this process of negative change. The long neglected and underdeveloped east has been further pushed to a worse level. Ethnic war took the lives of many, caused repeated displacement of several thousands, caused trauma to individuals and families, caused the destruction of properties and interrupted normalcy, affected the livelihood, broke the bond of ethnic cordiality that existed for centuries, and had many other negative impacts in the lives of the people of the east. The tsunami, on the other hand, added another layer of problems for the people who had already suffered a lot. However, one positive aspect that could be well observed among the people of east, and others in Sri Lanka, is the passion of having a strong individual, family and social capabilities of absorbing the burden while maintaining social order. It is very evident that with all these negative changes, people still are ready to face problems and resolve them individually and collectively. This is because of the tradition of culture that could be observed not only in rural East coast of Sri Lanka but also in many other Asian societies.

From the above analysis, it may be concluded that it is still not too late for resolving the problems of an Asian community that is taken as a case study in this paper. But, in order to resolve the problems faced by this region, it is necessary to understand the root causes that led to the present situation and to address those problems while addressing the immediate needs and concerns of the affected people. Development and other burning needs of the long neglected and underdeveloped east coast must be recognised. Meaningful power sharing is necessary for the people of the region to take development initiatives on their behalf. Ethnic relationships need to be rebuilt. The society is still capable of handling problems by itself.

References

Appathurai, E. 1983, "Communal Politics and National Integration in Sri Lanka", in M. Israel (ed.), *National Unity: The South Asian Experience*, New Delhi: Promilla & Co.

Casie, C.S. 1934, *The Ceylon Gazetteer*, Colombo: Gotta Church Press.

Colonial Government of Ceylon, 1937–1944, *The Economic Survey of Villages in Ceylon Seven Reports*, Colombo: The Department of Statistics of the Colonial Government of Ceylon.

Dasgupta, B.B. 1937, "Rural Economic Data from Kalutara District", *Ceylon Economic Journal*, December 19, pp. 65–79.

Department of Census and Statistics, Various Years, *Statistical Information*, Colombo: The Department of Census and Statistics.

ESCAP, 1976, *Population of Sri Lanka*, Bangkok: United Nations (ESCAP).

Hameed, N.D.A. et al. (eds.) 1977, *Rice Revolution in Sri Lanka*, Geneva: United Nations.

Leach, E.R. 1961, *Pul Eliya, a Village in Ceylon: A Study of Land Tenure and Kinship*, Cambridge: Cambridge University Press.

Obeyesekere, G. 1966, *Land Tenure in Village Ceylon: A Sociological and Historical Study*, Cambridge: Cambridge University Press.

Pieris, R. 1956, *Sinhalese Social Organisation*, Colombo: Ceylon University Press.

Peiris, G. 1970, 1972, Kalapura, The Colony of Craftsmen in Patha-Dumbara, A Paper Presented at the Ceylon Studies Seminar No. 7, University of Peradeniya.

Robinson, M.S. 1975, *Political Structure in a Changing Sinhalese Village*, Cambridge: Cambridge University Press.

Ryan, W. 1958, *Sinhalese Village*, Florida: University of Miami Press.

Wanigaratne, R.D. 1979, *The Minipe Colonisation Scheme: An Appraisal*, Research Study No. 29, Colombo: Agrarian Research and Training Institute.

Wiswawarnapala, W.A. and Woodsworth, D.E. 1987, *Welfare as Politics in Sri Lanka*, Centre for Developing Area Studies, Monograph Series No. 22, Canada: McGill University.

Weeramunda, A.J. 1982, "Transforming Peasants: Social Change in a Dry Zone Settlement Scheme", in *The Sociological Aspects of Rural and Regional Development*, Research Paper Series No. 1, Colombo: University of Colombo.

Wickramasekara, P. 1980, "Labour Absorption in Paddy Cultivation in Sri Lanka", in *Employment Expansion in Asian Agriculture: A Comparative Analysis of South Asian Countries*, Bangkok: ILO/ARTEP.

——. 1981, *Expansion of Employment and Income through Local Resource Mobilisation: A Study of Two Sri Lankan Villages*, Bangkok: ILO/ARTEP.

23

The 'Drum Beat' Heralds Schism in Dalit Movement

Intra-Dalit Rivalry and the Classification of Scheduled Castes in Andhra Pradesh

K. Sekhar and V. Sreemannarayana Murthy

The classification of scheduled castes (SCs) into ABCD categories in Andhra Pradesh has generated a nation-wide debate and added a new dimension to the discourse on the *Dalit* movement and *Dalit* consciousness. Protests against positive discrimination have been frequent occurrences since the implementation of the reservation policy. The demand for further inclusion into reserved categories by some castes is not uncommon either. However, the phenomenon of caste groups in reserved categories complaining about the preponderance of some other castes in the same categories, and consequently demanding some kind of re-arrangement of the reservation policies; to be more specific, the classification of castes into separate enclosures, with each group entitled to a fixed percentage of quotas within the broad category, is unique and relatively recent. A case in point is the *Madiga* community in Andhra Pradesh. The sustained agitation by the *Madigas* for classification within the SCs has extended the contours of the discussion on *Dalit* consciousness. The *Madiga* argument, for a just distribution of reservation benefits among the SCs in Andhra Pradesh, has sufficiently addressed the issue of the skewed policy which, over the decades, has facilitated the emergence of a new class among the untouchable castes. The contestation between *Malas* and *Madigas* is essentially for a space within the ambit of constitutionally guaranteed entitlements such as education and employment. This contestation has got further consolidated, intensified and sustained by the Madiga-led Madiga Reservation Porata Samiti (MRPS), meaning the organisation for protecting the Madiga reservation, and the Mala-led Mala Mahanadu (the great congregation of Malas).

Table 1 gives a detailed account of the classification of the SCs into ABCD categories:

Table 1

Group A

Relli Group

	Name of the Caste	*Traditional Occupation (24)*	*Total of Sub-castes*
1.	Havuri	Basket makers	756
2.	Chachathi	Fruit selling and scavenging	5,244
3.	Chandala	NA (25)	184
4.	Danadasi	Village watchman	5,410
5.	Dom, Combara, Paidi	Weavers, musicians, drum beaters	23,214
6.	Chasi, Haddi Relli, Chachandi	Fruit and vegetable sellers, sweeping and scavenging	1,872
7.	Godagali	Basket making, bamboo work	2,212
8.	Mehtar	Scavenging	4,553
9.	Paki, Moti, Thoti	Scavenging	7,876
10.	Pamidi	NA	5,647
11.	Relli	Scavenging, fruit sellers	76,329
12.	Sapru	Scavengers and fruit sellers	592
		Total	1,33,889 (1.68%)

Group B

Madiga Group

	Name of the Caste	*Traditional Occupation*	*Total of Sub-castes*
1.	Arundhatiya	NA	78,496
2.	Beda Jangam, Budga jangam	Hunting, flowers and cultivation	12,024
3.	Bindla	Priests of Madigas, appeasers of Goddesses	13,589

Cont'd...

...Cont'd

4.	Chamar, Mochi	Shoe makers and leather workers	12,881
5.	Chambar	Shoe makers and leather workers	519
6.	Dakkal Madiga, Dakkalwar	Mendicants, bards of Madigas, leather workers	1,598
7.	Dhor	Leather and tanning works	2,452
8.	Godari	Leather and shoe makers	834
9.	Jaggali	Leather workers and agriculture labourers	983
10.	Jambavulu	Foretellers, appeasers of Goddesses	961
12.	Madiga	Leather, tanning, chappal making	35,72,622
13.	Madiga Dasu, Masteen	Spiritual advisers, acrobatics, story tellers to Madigas	5,450
14.	Mang	Drum beating, basket making, mat making, tanning, jugglers, snake charmers	8,007
15.	Mang Garodi	Snake charming, buffalo shaving, acrobatics, juggling	107
16.	Matangi [g]	Begging, singing, tanning	323
17.	Samagara	Leather and tanning works	1,845
18.	Sindhollu, Chindlollu	Drama, dancing and prostitution	2,583
		Total	37,37,609 (46.94%)

Group C

Mala Group

	Name of the Caste	*Traditional Occupation*	*Total of Sub-castes*
1.	Adi Dravida	NA	1,00,382
2.	Anamukh	NA	76
3.	Arya Mala	NA	1,395
4.	Arvamala	NA	22,937
5.	Baniki	Village watchmen, palanquin bearers, watchmen	11,844
6.	Byagara	Watchmen, weavers of coarse cloth	1,740
8.	Ellamalwaru, Yallmmalwandlu	Vagrant caste	358

Cont'd...

...Cont'd

9.	Gosangi	Mendicants	7,653
10.	Holeya	Agriculture labourers, serfs, weavers of coarse cloth	665
11.	Holeya Dasari	Begging	620
12.	Madasi Kuruva	Sheep and goat rearing	3,550
13.	Mahar	Weaving coarse cloth, village watch, labourers	11,486
14.	Mala	Watchmen, labourers	28,94,643
15.	Mala Dasari	Spiritual advisers to Malas, agricultural labourers	18,416
16.	Mala Dasu	Spiritual advisers, acrobats, story tellers	8,335
17.	Mala Hannai	Vagrant caste	120
18.	Malajangam	Agriculture labourers	4,895
19.	Mala Masthi Acrobatics		474
20.	Mala Sale, Nethakani	Weavers, agricultural labourers	18,272
21.	Malasanyai	NA	300
22.	Manne	Village watchmen	64,668
23.	Mandala	Agricultural labourers	840
24.	Pambada, Pambanda	Devil dancers and musicians to Malas	2,333
25.	Samban	NA	3,233
		Total	32,63,6715 (40.99%)

Group D

Adi-Andhra Group

	Name of the Caste	*Traditional Occupation*	*Total of Sub-castes*
1.	Adi-Andhra (Malas and Madigas)	NA	6,98,860
2.	Masthi	Dancers, acrobats, carpenters	2,922
3.	Mitha Ayyalwar	Priests and spiritual advisors to Madigas and Malas	2,777
4.	Panchama, Pariah	NA	9,265
5.	Unclassified in Census	NA	1,12,933
		Total	8,26,757 (10.39%)
		Grant Total	79,61,780

The Madiga group is the largest among the scheduled castes in Andhra Pradesh. As per the 2001 census, it constitutes 49.2 per cent of the total scheduled caste population in the state. The *Mala* group constitutes 41.6 per cent and the Rellis 0.45 per cent of the scheduled castes in the state. The saga of the *Madiga* movement is replete with promises, victory, hopes, u-turns and disappointments. The MRPS movement, symbolically called 'Dandora', has been successful in carrying on a peaceful agitation and focusing on the need for more equitable distribution of social justice. No other social movement in the recent times, has been so massive in scale and yet is peaceful. In terms of mass mobilisation and sensitisation, the MRPS has set an example. The fact that their simmering discontent, at the real and perceived injustice being meted out to them, never led to any major crisis in public life stands a testimony to the organisation's forbearance and faith in Parliamentary methods.

The Place of Madigas in the Social Order

The earliest direct and contemporary record of *Madigas* was available only at the end of the eighteenth century through a survey of the border area (Dharmapuri and Salem districts of Tamil Nadu) by a Scottish officer Colonel Colin Mackenzie (1754–1821). Singh and Mathur (1974) described *Madiga* as the great family of Telugu leather related caste – or a constellation of castes. They point out that *Madigas* are represented by Jambhava. Intensive village studies portray the place of *Madigas* in the Hindu social order. In his study of village Shamirpet, in Rangareddy district Dube (1961) points out that *Madigas* are the lowest caste and *Malas*, who are also untouchables, are a degree higher than the *Madigas*. The *Malas* consider themselves superior to the *Madigas* by whose touch they are polluted. Dube (1961) further states that a narrow strip of land separates the colony of the *Malas* from that of the *Madigas*. The *Madigas* play drums on public occasion. They also make public announcements by the beat of the drum, dispose of the dead cattle and undertake leather work. They are skilled in curing and tanning hides.

Marie Larsson (2006) who has studied the Chintapalem village in Nellore district, also accounts for the social distance between the *Malas* and the *Madigas*, where the latter are despised by the entire village population including the *Malas*. Rao (1998), in a study of a village in Nellore district, found that Christian *Malas* stopped *Madigas* from beating the drums near the Church. Reddy (1950) explains the long standing antagonism between the two castes. A perceptible social distance is observed between the two castes. They live in separate *palles* (hamlets). Hence, spatial separation precludes the possibility of any substantial social interaction (Srinivasulu, 2002). The above studies clearly indicate that, though both the caste groups are regarded as untouchables, the *Malas* can claim superiority over *Madigas*.

The Significance of Drum Beat

The drum, a traditional musical instrument made of leather, is an inseparable cultural artifact of *Madiga* life. The *Madigas* beat the drum on public occasions in villages. The drum beating is popularly known as 'Dandora', which means broadcasting. Since the *Madigas* are the traditional messengers who communicate the messages of the village administration and make announcements in the streets by beating drums, the MRPS made the drum a symbol of its struggle for justice. The traditional occupation of drum beating has been a servile task performed by the 'lowly' in accordance with the norms of the village *jajmani* system. Hence, not surprisingly, the drum has become a cogent symbol for the arduous struggle of the *Madigas* (Muttaiah, 2004).

The Dalit Movement in Andhra Pradesh

Though the Malas and Madigas were ranked low in the social order, they exhibited clear signs of awareness, which could be attributed to the introduction of modern education. It may be assumed that the introduction of western education and the concomitant flow of western ideas not only inculcated a new spirit among Indians but also acted as a catalyst of 'social change' in modern India. While the privileged reasserted their hegemony over society, the underprivileged developed an urge to use education to acquire self-respect, equality and social prestige. In the colonial period, Dalit identity was constructed and articulated in terms of a critique of Brahminical Hinduism, caste ideology and philosophy. The Telugu *Dalit* leaders - Kusuma Dharmanna, Nakka China Venkaiah and Jala Rangaswamy - are credited with sowing the seeds of *Dalit* activism. Bhagya Reddy Varma, the leader and intellectual of Adi Andhra Maha Sabha, rejected the caste Hindu construction of untouchables as *Panchamas* and *Chandalas*, and coined the new name of *Adi Andhra*, advancing the theory that the untouchables were the original sons of the soil (Satyanarayana, 2005).

The Justice Ramachandra Raju Commission, appointed by the Telugu Desam government of Andhra Pradesh to study the classification of scheduled castes in Andhra Pradesh, identified 'Adi Andhra' as a caste and placed it in Group D without taking cognisance of the fact that Adi Andhra was only a euphemistic expression for *Mala* and

Madiga. By claiming Adi Andhra identity, some people from both the castes sought to disown their low status in society. Some of the *Dalit* communities tried to construct a new identity for themselves by changing the nomenclature of their caste, which was followed by a concerted action to get the new name officially recognised. The 1921 Census recorded only *Mala* and *Madiga* castes. But in 1931, some of the groups renamed themselves Matangi, Arundathi, Godari, etc. This assertion of self-respect indicated a growing *Dalit* consciousness during the colonial period. Some of the Brahmins of the Brahmo Samaj in coastal Andhra were instrumental in promoting a sense of self-awareness among the *Dalits* by establishing many schools and hostels for them (Satyanarayana, 2005).

The leadership of the *Mahasabha* was drawn from educated and reasonably well-off sections, viz., the *Malas* and Mala Dasaris. The Justice party nominated Sundru Venkaiah and Naralasetti Devendrudu to the decision-making. bodies. (Satyanarayana, 2005). Being in the vanguard of the *Dalit* movement, the *Malas* were the first to reap its fruits on the political front. The Bhakti movement also played a role in the awakening of *Dalits*. Potuluri Veerabrahamam and Vemana, who belonged to the non-Brahmin castes, spearheaded the fight against caste oppression and Brahminical dominance. The ideas of the Bhakti tradition (protest movements, Vaisnava cults) were embedded in the preaching of Christian missionaries. Reformers like Kandukuri Veeresalingam and Raghupati Venkatratnam Naidu also contributed to *Dalit* awakening. But the Christian missionaries, with the support of the state, played a pre-eminent role in the modernisation of *Dalits*. Operating on the ideal of humanitarianism, Christian missionaries could prepare the untouchables to attempt to get rid of caste oppression. Consequently, conversion was found to be an inevitable step, a definite means of escaping social disabilities and hierarchically structured caste society (Satyanarayana, 2005). Proselytisation, therefore, ultimately helped in delegitimising the traditional notions of purity and pollution.

Genesis of Dandora Movement

The *Madiga* movement makes a powerful appeal to civil society as well as the body politic. The *Madiga* grievance is not against caste oppression by the privileged castes but the overbearing domination of another caste with an almost equal ranking in the Hindu social hierarchy. Their consistent claim, that they are an excluded group within the larger excluded category, has to be thoroughly examined in the context of the growing importance of the studies of excluded groups. Exclusion within exclusion has paved the way for an acrimonious intra-*Dalit* rivalry.

The Madigas are the largest caste among the 59 SCs in Andhra Pradesh. They are mostly leather workers. Since their profession is considered unclean and demeaning by caste Hindu society, their status is lower than that of the *Malas*, who are not identified with any profession seen as polluting or unclean. The majority of *Malas* eke out their livelihood by working in agricultural fields. The *Madigas* trace their lineage to Jambavantha, an aboriginal king, and a pious woman called Arundhati, the wife of sage Vasistha. These characters are found in Hindu mythology. The *Madigas'* identification with Hindu mythological characters speaks of their inclination to glorify their caste and construct a well-defined history articulated by the Sanskritic oral tradition. Their relations with caste Hindus are very much ensconced in the *jajmani* system. In other words, the Madiga folk have been indispensable components of the village life for centuries as they alone can dispose off the carcasses.

The *Malas*, however were never close to the Brahminical scheme of things and hence, it can be argued, they were quick to embrace Christianity and make use of the opportunities thus accrued, charting a course of vertical mobility. Since they were not tied down to any profession, they could take up any activity that helped them better their situation in society. The *Malas* were always a majority in the Andhra region, which was prosperous. Christian missionary activity in the 19th century proved to be a boon to the untouchable castes and the *Malas* were the first among these castes to advance, educationally and economically. Massive irrigation facilities drastically altered the agrarian set-up of the delta region of present day Andhra Pradesh (formerly in Madras presidency).

In the year 1931, the *Madigas* started Arudhatiya Mahasabha at Hyderabad. The move to start such an association stemmed from the differences between the *Malas* and *Madigas* of Hyderabad. It was alleged that all the leaders of *Dalit* organisations in Hyderabad state, especially the Adi Hindu Social Service League in the 1920s, were *Malas*. They neither accommodated the *Madigas* in any of the bodies, nor involved them in organisational activities (Muttaiah, 2004). The prejudiced attitude of the *Malas* could be attributed to the inferior status accorded to the *Madigas* by the Hindu social system. It may be therefore, argued that the schism existed much before the enactment of the Indian constitution which provided reservations for the weaker sections in education and employment.

In 1981, the Arundhatiya Bandhuseva Mandali was established at Hyderabad by first generation *Madiga* employees under the Presidentship of Dr Kishan Lal (Muttaiah, 2004). With the publication of a document entitled 'Status of Arundhathiyas', it brought to light the glaring inequalities between *Malas* and *Madigas* with regard to the accrual of the benefits of affirmative action. The Mandali demanded the classification of SCs into ABCD groups for the distribution of reservation benefits in proportion to the population of each caste. The Mandali had chosen the 'prayers and petitions' method to ventilate their demands. For the first time, an assurance came from Telugu Deṣam party in the 1982 Assembly election. In 1982, Andhra Pradesh Madiga Sangam was established under the leadership of Dr Vidya Kumar (Muttaiah, 2004). It demanded the appointment of a Commission for the redressal of *Madigas'* grievances. After sometime the Sangam gave up its struggle as it understood that the power to enact legislation on 'classification' is vested with the parliament of India.

Dakshina Bharatha Adijambhava/Arundathiya Samakhya was established in 1990 to organise the *Madigas* of South India to launch a struggle for their rights, with Bangalore as their headquarters (Muttaiah, 2004). Dr N. Venkata Swamy and Dr M. Jagannath were elected as President and General Secretary of the Andhra Pradesh state wing. The then Chief Minister of Andhra Pradesh, N. Janardhan Reddy, promised to do justice to the Madigas. The most significant meeting organised by *Samakhya* was held on 2 May 1994 in the Nizam College grounds of Hyderabad, at the behest of the Congress government headed by Vijaya Bhaskar Reddy. The Congress government in Andhra Pradesh had become apprehensive after it witnessed the success of the Bahujan Samaj Party and the Samajvadi party combine in coming to power in Uttar Pradesh (Muttaiah, 2004). The Congress government was on a mollifying spree and, so, a few days after this public meeting, Koneru Ranga Rao, a *Madiga* leader, was made Deputy Chief Minister of Andhra Pradesh. The efforts of these organisations enabled the *Madigas* to capture some political space at various levels.

The *Madiga* movement entered its struggle phase with the 'drum beat' or *Dandora*. This phase was led by unemployed full-time activists, most of them former Marxists who left their party following the *Mandalisation* and *Bahujanisation* of state politics. The Madiga Reservation Porata Samithi (MRPS) was established by 20 youths in a small village, 'Eedumudi', in Prakasam District of Andhra Pradesh under the leadership of Manda Krishna Madiga, on 7 July 1994. The participants of the meeting vowed to build the MRPS state-wide. They resolved to adopt the philosophy of Dr B.R. Ambedkar and Babu Jagjivan Ram in their struggle for emancipation. A 52-day *padayatra* or great march (1,000 km trek) started at Naravaripalli (native village of Chandra Babu Naidu, the then Chief Minister of Andhra Pradesh) and passed through seven districts before reaching Hyderabad (Akhileswari, 1997).

The Grievances

Given their advancement levels, the *Malas* quite naturally made good use of the affirmative action policies and within a couple of decades they vastly outnumbered other scheduled castes, especially the *Madigas*, in employment as well as educational fronts in Andhra Pradesh. Though there are several other scheduled castes in the state, it is the Madigas who have effectively articulated their grievances against the *Malas*, as the *Malas* have been cornering the major share of the benefits that emanated from the reservation policy. The *Madigas* contend that the *Mala* group has been enjoying 80 per cent of the benefits of reservation since the enactment of the policy. The *Malas* are accused of occupying the entire political space. They are fielded as candidates by all the major political parties in most of the reserved constituencies. In some of these constituencies, the *Madigas* are in a majority. There have been Mala Central Ministers from Andhra Pradesh, while, except Bangaru Laxman of the BJP, no *Madiga* MP from any other political party in the state has found a berth in the Union Cabinet till date.

In all the formal and informal *Dalit* networks, the representation of the *Madigas* is minimal. Jayaraju (2007) states that the *Malas*, by virtue of their higher educational and awareness levels, have managed to secure some of the top positions in political parties. Prominent individuals from the caste are found in the entire political spectrum of the state, while the number of *Madiga* leaders in the political class is comparatively insignificant. Ambedkar, the Dalit icon, was against the Congress for most part of his life, whereas Jagjivan Ram, a Chamar by caste (*Madigas* are equivalent to Chamars of North India and Malas identify themselves with Mahars of Maharashtra) was a leading Congress man for more than four decades. Yet, the *Madigas* lament that the Congress, in its pronouncements and activities, project Ambedkar more than Jagjivan Ram. This is interpreted as the party's attempt to placate the *Malas* (Jayaraju, 2007). Jayaraju (2007) argues that the *Madigas*, in spite of being loyal to the Congress en masse, have been given a raw deal by being ignored at every forum. The *Madigas*, therefore, projected Jagjivan Ram as their icon and kept adding his name to the list of those who championed the cause of the weaker sections of society. It is, however, worth noting that, in their movement against *Mala* preponderance, they were never found slighting the sterling contribution of Ambedkar to the upliftment of Dalits.

Telugu Desam and Dandora Movement

The emergence of the Telugu Desam Party (TDP) signalled the crystallisation of factions and social tensions in the countryside. Till then the differential and conflicting socio-economic and political interests at the grassroots level were articulated through factional groupings within the Congress party. The TDP successfully attracted and integrated into its fold one or the other faction of the Congress party. The party thus provided a legitimate organisational basis for the factional divisions and conflicts. The *Malas*, who were numerically preponderant in the coastal districts, were historically ahead of the *Madigas*. In coastal Andhra Pradesh, under the British ruled Madras presidency, an educated *Mala* middle class existed since the late 19th century, owing to Christian missionary efforts and exposure to the process of modernisation. This historical advantage helped them to benefit from the special provisions for SCs after independence. Consequently, the *Malas* registered a relatively greater presence in education, employment and politics. This situation has been presented by the MRPS as a result of the *Malas'* cornering of the benefits of SC reservations, disproportionate to their population (Srinivasulu, 2002).

During the first decade of its existence, the TDP could not carve out any significant support among the SCs. In fact, the SCs displayed a strong preference for the Congress party. The division in the SC community on caste lines provided the TDP with an opportunity to garner the support of the *Madigas*. By supporting the demand for classification and by preferring the *Madiga* candidates in some of the SC reserved constituencies, the TDP (Naidu) carved out a space for itself among the *Madigas*, and made a dent into the vote bank of the Congress. Thus, the deep *Mala-Madiga* divisions among the *Dalits* helped the TDP to build a new support base (Srinivasulu, 2002).

All the political parties in the state are in favour of classification, excepting the BSP, whose stand is rather ambivalent, as it fears that such a move may open up a chain of demands across the country and erode its support base among the *Dalits*.

The Mala Reaction

The *Mala's* opposition to classification displays their repugnance to any kind of leverage being given to their fellow SCs. The *Mala* argument, though not buttressed with facts and figures, is based on rhetoric. Their contention, that the classification will spell doom for *Dalit* unity, is beyond dispute. Their pro-active role in mobilising public opinion against the Karamchedu carnage, in which eight *Madigas* were killed by the Kamma landlords, is ensconced in the *Dalit* 'collective conscious' and is seen as an act worth emulating. In the same manner, *Mala* dynamism came to the fore at the time of Chunduru massacre in which eleven *Malas* were brutally murdered by the Reddy gentry. These events spurred the *Dalit* conscience and, consequently, the *Malas* took the lead in consolidating the dalit identity. In 2001, however, when seven *Madigas* were killed in a village called Vempeta in Kurnool district by people belonging to Gandla caste (a backward caste), there was virtually no reaction from the *Dalits* as a whole and the *Malas* in particular. This could be interpreted as a direct fall out of the fragmentation of *Dalit* identity resulting from the classification. The *Mala* argument against the classification is couched in the Brahminical polemics that merit alone should count. The unstinted support of all the forward castes to the classification move can be interpreted in two ways. The well meaning among them support the move due to its distributive disposition, while those with a reactionary mind set support it for its capacity to drive a wedge among the *Dalits*. Jayaraju (2007) criticises the *Malas* for launching a number of organisations to counter the categorisation, through mass protests and legal suits.

Ambedkar's Views on Classification

Dr B.R. Ambedkar, in his numerous writings, vouched for some kind of reservation within reservation for the upliftment of the more depressed and disempowered among the weak. He was against castes/enjoying reservations cornering benefits disproportionately larger to their numbers. In a conference of the Mangs of Bombay Presidency in 1936, he assured the Mangs, who were more backward and numerically inferior to the Mahars, which the latter were prepared to guarantee their brethren their due quota out of the fifteen seats allotted to the depressed classes in the Bombay presidency (Moon, 1989). Endorsing Ambedkar's support to the depressed among the *Dalits*, Krishna Iyer (1990) argues that the scheduled castes themselves are made up of many layers of castes, some higher, some lower, within the hierarchy, leading to the higher layers gobbling up the benefits and leaving the lowliest always the lowliest. Therefore, it is imperative that a policy of providing sub-reservation to some definable sections is formulated (Krishna Iyer, 1990). According to John Rawls (1971), all social primary goods; liberty and opportunity, income and wealth, and the bases of self-respect cannot be distributed equally. An unequal distribution of any one or all of these goods is to be made for the advantage of the least favoured.

Implications of the Classification Move

It is hardly surprising that echoes of the classification are heard among several quarters which experience a sense of alienation despite enjoying some quantum of reservation. For example, among the scheduled tribes (STs) in Andhra Pradesh, it is the Erukalas and the Lambadas who have been the major beneficiaries of the affirmative action, leaving the other indigenous groups, who are more backward, gasping in the race. These discontented groups have organised themselves under the banner of *Thudumudebba* meaning drum (larger) beat in Telugu. These categories have declared their opposition to the preponderance of the aforesaid groups, and demanded a redesigned reservation policy which can accommodate all the tribes into its framework.

Another possible consequence of the classification of SCs in the state is a similar demand cropping up from the backward classes, among which some have already felt the overbearing presence of the more advanced classes. The classification is also likely to give rise to similar complex situations in other states. The Mala Mahanadu, which is stridently opposed to the classification, supports the bifurcation of the state into Andhra and Telangana. In view of the overwhelming numbers of *Malas* in the Andhra region, the demand for classification will wither away, while they have little to lose in the Telengana as their population in the region is comparatively low. Even without classification, the negotiating abilities of the *Madigas* are enhanced in the wake of the emotive appeal and the reason underpinning their movement. Krishna Madiga is able to influence many decisions of the government in favour of his caste; something which could not be thought of two decades ago. In a way, the delay in classification enabled some *Madigas* to draw mileage. In the same breath, it can be argued that even the *Malas*, whose discountenance of the classification is too well known, have been cajoled by the government on many occasions, since they are believed to be supporters of the Congress. For instance, J. Prabhakara Rao, one of the vocal Mala leaders, was made a Member of the Legislative Council by the Congress.

In 1975, the Government of Punjab issued orders that 50 per cent of the vacancies of the quota reserved for SCs should be offered to Balmikis and Mazhabi Sikhs, as a first preference among the scheduled castes' candidates. This was applicable only to direct recruitments. The Government of Haryana followed suit in 1994, dividing its SC population into two blocks, viz., Chamars and non-Chamars. It offered 50 per cent of the seats to non-Chamars on a preferential basis. This arrangement continued till 2005, when the Punjab and Haryana High Court directed the two state governments about the illegality of the order. This was done in response to a writ petition, which cited the Supreme Court judgment against the classification of scheduled castes in Andhra Pradesh (Jodhka and Kumar, 2007). The Punjab government, however, turned the 1975 order into an Act. However, the legal tangle persists.

The proportional distribution of reservation on the basis of population helps only in state-level recruitment and state-wide allocation of seats in educational institutions. But applying the same formula at the local level can lead to an asymmetrical distribution of the benefits, once again. Out of 15 per cent of the quantum of reservations, *Madigas* are demanding 8 per cent, based on their numbers in the state as a whole. But there are regions where *Madigas* are present in large numbers and, in proportion to their population, may need 10 per cent of reservation. In such a case, the proposed formula if applied, they may have to limit their benefits to just 8 per cent, which is less than what they deserve. Hence, the classification on the basis of population will be meaningful only for state-level recruitment or allocation of seats in educational institutes.

References

Akhileswari, R. 1997, *Deccan Herald*, June 8.

Dube, S.C. 1961, *Indian Village*, London: Routledge & Kegan Paul Ltd.

Jayaraju, T. 2007, *Madigas of Andhra Pradesh and Their Struggle for Social Justice*, Visakhapatnam: Intellectual Forum for Madigas.

Jodhka, S. and Kumar, A. 2007, "Internal Classification of Scheduled Castes: The Punjab Story", *Economic and Political Weekly*, Vol. 42, No. 43, October 27–November 02.

Krishna Iyer, V.R. 1990, *Dr Ambedkar and the Dalit Future*, Delhi: B.R. Publishing Corporation.

Larsson, M. 2006, *When Women Unite*, Stockholm Studies in Social Anthropology, Stodkholmiensis.

Moon, V. 1989, *Dr Babasaheb Ambedkar Writings and Speeches*, Vol. 1, Government of Maharashtra: Education Department.

Muttaiah, P. 2004, "Dandora: The Madiga Movement for Equal Identity and Social Justice in Andhra Pradesh", *Social Action*, Vol. 54, April–June, pp. 184–209.

Rao, S.N. 1998, *Organised Power and Unorganised Resistance*, New Delhi: Aravali Books International.

Rawls, J. 1971, *A Theory of Social Justice*, Cambridge, Massachusetts: Belknap Press of Harvard University Press.

Satyanarayana, A. 2005, *Dalits and Upper Castes*, New Delhi: Kanishka Publishers & Distributors.

Singh, T.R. and Mathur, K.S. 1974, "The Madiga: A Study in Social Structure and Change", *The American Anthropologist*, review by R.S. Khare, Vol. 76, No. 1, March, pp. 144–45.

Srinivasulu, K. 2002, Caste, Class and Social Articulation in Andhra Pradesh: Mapping Differential Regional Trajectories, Working Paper 179, London: ODI.

24

Public Hanging of Insurgents of 1857 and Social Construction of Folk Traditions in Haridwar Rural Areas

T.R. Singh

British rulers came down with a heavy hand on the activists of the 1857 insurgency or revolt. The authority of the *Raj* was firmly re-established with the punishment of those who had acted against the *Raj*. In Sunhra village of Haridwar a tall banyan tree, with self generating roots, is conspicuous. The tree had strong branches at adequate height to which the attachments of iron rings could provide a suitable arrangement for public hanging. Iron rings were tied around the necks of the 'culprits', hands bound in chains, and the attachment with the tree provided the last link to be released in the process of hanging. One of those hanged, put up physical resistance and the head got detached from the trunk, both the parts showing some signs of life jumping and tossing up for some time until they became inactive. The head got lodged in the territory of the village Mutallapur and the trunk in the fields of Salempur Rajputaan, about a mile from the site of execution. The two villages felt the after effects of these parts, associated with untimely death, and certain localised efforts got underway to keep the spirits calm. Local traditions cut across the two classical traditions; the Hindu and the Muslim and the two sects; the Arya Samaj and the Sanatan Dharma, and hold sway even a century and half after the event. The emergence and resilience of the local traditions, in spite of not being in accord with the major classical religions, and the non-secular after effects of an act of statement, to spread terror and instil the quantum of might in the minds of the subjects, were negotiated through indigenous practices and their rationale forms the crux of the paper. The site of the execution in Sunhra village, the village in which the head rested in Mutallapur and the 'Dargah' set up in village Salempur Rajputaan, all these sites have been visited by the author and contacts established with the caretakers of the last two sites.

I

The Sites

Sunhra, a place where collective execution of freedom fighters took place, is about 5 km from the town of Roorkee, and about 75 km from Dehradun and about 50 km from Saharanpur. It is about 200 km from Kurukshetra, about 50 km from Chandigarh and within a radius of five km from the town of Roorkee. Similarly, Mutallapur is at a walking distance from the rainy season stream that connects the two Sunhra and Roorkee.

There is a primary school, primary heath centre and provision for adult education, *Anganbari*, etc. All the houses, including those of *Kahars* (water carriers), are made of tallow and mud. All *Kahars* are illiterates and earn their livelihood by selling chat in the town. The *Dalits* are Chamars (leather work community) and earn their livelihood from sources associated with manual work; i.e., they are rickshaw pullers, drivers, and mechanics of all kinds. Only one family among them is well-to-do. The household head and his sons work in salaried jobs in Pawtis. The *Dalits* and the *Zannka* have better relations. The *Zamindar* gave 15 bighas of land to them and 60 bighas of land are under orchards that are grown and managed by the *Zamindar*. The *Zamindar* is a post-graduate and in a position to get programmes of rural development for his village. One such scheme was the establishment of Ambedkar Colony for the *Dalits*, road from *Dargah* to *Madhopur* and this connected the village to the neighbouring villages by *pucca* road. The *Dalits* are unhappy and grieved over the death of Ravi Mangal who was very kind to them. The *Zamindar* had sold all land where IIT constructed a massive hostel and the World Bank stopped renting out the rooms to public.

Salempur Rajputan is about a km from Sunhra. It is a multi-caste village. Caste groups inhabiting the village are Saini (cultivators involved in the cultivation of labour intensive crops), Nai (Barber), Sunar (goldsmith), Brahmin, Gadaria (Goatherder), Chamar and Bhangi (sweepers). We shall see how those castes are influenced by the *Sirkat*.

The Saini

In Western Uttar Pradesh, Saini means a caste of cultivators, vegetable growers and vegetable sellers. Today the Sainis are found in all occupations. They belong to backward class, and are good cultivators. In Rajasthan, Saini means an agricultural labourer. Sulempur Rajputan is so-called because the *zamindars* were formerly Rajputs. They sold half of Sulempur to the ancestors of a *gotra* called Janbuwal and the other half to the other *gotra* called Rana. The Ranas exceed in number and are in better positions. Sainis are found in several villages of Western Uttar Pradesh. The Sainis are the most troubled people because the *Sirkat* troubled them most. Other caste groups are insignificant as their number is small and therefore ineffective as they do not affect the social structure.

II

After-Effects and Rise of Caretakers

According to Muslim scriptures, the *rooh* or soul of a man after his death does not remain within the grave. On Thursday it raises and removes impurities, if any, it attends *Namaz* on Friday, says prayer to God and recommends anything to be done. In case of an immatured death, the case may be different. Among the Hindu scriptures it may be expressed as *akaal mrityu* (untimely death). If the hanged freedom fighters are Muslims, they were in Kartebala and *Sirkat* is no exception for Hindus.

A Saini of Mutallapur was preparing his plots for the coming season. The rains had stopped pouring. The cold wind had stopped and people all around were seen in their fields. This particular Saini took his bullocks to the field and as usual prepared his plough by putting it on the shoulder of his bullocks. Before he drove them straight, he felt like urinating. He sat facing the plot allotted to holy *Sirkat* and started urinating. Something knocked him down and he fell on his back with urine all over him. He became unconscious. His relatives observed the condition and took him to home to rest. He said to them, "Look here. I am *Sirkat*. I reside in the *babul* plots, the plots allotted to me. His urine brought impurities to the area where I live. Why should I not punish him?" The man died the next day.

The Sainis were terrified. The Saini who died was a respected member of his community. His house was larger than the others and also *pucca*. The members performed the function of purification as was promised to the *Sirkat*. The dead man was an Arya Samaji, but he had to comply. Who could avoid *Sirkat* and his verdict?

The village was peculiar in the sense that half of the inhabitants of the village were *Sanatan* and the other half were *Arya Samaji*. Sanskrit slokas were written on the walls of the houses. Sanatanis recited *slokas* praising the *Sanatan Dharma Vidhi* and the *Arya Samaji* households praised their sect and their leader, Dayanand Saraswati.

The trouble shifted from Mutallapur to Salempur, a Saini village. A Saini was advised to remove the *Dargah* installed in the house. Many Sainis promised to do so. The *Sanatana* Saini thought it improper to play with the sentiments of one sect. It so happened that the headman of the household climbed up a tree that was obstructing sunlight. He fell down the moment he started chopping off the branches. He fell down and in the unconscious state he said, "You know that I reside here. These neem leaves are good for my rest. You care so little and you are chopping off the branches of my rest. Secondly, you are thinking of removing the place from here. Remember, I will destroy your family and house, unless you promise not do so". He died within three days. He was an *Arya Samaji*. The Sainis of the village thought him to be one of the *Sanatana* leaders. He instructed his son and brothers to keep the place clean.

By this time, notions, ideas, beliefs and practices were settled. Whatever painful happened, it was attributed to the evil intentions of the *Sirkat*. There were beliefs about appeasement also. There sprang up an opera in the city who recited some parts of *Quran* to cool down the wrath of the *Sirkat* by scriptural methods. The *Maulwis*, on the one hand, and the *Operawalas* on the other, must be dealt with, if we try to understand the nature of disease and distress. The Vice-Principal of a private college came forward to please the *Sirkat* and cool him down. He was successful to a large extent but in several cases he was an utter failure.

It was held that a pregnant mother had to observe certain rules. She should not work too much in the pregnancy period. She should not undertake hard tasks. She should not go out when the sun is setting. Similarly she should not taste cheese and go to the field either on some important work or any other work prescribed for women for example, carrying food for the males working on the farm. A Saini woman got some cheese from a neighbour. This is also a very common practice as observed by Hardiman (1987). She put it on the oven and tasted some and went to the fields with some cheese for the man in the field. She was attacked by *Sirkat*. She became mad. The Vice-Principal of the private college could do nothing. At the most, the *Maulavi* gave a time prescription and the evil spirit became calm. However she died on the third day.

The villagers interpreted the two parts of the body as possessed of the spirits that actually brought ill luck to the wrong doers through physical harm including death. Persons so punished desired before their deaths that the family take care of the spirit and place associated with the same. *Sirkat* and *Sayed* became two referents for the trunk though questioned by one group on technical grounds. The spirits had great effect on the main ethnic groups, who irrespective of the classical levels of great religions continue to feel secure in the sacred sphere now after undergoing a few ill strokes.

Reference

Hardiman, D. 1987, *The Coming of the Devi: Adivasi Assertion in Western India*, Delhi: Oxford University Press.

25

Raij versus The *Raj*

The Phulaguri Mobilisation of 1861

Rabin Deka

This paper is an attempt to examine the local dynamics of the mobilisation of Phulaguri uprising in Nagaon district of Assam, which took place in 1861. As soon as the British annexed Assam in 1826, they started building the infrastructure of a plantation economy in Assam. The European tea planters faced a shortage of labour force to work in the tea gardens. To cope with the scarcity of labour, the planters urged the government to enhance land revenue so that the poor peasants could be flushed out of their land to work in the tea gardens as wage labourers. They also recommended putting a ban on the private cultivation and sale of poppy (opium) as a number of peasants were engaged in this cultivation. The peasants of Phulaguri reacted to this and mobilised under the 'Raij Mel' or the 'people's assembly' (traditional socio-political institution in Assam) to challenge the 'anti-people' policies of the British government. The protest took the form of violence as a manifestation of people's anger towards the exploitation perpetrated by the British *Raj*.

The peasant uprising of Phulaguri is an interesting case for study in the history of the peasant movement in India. The British *Raj* appeared on the scene in the guise of the saviours of the people who were suffering under the chaos, lawlessness and oppression that had persisted since the 1770s, starting with the Moamaria civil war and culminating in the Burmese occupation of the Brahmaputra valley. But, soon, people realised that the *Raj* had come to stay. Its purpose was to turn Assam into an agricultural estate of tea drinking England and to transform local traditional institutions to suit the colonial pattern of exploitation (Guha, 2006). In 1861 the peasants of Phulaguri of Nagaon district of Assam were mobilised against the British *Raj* to protest the enhancement of land revenue, modification in the revenue collection from the personal to the territorial base and the introduction of substantial changes in agrarian class relations. All these led to a severe burden on the peasantry. The officers and agents involved in revenue collection were given wide and extensive powers without any effective control on their unruly behaviour and arrogance. Consequently, tenants suffered under the coercion of landlords, *mauzadars* and other officials who were amply protected by the administrative machinery of the state. Under such circumstances, the economic condition of almost all strata of the peasantry of Brahmaputra valley started deteriorating during the second half of the 19th century. Such agrarian conditions led to massive discontent and resentment among the people that was eventually manifested in the uprisings that Assam witnessed during the period. The Phulaguri uprising, which took place in 1861 in Nagaon district, was one such major uprising. This paper is an attempt to focus on the local dynamics of the mobilisation of Phulaguri, the impact of the British agrarian policy on the economy of the peasants of Phulaguri, and their mobilisation to protest, which ultimately manifested in the form of 'insurgency'.

Socio-economic Profile of Nagaon District

The Nagaon district of colonial Assam, a district of central Assam, 50° 44° lying along the South bank of the Brahmaputra, is situated between 26 East 0° 54° and 93° 0° 0° North latitude, and between 92° 0° 47° and 25 longitude. According to the report of Sir Andrew John Moffatt Mills, the area of Nagaon was 8,769 square miles in 1853. The district is bounded by river Brahmaputra on the north, by the rivers Dhansiri and Doyang and the land occupied by the *Angami Nagas* were to its east, Dumuriah Mauza of Kamrup district was to its west and the Talingu river of Cachar and Jayantia hills that separate Assam from Manipur were to its south. The district was divided into fourteen *mahals,* namely, Nagaon, Chapari, Mayang, Kaliabor, Jamunamukh, Mikirpur, Mikirpahar, North Cachar, Jagi, etc. The Nagaon *mahal* was situated on both sides of the river Kolong. As per the census of 1871, the Nagaon district was prependarenlly populated by aboriginal tribes (81,770 persons), semi-Hinduised aborigines (80,793 persons), Hindu castes and people of Hindu origin (83,453 persons) and Muhammadans (10,066 persons).

Aboriginal and Hill Tribes

The most numerous and most important of the people inhabiting the district are the *Mikirs*, *Miris*, *Lalungs* and *Kacharis*. They were all formerly inhabitants of the hills and the last two settled down permanently in the plains. The *Mikirs* inhabited that part of the district which is known as the Mikir hills (which subsequently became Karbi Anglong district), and were the most numerous of the aboriginal tribes. Agriculture forms the principal occupation of the *Mikirs*, the chief crop being rice and cotton. They do not use plough or oxen for tilling the ground, their agricultural implements consists only of a hoe (*kodali*) and a hand-bill (*dao*). They cultivate their land on the *jhum* (shifting) system, by selecting a hill-side, clearing it of jungle by fire, and raising heavy crops for three or four years in succession until the soil becomes impoverished, when they abandon the land for newer soil, which they clear and cultivate in the same manner.

The *Miris* tribe in Nowgong, numbering, according to the 1871 census report, had only 225 persons. They originally emigrated from Upper Assam, and are now settled near Kaliabar. They are labourious people, living on the skirts of forests, and reclaiming lands from the jungle, which they cultivate year after year till the soil becomes unproductive, when they remove to another spot and select fresh land.

The *Kacharis* living in plains are said to have migrated into Nowgoan from Cachar during the rule of the Ahom kings. The census report gives their number at 8,828. They have a peculiar and distinct language of their own. The *Kacharis*, as rule, are an industrious race, their chief occupation being rice cultivation.

The origin of the *Lalung* tribe is obscure, but they are said to be aborigines of Cachar and indeed closely resemble the *Kacharis* in habits, customs, occupations, and religion. According to the census report their number in Nowgaon district was 32,813.

Castes

The following is a list of the prevailing castes and agrarian classes in the district: Brahmin (priestly caste), *Ganak* (next to the Brahmins in caste hierarchy), Rajput (employed in military or police service or as guards, doorkeepers, etc.), *Baidya* (physician), *Kayasth* (descendants of the servant originally came to Bengal with the five Brahmin imported by king Adisur from Oudh), *Kalitas* (next to the Kayastha in rank), *Keut* (an inferior caste but said to be not employed as fishermen), *Khatri* – merchants and traders, who claim to belong to the *Kshatriya* or military caste of ancient India, *Agarwala* (up-country traders and merchants), *Marwari* (also up-country traders), *Baniya* (the trading caste of Bengal), *Gandhabaniya* (a branch of the baniya caste, employed as spice dealers), *Oswal* (traders), *Kamar* (blacksmiths), *Napit* (barbers), *Kumbhar* (potters and dealers in earthenware), *Patia* (whose hereditary occupation is mat-making, but most of whom are now occupied as petty officials. *Goala* (milkmen, cow keeper), *Barui* (growers of betel leaf), *Mali* (garderners), *Ganrar*(preparers and sellers of parched grain), *Kansari* (coppersmith), *Sutradhar* (carpenters), *Sonar* (goldsmiths), *Halwai* (sweetmeat makers), *Kandu* (confectioners), *Madak* (confectioners), *Aguri* (cultivating caste), *Kaibartta* (cultivators), *Koeri* (cultivators), *Kurmi* (cultivators), *Shaloi* (cultivator), *Boria* (cultivators), *Sut* (cultivators), *Tanti* (weavers), *Katuni* (weavers), *Jogi* (originally silk manufacturers, but presently they do not confine themselves exclusively to this occupation), *Sunri* (a low caste), Teli (oil-sellers), *Dom* (fishermen untouchables), *Ahom* (the descendent of the former rulers of the Province), *Koch* (descendent of an ancient dominant aboriginal race), *Barahi* (descendent of the Ahoms), *Kahar* (domestic servants), *Dhoba* (washermen), Dhanuk (personal servents), *Chunari* (shell-lime makers for chewing), *Matiyal* (daily labourers), *Nuniya* (salt makers), *Mala* (fishermen), *Patuni* (fishermen), *Bagdi* (labourers and cultivators), *Baheliya* (labourers and cultivators), *Bauri* (labourers and cultivators), *Bhuya* (labourers and cultivator), Chamar (shoemakers and leather dealers), *Chandal* (labourers, cultivators and fishermen), *Chutia* (cultivators and labourers), *Dosadh* (Swineherds), *Hari* (originally sweepers but presently goldsmiths), *Khaira* (labourers), *Kharuwar* (labourers), *Mal* (snake-charmers), *Mihtar* (sweepers), *Rajwar* (labourers), and *Shikari* (hunters) (Hunter, 1879)

Revolt of 1857 and its Impact

Some members of the deposed local aristocracy became restless towards the close of July 1857, during the First War of Independence, and established contact with soldiers stationed at Dibrugarh and Guwahati under the leadership of Maniram Dewan (1806–1858). Dewan held many discussions on the *modus operandi* of the movement with the local elites of Nagaon and the tribal kings of Tapukuchi, Saragaon, Khaigarh, Barapujia and Mikirgaon; the seven tribal kings of Mayong, Kumai, Nellei, Baghara, Ghagua, Tetelia, and Sukhanagugia, besides the *kakatis* of Chahari, Uttarkhola, Gobhar, Gohain of Jagialia and *Laskars* of the

Kapili valley, specially from Kampur (Kalita, 2006). Dewan was able to unite these restless chiefs and princes and motivated them to launch a rebellion. Preparations began from 1855–56 and people belonging to *Tiwa* (Lalung) and *Mikir* tribes living in about 2000 square miles along the sparsely populated Kalong-Kapili valley prepared themselves to jump into rebellion whenever a call was given to them. The youth of different villages were given military training and prepared for a war against the Britishers. The planters and missionaries became panicky; and many took shelter at Guwahati. Marwari traders and moneylenders buried their properties in the apprehension of trouble.

New Taxation Measures

In the meantime, the British government introduced a series of new taxation measures. The officers and agents involved in revenue collection were given wide and extensive powers without any effective control on their unruly behaviour and arrogance. Consequently, tenants suffered under the coercion of landlords, *mauzadars* and other officials while the administrative machinery of the state amply protected them. Under such circumstances, the economic condition of almost all the strata of the peasantry started deteriorating during the second half of the 19th century. These measures resulted in the emergence of two agrarian revolts of a local nature; one in Jayantia hills and other in the Nagaon district of Brahmaputra valley. In the Jayantia hills, the people were not accustomed to any kind of money tax. House tax and stamp duty were introduced in 1860, further adding fuel to the already existing discontentment of the tribals of Nagaon. The *Khasi* people of the Jayantia hills stood united under the leadership of their traditional chiefs (Guha, 1977). Tribals inhabiting the Phulaguri area led a spontaneous and unstructured movement of the peasant masses of Assam.

Tea versus Poppy

Nagaon district was an ideal area for the cultivation of poppy as the floodwater of the rivers, Kolang and Brahmaputra, leave considerable amount of silt over the land. Abundant production of poppy induced the people to become opium eaters and encouraged them to export the produce for subsistence. The Assam Company, the first joint stock company of India, came into existence in 1939 and remained virtually the only tea planter in the field till 1850. The Jorehaut Tea Co. and several individual enterprises started growing tea plantation from 1859. The total area under tea plantation increased from 2,311 acres in 1841 to about 8,000 acres by 1859. The total output also increased proportionately. The planters faced an acute shortage of labour with the expansion of area under tea plantation. The planters urged the government in 1859 to further enhance the land revenue rates so that the poor peasants who fail to pay the enhanced revenue will be alienated from their land and could become wage workers on the plantation to earn their livelihood. More labour was required to cope with the labour requirements on the rapidly increasing area under tea plantation in the district. But, the planters failed to hire sufficient labour from Bihar and other states as the whole of Nagaon district was a malaria- and cholera-prone area. Malaria and cholera caused the death of many labourers working in tea plantation that created fear among the tea garden labourer. To manage the situation, the European tea planters suggested to the government that it should ban the cultivation of poppy by the local people. The planters suggested that the government could cultivate the poppy crop under its head and sell the produce, at higher price to the users. In case the implementation of the ban on the cultivation of poppy by the locals failed, then the revenue on such land needed to be increased manifold. The planters thought that the manifold increase of revenue on poppy cultivated land would compel the local people to sell off their land to the tea garden owners and work on tea gardens as wage earners. The government accepted the advice of the planters and imposed a ban on poppy cultivation in 1860. Such a ban on poppy cultivation, besides the hike in land revenue, caused resentment among the people of Nagaon.

Issue of Tax on Betelnut and Paan: The Immediate Cause of the Revolt

Although the Income Tax Act was amended in 1861, it did not touch a single agriculturist in Assam. It created misapprehension about the government's intentions as the earlier actions and policies of the government affected their lives significantly. People of Nagaon were aware of the peasants' resentment in the adjoining Jaintia Hills against the hike in taxes which they treated as unfair. In the meantime, the Bengal government called upon its officers in Assam to report on the feasibility of a tax on betel-nut and *paan* (betel leaves) cultivation. The peasants of Phulaguri treated betel-nut and *paan* as symbols of their culture and took the government's intention to impose tax on betel-nut and *paan* very seriously. The taxes on income, trade and profession affected the interests of the well-to-do to middle peasantry, *mauzadars*, traders, and government servants. This ultimately mobilised the tribal communities, traders, middle peasantry, traders and government servants against the Raj (Barpujari, 1993).

Mobilisation of 1861

The discontented cultivators about 1,500 of them, were first mobilised in the form of large gatherings in front of the Sadar Court on 17 September 1861 to raise their voices against the prohibition on poppy cultivation, imposition of taxes on betel nut and betel leaf cultivation, and increase in land revenue. They marched to the district headquarters to present a petition to the Magistrate containing the above mentioned grievances. The District Magistrate treated the demonstrating peasants casually and showed no sympathy towards the grievances. As per official records, the Magistrate always dealt with the cultivators in a high handed and provocative manner, and did not allow them even to enter into his office compound (Bengal Administrative Report, 1861) On 9 October 1861 they gathered for the second time but this too failed to receive a response from the District Magistrate.

Consequently, the peasants regrouped themselves and organised a *Mel* on 15 October, 1861. The *Mel* continued for five days at a stretch. Thousands of disgruntled cultivators attended the *Mel*. Many of them were armed with *lathis* (bamboo sticks) and everyday their number increased. The administration treated it as a law and order problem and attempted to disperse the gathering by force. The recalcitrant peasants were in open rebellion and declined to listen to the official appeals and warnings to disperse. The situation gradually became violent on the fifth day of the *Mel* as a British officer, Lieutenant Singer, came with a police party and ordered the police to disperse the cultivators. He tried personally to snatch the bamboo lathis from the recalcitrant peasants. He got himself inadvertently killed in the exchange of blows and his body was thrown into river Kolong. The police force accompanying him fled in panic.

The news of Singer's death reached Nagaon on the same evening. This made the District Magistrate panic and entrench himself at the treasury. An armed force was sent to the trouble-spot at Phulaguri. The troops fired indiscriminately, leading to the death of several persons in the collectivity. Narshing Lalung and eight other peasant leaders, mostly tribals, were punished with long term imprisonment. This heroic resistance is still very much alive in the folk memory as the 'Phulaguri Dhawa'. The Phulaguri resistance was the result of the particular conditions of outrage and oppression of subaltern groups (Karna, 2004) but colonial historians described it as an uprising against the ban on poppy cultivation. Similar outbreaks like the *Kol* and *Bhumij* revolts of 1831–33, the *Santhal* insurrection of 1855–56, the Birsa Munda uprising of 1899–1900 were some of the revolts by tribals in different parts of colonial India that stirred the tribal regions outside Assam. The revolt of *Lalungs* and *Kacharis* in Assam against colonial exploitation fall in the same tradition.

Role of Raij Mel, the Traditional Institution, in the Mobilisation

The *Raij Mel* was the people's assembly, an organisation of the peasantry with a rudimentary form of democratic element and style of functioning. It existed in different tribal and ethnic groups in Darrang, Nagaon and Kamrup where there had been no effective control of the *Ahom* monarchy (Kalita, 2006). The peasants usually assembled in the *namghar* (religious prayer house), an institution credited to neo-Vaishnavite saint Sankardev (1449–1564). From the time of Sankardev *namghar* became an institution of the village life of Assam where people assembled not only during religious ceremonies but also to hold discussions on matters of general interest. Thus, it can be treated as 'a venue of Village Panchayats' (Sarma,1966). It appears that out of this popular practice the *Raij Mel* emerged as a forum of public gathering totally distinct from the religious congregation. The study reveals that, as elsewhere, in the Phulaguri uprising *Raij Mel* played a crucial role in mobilising the peasants to revolt against the Government. The main participants in the *Raij Mel* were the tribesmen: *Lalungs* and *Kacharis* and *Kaivartas*, who occupied the lowest stratum in the caste hierarchy. The leadership of the *Raij Mel* emerged mostly amongst the peasants, the brass-metal artisans and the boatmen but not from the principal landholders or the rural intellectuals.

The *Raij Mel* discussed the issues of enhancement of tax, imposition of ban on poppy cultivation on private account, enhancement of revenue and imposition of tax on betel and betel leaves. Out of these issues, *Mel* took the enhancement of revenue more seriously which resulted in an antithetical relationship between the *Sarkar* and the *Mel*. It is clear in the words: the *Sarkar* told the *Ryot* (i.e., the peasant), 'If you don't pay the enhanced revenue, your property will be attached.' The *Mel* told the peasant, "If you do pay, you will be cursed and ex-communicated". The peasants could not disobey the *Raijer Hukum* (i.e., the order of the people) as disobedience was threatened with social boycott and excommunication, as well as imposition of fines.

Thus, the peasants, who were caught in the antithetical relationship between the *Mel* and *Sarkar*, finally followed the instructions of the *mel*. This suggests that the *Mel* succeeded in generating mechanical solidarity among the peasants and emerged as the dominant authority in the mobilisation.

Parallel to the domain of elite politics there always existed throughout the colonial period another domain of Indian politics in which the principal actors were the 'subaltern' classes and groups constituting the masses of the labouring population and the intermediate strata of people in the town and village. In case of Phulaguri uprising it has been found that the mobilisation of peasants took place horizontally among the *Lalungs*, *Kacharis*, and the *Kaivartas* unlike the mobilisation in the elite politics which takes place vertically. It has been found that the pull of primordial loyalties or sentiments of kinship, ethnic community ties and co-residence played a significant part in the peasant mobilisation of Phulaguri. Mobilisation took place mainly among the poor peasantry.

Political Character of the Uprising

The conventional discourses on peasant insurgencies attempted to understand insurgent movements with an aim 'to prevent their occurrences in the future'. The sense of history was thus converted into an element of 'administrative concern'. We should also be aware of the failure of Marxist historiography for not recognising the role of pure spontaneity in history. The recent studies on peasant movements have emphasised 'organisation', 'leadership', and 'ideology' as the key elements in the formation of rebels' consciousness. These studies have tended to treat the insurgencies as 'pre-political' phenomena. If we do not recognise the first glimmer of consciousness in this apparently spontaneous and unstructured movement of the peasant masses of Assam and brand it as 'pre-political', it will lead to the commitment of a serious error of judgment. The subaltern insurgents of Phulaguri were also trying to challenge the existing structure of power relationships as challenged in the uprisings of *Bhumij*, the *Kol* insurrection, the Santhal revolt of 1855, the indigo disturbances of 1859–62, and the Deccan riots of 1875. The influence of the Raij Mel was so strong that it emerged as the paramount authority, not the *Sarkar*. Hence, the collective action of the peasants of Assam was no less political than the politics of the liberal reformist struggles of the 'no-rent' or 'no tax' variety under the banner of the Congress or the Left-wing sponsored peasant struggles (e.g.,

Tebhaga or Telengana struggles) of the 20th century in India. It follows, then, that the peasant revolt of 19th century Assam was qualitatively different and decisively less advanced in terms of the level of consciousness, organisation, and ideological articulation, and failed to rise above localism and ethnicity. Demanding the restoration of old rates of revenue and not paying the enhanced revenue itself is a political issue or questioning the power of *Raj*.

Conclusion

Analysis of the facts of Phulaguri uprising reveals that the British *Raj* transformed local traditional institutions to suit their own interests and substantially changed the agrarian relations that adversely affected the traditional economy and culture of the peasantry, besides depriving the special administrative powers of tribal chiefs and princes that were given to them by the Ahom kings. Such changing material conditions gave rise to the feelings of relative deprivation that in turn resulted in organised protest against exploitation. The awareness of nationalism during the revolt of 1857 further acted as the formative background of the peasant revolt of the second half of the 19th century. The protest took the form of violence in Phulaguri where traditional institutions and primordial relations played a significant role in the mobilisation process. The autonomous and political aspects of consciousness of the peasants of Phulaguri make the uprising historically significant. This uprising is the first symptom of the peasant movement of Assam that is anti-British in nature.

References

Barpujari, H.K. (ed.) 1993, *The Comprehensive History of Assam*, Vol. V, Guwahati: Publication Board Assam.

Beteille, A. 1974, *Studies in Agrarian Social Structure*, Delhi: OUP.

Dhanagare, D.N. 1983, *Peasant Movements in India, 1920–50*, Delhi: OUP.

——. 1993, *Themes and Perspectives in Indian Sociology*, Jaipur: Rawat Publications.

Gait, Sir E. 1905, *A History of Assam*, Delhi: Surjeet Publications.

Guha, A. 1977, *Planter Raj to Swaraj*, Delhi: Tulika (revised edition).

——. 1983a, *Elementary Aspects of Peasant Insurgency in Colonial India*, Delhi: OUP.

——. 1983b, "The Prose of Counter Insurgency", in *Subaltern Studies I*, Delhi: OUP.

Hardiman, David, 1981, *Peasant Nationalist of Gujarat*, Delhi: OUP.

——. (ed.) 1992, *Peasant Resistance in India, 1858–1914*, Delhi: OUP.

Hobsbawm, E. 1959, *Primitive Rebels*, Manchester: Manchester University Press.

Hunter, W.W. 1879, *A Statistical Account of Assam*, London: Trubner & Co.

Karna, M.N. 2004, *Agrarian Structure and Land Reforms in Assam*, Shillong: NEHUP.

Kalita, B. 2006, *The Uprising of Phulaguri*, Nagaon: Krantikal Prakashan.

Miller, D.B. (ed.) 1978, *Peasants and Politics: Grass Roots Reaction in Asia*, New York: St. Martin's Press.

Mukherji, P. 1983, *Far Left Extremism or Electoral Politics*, Delhi: Manohar.

Namboodiripad, E.M.S. 1943, *A Short History of the Peasant Movement in Kerala*, Bombay: People's Publishing House.

Natarajan, L. 1953, *Peasant Uprising in India, 1850–1900*, Bombay: People's Publishing House.

Sarma, S.N. 1966, *The Neo-Vaisnavite Movement and the Satra Institution of Assam*, Guwahati: Lawyeri Book Stall.

Sen, S. 1979, *Agrarian Relations in India (1793–1947)*, New Delhi: People's Publishing House.

Thorner, D. 1956, *The Agrarian Prospect in India*, Delhi: Delhi University Press.

Wolf, Eric R. 1970, *Peasant Wars in the Twentieth Century*, New York: Harper and Row.

26

Feasibility of Social Capital and Collective Action in Villages of Uttar Pradesh

A Case Study

Pragyan and D.R. Sahu

Understanding Social Capital

The social capital perspective proposes a direct link between collective action and development via the increased participation of the local masses (Putnam, Leonardi and Nanetti, 1993) but requires a broader framework as social capital has different meanings for different scholars. The concept refers to engagements of co-operation, trust and reciprocity among people and network of collective action aimed for the pursuit of desired goal (Putnam, Leonardi and Nanetti, 1993). It means a network of social relations based on mutuality and interdependency that members use to achieve their common desired goals through coordination (Coleman, 1999). Thus, in the production of public goods and services from the existing resources, there is a need to (a) make investment in terms of time, skill, money and effort, (b) work out a strategy regarding the relatedness of stock and flow of that capital, and (c) some idea of substantial externalities. These externalities can be positive as well as negative ones. The positive externalities tend to expand profitability of the concerned resource in future. Negative externality enters accidentally in the formation and utilisation of resources and thus makes short the very range of positive externalities (Uphoff, 1999).

The social capital is additional to three other forms of conventional capital, i.e., physical capital (man-made), natural capital (natural resources), and human capital (Serageldin and Grootaert, 1999), and can easily be understood in relation to these three forms of capital. Like these three other forms of capital, social capital is also considered as a form of capital as it adds value by producing collective benefits in the form of assets that can be utilised for the betterment of society. Unlike the other three forms of capital, social capital is an intangible resource, as it lies in patterned social relations and is collective in nature. One can use the other three tangible forms of capital individually. But social capital implies reciprocal interpersonal exchange, with "some degree of mutuality, common identity, co-operation for mutual benefit, not just for personal benefit" (Uphoff, 1999). Thus, social capital refers to those social relations that promote collective action in the pursuit of commonly desired goals. The relationship between social capital and purposive action can be better understood after the comprehension of collective behaviour and collective action conceptually.

Comprehending Collective Behaviour and Collective Action

Blumer (1951, 1971) classified behaviours of collective groupings into four types, viz., (i) the acting crowd (a mob), (ii) the expressive crowd (the dancing crowd), (iii) the mass, and (iv) the public. Acting crowds' actions are aimed at the pursuit of certain defined objectives. Unlike this, the expression of emotions is the objective of expressive crowds. According to Blumer (1951), mass is "more heterogeneous, more anonymous, less organised, and less intimately engaged in interaction. Mass behaviour is in fact a convergence of a large number of individuals on the basis of 'vague impulses and feelings'. The public constitutes a group of people who focus their actions on some issue, disagree on the means, engage in discussion, and move towards a decision". It means "the public differs from the crowd in terms of its emphasis on disagreement (rather than unanimity), and rational consideration (rather than spectacular suggestion) and occupies a prominent place in the development of a public". Thus, a sociological perspective of collective action includes the public, and excludes the former three types of collective groupings. Parsons and Shils (1951) further consider four characteristics as essential to conceptualise collective behaviour and collective action. They are: (1) collective behaviour is oriented in the attainment of ends or goals or other anticipated state of affairs. (2) It occurs in social situations. (3) It is normatively regulated. (4) It involves expenditure of energy or effort in motivation. Thus collective action needs to be seen as a process, i.e., as a recurrent phenomenon but not episodic. It is inextricably interwoven with a social context and its dynamics need to be comprehended. The relationship between collective action and its effect, externality, in a society is mediated through the dynamics of relationships in the attainment of a collective goal. Secondly, the process of collective action is a dynamic interplay between society and action oriented to development. It also tends to get influenced by the structure of a society. On this there is a full range of empirical studies conducted in India (Rudolph, 2000; Blomkvist and Swain, 2001; Jayal, 2001; Mayer, 2001; Serra, 2001; Mohopatra, 2001; John and Chathukulam, 2002; Chopra, 2002; Mukherjee, 2002; Pai, 2001; D'silva and Pai, 2003). Although we would attempt to pave the way for discussion by extrapolating issues from these empirical studies so that we can have a debate with a logical mind rather than captive mind (Alatas, 1974; Dube, 1982; Mukherji, 2005) through the relation between social capital and collective action and the conditions under which the formation and sustenance of social capital is emphasised.

Understanding the Problematic of Social Capital and Collective Action in Indian Context

Individual factors of trust and reciprocity cannot be acknowledged to comprehend collective behaviour and collective action as the social capital theorists reduce the manifold complexities of trust to an unviable general scheme (Prakash and Selle, 2004) and take more interest in the individual side of trust rather than collective collaboration (Rothstein, 2004; Caulkins, 2004; Dekker, 2004; Stolle, 2004). Besides, this trust cannot be assumed as a viable precedent of actual behaviour as disparity exists between preferences for being trustworthy and actual participation in collective action (Hardin, 1993; Moore, 1999). The concept of collective action provides a viable scheme for understanding collaboration through an association between individuals of different age categories, gender and profession besides the participants' social identities in terms of caste, class, religion, language, etc. These identities may affect performance of a collective collaboration and its results. Thus, collective action is incorporated as the central concern in the paper. In the context of Indian society, basic propositions of social capital perspective need minute observation as the society is segmented with 'homo-hierarchicus' (Dumont, 1970). The segmental nature of society may in turn put forward a different tone and tenor to the process of social capital and collective action. This paper examines two of the main propositions (Mohapatra, 2001; John and

Chathukulam, 2002; Chopra, 2002; Mukherjee, 2002; Pai, 2001; D'silva and Pai, 2003) of social capital perspective.

Proposition 1: Social capital theory emphasises on the horizontal framework of social relations for the formation and sustenance of social capital

According to Blomkvist and Swain (2001), boundaries of social groups in a social interaction are porous in accordance to the point of reference. The reference point may be related to the observance of linkages within and between groups in a society. Secondly, the impact of these linkages on macro phenomena in terms of its functionality and dysfunctionality to groups and the whole society for development or democracy, etc., needs a clear comprehension. In a segmented society like India, the social capital of a group cannot be necessarily treated as functional for society as a whole. For instance, Dalit assertion and collectivity may create tension and conflict between Dalit and non-Dalit castes in a social setting. So conflict is not excluded at all from a social capital perspective. Besides, this conflict can generate a negative or positive aftermath for macro phenomena, i.e., segmentation and distrust in a community and people's mobilisation, respectively (Pai, 2001).

Proposition 2: Generation and functioning of social capital promotes participation of actors due to increased trust and reciprocity; thus social capital affects development positively

Social processes, like social capital and development, coexist in society and may either reinforce or cross-cut each other. The linkage between social capital and development is a two-way relation. Blomkvist and Swain (2001) assert with Jayal (2001) that state intervention may deteriorate people's collective responsibility towards natural resources and may thus lead to a social milieu of distrust. Thus, generally, one can not foresee the relationship between social capital and development as positive and functional in a segmented society. Analytical understanding of both the propositions mentioned above may be better comprehended in the light of field study.

On practical grounds, these propositions spell out that societies with egalitarian frameworks or those with multiple voluntary associations will act as prerequisites for development but development will be hindered in the context of societies based on vertical solidarity and with fewer voluntary organisations. The first view point is further divided into two sub-streams. One stream of thinkers on social capital argues that the formation and sustenance of social capital are dependent on the cultural and historical civil traditions of society and it affects development (Putnam, Leonardi and Nanetti, 1993; Fukuyama, 1995; Locke, 1995). Another stream views that social capital can be constructed, and enhanced and its steering capacity utilised for development (Ostrom, 1994; Lam, 1996; Schneider and others, 1997; Chopra, 2002; Mukherjee, 2002; Weitering and Nooteboom, 2004).

With this juxtaposition, the next part attempts to understand structural conditions for social capital and scope thereof in a vertically organised rural setting of Uttar Pradesh. Here, the main counter-logic originates from the idea that whether social capital is engrained in the historical conditioning of a society or a subject of creative alterations with a deliberately designed framework, there is always a need for social capital to accumulate, work and sustain in a society. Flow, i.e., emergent benefits of social capital, cannot be produced without purposive action. If the members of a society have inherited a certain extent of social capital, they have to earn it in order to own it. In case they don't earn social capital by investing their collective efforts to work out their respective roles, they will lose the flow of social capital. On the obverse, in a consciously planned framework, members are assigned to perform reciprocal roles, necessary to inculcate individuals' efforts into one collective collaboration/collective action. There is a prior need to pay heed in the social context of the present rural setting. This socio-structural context serves as a general context wherein the process of social capital and its externality for collective action are being observed as part of the societal reality of the field.

The Field

Fieldwork was conducted in Narayanpur and Binaura villages located in Sitapur district of the central region of Uttar Pradesh as a part of doctoral work. The distance between these two villages is only one and a half km. Inter-village network between these villages is found in the agrarian relations as some landlords of village Narayanpur have tenants/sharecroppers from the village Binaura. Agriculture is the main source of livelihood of both the villagers and they predominantly cultivate two main crops, i.e., sugarcane and wheat. These villages belong to two different Village Panchayats and were deliberately selected in order to understand the functioning of Panchayat Raj Institutions (PRIs) in terms of the implementation of developmental programmes and interaction with social capital in more than one village situation.

Village Narayanpur is comparatively more homogeneous than village Binaura in terms of caste composition and occupational diversity. The former has only two castes, Thakur (warrior caste) and Pasi (scheduled caste) while the second village has 13 castes Thakur (warrior caste), Bania (business caste), Chamar (leather worker), Pasi (fishing), Dhanuk (child delivery services), Gadari (goat herder), Lohar (blacksmith), Teli (edible oil presser), Murau (vegetable seller), Gaddi (dairy farming), Manihar (bangle seller), Dhobi (washerman), and Pathan (warrior caste of Muslim community). Similar trend in case of occupational structure is also observed. Larger proportion of Narayanpur villagers is engaged as cultivators while a smaller proportion of its population has been employed as wage labour in agriculture and non-agriculture activities. Occupational heterogeneity is more pronounced in the village Binaura as most of them are engaged in non-agricultural occupations like tailoring to painting houses in the nearby cities besides engaging in agriculture The intensity of migration in the village Narayanpur is less than the intensity of migration from the village Binaura. The villagers of Binaura migrate to cities like Delhi, Kanpur and Sitapur.

In both these villages' higher castes, Thakur and Bania, are not engaged in direct cultivation of land but are dependent on the lower castes for the cultivation of land. These castes in the studied villages predominantly earn income either exclusively from agriculture or from both agriculture and service. In the village Narayanpur, Thakurs own a large proportion of arable land and are politically dominant while lower caste (Pasis) are landless or owners of smaller pieces of land but also ritually lowest in caste hierarchy. In case of village Binaura the two higher castes, i.e., Thakur and Bania, are engaged in continuous competition with each other for occupying positions of power in the Village Panchayat. These two castes have different sources of power and influence. Banias own most of the arable land while Thakurs' political influence and support is based on bureaucracy. Neither of them hold both these resources of power and influence. Reservation in PRIs for SCs and OBCs has given a fresh boost to the competition between Thakurs and Banias as both require the support of numerically preponderant lower castes.

These facts reveal the structural locations of different groups in these villages and the cultural stocks of society became both functional and dysfunctional in the production and sustenance of social capital. Network of social relations of different groups within a society is deeply rooted in its normative structure while status and role provides a behavioural base to the normative reality. Thus, field narratives facilitate a deeper insight into processes of continuity and change in the structure of social capital. It may also enable us to understand the field reality and collective action as a part thereof.

The following data will provide the base for the comprehension of the production and sustenance of social capital within and between groups in the villages under study. They are illustrated through four illustrations.

Case 1

The place of inhabitation of Pasi (SC) caste is geographically segregated from the inhabited place of Thakurs (higher caste) in the village Narayanpur. Thakurs in general maintain social distance in terms sitting place hand maintenance of separate arrangements on the occasions of ceremonial feasts organised by Thakurs. Let us illustrate this with one of the cases as observed in the field study.

(i) Most of the Thakurs are literate and fond of Sanskritic names for their family members. In close contrast, Pasis are mostly illiterate and try to pick-up Sanskritic names from Thakurs and this practice is stiffly resisted by Thakurs. The resistance is ranged from making sarcastic comments to that of the bickering and finger pointing until they changed the borrowed names. If such a name is not change even after such resistance, then the name is deliberately 'mis-pronounced'. For instance, it is observed that name '*Uttam*' (means good) is pronounced as '*Uttim*' (meaningless word) and name '*Anupa*' (means special) is replaced by '*Anupha*' (another meaningless word).

(ii) Most of Pasis are either landless or owners of small pieces of land. Some of them also have buffaloes and goats. Mostly, these Pasis become subjects of Thakurs' anger in case of animal trespass and grazing in Thakurs' fields by their cattle. In case the grazing is done by cattle belonging to a Thakur on the lands of Pasi such humiliation is not meted out to the former.

Case 2

In general, the plurality of interacting endogamous units, arranged hierarchically, is a unique feature of Indian society. Besides this, each caste has multiple lineages that are also hierarchically arranged. Deviance from endogamous practices results in further lowering of status, as observed in the case of a Thakur lineage within the village; the offending members are excluded from participation in different ceremonies organised by other *Thakurs*, thus affecting the social capital formation and its sustenance within and between groups

Case 3

In any ceremonial feast, guests are served by the host in a *pangat. It* means that the guests sit on a long and narrow piece of woven cloth, side-by-side in a row and then the host serves food to the host. The *pangat* system is prevalent and popular in this area. Lower castes, including untouchables, are served in separate *pangats* which usually occurs in the last turn or they are given food in their own utensils so that they can carry it to their homes. It is known as *persa*, i.e., the served (food). Thus the *pangat* system facilitates a practicable scheme to maintain social distance between castes, along the lines of purity and pollution, and thus creates fission and fusion among castes. A dominant Thakur family, with an intention of gaining political mileage in the panchayat elections of 2006, organised a buffet system in the *tilak* ceremony (pre-marriage function from groom's side) in village *Narayanpur* in 2005. Lower castes, from neighbouring five villages that fall under the Narayanpur Statutory Panchayat including untouchables, which are close to the Brahmin contestant, were also invited. The practice of the buffet system was not only criticised but a few Thakur families also did not accept food when the host made it available at their residences. The self-service system was completely different from the traditional *pangat* system and thus affected social capital within the group though extended it beyond the group.

Case 4

Lokvani is an e-governance initiative by the combined efforts of district administration and National Informatics Centre in Sitapur district of Uttar Pradesh to promote public-private-partnership programme and to reduce bureaucratic hassles. It was conceptualised in September 2004 by the then DM Sitapur and by December 2004, 13 Lokvani centres were set up. By December 2006 this number has gone up to 90. It is a kind of modern organisational arrangement, for the redressal of public grievances related to irregularities in land records. The cultivators can make complaints, in case of irregularities, to Lokvani. It provides easy access of land records to rural masses. Private professionals have emerged, on paid service, to help computer illiterates in lodging complaints and getting information. It has become a strategy to show loyalties in factional politics. Secondly, the pace of development is being hampered as manipulations are practiced in official procedures. Factional conflicts have hindered the appointment of the *'Panchayat Mitra'*, an associate to village *Pradhan*, for more than six months through fake candidatures and complaints.

In order to understand the role of social capital in collective action and its effect on development, the collective actions are categorised on the basis of its nature, as formal and informal and, in terms of its functionality, articulation and mobilisation. Informal kind of collective action deals with articulation along the lines of primary relations such as neighbourhood, kinship, friendship, etc. These primary relations produce intimate ties which can turn into social capital in the hour of need. In the informal collective action, there exists a mutual social network among its members at first and thereafter the social capital is used in the articulation of collective action. Formal kind of collective action originates from common needs and objectives of a group of people which facilitates collective collaboration and coordination among the members. Unlike informal framework, formally articulated collective action has a clearer set of rules and regulations. So the common sharing of cost and benefits can be produced and distributed evenly. The extent of flexibility regarding norms is more in the informal rather than in the formal kind of collective action. Sustenance of a collective action is attained differently in both kinds of collective actions. Informal collective action is more flexible and implicit set of sanctions are imposed to check the habit of free rider choice, such as peer pressure, etc. In contrast, formal collective action has a codified set of sanctions as the formation of collective identity of this group is based on a verified social base.

Oral history and focused group discussions, conducted in the field, have pointed out a relevant incidence in this regard. After *chakbandi* (land consolidation) implementation in 1950s, the small pieces of land segregated at different places in the village were consolidated at one place that promoted the adoption of commercial agriculture. After nearly six decades, the land holdings are currently fragmented and also scattered. Management of such land was a real challenge for labour power as cultivation was labour intensive as mechanisation was low. In village Narayanpur two Tomar families belonging to the same lineage had maintained the practice of joint pattern of management of the scattered landholdings as they were before *chakbandi,* for almost a decade after 1950s. The members of one family got jobs outside and emigrated from the village. So, they were unable to put their efforts into cultivation. Another family lacked monetary resources but had man power. *Chakbandi* worked as a catalyst in the consolidation of landholdings of both these families. Joint land management became feasible as both the families informally worked out the rights and obligations in the joint management of the land. Chopra (2002) also acclaimed a similar formation and functioning of joint land management among farmers of a village who have their small landholdings at one place although they are not kith and kin.

It is evident from the above illustrations that formal collective action is primarily purposive and deliberate in the formation of the group and the articulation of its needs while informal collective action predominantly utilises the existing intimate and familiar social bonds. But the types of collective action will become different from each other, depending on whether the collective precedes the formation of group or vice-versa. Formal collective action is initiated because of some common problem. The common problem turns into a mediation of a common need and thus, the articulation of the shared need and the collective response to it, become the root causes of a formally organised collective action. Such a classification of collective action into two analytical categories promotes a better understanding of the processes in collective action, which is substantiated through the following cases in point.

Analysing Continuum of Collective Action

In collective action voluntary actions as well as those resulted from policy of state intervention for developments are incorporated. Collective action is treated as a process, that can help in segregating cause from consequence and the emergent recurrent social phenomenon can be understood in terms of its functional and dysfunctional consequences. Collective actions are classified on the basis of its organisation, i.e., formally or informally organised collective action and with functional or dysfunctional externality. The scheme is applied in operational terms so that the ongoing pattern of collective action can be comprehended easily as observed in the studied villages. Due to the absence of any voluntary organisation in the field, only four possible patterns of collective actions are observed. However, there are two significant analytical problems with this model which are required to be discussed beforehand. First, a scheme of collective action is primarily dependent on the formation of a group. The formation and sustenance of groups in a society seems to be complicated because of the internal dynamics of groups. Studying the emergence of factions within a group is important to understand interrelationships between groups. Therefore, the first challenge is to frame units of analysis in order to understand the collective action because the manifest boundaries of a group may have unstated engagements with factions of another group. Secondly, formally organised collective action can not be expected free from informal structure, i.e., caste and kinship, etc. Henceforth, a third category may come into existence because it incorporates both formal and informal aspects into one entity. Thus, there can be more logical possibilities, of which only four are attempted and observed in the field study.

The functional and dysfunctional consequences can be better understood within the framework of formal and informal kinds of collective action in following way:

Externality/Collective Actions	Functional (A)	Dysfunctional (B)
Formal Collective Actions (X)	Type1–AX	Type3–BX
Informal Collective Actions (Y)	Type2–AY	Type4By

In a segmented society analytical categories of collective action, i.e., formal and informal framework, tend to get blurred and produce permutation and combination of these categories. Henceforth, collective action emerges as a multi-dimensional reality because social capital becomes segmented in itself. Due to differentiation among groups within a society, the relationship between social capital and collective action seems quite complex. In such a situation both kinds of collective actions are found socially alloyed with functional and dysfunctional externalities.

Type 1–AX is a logical representation of functional externality of formally organised collective action. The establishment of a private primary school at Kishunpur in 1992 and its functioning over a period of more than fifteen years is a significant pointer in comprehending the dynamics of collective action. Although this school is not located in our rural setting, two staff members of the school (one out of the six teachers and the principal) are natives of village *Narayanpur* and *Binaura*. Besides the staff members, school going children of both the villages are enrolled in this school. At present, it is a primary school, i.e., up to class fifth, and named after its founder. The school, with strength of 183 students, is well known in the vicinity for its high quality education. Since its establishment, a group of dedicated teachers has been making collective efforts to enhance the quality of education. Moreover, from time to time, other villagers have helped this dedicated staff with men and material. The Member of Legislative Assembly (MLA) of the constituency provided funds from his '*vidhayak nidhi*' (MLA's funds) for the construction of the school building in 2003. But, now, it has come to an impasse. The teachers are keen to get government sanction, so that they can get the grant-in-aid and are otherwise unable to raise the required amount of money to run the school. In such a situation, a few powerful persons, like politician and influential peasants want to own this school, as it has become a kind of capital in itself. The teachers are under pressure and quite apprehensive. Lack of funds and bureaucratic bottlenecks have become main impediments in the continuity of the school. Thus the teachers are feeling insecure not only about the fate of the school but also their own.

Type 2–AY is a logical category of functional externality of informal collective action. A small scale lending group is organised informally among a group of neighbours, and kins in village Binaura. The formation and functioning of this group is based on familiarity. In fact, this strategy of inculcating reliance through personal relationships is working favourably for this lending group on a micro level. In the absence of institutionalisation of a wider social arena, this collective group works like a small pocket of social capital. It is a voluntary group, where initiative has been taken on a purely voluntary (Self-Help Group, SHG) basis by its members without NGO and government involvement. The group is comprised of twelve members. They have been working together since 2002. The self-help group has a fixed tenure of five years and completes its tenure in 2007. This group makes a joint pool of money, from each member every month, which is then used for lending. In case a member is not able to contribute its monthly share, then he must pay two month's share along with a fine of ₹ 10. Interest rate is fixed at 10 per cent. As per the rule, if a member wants to quit before the fixed term, i.e., 2007, then he can withdraw his money, although he/she cannot claim a share in the accrued profit. So each member gets a profit if he/she continues till the end of the term. During the four years of its existence it has more than ₹ 40,000 balance in a bank on the group's account.

Register is maintained with minute details of every borrowing. They lend money on personal basis, i.e., clients come through members specifically and thus it ensures that a stranger is strictly prohibited. For villagers, it is a good and easy access to borrow money, as villagers need short-term loans for non-productive purposes, like paying the fees of a veterinary doctor, or buying some pesticides or fertilisers. Although, the interest rate is quite high, villagers prefer to borrow money from this group. One significant hallmark of this lending group is that members need not mention a reason for borrowing money. One more self help group has been formed along these lines and has also been working successfully for three years. As per the rule, at the end of the stipulated time, the money will be distributed equally among its members, but challenges lie ahead in the equitable distribution of profit.

Type 3–BX presents another type of formal collective action, which results in dysfunctional externality. Unlike the functional one, the dysfunctional externality works as a negative factor for the process of development. In village *Binaura*, two SHGs were formed on the initiative of a government sponsored microfinance scheme to earn livelihood collectively. These SHGs have fifteen members each and they mainly belong to the SC category (Chamars in particular). A loan of ₹ 1 lakh each to be received in four instalments was sanctioned for these two SHG for animal husbandry and dairy. The loan is meant to purchase the buffaloes. But both the SHGs could not take off. Some of the reasons for their inability are mentioned below. First, the scheme itself is not compatible with the wishes of the participants. Actually, the formation of both these groups was not based on a voluntary basis by the participants, according to their felt needs but by manipulating technicalities, worked out by a Panchayat Secretary of Thakur caste (one of the most influential persons of village). The manipulative techniques can be summarised in the following points. First, only two out of fifteen members in the SHG were comfortable with the rearing buffalo. As a result the remaining members were suspicious about providing substantial inputs regarding dairy management. Secondly, five participants were well known for their strong backing by this Panchayat Secretary. This Panchayat Secretary was interested in appropriating an amount out of the sanctioned loan. Consequently, other members of self-help group were also apprehensive of free rider choice being applied by these five men. So the members withdrew from the SHG before it could receive the second instalment of loan. At present, most of the members are scared of taking loans from governmental schemes as their nominal landholdings will be confiscated in the context of non-payment of loan.

Therefore, the government initiative of promoting organised SHGs for income generating activities on a collective basis, was severely fractured. Strategic manipulation of rules, for narrow interests by a higher caste Panchayat Secretary, had affected the implementation of the government scheme adversely. In addition, it had shattered the potential of voluntarism among the members of that group, who were involved in the collective action.

Type 4–BY describes the informally organised collective action of two families that acted as impediment in the implementation of a *khranja* (a road/pavement with upright bricks) and *nali* (a fully covered drain) project in the village. In village Narayanpur, the construction of *a kharanja* and *nali* was planned and sanctioned under the purview of Panchayat Raj institution. But it became a bone of contention that led to a division within the village and the emergence of two factions. On the one hand was the majority of villagers, facing problems of waterlogging and completely blocked route, particularly in rainy season, and on the other hand, a group of people who were opposing this project tooth and nail, as the drainage passed through their *duwars* (a part just in front of the house).

The proposed drainage channel would be the main drainage channel, in which the drains of other houses would merge and it would end at a nearby pond. Two families had their drains leading to the same direction but they did not agree to construct the main drain. The village *Pradhan* and government officers tried to negotiate with these two families on the issue and to convince them that the drain would be completely covered and would not cause any kind of disruption in their lifestyle. This issue had a longer history of bloodshed in late 1980s. Intense and violent conflicts occurred in the village when villagers tried to solve the issue carrying *lathis* (a strong piece of bamboo seasoned with pure mustard oil, which makes a strong impact on hitting) in their hands. However, in the last two decades, there occurred only two minor changes. First, the issue reemerged as dwelling density increased considerably, so that it became completely impossible to avoid this problem and to let it remain unsolved. Secondly, a few faces within the contending parties changed but the issue of confrontation itself did not disappear. Thus, this pattern of informal collective action hampered the developmental activities in the village.

All these case studies, taken together, highlight the possible range of collective actions and their externalities in terms of negative as well as positive contributions in development. Thus, sometimes, collective action, as propelled by social capital, may prove to be a detonator rather than facilitator of development in the society. Thus, the contribution of heightened social capital ranges from 'promising' to 'fractured' potential for development.

Unlike Putnam's study (1993), our study exhibits the negative externality/effect of collective action. Collective action appears to be a fragile input for development in a society. This aspect of collective action is in clear contrast to the naive optimism associated with social capital approach. Our findings are closer to the doubts raised by Rudolph (2000), Mohopatra (2001), and Blomkvist and Swain (2001). Similar realities regarding the social capital approach have been substantiated in studies conducted by Jayal (2001) and Pai (2001). A polemical situation can be seen between the 'externality of collective action' and 'continuity of structure of caste inequality'. This is polemical situation, because on one extreme, collective action works, while, on the other extreme, the caste structure is functioning continuously with adaptive changes in its role. In fact, both these forces crosscut one another. Mutual interplay between 'process of collective action' and 'continuity of structure' is significant to observe. It does not only cut short the promising scope of collective action but also promotes dysfunctional externalities by reinforcing uneven stake-holding in development.

Caste-based structural inequality is accrued in the form of unevenly distributed resources and life chances. One can easily understand that the upper strata may not be willing to volunteer, because it may offer an opportunity to overcome the personal constraints of the downtrodden masses and enhance their life chances. On the face, if the down sections are willing to attain a development goal they are not only vulnerable because of the poor availability of resources but can but can also become victims of development, because of their low positions in the local power structure. In case of rural setting in Uttar Pradesh, impediments are clearly visible along the lines of caste. Collective action seems promising on a small scale, for instance, in the lending of money through self-help groups in the village Binaura (case study 2). However, the transcendence of social capital and collective action for developmental goal, from micro to meso and macro levels, may not occur spontaneously or naturally in a homo-hierarchicus society. Macro scale collective action requires larger investment of men, material and, power. This is the level where the potential and scope of collective action can exhibit its limits. The permeation of caste into new institutional arrangements can be understood through *Lokvani*, which has been adopted in cases of factional politics. As regards the caste structure, Srinivas (1966) and Beteille (2002) have pointed out the adaptive capacity of caste to alter its role with the changing demands of the modern era, too. Srinivas (1966) has emphasised the need to be cautious about the working matrix of a vertically organised caste structure, which tends to give a particular tone to the development process.

One additional distinction, of 'deliberate endeavour' versus 'natural course', also emerged in our field study. Collective action is characterised by the deliberate efforts of a group of members. The rules of distributing cost and benefits of collective action among members are deliberately designed on a day to day basis. Unlike this, the continuity of structure works in terms of its natural course of occurrence, from all mundane things of everyday life to the macro level of village life. Study reveals that rules of marriage and inter-dining are significant for the sustenance of unevenly organised caste structure. From minor issue of animal grazing to the major one of social boycott caste is all-pervasive through networks of social institutions and sanctions.

Thus, within the caste-based society of rural India, the set of status and role produces working matrix for norms and values via the system of social institutions and the normative base. In this way, continuity of structure is sustained even with the further amalgamation of traditional forms of social institutions and organisations, with new institutional arrangements. The findings of this study can be enumerated in the following way:

- The dynamics of social capital process in a rural social setting require a comprehensive understanding of intra-caste and inter-caste social capital.
- Link between social capital and collective action may not necessarily contribute in a positive way to development. It may hamper development through the negative externality of collective action.
- Mediation of volunteers and collective action towards the attainment of goals, in a caste-ridden society, cannot be assumed as being free from social conflict. Social retaliations may be produced and counter-produced in the hierarchically organised society.
- The structure of caste inequality emerges in this field study as being all pervasive. Though collective action is not absent from the scene but it is emerges as a corrigible input for development in a segmented society.
- This whole dynamics of social capital, collective action and development can be called a continuum of collective action. So, the continuum comprises functional externality and working potential of collective action for development, on the one end, with dysfunctional externality and limited scope on the other end.

Lastly, it may be summarised that the caste structure is experiencing forces of continuity and change. A network of social institutions and organisations facilitates the socially alloyed existence of this continuity of structure. The link between social capital and collective action requires a close scrutiny of social structure so that one may distinguish naive optimism from ground reality and the captive mind from the creative one.

Note: This paper is a revised version presented in the Seminar on 'Intensive Village Studies of Uttar Pradesh', held at Govind Ballabh Pant Social Science Institute, Jhusi, Allahabad from 29th February to 1st March, 2008. We are grateful to Prof. B R Chauhan and others for their suggestions and comments that have been incorporated in this article.

References

Alatas, S.H. 1974, "The Captive Mind and Creative Development", *International Social Science Journal*, 26 (4).

Atal, Y. 1981, "The Call for Indigenisation", *International Social Science Journal*, 33 (1).

Beteille, A. 2000, *Sociology: Essays on Approach and Method*, New Delhi: Oxford University Press.

—. 2002, "Hierarchical and Competitive Inequality", *Sociological Bulletin*, 51 (1).

Blomkvist, H. and Swain, A. 2001, "Investigating Democracy and Social Capital in India", *Economic and Political Weekly*, February 24.

Blumer, H. 1951, "The Field of Collective Behaviour", in *Principles of Sociology*, edited by Stanford Lyman, New York: New York University Press, pp. 167–222.

—. 1971, "Social Problems as Collective Behaviour", *Social Problems*, 18: 298–306.

Bo, R. 2004, "Social Capital and Institutional Legitimacy: The Corleone Connection", in *Investigating Social Capital*, edited by Sanjeev Prakash and Per Selle, New Delhi: Sage Publications.

Bourdieu, P. and Wacquant, L. 1992, *An Invitation to Reflexive Sociology*, Chicago: University of Chicago Press.

Caulkins, D. Douglas, 2004, "Organisational Memberships and Cross-cutting Ties: Bonding or Bridging Social Capital?", in *Investigating Social Capital*, edited by Sanjeev Prakash and Per Selle, New Delhi: Sage Publications. CHECK NAME

Chopra, K. 2002, "Social Capital and Development Processes: Role of Formal and Informal Institutions", *Economic and Political Weekly*, July 13.

Coleman, J.S. 1990, *Foundations of Social Theory*, Massachusetts, Cambridge: Harvard University Press.

——. 1999, "Social Capital in the Creation of Human Capital", in *Social Capital: A Multifaceted Perspective*, edited by Dasgupta Partha and Serageldin Ismail, Washington, DC: The World Bank.

Dekker, P. 2004, "Social Capital of Individuals: Relational Asset or Personal Quality?", in *Investigating Social Capital*, edited by Sanjeev Prakash and Per Selle, New Delhi: Sage Publications.

D'silva, E. and Pai, S. 2003, "Social Capital and Collective Action: Development Outcomes in Forest Protection and Watershed Development", *Economic and Political Weekly*, April 5.

Dube, S.C. 1982, "Social Sciences for the 1980s: From Rhetoric to Reality", *International Social Science Journal*, Vol. 34, No. 3.

Dumont, L. 1970, *Homo Hierarchicus: The Caste System and Its Implications*, London: Weidenfeld and Nicolson.

Fukuyama, F. 1995, *Trust: The Social Virtues and the Creation of Prosperity*, London: Penguin.

Hardin, R. 1993, "The Street-Level Epistemology of Trust", *Politics and Society*, 21 (4): 505–30.

Jayal, N.G. 2001, "Democracy and Social Capital in Central Himalaya: Tale of Two Villages", *Economic and Political Weekly*, February 24.

John, M.S. and Chathukulam, Jos, 2002, "Building Social Capital through State Initiative: Participatory Planning in Kerala", *Economic and Political Weekly*, May 18.

Krishna, A. 1999, "Institutional Analysis: Creating and Harnessing Social Capital", in *Social Capital: A Multifaceted Perspective*, edited by Dasgupta Partha and Serageldin Ismail, Washington, DC: The World Bank.

Lam, W.F. 1996, "Institutional Design of Public Agencies and Coproduction: A Study of Irrigation Associations in Taiwan", *World Development*, 24 (6): 1039–54.

Locke, R.M. 1995, *Remaking the Italian Economy*, Ithaca: Cornell University Press.

Maheu, L. (ed.) 1995, *Social Movements and Social Classes: The Future of Collective Action*, Sage Studies in International Sociology 46, Sponsored by the International Sociological Association/ISA.

Mayer, P. 2001, "Human Development and Civic Community in India: Making Democracy Perform", *Economic and Political Weekly*, 36 (8), February, p. 240.

Mukherjee, N. 2002, "Measuring Social Capital: Forest Protection Committees in West Bengal", *Economic and Political Weekly*, July 20.

Mohapatra, B.N. 2001, "Social Connectedness and Fragility of Social Capital: View from Orissa Village", *Economic and Political Weekly*, February 24.

Moore, M. 1999, "Truth, Trust and Market Transaction: What Do We Know?", *Journal of Development Studies*, 36 (1): 74–88.

Mukherji, P.N. 2005, "Sociology in South Asia: Indigenisation as Universalising Social Sciences", *Sociological Bulletin*, 54 (3), September–December.

——. 2006, "Sociology for What? Rethinking Sociology in an Era of Transformatory Changes", *Sociological Bulletin*, 55 (2), May–August.

Ostrom, E. 1994, "Constituting Social Capital and Collective Action", *Journal of Theoretical Politics*, 6 (4): 527–62.

——. 1999, "Social Capital: A Fad or a Fundamental Concept?", in *Social Capital: A Multifaceted Perspective*, edited by Dasgupta Partha and Serageldin Ismail, Washington, DC: The World Bank.

Pai, S. 2001, "Social Capital, Panchayats and Grass Roots Democracy: Politics of Dalit Assertion in Uttar Pradesh", *Economic and Political Weekly*, February 24.

Parsons, T. and Shils, E. 1951, *Toward a General Theory of Action*, Cambridge: Harvard University Press.

Pathy, J. 1995, "The Consequences of the New Economic Policies on the Peoples of India: A Sociological Appraisal", *Sociological Bulletin*, 44 (1), March.

Prakash, S. and Selle, Per, 2004, *Investigating Social Capital: Comparative Perspectives on Civil Society, Participation and Governance*, New Delhi: Sage Publications.

Putnam, R.D. 1993, "The Prosperous Community: Social Capital and Public Life", *The American Prospect*, 13: 35–42.

——. 1996, "The Strange Disappearance of Civic America", *The American Prospect*, Vol. 24.

Putnam, R.D., Leonardi, R. and Nanetti, R.Y. 1993, *Making Democracy Work: Civic Traditions in Modern Italy*, Princeton: Princeton University Press.

Raj, P. Mohan and Graham, C. Kinloch, 2004, "Contemporary Professional Sociology in America", *Sociological Bulletin*, 53 (3), September–December.

Rothstein, B. 2004, "Social Capital and Institutional Legitimacy", in S. Prakash and P. Selle (eds.), *Investigating Social Capital*, New Delhi: Sage Publications.

Rudolph, S.H. 2000, "Civil Society and the Realm of Freedom", *Economic and Political Weekly*, May 13.

——. 2004, "Is Civil Society the Answer?", in *Investigating Social Capital: Comparative Perspective on Civil Society, Participation and Governance*, edited by Sanjeev Prakash and Per Selle, New Delhi: Sage Publications.

Schneider, M. et al., 1997, "Institutional Arrangements and the Creation of Social Capital: The Effects of Public School Choice", *American Political Science Review*, 91 (1): 82–93.

Serageldin, I. and Grootaert, C. 1999, "Defining Social Capital: An Integrating View", in *Social Capital: A Multifaceted Perspective*, edited by Dasgupta Partha and Serageldin Ismail, Washington, DC: The World Bank.

Serra, R. 2001, "Social Capital: Meaningful and Measurable at State Level", *Economic and Political Weekly*, February 24.

Smelser, Neil J. 1962, 1967, *Theory of Collective Behaviour*, New York: Free Press.

Srinivas, M.N. 1966, *Social Change in Modern India*, Berkeley: University of California Press.

Stiglitz, Joseph E. 1999, "Formal and Informal Institutions", in *Social Capital: A Multifaceted Perspective*, edited by Dasgupta Partha and Serageldin Ismail, Washington, DC: The World Bank.

Stolle, D. and Rochon, T.R. 1998, "Are All Associations Alike? Member Diversity, Associational Type, and the Creation of Social Capital", *American Behavioural Scientist*, 42 (1).

Stolle, D. 2004, "Communities, Social Capital and Local Government: Generalised Trust in Regional Settings", in *Investigating Social Capital*, edited by Sanjeev Prakash and Per Selle, New Delhi: Sage Publications.

Turner, J.H. 1999, "The Formation of Social Capital", in *Social Capital: A Multifaceted Perspective*, edited by Dasgupta Partha and Serageldin Ismail, Washington, DC: The World Bank.

Uphoff, N. 1999, "Understanding Social Capital: Learning from the Analysis and Experience of Participation", in *Social Capital: A Multifaceted Perspective*, edited by Dasgupta Partha and Serageldin Ismail, Washington, DC: The World Bank.

Wade, R. 1994, *Village Republics: Economic Conditions for Collective Action in South India*, Cambridge, UK: Cambridge University Press.

Weitering, D. and Nooteboom, G. 2004, "Railway Porters of Mumbai: Social Capital in Practice", *Economic and Political Weekly*, May 29. http://www.sitapur.nic.in/lokvani.

World Bank (http://www.worldbank.org/poverty/scapital/index.htm.).

Index